# Oriental Experience

# Oriental Experience

A SELECTION
OF ESSAYS AND
ADDRESSES
DELIVERED ON
VARIOUS OCCASIONS

**SIR RICHARD TEMPLE, BART**
Late Governor of Bombay,
Lieutenant Governor of Bengal
and Finance Minister of India

WITH MAPS AND ILLUSTRATIONS

**Gian Publishing House**
29/6 SHAKTI NAGAR • DELHI-110007 • INDIA

GIAN PUBLISHING HOUSE
PUBLISHERS OF BOOKS ON HUMAN CIVILIZATION
29/6 SHAKTI NAGAR, DELHI-110007

First Reprint in India, 1986

*Printed at Goyal Offset Printers, Delhi-110035
and published by Smt. Gayatri Garg
for Gian Publishing House, Delhi-110007*

# PREFACE.

THIS book is intended to be a continuation of my two former books, 'India in 1880,' and 'Men and Events of my time in India.' The volume comprises a collection of addresses and speeches delivered before Societies or Associations in Great Britain, and articles contributed to English magazines, by me since my return to England in 1880. They all relate to one great subject, namely, the East, and in that sense are all connected together. Almost all of them are the results of my personal experience. Though they are entirely pervaded by the one idea of that duty which we British people owe to ourselves and to others in the East, yet there is no sameness about them. On the contrary, there will, I trust, be found in them a ceaseless variety. In this loom, so to speak, are extended numerous threads of divers hues, but they are crossed by a woof of one colour, and that represents British responsibility. Thus the texture has an uniformity in general appearance with an endless diversity in detail. While British India naturally occupies a considerable portion of the volume, other regions of the East come into view. Out of the twenty-one chapters in the book, eleven refer to Indian affairs, and the remainder to different subjects in the East.

These latter chapters relate to the progress of survey and exploration throughout Asia by European and American travellers who, in adventure, in peril, in suffering, have widened the limits of human knowledge, and of whom some have been steadfast unto death in the cause of science;—to the physical features of that Central Asian plateau which is replete with marvels of scenery, of climate, of social cataclysms, of natural products;—to the lessons of Chinese history, showing the unchanging polity, the deep-rooted institutions, the contradictory qualities, the unfathomable mind, the despairing courage, of a people whose part in Asiatic politics is not yet played out;—to the lovely lake-district on the frontier of East Tibet, near the dividing line between the British and Chinese dominions, and between the two most populous empires on earth;—to the railway alignment through the Indus desert into the mountain flanks of the region still called Khorasan, up to the border of southern Afghanistan;—to the inner disposition, the stern faith, the proud aspirations, the declining forces, the waning hopes, of the Muhammadan world in which England has a pre-eminent interest politically;—to the situation and prospects of Egypt and the principles of administration in a land whose destinies are to be guided by British policy;—to the outward objects and inward associations of the Holy Land as they actually present themselves before the student on the spot and the pilgrim of to-day;—to the diffusion of social science from its centre of enlightenment in the United Kingdom to the remotest parts of the British empire abroad.

Of the Indian topics dealt with in this volume, some, such as the question of local self-government for the natives, have arisen since I left that country. The three chapters regarding the Mahrattas constitute a monograph on a remarkable nationality with which I have enjoyed peculiar opportunities of being acquainted, and which, having fulfilled a great destiny in the past, might rise into embarrassing prominence under future contingencies. Further, there is a disquisition regarding the political economy of British India, the condition of its people, the expansion of its trade, banking and industry, the soundness of its finances. The objections sometimes urged against missionary enterprise are answered by a statement of the facts concerning the success of private effort in the most sacred of causes. The under-currents in the minds of natives, and the tendencies of their religious thought, are examined. The duty of British people towards their Eastern fellow-subjects is urged at the bar of national conscience. The happy promotion of Temperance among Europeans in the East is set forth. The professional instruction in engineering, and technical education generally, are advocated by reference to example. The preservation of forests, for the sake of climatic benefit as well as material wealth, is inculcated.

In the various parts of the book there will be found much diversity of style and composition, because some are reports of speeches, while others are written essays. Though the speeches have been carefully revised, no attempt has been made to modify the form they naturally have as oral deliverances.

Three chapters, being addresses on geographical characteristics, are abundantly illustrated. Besides the illustrations, there is prefixed to each of these chapters a special map, copied from that which was prepared by the Royal Geographical Society for the addresses. Further, to the chapter on Chinese history a map is appended for particular reference concerning the events described. At the beginning of the book, too, there will be found a map displaying the progress of geography, and the physical configuration, of Asia generally. This has been compiled from two large diagrams that were prepared for the British Association for the Advancement of Science, in order to illustrate the addresses included in the volume.

If my topics shall seem many-sided and multifarious for a single author, it is to be remembered that these works represent the outcome of a thirty years' preparation, and embody the result of an almost life-long labour.

I am under a pleasant obligation to the several Societies and Associations in Great Britain, and to the several English magazines, that have permitted me to re-publish the addresses and speeches I have delivered before them at their invitation, or the articles I have contributed to them. Thus my thankful acknowledgements are rendered to the Royal Geographical Society, the Royal Historical Society, the Royal Colonial Institute, the Society of Arts, the British Association for the Advancement of Science, the National Association for the Promotion of Social Science, the Society for the Propagation of the Gospel, the Presbyterian Board of Missions in America, the Baptist Missionary Society in London, the East India Association, the Institute of Bankers in London, the Scottish Arboricultural Society, the Temperance Association in Liverpool, the 'Encyclopædia Britannica,' the 'Contemporary Review,' the 'Fortnightly Review,' and the 'Evening News,' in London.

I am specially indebted to Sir Thomas Wade for advice of the utmost value to me in my estimate of Chinese tendencies: and to Mr. Trelawny Saunders for much geographical verification respecting Mid Asia.

The composition of these papers, and the reproduction of these speeches, while recalling many bright associations of the sunny land, and many memories of national triumphs won by Britain in Asia, must yet awaken a sorrowful regret for those whose place knows them no more, and for those who, though still in active existence, will probably not be seen by me again. However keen may be our interest in the events now passing before us, and in the wondrous prospect of the time coming, we can hardly escape from pensive reflection after a retrospect of the momentous circumstances which this generation has witnessed in the East. While the thoughts of that noble past crowd around us, we call to mind the lines in the dedication of 'Faust,' some of which I translate literally.

"Ye draw near again, ye wavering forms, that once before showed yourselves to my troubled sight; shall I really essay this time to hold ye fast? . . . . Ye bring with ye the images of happy days, and many beloved shades rise up; like an old Saga lay half-expired, first love and friendship come forth together: the grief is renewed, the wailing repeats the labyrinthine erring course of life, and calls up the Good, who, by Fortune disappointed of their shining hours, have vanished from before me. . . That which I grasp I see as in the distance, and that which has disappeared, to me becomes reality."

R. T.

THE NASH, KEMPSEY, *near* WORCESTER,
*October* 1883.

# CONTENTS.

## CHAPTER I.

### GEOGRAPHY IN ASIA DURING THE LAST FIFTY YEARS.

[*Paper read before the Jubilee Meeting of the British Association for the Advancement of Science, at York, September* 1881.]



## CHAPTER II.

### THE CENTRAL PLATEAU OF ASIA.

[*Paper read before the British Association for the Advancement of Science, at Southampton, September* 1882, *as Presidential Address in the Section of Geography.*]

## CHAPTER III.

### POLITICAL LESSONS OF CHINESE HISTORY.

[*Paper read before the Royal Historical Society, in London, April* 1883.]



## CHAPTER IV.

### LAKE REGION ON THE FRONTIER OF EASTERN TIBET.

[*Speech delivered before the Royal Geographical Society, in London, February* 1882.]



## CHAPTER V.

### RAILWAY FROM THE INDUS TOWARDS CANDAHAR.

[*Speech delivered before the Royal Geographical Society in London, June* 1880.]

## CHAPTER VI.

### LOCAL SELF-GOVERNMENT IN BRITISH INDIA.

[*Reprinted from the 'Contemporary Review' for March* 1883.]



## CHAPTER VII.

### RELIGIOUS MISSIONS IN THE EAST.

[PART I. *Speech delivered before the Society for the Propagation of the Gospel in Foreign Parts, at Lincoln, November* 1881. — PART II. *Speech delivered before the Board of Foreign Missions of the Presbyterian Church in the United States, at New York, November* 1882.—PART III *Speech delivered before the Baptist Missionary Society, in London, April* 1883.]



## CHAPTER VIII.

### EFFECT OF RELIGIOUS THOUGHT AMONG INDIAN NATIVES.

[*Reprinted from the 'Fortnightly Review' for January* 1883.]

## CHAPTER IX.

### THE DUTY OF BRITISH PEOPLE TOWARDS INDIA.

[*Speech delivered before the East India Association, in London, March* 1882.]



## CHAPTER X.

### POLITICAL ECONOMY OF THE INDIAN EMPIRE.

[PART I. *Speech delivered before the Royal Colonial Institute, in London, December* 1880. — PART II. *Speech delivered before the Institute of Bankers, in London, March* 1882.]

## CHAPTER XI.

### INDIAN FORESTRY.

[PART I. *Speech delivered before the Society of Arts, in London, January* 1881.—PART II. *Speech delivered before the Scottish Arboricultural Society, at Edinburgh, October* 1881.]



## CHAPTER XII.

### MONETARY PRACTICE AMONGST THE NATIVES OF INDIA.

[*Speech delivered before the Institute of Bankers, in London, May* 1881.]



## CHAPTER XIII.

### COOPER'S HILL COLLEGE OF ENGINEERING.

## CHAPTER XIV.

### PAN ISLAMISM OR POLITICAL MUHAMMADANISM.

*[Reprinted from the 'Evening News,' London, July* 1882.]



## CHAPTER XV.

### THE MAHRATTA NATIONALITY.

*[Reprinted from the 'Encyclopædia Britannica,' New Edition,* 1883.]



## CHAPTER XVI.

### BIRTHPLACE AND CRADLE OF MAHRATTA POWER.

*[Speech delivered before the Royal Geographical Society, in London, February* 1882.]

## CHAPTER XVII.

### PERSONAL TRAITS OF MAHRATTA BRAHMAN PRINCES.

*[Paper read before the Royal Historical Society in London, June* 1883.]



## CHAPTER XVIII.

### THE TEMPERANCE MOVEMENT AMONG THE BRITISH IN INDIA.

*[Speech delivered before the Temperance Association at Liverpool, February* 1881.]



## CHAPTER XIX.

### PRINCIPLES OF BRITISH POLICY IN EGYPT.

*[Reprinted from the 'Contemporary Review' for October* 1882.]

# LIST OF MAPS AND ILLUSTRATIONS.

# ORIENTAL EXPERIENCE.

## CHAPTER I.

### GEOGRAPHY IN ASIA DURING THE LAST FIFTY YEARS.

[*Paper read before the Jubilee **Meeting** of the British Association for the Advancement of Science, at **York**, September* 1881.]

Physical features of the Asiatic **continent** — General state of our knowledge — Scientific surveys in British **India** — **Military** surveys in Afghanistan — French investigation in Cochin China — Chinese geography — Japanese surveys — Russian surveys in Caucasus, Siberia and Turkestan — Maps of Persia — Travels in Asiatic Turkey and Arabia — Palestine exploration — Progress of Asiatic geography — Vast work remaining to be done — Zeal and fortitude of explorers and travellers.

THE area of Asia contains seventeen millions of English square miles. Out of this, about two-thirds consist of mountains and table-lands, whereof a large part is desert; and one-third of lowlands, wherein a small part is desert: the rest of the lowlands being arable, of which again a considerable portion is cultivated. Thus out of the whole area not more than one-sixth is under cultivation; among the populated tracts, however, some are the most densely peopled in the world. As regards climate, Japan and a part of China proper can be called temperate. The southern peninsulas of Asia have great heat, with but little relief from cold. The main Asiatic continent has extreme cold of varying duration in the year, followed by equally severe heat. Although some nomad tribes show kindness and hospitality to Europeans, and even to European ladies, still for travellers the fierceness of Man is but too often added to the wildness of Nature. The geographers in Asia therefore need not only intellectual ability and persistent diligence, but also the sternest moral qualities and the stiffest physical strength. In recounting their deeds we may adopt the Virgilian words "Arma virumque cano;" that is, we celebrate the work and the men who did it. We remember, too, the maxim, "Nil mortabilus arduum," which to us means that nothing is too hard for geographers to attempt.

On the map which illustrates this paper, and which has been prepared with the assistance of Mr. Trelawny Saunders, Geographer to the India Office, you will see clearly marked in the midst of the continent a great Central Plateau, more than two millions of English square miles in area, rising to great altitudes, which dominates the river systems and the drainage of the greater part of Asia, and which is bounded by the Himalayas towards the Indian Ocean, by the Yun-ling and the Inshan mountains towards the Pacific Ocean, by the Altai and Yoblonoi ranges towards the Arctic Ocean, and by the Pamir mountains towards the inland seas, the Aral and the Caspian. The Pamir mountains constitute a group connecting the great ranges of Himalaya and Altai.

Branching off from this Central Plateau is another extensive plateau, with an average altitude of 5000 feet above the sea, which includes Afghanistan, Beluchistan, Persia, Armenia, and Asia Minor, and from a small part of which the drainage is towards the Atlantic Ocean, through the Black Sea, and the Mediterranean. It is through Asia Minor and the Caucasus that the Asiatic mountains are connected with the ranges of southern Europe.

It is remarkable that from within this Central Plateau, walled round as it is by mountain ranges, there rise most of the greatest Asiatic rivers, which burst through the mountains in order to make a passage towards the sea. Such, for instance, are the Indus, with its affluent the Satlej, the Brahmaputra, the Ganges, the Irawady, the Salwen, the Cambodia or Mekong, all flowing into the Indian Ocean; the Yang-tsze Kiang, the Hoang-Ho, the Amûr, flowing into the Pacific Ocean; the Lena, the Yenisei, and the Ob, flowing into the Arctic Ocean; the Jaxartes and the Oxus, flowing into the inland sea of Aral. Many other rivers, which though lesser are still very great, take their sources from the outer slopes of the mountains which surround the Central Plateau.

Next after the oceanic drainage, the inland Asiatic drainage, which finds no vent towards the ocean, may claim attention as being the largest in the world, and as occupying nearly four millions of English square miles, or nearly one-fourth of the Asiatic continent. This extraordinary drainage area may be divided into the following categories:—1st, the Caspian; 2nd, the Aral; 3rd, the Balkash (Siberian); 4th, Lake Lob (Yarkand); 5th, Kuku-Nor; 6th, the lesser lakes of Tibet; 7th, the lesser lakes of Altai; 8th, the Helmand, draining nearly all Afghanistan into the Seistan swamps; 9th, the Kavir or saline deserts in eastern Persia; 10th, the lake of Urumiya in north-western Persia; 11th, Lake Van in Kurdistan; 12th, the Dead Sea.

The Central Plateau is made up of several plateaux having different altitudes. The highest is that of Tibet, on the average 15,000, above the sea, the loftiest in the world; next, that of Pamir, 13,000 feet; then that of Kuku-Nor, 10,000 feet. Next we see a sudden dip or depression, namely, that of Yarkand, or Western Gobi, only 3000 feet above the sea; then there follow two steps upward, namely, that of Eastern Gobi, 4000 feet; and lastly that of Altai, 5000 feet.

The Central Plateau has been the home of most of the nomad and pastoral tribes which have successfully overrun the rest of Asia. It now belongs (with the exception of one tract) to the Chinese empire.

I next invite your attention to the political divisions of Asia, indicated on the map, as they are now recognized to exist, namely:—I. India and Ceylon; II. Afghanistan and Beluchistan; III. Siam and Cochin China; IV. The Chinese Empire; V. Japan; VI. Asiatic Russia; VII. Persia; VIII. Asiatic Turkey and Arabia.

Upon the map there are separately marked those portions which have been professionally and scientifically surveyed, those portions which have been surveyed non-professionally or roughly, and those portions which have been explored only, without surveys; while the remaining portions, being unexplored, are left white.

For the southern coast of Asia, 15,000 miles in length, the geography is based on professional surveys. For the shores of the Red Sea, Southern Arabia, the Persian Gulf, Beluchistan. British India, Ceylon, and Siam, there are the scientifically framed charts of the British Admiralty or the Indian Marine. For the shores of Cambodia and Cochin China, there are the French surveys; for the Chinese coast, the British surveys with a few intervals only; for the shores of Japan, several surveys; and for the East Siberian coast up to Behring Strait, the Russian surveys at a few points only. The Arctic shore of Siberia, though explored, and at some few points partly surveyed, is for the most part unsurveyed.

I shall now advert very briefly to the work accomplished in each country during the time under review, the last fifty years, that is, since 1830.

I. INDIA AND CEYLON.—As this area, having a million and a half of square miles, and a population the largest in the world, next after that of China, forms part of the British Empire, we may expect to find that here the progress of geography has been during the last fifty years, or since 1830, far greater than in any other country of Asia. Seven great operations have been carried on, namely, the Great Trigonometrical Survey, the Topographical Survey, the Land Revenue Survey, the Field or Cadastral Survey, the special surveys for railways, canals, and roads, the Marine Survey of the coast, and the Geological Survey. From the base of the Himalayan range down to the southernmost cape near

Ceylon the British territories are delineated and depicted, not only mountain by mountain and river by river, but also village by village, even field by field, and are as minutely known as the most highly civilised districts on the globe, or the best-managed estates in Europe. The classic streams of the Indus, the Ganges, the Jumna, and the Brahmaputra, immediately on issuing from their rock-bound beds in the main Asiatic range, aptly termed in all ages "the Abode of Snow," are brought within the grasp of the geographer along their whole course, their banks being described, their velocity and fall per mile calculated, the volume of their waters measured. Similar processes have been adopted with the densely peopled basins of the rivers which rise in the purely Indian ranges. The altitude has been precisely determined of many of the loftiest peaks yet discovered on the earth, and of every range that is pierced by a railway or crossed by a road. The country has been covered by a network of triangles, a large arc of the meridian has been measured, the curvature, contour, and configuration of the land have been ascertained by geodetic work. Every spur, ravine, and torrent-bed has been examined in the hills, which are studded with tea or coffee plantations, or with gold mines, or with coal beds. In the field-maps of the cultivated plains and valleys, every land-mark in the fields, even every cottage or tenement, is noted down. In two provinces only, Bengal and Behar, is the field-survey wanting.

The Himalayan ranges are indeed under British domination, but have not been fully surveyed. Herbert was the pioneer; afterwards Brian Hodgson followed with excellent geographical analysis. The central portion of this region belongs to the Nepal State, which has for the most part successfully resisted the advance of exploration within its limits. In the eastern portion, Sikkim was mapped by Dr. (now Sir Joseph) Hooker, and some knowledge was gained of Bhûtan through the mission of Pemberton and Griffith, and later through the mission of Eden and the subsequent war. In the western portion, Kashmir has been topographically surveyed by Montgomerie; Ladakh has been explored by Shaw, Gilghit by Biddulph, the Pangong basin and the Mustagh by Godwin-Austen; Dr. Thomas Thomson was the first to reach the Karakoram pass; much original work has been performed in various directions by native Indian surveyors of high qualifications; something has been ascertained regarding Kafiristan by Tanner; Basevi and Stolicska fell victims to their scientific labours near the Yarkand border. Surveyors have carried their instruments to altitudes of 21,500 feet above the sea; and year by year fresh passes are crossed by individual travellers.

Among the chiefs of the geographical department in India the names of Everest, Waugh, Walker, and Thuillier are conspicuous. Markham's memoir on the Indian Surveys furnishes a condensed history of the labours of those distinguished surveyors; and the catalogue of maps preserved at the India Office in London shows the results of their work.

The surveys of Ceylon are also in a nearly complete state, and the excellent map by Fraser, the Surveyor General, and his successors supplies full information.

II. AFGHANISTAN AND BELUCHISTAN.—Although these countries have been for more than one generation connected with the British Government, their geography is utterly incomplete. The territory indeed offers the utmost difficulty to surveying, being for the most part mountainous, with extreme cold in many quarters, the remainder being desert. It is not this difficulty, however, which prevents surveying. The real obstacle is the fierce and intractable character of the inhabitants, who would treat any attempt at surveying as a *casus belli*. The Government, then, has always to consider the alternative of fighting; because geographical efforts, unless backed by armed force, would end only in failure and bloodshed.

Some general account of the region was obtained by Mountstuart Elphinstone's embassy to Cabul in 1808, together with a map by Macartney. Many details have been subsequently supplied under circumstances of a stirring and adventurous character, by men whose memory will not be forgotten so long as the record of British zeal, constancy, and resolution shall endure. Alexander Burnes, Arthur Conolly, Eldred Pottinger, Henry Rawlinson, James Abbott, John Wood, have obtained particulars of Afghanistan and its dependencies from the sultry marshes of Seistan to the sources of the Oxus. These being officers of the Indian Government, had before their eyes the goal of a career in the public service. Others, however, travelled in a private capacity, holding their lives in their hands at all hours of the day and the night during weary months, and often subject to insult from cruel and barbarous people. Such were Moorcroft, Trebeck, Masson, Vigne, and the Frenchman Ferrier.

Little of surveying was effected during the first occupation of Afghanistan by the British from 1838 to 1841. The mission of Harry Lumsden to Candahar in 1857, and the arbitration regarding the Seistan boundary in 1872, added something to our topographical knowledge. Much of recent information respecting the southern and western districts was embodied in the work by Dr. Bellew in 1874.

During the recent Afghan war from 1878 to 1880, a professional surveying staff was attached to the military establishments, and thus routes were surveyed and altitudes taken, on the lines for the march of troops. The results of this work have been embodied in the reports by Captain Holdich. On the whole, considerable data exist for the maps which have been issued by Thuillier and Walker in India, and by Wilson in England. Still it is to be remembered that no comprehensive surveys have been possible, that in a few parts only of the country has the work been completely scientific, and that many parts (especially the Hazâra country and the Zhob valley) remain unexplored.

The geography of Beluchistan is even less advanced; of the north-eastern portion some knowledge has been obtained from the political and diplomatic proceedings of the last few years, and by the surveys for the railway from the Indus towards Candahar.

The interior of this vast area is known only from the daring journey of Henry Pottinger, the travels of Masson, and the explorations connected with the Seistan mission.

III. SIAM AND COCHIN CHINA.—The country of Siam is known to English readers chiefly through the descriptive works published by Crawfurd of his mission in 1821, and by Bowring of his mission in 1855; these descriptions were not, however, derived from personal explorations in the interior. In 1854 the French Bishop Pallegoix published a map of his journeyings. Again, in 1864 another Frenchman, Mouhot, undertook under English auspices a scientific expedition up the course of the Meinam, the principal river of Siam, penetrating to a point near its source, and died from his fatigues.

In the deltaic region of Cambodia the French authorities are duly surveying their settlements around Saigon; and a French geographical literature for this district together with the adjacent territories is fast accumulating. In 1866 a geographical and scientific expedition was undertaken by the French Government along the Mekong, the great river of Cambodia, right up to the regions near its source within the Chinese border. Of this important exploration some account was given by Carné in 1872, and a great report was published in 1873 by Garnier, splendidly executed and embellished with an album of pictorial illustrations. Garnier was, while still comparatively young, murdered by Chinese rebels. Further, these operations were connected with the Chinese coast by the explorations of Harmand in 1877.

For the rest of Cochin China, now called by its local name Anam, French authors have published several descriptive works. Here also explorations have been made by the French along the course of the Red River of Tonkin on the north near the frontier of China proper.

IV. THE CHINESE EMPIRE.—In this area, which has four millions of square miles, and the largest population of any country in the world, are included four main divisions, namely, 1st, China proper; 2nd, Manchuria,; 3rd, Mongolia, Kulja, and Yarkand; 4th, Tibet. The Chinese have bestowed upon topography that marvellous aptitude for details which they evince in other subjects. For their enormous territories they have, through centuries of research, compiled monster gazetteers comprising several hundreds of maps and of volumes. But the examination was not conducted with anything like a scientific survey, the maps were not precise, nor was the general geography exactly determined. In the seventeenth century, however, one Chinese emperor employed the Jesuit missionaries to make the best surveys possible with the then existing appliances; and the results were collated by D'Anville in his famous 'Atlas de la Chine,' published at the Hague in 1737. In the eighteenth century another emperor caused further surveys to be made by the Roman missionaries, who fixed many points by astronomical observations about the year 1755; and these points were a century later presented to the English public by the appendix to Michell's book upon the Russians in Central Asia. The Jesuit surveys were also published in Europe by Du Halde. Those who know the persevering zeal of the Roman Catholic priests in Asia, will readily imagine how steadily these missionaries must have prosecuted their surveying operations. After them there was a lull in the advance of Chinese geography for three generations. Within the last generation, however, the Chinese empire has been the scene of many wonderful explorations. Again Roman Catholic missionaries, two Frenchmen, Gabet and Huc, led the way by toilsome marches of more than 7000 miles right through China proper and Mongolia, between the years 1845 and 1850. Gabet died from infirmities caused by his sufferings during this journey, but Huc survived to relate their proceedings in one of the most entertaining books of travel ever written. But in gauging the value of his information it must be remembered that he was not a surveyor nor a trained geographer. The Russian military officer Prejevalsky, the most scientifically trained, persevering, and capable traveller that has yet entered Mongolia, went over a part of the same ground in 1870, in the course of his successive explorations. He finds fault with some of Huc's observations and descriptions; but Colonel Henry Yule, one of the best of living English authorities on such subjects, has stated that Huc's word-pictures, brightened perhaps by a lively fancy, appear to have been drawn from nature, though errors had crept into them from imperfect recollection. Still such books as that by Huc, however interesting, are not to be compared in solid merit with the exact and well-weighed work of Prejevalsky. In Mongolia also the journey of Ney Elias in 1872 proved to be very important; and the routes taken by the Russians, Potanin and Rafailoff, have been recently published by Petermann. The work has been carried on by the visit of Delmar Morgan to Kulja.

Further, the topography of Yarkand and Kashgar was elucidated by the mission of Sir Douglas Forsyth in 1873. Of this a full report has been written by Trotter, whose explorations were remarkable and extended to the Pamir lake. Yarkand was visited by Shaw twice, and once by Hayward, who lost his life. Further, Johnson penetrated to Khoten.

In the elevated plateau of Tibet no explorations have been made since the political missions of Bogle and Turner in the eighteenth century, which were despatched by Warren Hastings, the Governor-General of India, and the journey of Manning to Lhassa. Recently, however, in 1870, the French missionary Desgodins published the result of his Tibetan journeys extending over several thousands of miles. Here again the native Indian surveyors, trained by Montgomerie, have taken accurately many altitudes, determined the lacustrine characters of the plateau, and followed the course of the San-po, till it disappears amidst the Himalayas.

For China proper, another French missionary, David, in 1874 gave to the public the results of his ten years of travel extending over some 6000 miles. The Chinese nowadays offer the most liberal facilities to Christian missions for evangelistic tours, and many missionaries, English and French, are availing themselves of these opportunities. The best example of travel in China is the work of the German Richthofen, who, after covering the country with a network, as it were, of his journeyings, published in 1877 the most scientific, systematic, and elaborate of the books yet written on that country. In this work, among other things, much geological information is embodied. As might be expected, the English have made use of the advantages they possess in China for geographical exploration. A generation has passed since Fortune paid to the tea-districts those visits which have proved so fruitful in economic results. Blakiston has minutely determined the course of the lower Yang-tsze Kiang. Within the last few years, Cooper, Margery, Ney Elias, Gill, and Baber have courageously and laboriously passed from China across perilous regions straight through to India or to Burma. Of these, Cooper was killed by a half demented native soldier of his own escort, at Bahmo in Upper Burma. Margery and Gill were murdered, the former with the collusion of the officials on the Chinese frontier, the latter by the Bedouins of the Egyptian desert. But Ney Elias and Baber are still in the van of geographers.

Adjoining China, there is the comparatively small peninsula of the Corea, of which little is known except from the explorations of Dallet, the French missionary. The Corea is about to be visited by a surveying vessel, on board of which is our accomplished young Associate, Lieutenant Pirie, R.N.

V. JAPAN.—We next glance at the chain or group of picturesque, fertile, and populous islands—sometimes divided one from the other only by narrow streaks of water—which constitute the dominion of Japan. Under their ancient and, as it would be called by some, their uncivilised system, the Japanese collected a mass of topographical information. All that was most valuable in this was collated by Siebold, a distinguished officer who was despatched by the Dutch Government of Java in 1823 on a commercial mission to Japan, where he resided till 1830. During his eight years of residence or travel in this country, he supplemented the Japanese geography by observations of his own, many of which bore a scientific character. He then embodied the results in a large work of several quarto volumes. This work was completed in 1832, and is beautifully illustrated with pictorial representations which bring before the reader's eye a scenery which remains ever the same in its beauty, and national costumes or characteristics which are fast passing away under a new civilisation. From these data was the map prepared by Commodore Perry, of the United States Navy, for his work describing the commercial mission on which he proceeded twenty years later, in 1852. He again added much information, on scientific authority, for the extensive coasts of this island dominion. In 1863 Sir Rutherford Alcock, after an official residence of several years, published his work entitled 'The Capital of the Tycoon,' which embodied, among other things, the geographical results of inland travel and the ascent of lofty mountains. Subsequently the world has been astonished by the wave of quasi-European civilisation which is sweeping over many of the old institutions in this country. Among the consequences of this is the introduction of projects for postal roads, electric telegraph lines, railways, and other purposes of an administration framed after European models. For the railway lines, surveys have been or are being made. A line across the principal island has been determined by trigonometry. Some geological surveys have also been carried out. From these, combined with the former data, a map was made by Mr. Brunton, in the Japanese service, and more recently a still better map has been prepared by Knipping, a German, also in the Japanese service, and engraved by Stanford of London. A handbook has been prepared by Mr. Satow, on the staff of the British embassy, and by Lieutenant Hawes of the Royal Marines. Lastly, an English lady, Miss Bird, having traversed important tracts in solitude and hardship, with amazing constancy and endurance, has set forth her observations in a graphic and life-like narrative.

VI. ASIATIC RUSSIA.—In this area, which contains six millions of square miles, are included, first, Siberia and Russian Manchuria; secondly, Caucasia, including the Caucasus mountains, together with the region lying between them and Armenia; thirdly, Western Turkistan, now extending to the northern boundary of Persia.

For Siberia, the meritorious travels of Pallas at the end of the eighteenth century, of Wrangel, of Middenorff, of Erman, of Alexander Humboldt during the first half of the present century, are still of value. But systematic modern exploration, combining geology and zoology with geography, began in 1854 with the operations of Schwarz, Schmidt, and others in the upper basins of the Lena and Amur rivers. This work was followed up by the expedition under Prince Kropotkin (a good geologist) to the same region in 1873, and by Poyarkow's explorations of the Amûr. A further examination was made of the river Lena by Lopatkin, of the Amur by Maack the naturalist, and by Schrenck (whose work has fine zoological illustrations), and of the Lower Amûr by Bolshev in 1874. The basin of the river Ob was visited by Polyakoff, and of the Yenisei by Krivoshapkin. The mountain region of the Altai and the north of Siberia have been described by the works of Radde (rich in pictorial illustration), and by the book of travels undertaken by the German Finsch in connection with the North Polar expedition of Germany; also by the works of many other travellers. In short, the Russians have within the last thirty years accumulated quite a geographical literature and published a series of excellent maps regarding Siberia and Kamchatka, the particulars of which would exceed the space at our disposal. Thereby the principal points have been scientifically fixed, the altitudes of many of the mountains have been ascertained, and the basins of the principal rivers have been examined. But it is hardly to be expected that regular surveying can as yet have been extended throughout a region so vast, inclement, and inhospitable. The survey of the country must be regarded as still unfinished, and the information as approximate only for many places. Still the geographical results already obtained are honourable to the Russian Government, and prove the skill and resolution of the explorers.

The voyage of the distinguished Swede Nordenskiöld along the northern coast of Siberia resulting in the discovery of the North-east passage, and the rectification of the coast-line by his colleague Pallander, are fresh in the memory of all; but it ought not to be forgotten that here the way was led by Wiggins of Sunderland.

The borders of Western Siberia have been trigonometrically and geologically surveyed, and with those operations the great name of Sir Roderick Murchison is honourably associated.

For English readers, several parts of Siberia have been recently described by the Rev. Henry Lansdell, after a journey of 8000 miles from the Urals to the Pacific. The Altai mountains, even within Mongolian limits, and the Siberian plains, also have been graphically illustrated by Atkinson, a portion of whose toils was shared by his courageous wife, and whose life was prematurely ended by the hardships he endured during his travels. Among the precursors of travelling on the Amur was Collins the American. Then Kennan published the story of his tent life in Siberia, and Bush an account of reindeer dogs and snowshoes; both these travellers were American. The Englishman, Seebohm, descended the Yenisei to the Arctic circle, in the prosecution of ornithological studies.

Next, for Caucasia, trigonometrical surveys have been made by the Russian Government between the years 1830 and 1860, and a large map has been prepared by the topographical staff. Here we meet again with pictorial illustrations by Radde, adorning his geographical work on this region. The Caucasus itself has been visited by English travellers, Moore, Grove, and especially by Freshfield, who ascended apparently for the first time the summit of Elbruz, and has presented to English readers a charming narrative of his proceedings.

Lastly, for Western Turkistan, the Russian Government has

caused some important surveys to be made and several scientific expeditions to be undertaken within the last fifteen years. This geographical literature has become so varied and extensive that the names of the distinguished Russian officers connected with it are too numerous to be mentioned in our limited space. One of these Russian surveys arrived at a point only 30 miles distant from the farthest English survey from India. It appears from Trotter's account that the English and Russian surveys were never joined; and thus a trigonometrical line right through Asia from north to south remains to be accomplished. For the eastern shores of the Aral and Caspian seas, for the basin of the great river Oxus, for the course of the lesser though important river Attrek, the surveys, if not scientifically complete, are very considerable; many points of consequence have been astronomically determined, and quite 2000 altitudes have been taken with the barometer. Admiral Boutakoff was the first to navigate ships on the sea of Aral. About four-fifths of the elevated steppes of Pamir and of the neighbouring Alai mountains have been roughly surveyed. The old course of the Oxus towards the Caspian has been ascertained, and the oscillations of that river between the Aral and the Caspian in former centuries have been verified.

The exploration of the Thian-Shan mountains was begun in 1856, and has been since continued at intervals by eminent Russian officers. Notwithstanding their efforts, however, the barometrical observations are understood to be of doubtful accuracy, and the estimates of altitudes are approximate only.

Other nations have shared with Russia in the honours of travel in this region; the works of the Hungarian Vambery, the Frenchman Ujfalvy-Bourdon and his talented wife, the American Schuyler, the Englishman Burnaby, shine brightly in the memory of geographers. It was here that the German Schlagintweit lost his life in the midst of his work, a martyr of science. Here also the war correspondents of the newspaper press, Macgahan and O'Donovan, added to our topographical knowledge while following their arduous profession.

It is not to be forgotten that some of the earliest explorers in Western Turkistan were English. The travels of Burnes and Conolly in this quarter formed part of their journeys already mentioned in reference to Afghanistan. Afterwards Conolly in company with Stoddard proceeded to Bokhara, where they both were barbarously killed by the Khan. James Abbott marched through the Merv desert to Khiva and thence to the shore of the Caspian, and has recorded his adventures in one of the most remarkable narratives of modern travel.

VII. PERSIA.—For Persia, a new map in six sheets has recently been prepared under the orders of the Secretary of State for India, by Major (now Sir Oliver) St. John (R.E.), whose reports embody much information regarding the geological formations, the altitudes of some of the mountains, and the physical geography. This map is based in part upon surveys taken for the purpose; there are also the data furnished by the surveyed lines of the Indo-European telegraph, of the political mission through Southern Persia to the south-western corner of Afghanistan, and of the border between Persia and Turkey. Much of the country, however, remains unsurveyed; the altitudes of many points among the mountains towards the Caspian Sea, the Persian Gulf, and the Euphrates basin have been but approximately estimated; and the levels of the depressions called salt deserts are only known roughly. Though some districts remain unexplored, there have been many explorers within the last fifty years, mostly servants of the British Government. Besides the men of the last generation, Morier, Malcolm, Porter, Fraser, and others whose writings are monuments of talent and industry, and above all, Kinneir, the great topographer,—many English travellers have arisen in recent times to illustrate a country so primeval in its associations and yet so fraught with modern interest. Such men are Layard, Goldsmid, Valentine Baker, Eastwick, Mounsey, Macgregor, Bellew, C. E. Stewart.

Much light has been thrown on the whole subject by the writings of Sir Henry Rawlinson. The representatives of other nations also have shared in this interesting work; such are the Frenchman Ferrier, the Russian Khanikoff, the German Schindler. The geology of the country has been in part elucidated by the writings of Loftus and Blanford.

VIII. ASIATIC TURKEY AND ARABIA.—It will be remembered that the Asiatic dominions of Turkey comprise, 1st, Asia Minor and Armenia; 2nd, Mesopotamia and the adjacent territory; 3rd, Arabia, for the most part; 4th, Syria and Palestine.

For Asia Minor and Armenia the standard map is that by the German geographer Kiepert, based largely on surveys made and information collected in 1838 by Moltke, who was then a major on the general staff, and who has since become celebrated.

The several archæological explorers starting generally from the Mediterranean coast, have, while exhuming remains or excavating ruins, rendered incidentally great service to geography. The work by Fellowes in 1838, supplemented greatly the knowledge of that time. Later on, the finely illustrated book by the Russian Tchihatcheff threw light on the circumstances of the country. Members of the British Consular Service have, by journeys undertaken for the better preparation of their official reports, promoted the advance of geography; conspicuous among these are Colonel (now Sir Charles) Wilson and Mr. Chermside. Considerable investigations into the topography and geology of the country were made by Richardson and MacCoan. Recent years have been fruitful in travel, consequent doubtless on the awakening of general interest in this region. The Rev. Mr. Davis has published excellent records of two journeys, one relating chiefly to Anatolia, the other chiefly to Cilicia. Burnaby's ride through the middle plateau, along the Upper Euphrates, and round Lake Van, is fresh in the public recollection. Freshfield's explorations in the neighbourhood of Ararat added much to the public knowledge of that noteworthy region.

Subsequently, Bryce's ascent of this mountain, when, deserted by his native guides, he advanced alone amidst the clouds and darkness to the summit, setting marks on the ice and snow for recognition of the way on his return descent--forms a striking episode in the history of travel.

For Arabian geography during many years the standard authorities were the careful results made by Niebuhr and Burckhardt. They were followed first by Wellsted, and subsequently by Burton with the vivacious narrative of his pilgrimage to Mecca. The northern tracts have more recently been described by the Italian Arconati Visconti, with many large illustrations, and by the German Hüber; also the southern tracts by the Frenchman Halévy, the German Müller, and the Italian Manzoni. The tracts belonging to the Arab tribes under the control of the British settlement of Aden are being fast explored and mapped. The independent Wahhabi kingdom around Riad, lying far inland in the heart of the arid peninsula, has been understood for the first time since the wonderful journeys of the Englishman Palgrave and the German Wallin. Collaterally, much information on the subject has been gathered by means of Sir Lewis Pelly's journey inwards from the Persian Gulf, by marches conducted under frequent peril of death from thirst. Lastly, one of the most talented among lady travellers, Lady Anne Blunt, has performed much original work in Nejd or Central Arabia, correcting parts of the previously received topography, and determining altitudes with barometrical readings.

For the rivers of Mesopotamia many geographical data have been furnished by the surveys of the Indian Navy. The greatest geographer in this region was Colonel F. R. Chesney, who in 1835 conveyed a steamer in pieces from the Mediterranean shore across the desert, and set it up on the Euphrates. He thence extended his inquiries over all Western Asia and prepared a record which constitutes a monument of amazing industry. The Assyrian excavations, first by Layard and Botta, and afterwards by George Smith, Rassam, and others, have incidentally afforded help to geography. Here also Lady Anne Blunt's journeys have added much to our knowledge.

For the map of Syria and Palestine, data of the best sort are being gradually furnished from the inquiries begun by the Palestine Association in 1832, and from the surveys prosecuted by the Palestine Exploration Fund since 1865, on which Wilson, Warren, Palmer, Conder, and other able officers have been engaged. These surveys, which are still in progress, are directed scientifically, and have for their objects among other things the topography, geology, and physical geography of the Holy Land. Already a detailed map on a large scale of Western Palestine has been issued, and an expedition is now in the field for the survey on a similar scale of the region beyond the Jordan. Among the separate and independent explorers, the names of the Frenchman Guerin, and of the Englishmen Porter, Tristram, Robinson, Burton, Beke, are conspicuous. Lastly, a melancholy interest is now aroused when we mention the charming book by Arthur Penrhyn Stanley.

Finally, it will be observed that the Eastern Archipelago, including Java, Borneo, and Sumatra, has not been embraced in this review, as that is by the latest geographers included in Australasia.

In conclusion, from this rapid review, which is summary only and not exhaustive, it will be seen how much has been accomplished absolutely during the last fifty years, say since 1830, and yet how little relatively. Geographers from most of the European nations have laboured for a common end. A geographical literature has been gathered together, comprising many names besides those which have been mentioned in this paper. Yearly additions are made to our knowledge by the reports of the British Consular Service. The efforts of governments, of societies, and of individuals have been combined. The results have been on the whole commensurate with the cost in money and resources, and with the wear and tear in human life and strength. The great share borne by England and

Russia is only proportionate to the magnitude of their stake in Asia; other European nations have also earned a title to geographical fame. Respecting the literature in several languages on this subject, Englishmen may well remark the attention which foreign travellers pay to pictorial illustration. Hardly any recent English books of travel are so richly illustrated as the works in French by Garnier, in German by Richthofen, in Russian by Radde, in Dutch by Siebold.

Still it must be admitted that the greater part of Asia has not yet been touched by scientific operations on a complete scale. In the whole of Asia, only India, Ceylon, Cyprus, Western Palestine, Caucasia, the Caspian basin, part of Western Siberia, and part of Japan, also many points in the Asiatic coast-line, have been subjected to trigonometrical observation. The altitudes of mountains have been determined only in the Himalayas, the Caucasus, and the Urals by trigonometry. But in many ranges the heights have been approximately ascertained by the barometer. Professional surveys in details have been completed only in India, Ceylon, Western Palestine, Caucasia, parts of Western and Eastern Siberia, the Thian-Shan region, the greater part of Western Turkistan, Cambodia, parts of Cochin China, parts of Afghanistan, also on certain lines of Persia, Mesopotamia, and Asia Minor. Even in the professionally surveyed territories many defects and imperfections are acknowledged to remain.

Non-professional surveys have been carried out in Japan, in China proper, in parts of Arabia, on the frontiers of Tibet, China, and Burma, and on certain lines in Afghanistan and Beluchistan. Explorations without any actual survey have been made in Mongolia, Siam, the interior of Arabia, most parts of Persia, the Turkoman country, the Ust-urt plateau between the Aral and the Caspian, Manchuria, and in some parts of Afghanistan and Beluchistan.

Though, as already stated, the southern coasts of Asia have been surveyed in sufficient detail for geographical purposes, yet according to the demands of a growing traffic and of maritime resort, these surveys need frequently to be amplified in detail. The old surveys by the Indian Navy were good in their day, reflecting honour on Moresby, Ross, and others; still the Government have ordered a new survey to be made for nautical purposes. A fresh survey, like that done by Sir George Nares for the Gulf of Suez, may have to be ordered one day for the whole of the Red Sea, and the Persian Gulf. The British Admiralty are making yearly additions to the surveys of the Chinese coasts, of which the work done by St. John (R.N.) is an example. Whether the Russians will see fit to attempt a scientific survey throughout the Arctic coast of Siberia remains to be seen. This branch of the subject will be best understood on a reference to the paper on oceanic explorations and research, by the highest authority, namely, Sir Frederick Evans, Hydrographer to the Admiralty.

Of geological surveys, the largest example is that in India, which, though well advanced, is far from complete. Very much remains to be done in this respect for the Himalayas. Geological surveys have been made in the Caucasus, the Urals, the Thian-shan and Altai ranges, Kamchatka, many parts of China and Japan, Cambodia, Ceylon, some parts of Arabia and Persia, much of Asia Minor and Palestine.

But there remain unexplored, parts of the Himalayas, of Afghanistan and Beluchistan, of Arabia, and nearly the whole Kuen-Lun region north of Tibet, in the very heart of Asia.

Further, the following are among the principal geographical problems still awaiting solution:—The connection of the Tibetan San-po with the Indian Brahmaputra; the existence of mountains connecting the Kuen-lun range eastwards with the Chinese ranges; the sources and upper courses of the Irawady, Salwen, Mekong, and Hoang Ho; the disposition of the mountains between the Ladakh passes and the Hindu-Kush or Indian Caucasus north of Cabul, near to the culminating region of the entire continent.

When recounting the deeds of explorers and geographers in Asia, we ought to cherish the memory of the Italian Marco Polo, the mediæval traveller whose amazing journeys in Asia have never been equalled even by the great tra' ellers who have succeeded him in modern times. The record of Marco Polo's travels has been recently familiarized to English readers by the learned labour of Henry Yule.

A retrospect of brave and successful achievement should encourage travellers to do and to dare more and more. Of the men thus engaged, many indeed have injured their health, and some have lost their lives. But all have been sustained under trials by their sense of natural beauty, their aspirations for the progress of civilisation, and their zeal in the pursuit of knowledge. It is the masterful force of these high and noble sentiments which impels them, "tot volvere casus, tot adire labores." *

* Subsequently to the reading of this paper additional information has been presented by the Royal Geographical Society regarding Russian surveys between the Turkoman country and Herat; which surveys shew that the route across the continuation of the Hindu-Kush range is much more easily passable for armies than has been generally supposed.

# CHAPTER II.

## THE CENTRAL PLATEAU OF ASIA.

[*Paper read before the British Association for the Advancement of Science, at Southampton, September* 1882, *as Presidential Address in the Section of Geography.*]

Grand mountain system — Series of heights and depressions — Sources of great rivers — The lake regions — The home of warriors and conquering races — Mighty achievements of the Mongols — Their cavalry resources — Variety and value of natural products — Pastoral wealth — Strange phenomena of Nature — Enormous field awaiting research — Imperial jurisdiction.

THE subject chosen for this address is the Plateau of mid-Asia. This area, which is one of the most wonderful on the surface of the earth, contains nearly 3,000,000 of English square miles, and is equal to three-fourths of Europe. Its limits, its exterior configuration, its central and commanding situation in the Asiatic continent, will be clearly perceived from the subjoined map of Asia.* As compared with some of the more favoured regions, it is singularly destitute of natural advantages. Though it has several deep depressions of surface, yet its general elevation is very considerable, and some of its large districts are the most elevated in the globe. It is walled in from the outer world, and excluded from the benign influences of the sea, by mountain chains. Its climate, then, is very severe on the whole, more distinguished for cold than for heat, but often displaying extremes of temperature high as well as low. It offers, from the character of its contour, extra-

* See map prefixed to Chapter I.

ordinary obstacles to communication by land or water. Though seldom inaccessible to courageous explorers, it is generally hard of access, and in several respects very inhospitable. In the progress of civilisation it is, with reference to its historic past, excessively backward. Its capacities for the production of wealth have been but little developed. Its population is scanty, scattered, and uncultured. Its agriculture comprises only a few areas widely segregated from each other, and many of its largest districts are amazingly desolate.

Nevertheless this plateau has eminent claims on the attention of geographers, for several reasons which may be summarised thus:—

1. A mountain system which dominates the greater part of Asia, and includes stupendous ranges with the loftiest peaks yet discovered in the world.

2. A series of heights and depressions almost like the steps of a staircase within the mountainous circumvallation of the plateau.

3. The sources and the permanent supply of rivers which, passing from the plateau, flow through densely populated regions, and help to sustain the numerically greatest families of the human race.

4. A lacustrine system, comprising lakes, of which some are saline while others have fresh water, and of which many are situated at great altitudes.

5. The home of conquering races, whence warrior hordes poured during several centuries over nearly all Asia and a large part of Europe.

6. Natural products of value, variety, or interest, and pastoral resources susceptible of indefinite development.

7. An enormous field for scientific research, with many regions which, though not wholly undiscovered, yet need much further discovery.

8. An imperial jurisdiction offering many problems for the consideration of social inquirers.

I shall now offer a brief explanation regarding each of the eight points stated above.

In the first place it will be seen from the map that the plateau, in shape somewhat of an irregular rhomboid, is completely enclosed by six grand ranges of mountains, namely the Himalayas looking south towards India, the Pamir looking west towards Central Asia, the Altai looking north towards Siberia, the Yablonoi looking north-east towards Eastern Siberia, the Yun-ling and the Inshan (inclusive of the Khingan), looking towards China. These several ranges preserve generally a considerable altitude varying from 6,000 to 25,000 feet above sea-level, and reaching in the Himalayas to more than 29,000 feet. The tallest of these summits have been accurately measured by the Great Trigonometrical Survey of India. Their altitude is about double that of the highest mountains in Europe, and surpasses any altitude yet observed in any quarter of the globe. But as a great part of these several ranges is as yet unsurveyed by trigonometry, it is possible that still greater heights may be discovered, and that "excelsior" may be the proud answer rendered by the everlasting hills to human investigation.

Regarding these and the other chains yet to be mentioned, it must be borne in mind that there are many cross ranges and transverse lines of mountains. Even the chains often consist of detached groups separated by deep valleys. It is by observing the position of the groups relatively to one another that the tendency of the chain can be discerned.

Such being the outer barriers of our plateau, there are within it two great ranges mainly parallel and running from west to east, namely the Kuen-lun and the Thian Shan.

While the Himalayas form the southern flank of the great Tibetan upland, the Kuen-lun constitutes the northern. The modicum of knowledge possessed by us regarding the Kuen-lun, a most important factor in the geography of our plateau, is largely due to the praiseworthy travels of the Russian Prejevalsky. This range may be said in a certain sense to overlook the Tarim basin ending in Lake Lob, though the mountains are actually distant more than a hundred miles from that lake. It forms the southern boundary of the Tarim basir, which contains some of the few beautiful tracts in our plateau. If there be such a thing as a backbone to these regions, or anything like a dorsal ridge, it consists of the Kuen-lun.

The Thian Shan starts from the Pamir, and runs westward for full 1500 miles, till it joins with some of its spurs the uplands of Mongolia proper, or touches with others the dreary desert of Gobi. As the Kuen-lun forms the southern boundary of the Tarim basin, so the Thian Shan constitutes the northern.

Connected with the north-western part of the Himalayas is another range which some regard as an offshoot, but which others treat separately under the name of Karakuram. Together with the Himalayas it joins the Pamir.

Thus three of the greatest mountain ranges in Asia converge upon the Pamir, or, according to some, are there interlaced; namely the Himalayas, the Kuen-lun, and the Thian Shan; to which perhaps two others might be added, namely the Karakuram just mentioned and the Altai. But it may be more accurately said that the outer border of our plateau north of the Pamir is formed by the terminal spurs of the Thian Shan. It is to be remembered also that the Indian Caucasus—which does not concern our plateau directly enough to fall within this address—probably joins the Pamir. In general terms, the convergence of mountain ranges on the Pamir renders it geographically the most important position in Asia. The uninstructed Asiatics have evinced a hazy admiration of its grandeur by calling it "the roof of the world." The comparatively instructed Europeans have revered it as the source of the classic Oxus and as fraught with political considerations. Unless further discoveries shall alter existing information, we may expect that completely informed geographers will consider that this Pamir is the mother of mountains, that other ranges are to it as the branches are to the root, and that here if anywhere is the true boss of the Asiatic shield.

In the second place, the vast surface of our plateau, though almost uninterruptedly environed by its rocky walls, presents an extraordinary series of elevations and depressions. In the heart of the plateau there is the depression known to geographers as the Western Gobi, sometimes called the Tarim basin. Within this there is the Lob Lake or Lob Nor, truly an inland sea into which the waters of several rivers ultimately flow, finding no vent towards the ocean. The total length of the Tarim river with its affluents debouching into Lob Nor, cannot be less than 800 miles. This curious and interesting lake is not more than 2,000 feet above sea-level, and forms almost the lowest dip in our plateau. It is like the bottom of a vast platter, or the centre in the hollow of a mighty hand. Around this depression there are on all sides uplands of various heights, like gradations in the Asiatic terrace, terminating in the intermediate ranges, or in the outer circumvallation of mountains already described. On the east of it there is the tract called Eastern Gobi, partly desert, and Mongolia, averaging 4,000 feet above sea-level; on the north the Altai uplands, exceeding 5,000 feet. On the west the Pamir rises abruptly, exceeding 13,000 feet; on the south is Tibet, with equal abruptness, having an average altitude of 15,000 feet above sea-level, thus being the loftiest expanse in the world; and on the south-east lies the tract around the Kuku Nor Lake, 10,000 feet.

Further, there is a detached depression known as the Zungarian strait, extending to the northern confine of our plateau between the Thian Shan and the Altai ranges. This strait, hardly exceeding 2,000 feet above sea-level, is as low as, perhaps even lower than, any part of our plateau, and is very near breaking its continuity, which may be considered as being just saved by the comparatively humble altitude above mentioned.

The depression is geographically important as forming the only broad pass between our plateau and the world without. It runs from Mongolia, the most important tract within our plateau, to Siberia outside. Great value was, in early times, attached by the Chinese to it, as being the only natural highway on a large scale between Northern and Central Asia.

The existence of this and the other depressions above described has led to interesting speculations among geologists as to there having been, in primeval times within our plateau, at least one inland sea as large as the Mediterranean of Europe.

Be that as it may, there is no doubt that a process of desiccation has been going on within our plateau during historic ages, whereby the climate is considerably affected, and many signs or evidences show that this process is still in operation.

On most of its sides our plateau is extraordinarily inaccessible, the passes being steep in the extreme, and culminating in ridges 18,000 to 20,000 feet above sea-level. Towards Siberia the Altai passes are easier, and on the north-east between Mongolia and China there are several passes that have witnessed the historic outpourings of the Mongol hordes, and that are ominously remembered by the Chinese as the openings through which their invaders rushed like the great river in flood, or the landslip from the mountain side, or the avalanche sweeping along the boulders and *débris* to the destruction of the valleys beneath.

The great desert of Eastern Gobi occupies the eastern portion of our plateau. With its accumulating forces of sand and powdered earth it has a tendency to encroach, and is regarded by man with a vague awe. Its present extent is enormous, being not less than half a million of square miles. Nor does it exist alone within our plateau, for between the Tarim basin and the Kuen-lun spurs there is a lesser desert called Takla-makan with 100,000 square miles of area. It may probably be found that these two deserts join or are otherwise connected.

In the third place we have noted that while the prevailing

characteristics of our plateau are wildness, ruggedness, or desolation; yet within it are the sources of several great rivers which sustain the most teeming peoples on the face of the earth. The monarch as it were of all these noble waters is the Yang-tse-Kiang. Though its head streams have been but imperfectly explored, yet its true source is known to be in the Kuen-lun mountains already mentioned. After quitting our plateau and passing out of its prison-house in the mountains through natural gates of the utmost magnificence, it permeates the most thickly-peopled provinces of China—provinces inhabited by about 120,000,000 of souls.* It sustains the life of this enormous population by supplying the necessary moisture and by affording the means of irrigation and of water traffic. No river has ever in ancient or modern times played so important a part in the increase of the human race as the Yang-tse-Kiang. Its supply of water is immense and unfailing, and this most essential characteristic is caused by its connection with the snow-clad and ice-bound regions of our plateau, within which it has a course of 700 miles before entering China proper. Amidst the same Kuen-lun range, the Hoang-ho rises, from unexplored springs, which the Chinese figure to themselves as "the starry sea." After bursting through several watersheds, making wondrous bends from its main direction near the base of our plateau, and changing its course more than once to the confusion of comparative geography, it traverses Northern China and confers agricultural prosperity on some 70,000,000 of souls. It also has a course of some 400 miles within our plateau, in consequence of which its water supply is perennially snow-fed. Again, the Irawady and the Mekong, the former watering Burma and the latter watering Cambodia, rise in the offshoots of the Kuen-lun. That region, then, in respect of the parentage of important rivers stands in the first rank. This

* The doubts have recently increased regarding the trustworthiness of the statistics of Chinese population; and the real number, though certainly vast, may be somewhat less than that which is here stated.

beneficent circumstance arises from the direction of subsidiary ranges which admit to this part of our plateau some of the moisture-laden breezes from the Pacific Ocean.

Similarly the two Indian rivers, the Brahmaputra, and the Indus with its affluent the Satlej, have their origin at a great distance within our plateau, and their water-supply is indefinitely augmented in consequence. Notwithstanding the vast volume of their waters, these rivers play an economic part which, though great, is less than that of the main Chinese rivers. The Brahmaputra above its junction with the Megna cannot be said to sustain more than 15,000,000 of people; and the Indus, together with the Satlej, may support 12,000,000. The Ganges and Jamna, issuing from masses of snow on the southern scarp of our plateau, sustain before their junction at Allahabad a population of 30,000,000—quite irrespective of the deltaic population of the lower Ganges for whom moisture is supplied from other sources. Of these Indian rivers the waters, perpetually snow-fed, are largely drawn away for canals of irrigation on a grand scale. Taken all in all, despite defects, the Ganges Canal is the most imposing example of hydraulic engineering that has yet been seen. From the glaciers of the Pamir and the western terminus of the Thian Shan there spring the head-streams of the Oxus, the Jaxartes, and other rivers, ending in the inland sea of Aral. To these, in Persian phrase, the epithet of "gold-scatterer" or "wealth dispenser" is felicitously applied by the natives.

Of the rivers rising in the northern section of our plateau, the Amur has possibilities of which the future may see the development. But the great rivers of Siberia, such as the Ob, the Yenisei, and the Lena, though flowing through rich soils and affording marvellous facilities for several systems of inland navigation to be connected with each other, yet have their long estuaries in the permanently frost-bound lands of the Tundra, and their mouths in the arctic waters frozen during most months of the year. Therefore they can never, in economic importance, vie with the rivers above mentioned, which flow into the Pacific and Indian Oceans.

In the fourth place, the lacustrine system, though not comparable to that of North America or of Central Africa, and not approaching in beauty or interest that of Southern Europe, is yet very considerable. It is not, however, the only one in Asia, and from it must be excluded the three great Siberian lakes of Issykkul, of Baikal, and of Balkash, which, though connected with our plateau, are beyond its actual limits. Exclusive of these, however, the lakes, great and small, within our plateau, are extraordinarily numerous. Not less than a hundred of them may be counted on the maps of this region. Of these lakes, however, some are insignificant, being little more than saline swamps. Others, again, as the Pangong, though romantically beautiful—reposing at an altitude equal to that of the highest European mountains, and reflecting the perennial snow of surrounding peaks—do not illustrate specially any geographical problem, nor produce any economic result. But some may be selected as having a scientific interest irrespective of beauty or of strangeness.

The Lake Victoria, discovered by Wood in 1838, rests in the heart of the Pamir, already mentioned, at an elevation of 14,000 feet above sea-level. It is frozen over during the greater part of the year, and lies with a glistening and polished surface in the midst of a snow-whitened waste. In that state it powerfully affects the imagination of the spectator who reaches it as the final goal, after a protracted and toilsome ascent from the barren or deserted plains of Ariana. It is the source of the Oxus, and is near the point of contact between the British and the Russian political systems in Asia.

In the sharpest contrast to the highly-placed Pamir lake is the lowly Lake Lob, already mentioned. Shallow water, sedgy morass, dreary sands, parched forests, the monotony of desolation, are reported to be its characteristics. It apparently consists of the dregs of an inland sea that has become mostly dried up, and is, as it were, kept alive only by the Tarim river, which has its sources in the everlasting snows of the Pamir. Despite the proximity of saline tracts, the lake has fresh water. Near it is a great desert, of which the soil, though now arid and friable, owing to the gradual desiccation, was once more or less productive, and where a population has probably become extinct or has disappeared by migration.

The Pamir then is a water-parting for two inland seas, one the Aral, beyond our plateau, the other Lake Lob within it—both saved from speedy desiccation only by the influx of rivers from the snow-line.

Again in contrast is the Kuku Nor, a sheet of water 10,000 feet above sea-level, in the eastern section of the Kuen-lun mountains, near the source of the Hoang-ho. Its waters, profound and saline, have a dark azure hue, which is compared by the natives to that of the exquisite silks in China. It is in the Tangut region, mentioned by Marco Polo in his Itinerary. In respect to the lakes in this region, and especially the morasses of Tsaidam, there are geological speculations as to another Asiatic Mediterranean (besides that already mentioned), long since dried up, whereof there are a few widely scattered remnants, among which the Kuku Nor is one.

Lastly, a word of passing notice may be devoted to two among the Tibetan lakes, that of Tengri, near Lhassa, on the shore of which stands a venerated Buddhist convent, and the Bul-tso, from which have been obtained quantities of the best borax.

In the fifth place, the north-eastern part of our plateau was during remote ages, beyond the ken of history, the home of hardy and aggressive Tartars. These Tartar races, dwelling among the uplands in the lee of the mountains, used for many centuries to emerge and harry the fertile Chinese plains lying between the mountains and the Pacific Ocean. It was to ward off these incursions that the Great Wall was constructed, winding like a vast serpent of stone along the ridges of mountains for 2000 miles from the Pacific coast to the Siberian confines. The cost and labour expended on this amazing work attest the dread with which these Tartar highlanders had inspired the Chinese lowlanders. Some centuries after the building of the Great Wall, the most warlike among the Tartar tribes, in the council of their national assembly, acclaimed Temujin as their king, in the year 1206 A.D. He took a title which is translated by Europeans as Chinghiz Khan, or Genghiz Khan, a title which for two centuries or more was the best known name in the whole world. At the head of his Tartar adherents, he first subdued the other kindred tribes of our plateau. Then he organised and disciplined the whole Tartar manhood into an army of horsemen. This is the most wonderful instance of military mobilization known to history ancient or modern. Its results too were equally appalling. In mediæval times the marches of the Arabs and the Saracens, in modern times the expeditions of Napoleon, have dazzled Asia or Europe. These were hardly, however, equal to the distant conquests of Alexander the Great in ancient times. But even the wars of Alexander were perhaps surpassed by the ravages of Chinghiz Khan and the Tartars of our plateau. The countries of China, India, Afghanistan, Bactria, Persia, the Aral-Caspian basin, Siberia, Asia Minor, Russia, were overrun within a hundred years by Chinghiz Khan, his lieutenants, and his immediate descendants. Thus, by the hordes of our plateau, there was established a dominion stretchi from Cape Comorin, near the equator, to the Arctic Ocean, and from the Pacific shores to the banks of the Vistula in Poland. The latest historian of the Mongols considers that nothing but the unexpected death of the Tartar sovereign, and the political combinations arising in consequence within this very plateau of ours, prevented the Tartar invasion from spreading even to Western Europe. Though it is often held that these terrific events have been overruled by Providence for the progress of mankind, still at the time they caused what Gibbon truly calls a shipwreck of nations. Notwithstanding this, the Tartars won, in a certain sense, an unparalleled success, which is attributable to the geographical circumstances of our plateau.

The influence of the precipices, the forests, the prairies, the wild sports, in forming the national character is so obvious that it need not be specified. We readily understand how the sturdy mountaineer, the daring hunter, the practised archer, becomes the able soldier. In Mongolia, however, the local specialty was this, that the practically boundless extent of the pasturage and the nutritious richness of its quality, induced the people to maintain countless horses, cows, buffaloes, sheep, goats, and camels,—neglecting the tillage of the soil, never building houses, but living in tents made of warm felt, accumulating a certain sort of rude wealth, still roving and roaming about at some seasons incessantly from one encampment or one grazing-ground to another, dragging with them their families and their effects by means of the pack animals and the roomy waggons drawn by many oxen yoked abreast. Thus was a truly nomadic existence practised on the largest scale ever known. Mongol armies, better drilled, armed, accoutred, and equipped than any forces then known in the civilised world, would march from our plateau into the inhabited plains around, and would observe houses and towns for the first time. It is even alleged that some of them had never seen cultivated crops before.

In this state of existence the temptations to depredation of all sorts were excessive, and the danger from the climate, the savagery of nature, and the wild beasts, was always imminent. Consequently the Mongols were obliged to hold themselves together by the cohesion of families, clans, and tribes. Thus by the force of circumstances a social organisation was established which proved the foundation of a military discipline, suitable to the genius of the people, almost self-acting, and unfailing even in the remotest expeditions. The horses, too, upon which the Mongol warriors mainly depended, naturally fell into the training; being always turned out to graze in herds, they habitually kept together, and the field manœuvre fixed habits which had been already acquired. It used to be remarked that a line of Mongol cavalry was like a rope or a chain perfectly flexible but never parted.

The Mongolian food included little of cereals or vegetables, but consisted mainly of cheese and meat. For stimulating drink there was the fermented mare's milk. The name "koumis" or "prepared milk," apparently much esteemed medically now-a-days, is a Mongolian word. Manifestly, men thus nurtured could live in the saddle day and night, carrying with them their sustenance in the smallest compass, and scarcely halting to eat or drink. Thus the hardihood evinced on protracted marches, which would otherwise be incredible, can be accounted for.

It is probable that this diet, while sustaining vivacity, produced also a violence of disposition. Certainly, ruthlessness, cruelty, indifference to suffering, characterised the Mongols and marred the effect of their grand qualities. Massacres, holocausts, conflagrations, marked their warlike operations. Even famines and epidemics have hardly done more for depopulation than the Mongol conquests. A Mongolian chief would say that the keenest enjoyment in life was to stamp upon a beaten enemy, to seize his family, and despoil his encampment.

It is not the purpose of this address to describe the policy of the Mongols or the institutions which they founded in conquered countries. A few salient points only have been indicated in reference to the geography of our plateau. It is here, near what is now known as the upper region of the Amûr, that the Onon, the Orkhon, and the Kerulen, classic streams in Mongol story, take their source. Here is the site of Kara Koron, the emperor's headquarter encampment. Here the Kurultai assemblies were held to decide the fate of nationalities. Here were the camps, the Urts and Urdus, rude names at first unpronounceable in the civilised world, but soon to become terribly familiar. Here were the hordes mustered under their banners, each standard having its distinctive colour, the supreme ensign being, however, the yak's tail raised aloft. Hither, also, the corpse of Chinghiz

Khan was borne in a cumbrous catafalque, dragged through the deep loam by oxen yoked twenty abreast, while his henchman chanted a dirge which was a pathetic effusion from the heart of a valiant nation, and was full of poetic images drawn from the Mongolian surroundings.

In the sixth place, though our plateau has possessed, and still possesses, some patches of fine cultivation, such as those in the Upper Tarim basin, near Yarkand and Kashgar, and some near Lhassa in Tibet, still it has comparatively but little of agriculture, of trade, or of industry. Nevertheless it has many natural resources of value and interest, while its pastoral resources have proved astonishing. Its breed of horses, though by no means the finest, has yet been quite the largest ever known. These horses have never displayed the beauty of the Arabian or the size of the Turkoman breed. They are middle-sized, and do not attain the speed of thoroughbreds. But in nimbleness amidst rugged ground, in endurance over lengthened distances, and in preserving their condition with scanty nourishment, they are unrivalled. Their numbers too may well exercise the imagination of modern breeders. For many years the Tartar emperors maintained in the field at least 500,000 cavalry, for which the horses were drawn chiefly from our plateau. This enormous cavalry force was engaged in fighting over an area of many thousand miles in length and breadth, during which operations much desperate resistance was encountered. It was occupied in steep ascents and descents, in traversing deserts, in crossing frozen lakes, in swimming rapid rivers. How vastly numerous then must have been the casualties among the horses, and how immense the breeding studs. The pasturage too was so potent in nutritive qualities that ordinarily there was risk of animals suffering from repletion, and emaciated creatures rapidly gained flesh and strength.

In other respects too the fauna are noteworthy—the sheep and goats, with wool or down of the softest texture—the buffalo herds and the yaks inured to the sharpest cold—the gazelles careering in thousands—the untameable camel of the desert having a speed and agility unknown in other species—the wild asses and the white wolves—the waterfowl at times like clouds darkening the air.

The flora too, though less abundant, has its specialities—the pointed grasses sharp enough to pierce leather, the gigantic rhubarb, the magnificent holly, the branching juniper.

The mineral resources of the Kuen-lun are certainly enormous; nobody yet knows how great they may prove. Indeed our plateau is remarkable for the antimony, the sulphur, the saltpetre, the borax, the gold-washings, the turquoise, and the classic jadestone.

In the seventh place, the field offered by our plateau for scientific research will be apparent from even a cursory consideration of the stage to which our knowledge has reached. From the map,* which shows with separate marking those portions ot Asia that have been professionally surveyed, those that have been roughly surveyed, those that have been explored only, and in white those that are unexplored—it will be seen that almost the whole of our plateau is unsurveyed, and that while much of it has been explored more or less, some portions yet await exploration. For some time, however, it has been the sphere chosen by many among the most skilful, enduring, and intrepid travellers of Europe. The journeys of the Russian Prejevalsky in the Tarim basin and Mongolia, of Potanin and Rafailoff in the same region, of Malussovski near Kobdo, of the French missionaries Gabet and Huc in Mongolia, of the Bishop Desgodins in Tibet, of the German Schlagintweit in Turkestan, of the Englishmen Forsyth, Trotter, Johnson, Shaw, Hayward in the Tarim basin, of Wood in the Pamir, of Ney Elias in Mongolia, of Delmar Morgan in Kulja, of Bogle and Manning in Tibet, while teaching us very much, have yet left our minds dazed with a sense of what remains to be learnt. Even the trigonometrical determination of the Himalayan summits by the English Surveyors General

* See map prefixed to Chapter I.

namely, Everest, Waugh, and Walker, the researches of Basevi, Stolieska, Godwin-Austen, Thomson, Biddulph, in the same quarter, and the Siberian surveys by the Russians among the Altai and Thian Shan mountains, have brought us only to the verge of half-discovered or undiscovered countries. The greatest unexplored region in all Asia, namely, the Kuen-lun range, lies in the very heart of our plateau. It is remarkable too that if the principal geographical problems awaiting solution in Asia be specified, such as the true and ultimate sources of the Hoang-ho, the Irawady, the Salwen, the Mekong, the relation of the San-po with the Brahmaputra, the connecting links between the Kuen-lun and the Chinese mountain chains, they will be found to concern our plateau.

At a few points only has our plateau been penetrated by geological surveys, namely, in some parts of the Altai and at the western end of the Thian Shan; and these surveys are Russian. But the formations, the strata, the upheavals, the denudations, the fluvial action, awaiting scientific examination, are indescribably great. A notion of some of the questions inviting inquiry from the geologist and palæontologist may be gathered from what has been already said under previous headings in respect to the general desiccation and the subsidence or evaporation of the primeval waters.

To the naturalist few regions present more surprising opportunities for the observation of the coming, the resting, the departing of migratory birds.

To meteorologists many of the natural phenomena must prove highly interesting—the causation of the wondrous dryness, the effects produced on animal comfort by the rarefaction of the air, the mummified bodies dried up without undergoing putrefaction, the clouds of salt particles driven along by furious gusts and filling the atmosphere, the fires in the parched vegetation of the desert, the spontaneous ignition of coal-beds, the caves emitting sulphurous gases, the rocky girdle of syenite bounding the Gobi desert, the gradual contraction of the glaciers, the ordinarily rainless zones sometimes invaded by rain-storms with a downpour like that of the tropics.

In the eighth place, our plateau is now under one imperial jurisdiction, and offers many problems for social inquirers. It belongs entirely to the Chinese empire with the exception of one small tract where the Russian authorities have crossed the mountain border. The geographical features for the most part favour national defence and territorial consolidation. The old Chinese Wall is still suitable to the political geography of to-day. In the Zungarian strait, however, in the Ili valley near Kulja, perhaps, also, in the line of the Black Irtish, near Zaisan, the Chinese empire, in its contact with Russia, has weak points strategically, or chinks in its armour. Though the plateau was originally under the Chinese suzerainty, it became, under the Mongolian emperor Chinghiz Khan and his successors, the mistress of China, as indeed of all Asia and of Eastern Europe. As the Mongol power, however, shrunk and withered, the Chinese reasserted themselves. At length, under a dynasty from Manchuria outside the mountain border, the Chinese became lords over our plateau. The Zungarian tribe of Eleuths rose, and after severe military operations were suppressed. The Muhammadan inhabitants of the Tarim basin rebelled against the Chinese government, and for a while maintained an independent principality for Islam. It was during this time that the British sovereign sent an envoy to Yarkand to conclude a commercial treaty, in 1873. Subsequently the Chinese broke down this rising independence, and the whole region of the Tarim receives its orders from the emperor at Peking.

The decline and fall of the Mongol empire, the disruption of that wide-spread dominion, like the breaking up of the ice on its own frozen rivers, are historical themes beyond the scope of this address. But the changes which have gradually come over the national character of Mongolians are cognate to the studies of geographers. As already seen, the annals of the Mongols reveal one of the many examples of the theory of causation, explaining how geographical surroundings mould or affect the human character. There remain the mountains, the sea of undulating uplands, which are still among the few important regions not essentially modified by human action. The pine forests, though hardly intact, have not been extensively cleared. There is the dread desert, where to the ears of superstitious Mongols the roll of the mustering drums and the shouts of victorious battle are audible, and which has engulfed in sandy waves additional tracts once productive. The pastoral resources, the nomadic diet and exercises, the tribal organisation, are in kind the same as of yore, though perhaps modified in extent or degree. The short-lived heat may perhaps be gaining strength as the ages advance; but the winters must be nearly as long and hard as ever. Thus the same physical and climatic conditions, which once caused the Mongolian nation to become one of the mightiest engines ever directed by man, are still surrounding the politically degenerate Mongols of to-day, who are best represented by the tribe of Khalkas. Once audaciously ambitious, the Mongols are now sluggish and narrow-minded; once passionately fond of an independence as free as their mountain air, they are now submissive to the domination of races formerly despised by them as inferior; once proud of a tribal organisation and a voluntary discipline that wrought world-renowned wonders, they are now split up into factions like a faggot of sticks that has been unbound. A man who, though the feeblest of pedestrians, grips with his bowed legs the saddle of the most restive horse as with a vice, is all that remains of the historic Mongol. It is for the social inquirer to determine what have been the circumstances counteracting the climatic and local causes which made this nation potential in moulding medieval history.

Here too may be observed the tendencies of Paganism, Buddhism, and Muhammadism respectively. Of all religions our plateau offers the best means of studying Buddhism, which still is supposed to count more adherents than any other faith. Though the mid-Ganges Valley was the birthplace of this wide-spread religion, and was for ages regarded by pious Buddhists as their holy land—yet during recent centuries the active centre of the faith has been in Tibet. Of the four incarnations of Buddha now held to exist, three are within our plateau, namely, two in Tibet near Lhassa and at Teshu Lumbo, and one in Mongolia at Urga, near the spot where mounds attest the burial of heaps of slain after one of Chinghiz Khan's earliest battles. In Tibet may be seen to the best advantage those religious ceremonies, the sight of which has always attracted the observation of Roman Catholic missionaries.

In conclusion, this brief summary of our geographical knowledge regarding the plateau of mid-Asia is provisional only. For it avowedly deals with regions mostly unsurveyed and seldom even explored completely. Further exploration or discovery therefore may reverse some of our specific conclusions, or may modify the current of our topographical ideas. It is probable indeed that there will be such changes, inasmuch as almost every investigation within this vast area has revealed something unimagined before, or has caused disbelief of something previously believed. This address, then, is limited to a *résumé* of things imperfectly known, with a view of bringing into strong relief two matters which are unquestionable, namely, the importance of our plateau and the grand field it offers for research. If the public consideration of these matters shall induce enquirers to direct their enterprise towards this grand region, we may hope that by degrees the errors in our facts may be removed, the misdirection of our conclusions remedied, the vagueness of our notions made definite. At present the physical obstacles in the path of such enquiries are so grave as to be almost deterring. But they do not finally deter those who after forethought decide to brave peril, distress, sickness, suffering, in order to enlarge the bounds of knowledge. Each enquirer, however, has the consolation of reflecting that he makes the rough ways smoother for those who shall come after him. Every journey that is accomplished must facilitate successive discovery in the same line of country. Probably as fast as one line is made good geographically, fresh lines may present themselves, and new vistas will be opened to the astonished gaze of geographers. At length, with all the constancy and courage which arduous travel never fails to inspire, the enquirers of the future will doubtless explore this plateau till it becomes as well known as the Alpine regions of Europe.

# CHAPTER III.

## POLITICAL LESSONS OF CHINESE HISTORY.

[*Paper read before the Royal Historical Society, in London, April* 1883.]

Political and strategic geography of China — Mongol invasion turning-point in Chinese history—Early Chinese civilization before that event—Gallant and patriotic resistance on the part of the Chinese against their Mongol invaders—Mongol conquest of China completed A.D. 1270—Character of Mongol rule there — Restoration of native Chinese dynasty — Its decay after lasting two centuries — Local insurrection of a strange character arising — Prepares the way for accession of the Manchus — Origin of the Manchu Tartars — They overrun China after a noble resistance by the people — Their dominion established over China — Character of their rule up to the nineteenth century — Eminent sovereigns of their race — Beginning of their degeneracy.

In undertaking to address you regarding the political lessons derivable from the history of China, I must ask you to allow me to bring my survey down to the end of the eighteenth century only, and to stop at the commencement of our present nineteenth century. The reason is this, that Chinese history, from about the year 1800, involves several problems which have been and still are agitated among politicians, and some controversies of a moral, social, or economic character, which are far from being exhausted. Such topics would, doubtless, be regarded by you as unsuitable in the present address. Still, an impartial retrospect of the past cannot fail to assist us in understanding the present, and gauging the immediate future of a vast people in whose affairs British interests are largely concerned.

Moreover, to essay such a task is all the more desirable, in that Chinese history, though striking and interesting when its leading features are grasped, is but little known popularly, and even to the sight of cultured people is perhaps involved in mist and confusion. Yet with many there is springing up an uneasy consciousness that as China is growing fast in importance, its antecedent conditions merit examination.

Before presenting to you those parts of Chinese history which are really the turning-points in the career of the nation, I must call to your remembrance certain salient points in the political and strategic geography of China. These points will immediately be apprehended from a glance at the map prefixed to this address. In the first place, beginning at the north, pray observe the head-waters of the river Amûr and its affluents. There was the birthplace of the Mongolian power, probably the most destructive and terrific force that has ever appeared in human history, and which overcame China together with many other countries. In the next place, let your attention be turned to a comparatively small river which flows into a gulf to the north-east of Peking. Its valley was the original home of the Manchus, who, from the humblest beginnings as a petty Tartar tribe, conquered China after a contest lasting only a single generation. In the third place your notice must be claimed for the range of hills immediately north of Peking, stretching from the sea-coast westwards till they join the mountains which overhang the desert of Mongolia. These mountains formed the line of demarcation between the Chinese proper, who were people of the plains or valleys, and the Tartars, including the famous Mongols, the Manchus, and other cognate tribes, who were people dwelling in the mountains or the elevated plateaux. The tribes dwelling beyond this range were to the Chinese what the barbarians beyond the Alps were to the Romans—at first subdued by civilised force, but ultimately rising against the civilisation to which they had bowed, and victoriously overthrowing it. It was along the winding ridge of this range that the great Chinese Wall was built. In the next place I must beg you to note the course of the Hoang Ho. This river, rising in the eastern spurs of the Kuen Lun mountains, runs northwards, then, after turning eastwards, wends straight south—its course resembling a bent finger—and finally pursues an easterly course to its mouth. It is in the middle valley of the Hoang Ho, near the two great bends above described, that some of the crucial struggles for possession of the Chinese empire have occurred. This province has been to China what the Panjab was to India; and in the province adjoining it on the east, the Chinese nationality was originally formed. Near the point where the river on completing its last bend passes between the hills towards the plains—is situated the fortified pass of Tung Kwan, for the possession of which several historic contests have been waged. To the Chinese this position resembled in importance the Khyber Pass, with Peshawar or Attok, on the British Indian frontier.

Further, I invite you to mark the course of the Yang-tsze-Kiang, which rising in the same spurs of the Kuen Lun mountains as the Hoang Ho, follows a south-easterly and then an easterly course to the sea. This river, together with its affluents, sustaining a population of 100 millions, has contributed more to the multiplication of the human race than any other river under the sun. But, apart from this, the Yang-tsze-Kiang valley must be remembered by us at this moment, because it has been the central domicile of the Chinese proper, the home of their best civilization, and the scene where their supreme efforts have at times been organized for national defence.

There is yet a river in the south which joins the sea at Canton. For the surrounding district a future of indefinite greatness is perhaps reserved. Within its limits, as we shall presently see, Chinese nationality on two separate occasions made a last stand for independence.

Further, I suggest that you let your glance sweep round the outer limits of the Chinese empire, and then down the mountain range (the Inshan and Khingan) which divides the empire into two unequal parts. You will perceive that there are included two distinct areas in the empire; one the Central Plateau of Asia, the other the comparatively lowland country between that plateau and the sea, or China proper. The plateau is regarded by geographers as the most remarkable on the surface of the globe. I have elsewhere (that is before the British Association for the Advancement of Science) * described its physical geography, and need here only advert to its political effect on China. It constitutes two-thirds of the total Chinese area, that is, upwards of 2½ millions of square miles out of 4 millions of square miles and upwards. But it has only one-thirtieth of the total population, or 15 millions of souls, out of a possible total of 350 millions. Nevertheless, this plateau, which at one epoch grievously affected the fate of all Asia, and a part of Europe, has constantly affected the fortunes of China. It includes Tibet, the centre of Buddhism, the established religion of China. On some occasions the Chinese subdued the barbarous and brave inhabitants of the plateau. On other occasions some sections of these inhabitants, notwithstanding the low state of their general civilization, have acquired the art of war far better than their more civilized contemporaries, have burst into China proper with forces that with martial superiority more than compensated for their inferior numbers, and have held down the populous provinces of China with an iron hand. Nevertheless, whenever the barbarians of the plateau have been settled as conquerors in China proper, one of two things has happened to them. Either they have lost their hardihood among soft surroundings, and, becoming degenerate, have been relegated by Chinese patriotism to their native mountains, or else they have adopted the Chinese civilization. In the latter case they have illustrated the truth of the classic line,—

> "Græcia capta ferum victorem cepit."

Thus history has repeated itself here on a gigantic scale.

* See the preceding Chapter II.

The population, then, of China proper is different from that of the Plateau, and, ethnologically, the two peoples are distinct branches of the same family. Thus with the mental culture of the Chinese there has generally been a mingling of northern vigour and genius in the dynastic, the military, the political achievements.

I have troubled you with this preface of political geography because it is necessary to fasten on these points in order that the events, which I shall have to marshal, may rise up in due procession before the historic imagination.

Now let any one look back over the events of Chinese history for nearly three thousand years, and say what is the train of political circumstances that has modified most the national destiny? The answer would probably be, the Mongol conquest shortly after the year 1200 A.D. Before that fatal year, the Chinese nationality had developed those characteristic peculiarities which, uniformly distinguishing the entire nation, have proved to be almost immutable. Since that time, it has passed through tremendous vicissitudes, and partially righted itself, retaining or restoring many of its pristine features. But it can hardly have been quite what it was before.

> ". . . Nec amissos colores
> Lana refert medicata fuco."

Hence it is primarily interesting to consider what was the stage of Chinese development before the cataclysm of A.D. 1200 tore up the medieval world. For our present purpose this development is regarded from a political point of view only.

In the first place it is very remarkable that the Chinese originally lived under a feudal system. The country consisted of several states (seven in number), over each of which there was a local lord, under whom there were lesser chiefs holding lands by laws of sub-infeudation. The states were federated under one lord as emperor, who had some territory in his own direct administration. Several dynasties of emperors really represented the headship of a feudal confederation. Under this feudalism there arose many of the ancient heroes, statesmen and sages of China, while many of its characteristic marks were stamped upon the civilization, the institution, and the habits of the Chinese. The system was destroyed 200 years before the Christian era by a sovereign who has been very properly styled the Chinese Cæsar,* and who established a real empire to last for centuries. At times this empire became disunited, to be again united; but the principle of absolute and centralized power remained in force.

This suppression of feudalism is regarded by some authorities to have been the only revolution that has ever occurred in China, inasmuch as it warred against a principle. The political movements, to which we shall presently advert, were rebellions only as warring against individual rulers.

The confines of the Chinese empire were always fluctuating, now receding, and now advancing. At times they reached to the western end of the central plateau, and tribute was probably received even from tribes dwelling near the Caspian. A system of frontier defence was organized by the construction of the great Wall already mentioned, with fortifications at intervals upon a line at least 1200 miles in length; together with a strange line of palisades towards Manchuria and the Corea, 800 miles long. The combined length of fortified frontiers amounted to 2000 miles. Similar lines have been constructed elsewhere, by the Romans in Central Europe, by the Russians in Siberia, by the British near the Indus, but none of them have approached the mileage and the completeness of the Chinese defence. The towns in the interior were encompassed with fortifications, the places thus fortified being numbered by many hundreds. In no country has the system of internal defence been ever carried out more thoroughly. Besides a sea-going fleet, organised mainly for service in Corean or Japanese waters;

* See Boulger's 'History of China,' vol. i.

a special marine was maintained for service in the great rivers; the river war-vessels numbering many hundreds. A code of army regulations was drawn up, relating to pay, promotion, drill, discipline, and all the minutiæ of military service. The vast territories were divided for administrative purposes into provinces, districts, and townships. Feudalism was superseded by the appointment of provincial governors and district magistrates. From time to time censors were deputed by the central authority for peripatetic supervision. For the central authority itself something like a constitution was established, in which the leading features were a council of state, and several departmental boards. The civil legislation was most voluminous; the penal code was comprehensive in scope, and lucid in arrangement; the moral precepts were definite, and the religious ritual minute. There were codes for all branches of human conduct and relationship. The official deference paid to literature has hardly been equalled in any other age or country; the lettered classes in their capacity as literati formed a power which could make revolutions, and which emperors on their accession were obliged to conciliate. The patronage of letters, and the preparation of chronicles ranked high among public duties. A kind of rude printing with wooden types was invented at an early time; public libraries on an immense scale were maintained; a tribunal of history, and an official gazette were instituted. Extraordinary attention was paid to popular education; the central colleges were among the most influential institutions of the land. Competitive examinations were essential preliminaries for admission to that public service which conferred the highest social status attainable. The official class, indeed, constituted the real aristocracy. Surveying and map-making received close attention; the cartography included topographical and cadastral particulars. Gazetteers and encyclopædias were compiled. An elaborate lexicography was instituted, and a statistical bureau was set on foot. Interminable voluminousness was the awful feature of Chinese literature. On each topic the volumes were counted by hundreds, and the chapters by thousands.

In China (as in India) there was always a question whether the land belonged to the Emperor or to the people. In theory it belonged to the Emperor, while in practice the people had a perpetual lease, which was tantamount to property. But this property being liable to taxation, might be rendered valuable or valueless, according as the administration might be moderate or extortionate. In China, practically, there was moderation. As a rule there was peasant proprietorship; small landed properties were also common; but large estates, though existing here and there, were comparatively rare. The rules for mortgages and temporary transfers were complete, and there was a registration of landed occupancy. A communal system existed somewhat resembling the village communities of India.* In towns there appear to have been municipalities managing conservancy and police.

It is observable that, with all the legislation, there were no institutions like juries to protect the subject, and trials were left to the discretion—or but too often to the will and pleasure—of the judge.

The construction of public works was recognised as a duty of the state. Canals of navigation, of a length never equalled elsewhere, were begun; irrigation works were undertaken, which—though not comparable to those which the British Government has constructed in India—have yet challenged the admiration of observers in subsequent ages. Roads were engineered in the midst of mountains, and passes were hewn through rocky crests. Even valleys were spanned by bridges with lofty piers. Embankments were raised to restrain the flowing rivers, one of which rivers was declared by the last testament of an Emperor to be "China's sorrow."

All this represents an aggregate of administrative achievements fully justifying the ancient repute of China, and, at first sight,

* Maine on "Village Communities and Early Law and Custom."

seeming to anticipate some parts of our modern civilization. But a closer examination will reveal defects fatal to national progress and political stability.

No standard of public conduct is higher than that which was recognised by the Chinese emperors, who ascended the throne not by the right of primogeniture or even of birth, but by a commission from heaven. This standard was followed by many of them in some degree, while by a few of them it was observed to a degree which has rendered their names household words among succeeding generations. But the sovereign was expected to hold in his own hands the threads of countless affairs and to be the administrator in chief. Never was the doctrine of everything for the people and nothing by them, carried more rigidly to its conclusion. Their right to paternal care from the government was asserted as having been bestowed on them by a charge from on high. They looked to the state for support and guidance in matters relating to material prosperity, as well as to moral advancement. Economic doctrines were sometimes preached which taught even the agriculturists to depend on the government for sustenance. The first consequence was an excessive centralisation of authority. The effect was intensified by the want of local institutions strongly rooted, and the paucity of territorial chiefs or landed gentry. The weight of the administration hung too much on a single rope. If that rope snapped, then political ruin ensued. Thus, China, from time to time, displayed the phenomena of movements arising suddenly and mysteriously which the state seemed unable to withstand. A robber chief would spring up, insurrectionary forces would gather round him, and he might even scale the seat of empire. In China, as in India, brigandage, beginning with success, ends with political significance.

An occasion for convulsion would be offered by the bad surroundings of an emperor. For although polygamy is not a Chinese institution, yet something tantamount to it must have prevailed in the imperial families. Nowhere have the palace guardians exercised a more baneful influence upon the national history than in China. It is not to be hence inferred, however, that the imperial ladies were always kept in seclusion, for in China many widowed empresses, or empress mothers, have ambitiously seized opportunities of displaying patriotic resolution and governing capacity.

But, irrespective of such grave interruptions, there seems to have always been a difficulty in securing good administration. While an elaboration of theory and system was carried to an extreme, the practice and execution were seldom successful. While the doctrines of the ethical code were sublime, plain honesty appears seldom to have been observed even to an average extent in the affairs of the nation. Corruption is alleged to have been ever the rule. The ancient Chinese never dared to pride themselves on the favourite quality of the ancient Persians, namely, truth-telling. Notwithstanding the selection by competition, good administrators were not always forthcoming even for the collection of the revenue. The evil failed to be checked by the permanent supervision of departmental boards and the occasional inspection of imperial censors. The master instinct was that of formalism, and there was not enough of vitalising spirit to make the dry bones of regulation live with efficiency. The rust thus engendered began to spread with the army as well, despite all the nominal organisation; and before the irruption of the barbarians, a cry had arisen that the precisely drilled troops would not in action either stand or charge.

The educational method generated a power of intense mental application, in which the Chinese have been rarely equalled, also a faculty of refined perception and subtle discrimination. A round of distressful tasks, intellectually, was prescribed, to which the sufferers addressed themselves with marvellous patience. Still the reasoning aptitude was not developed *pari passu* with the memory. While an excessive strain was put on the memory, the logical aptitude became shrunken and the scientific spirit was quenched.

Though ordinarily averse from suffering, and often failing in battle, the people had a certain sort of courage. None would endure mortal pain with more fortitude than they; none would face death more stoically. Their history too is adorned by many passages of self-denying heroism. Still it may be doubted whether by temperament they ever had "a stomach for the fight." Their original impulse would always have been to seek peace and avoid conflict. Their religion may be described as Buddhism and Lamaism combined with the ethics of Lao, of Confucius, of Mencius, and of the commentators. In so far as that affected their disposition, the tendency was towards quiet at any price. The precepts relating to charitable forbearance were noble indeed, but proceeded to what might be called an unpractical extreme.

Veneration was set before them as being among the foremost attributes of humanity. Obedience to authority—first that of parents, then that of existing rulers, and finally that of the emperor as vice-regent of Heaven—was accepted as the first of duties. Being in the main sincere and single-minded, they were loyal to existing dynasties for periods of some duration. They were also long-suffering under oppression and extortion up to a certain limit. But when that limit was over-passed, they would deem that the time had come to be angry and sin not. Then discarding their habitual tolerance, they would turn and rend their oppressors. The knowledge that this might happen doubtless operated as a permanent check on oppression.

Furthermore, with the philosophic and speculative tendencies pervading large classes, there was something fanciful, something restless in the popular imagination. Movements were from time to time arising and predisposing the people to change, of all which circumstances advantage would be taken by daring and desperate men. Indeed periodicity of revolt is alleged by a recent authority to be an abiding characteristic of Chinese history.

On the whole it will be seen that the Chinese nationality

abounded in inconsistencies which cannot be reconciled in a brief analysis. Side by side with gentle virtues there was nourished a national self-sufficiency and a desire to stigmatize with barbarism all those not falling within the pale of a peculiar civilization. The obligatory duties at the ancestral tombs prevented permanent emigration. Though Chinese traders went far afield they returned to the mother land. In the depths of the national mind there lay a faith not only in the moral government of the world, but also in a theocratic supervision of human affairs. Combined with this was a belief in the dignity of the individual man. Though the investing of chosen persons with august authority was a divine institution, still the choice was to follow personal merit. Every man, however humble, was to have his chance of rising to a bright career by conduct and learning. This idea is the parent of the educational system unapproached by any other Eastern race, and has conduced to the individuality distinguishing Chinese annals.

It is a hopeless task to state the population of this empire; the estimate ranges from 300 to 430 millions of souls. The area of China proper, 1½ million of square miles (exclusive of the Central Plateau), is the same as that of India. The Indian population, being 260 millions, might be taken as a basis for estimating that of China, to which might be added 15 millions for the Central Plateau, making the total 275 millions. The distribution of population dense and sparse in the two countries is not dissimilar. If, however, the proportion of densely peopled tracts be larger in China, the total might be raised to 300 millions. But how far it should be raised above 300 millions, may be a question for statisticians to consider.

This chequered view regarding the outcome of Chinese civilization before the era of the Mongol deluge, A.D. 1200, shews that in the massive and unwieldy empire there were enfeebling and disintegrating causes at work. Still there remained, as we shall presently see, enough of vitality and energy in the mass to cause the conquering Mongols more trouble than they ever experienced in all their widespread and diverse conquests.

At this epoch, the Chinese empire, or rather the Chinese kingdom as it should be called, had shrunk from its imperial proportions, and was restricted to China proper. The tribes making up the Mongolian nationality had gained such an independence throughout the Central Plateau as threatened all neighbouring countries. One of these tribes named the Kin, or "Golden," had established a dynasty in northern China with Peking as its capital. Another tribe, the Hia, had a strong principality in the upper valley of the Hoang Ho. To the native Chinese dynasty of Sung there remained central and southern China, about two-thirds of the whole country, with its seat of power and resource in the valley of the Yang-tsze-Kiang, and its capital at Nanking.

As might be expected, the Mongol leader, Chinghiz Khan (or Genghiz), caused the divided Chinese kingdom to be attacked in detail. It would require the burning language of Edmund Burke to describe how the Mongol war-cloud burst upon the Kin defences in the Great Wall and, passing round the Chinese flank on the north-east, swept over the devoted country. The fortified places were overthrown like nine-pins by hundreds, and the conquerors boasted of the numberless habitations that had been razed level with the earth. The Kin, however, rallied his resources; his capital Peking, and his western stronghold (Tung Kwan already mentioned) remained to him; and the Mongols received their first check in northern China. The Hia kingdom, commanding the upper valley of the Hoang Ho, also held out. The conjuncture was so serious that Chinghiz Khan, after having overcome many nations, came down in person from Mongolia to command the operations. He defeated the Hia army in a battle fought amidst the frosts of winter, and so conquered the north-western corner of China. This was the last of his many battles; for he shortly afterwards died, adjuring his successors to continue the conquest of northern

China. The Kin, however, contested his territory bit by bit; the Mongols met with a resistance stiffer than any they had as yet experienced in the various countries which they had subdued; and the stand thus made was marked by several heroic episodes. The Mongols, accustomed to overrun countries in Asia and in Europe as with an avalanche, were occupied for twenty years in reducing northern China; and the Kin succumbed, sinking under superior force, but leaving behind him a memory destined, as we shall see presently, to animate his descendants to deeds grander than his own. In all this patriotism the impulse and the direction were due to the Kin, and many of the troops were of that nationality; still, many of the troops and officers were Chinese, and the part then played must be reckoned among the glories of China.

Indeed, northern China might have kept the Mongols at bay for an indefinite time, had it not been for the conduct of the southern Chinese under the Sung dynasty. In an ill-fated hour, national jealousy of the Kin induced the Sung to make an alliance with the Mongols on the condition of his having a share in the Kin spoil. Thus, although the Mongols were then equal, unaided, to any enterprise, it is the fact that in subduing northern China they had the aid of southern China. The Sung doubtless hoped by making common cause with the destroyers to put off the day of his own destruction. But the usual quarrel ensued over the spoil, and the Mongols formally issued the fiat of "delenda est" against the Sung dynasty. Then came a memorable passage, in which native Chinese may claim the undivided honour, and which is the most illustrious chapter in the record of Chinese patriotism.

The Mongols, flushed with a victory extending from the Amûr in the east to the Volga and the Danube in the west, now bent their best resources to the reduction of that Chinese kingdom which they perceived to be far richer and more populous than any region they had ever invaded. As might be expected, everything went against the Sung. First, his front which stretched along the lower valley of the Hoang Ho, was driven in right and left. Next his left flank, resting on the eastern slopes of the Central Plateau, was turned. Then his rear in Yün Nan was successfully occupied by that sweeping movement and that masterly strategy in which the Mongol commanders emulated the traditions of Alexander and Cæsar. Two lines or points alone remained to the Sung, namely, his right resting on the sea, and his centre resting on the Yang-tsze-Kiang, the river regarded by the Chinese as of all their rivers the most national. Some of the ocean-going fleet, and much of the inland river fleet were still in his possession. Along the sea coast, however, the Mongols were soon beforehand with him. For the conquest of northern China had placed at their disposal the marine in the Gulf of Peking and the estuary of the Hoang Ho. Thus they, for the first time in their political life, stepped straight into the position of a maritime power. The manner in which these Mongols—newly emerging from barbarism, dwelling amidst mountains far inland, never having beheld any sea except the Caspian or the Euxine, not possessing at home any navigable river, not trained to any pursuit whatever, except that horsemanship in which their proficiency was consummate—at once brought naval means into play, just as if they had been born to the business, is one among many proofs of the capacity which at that period belonged to them. So the Sung with his native Chinese, beaten at all sides on land, and sorely hindered at sea, made a crowning effort. He took to the inland waters of his national river. He placed his fighting men on board the river war vessels, which swept the course of the Yang-tsze-Kiang for several hundred miles. On or near both banks he had cities, which had been strongly fortified, and were fondly venerated by the Chinese as being the most splendid places under heaven. Subject to the control of these river squadrons and these strongholds, he had strips of the richest lands from which to draw supplies. He was enthusiastically sustained by civil administrators and military commanders, by soldiers and sailors, by citizens and peasants. Thus he took up a position from which the Mongols by land forces alone would never have expelled him. Their invincible cavalry, after overrunning most of Asia and a part of Europe, must have stopt at last baffled in sight of the Yang-tsze-Kiang waters. But, alas! the Mongols now had at their disposal the boats and sailors of northern China. Thus they forced the mouth of the Yang-tsze-Kiang, and challenged the Sung on his native element. Then there ensued and lasted for several years an amphibious warfare hardly paralleled in military annals. Furious river-fights were fought; often the banks of the Yang-tsze-Kiang were lit up with the glare of burning war-boats, while its waters rolled red with the blood of Mongol and of Sung. The Sung was, however, gradually overpowered; squadron after squadron, fort after fort, city after city, were lost to him; and the Mongols were at length masters of the Yang-tsze-Kiang. The Sung at last pushed his way out to sea; and the emperor plunged into the waves to escape gracing the Mongol triumph. But his cause survived; his followers still held tracts far south in the Canton valley. When driven from these they sought a final refuge in neighbouring islands. The last of their commanders organized an insular force, probably enlisting the privates that swarmed in the archipelago, and prepared to descend upon the Canton coast and to strike yet one more blow for the Sung. But he and his were overtaken by a hurricane within sight of their native shores, for which they were fighting so well, and the last of the Sung patriots foundered at sea.

Now it is not to be understood that this record of Chinese glory is spotless. Indeed there are spots left by flagrant instances of neglect, of incapacity, and of unworthy surrender. But it is also noteworthy that this long-sustained struggle of patriotism was not at all the work of individual emperors specially gifted with genius. On the contrary, the emperor in these crucial times happened to be sometimes an imbecile, and sometimes a boy. The war of independence was really maintained by whole classes of faithful ministers and brave generals. Had the Sung at that moment possessed a supreme head of adequate ability, the Mongols might, after all, have been foiled at the Yang-tsze-Kiang line of Chinese defence. The fact, however, that such a defence was made without the advantage of one guiding hand, is a proof of the patriotic vitality which the Chinese nation still possessed up to this fatal year A.D. 1270.

The Mongols were now masters of China, having been occupied for more than half a century of ceaseless fighting in that conquest — that is to say, full twenty years in conquering northern China under the Kin, and upwards of thirty years in subduing southern China under the Sung. When estimating the calibre of Chinese nationality in the middle ages, let the historical student compare the above-named time with the time taken by the Mongols in reducing many of the classic regions of the world, Ariana, Bactria, Persia, Asia Minor, old Russia, and South-Eastern Europe. Then let judgment be formed as to whether the Chinese resistance was not the stoutest that the Mongols ever encountered.

The commander of the Mongols in the operations against the Sung was Kublai, one of the three or four men of genius whom the Mongolian nationality produced. He established a Chinese kingdom in China proper, as distinguished from the Central Plateau. Other branches of what had now become the imperial family of the Mongols reigned in that Plateau, to which the eyes of European civilization were turned with awe, and to which the Christian Powers were fain to despatch ambassadors.

In China proper, the Mongol dominion was consolidated under Kublai by scrupulous attention to nearly all the ideas, the peculiarities, the prejudices, the institutions of ancient China, which have been already described. Great as a warrior, he was equally great as a civil ruler. He improved and enlarged the grand canal, which, uniting the deltas of the Hoang Ho and the Yang-tsze-Kiang, in the rear of the Shan Tung promontory, supplied inland navigation, saving a difficult detour by sea. He never tried, or at least he failed, to establish any new institutions which should give stability to the ancient Chinese polity. Whether the Muhammadan religion was introduced into China under his rule may be doubtful; at all events during his time the faith of Islam pushed itself like a wedge into the midst of the Buddhist population, constituting a sect of some millions of adherents. This sect has on occasions asserted itself, but there is doubt as to whether it would have to be reckoned with seriously by those who aspire to govern China.

The successors to Kublai's throne, nursed in the soft Chinese atmosphere, lost the ancestral vigour which had been braced in the rigorous clime of the Central Plateau, and soon their degenerate reigns were disturbed by those Chinese movements which, as already explained, have periodically destroyed even the best founded dynasties in China. Thus the Mongol rule, after lasting just one century in China, and being beset by popular risings under really national guidance, and by banditti acting merely under impulse of spoliation—collapsed ignominiously. Had there then been a presiding genius like Chinghiz Khan in the national council of Mongolia near the head-waters of the Amûr, the day might still have been retrieved for the Mongols in China. But no succour came from the Central Plateau. For by this time the Mongol authority was cankered to the core in Mongolia itself. That monstrous upas tree, which had overshadowed half the world, still stretched out branches in which the sap ascended, but its roots, which really sprang from the Central Plateau, were decayed and withering.

The revolution which now restored the native sovereignty of China, was characteristic of the Chinese. A man of the humblest class, who began life as a menial in a Buddhist monastery, and afterwards enlisted as a private soldier, carried in his knapsack not only the baton of a marshal, but also the sceptre of sovereignty. He founded, on the Mongol ruins, the next, which also proved the last, Chinese dynasty under the title of Ming. Ascending the throne he, like every preceding founder of a dynasty in China, was careful to confirm all the ancient institutions, civil, educational, literary, of the Chinese. The merits of the Chinese Ming ruler have been elaborately described by one of his successors, who, being a Manchu, and belonging to a different nationality, was free from any partiality towards the Chinese. The virtues of the Ming, then, have been set forth with extraordinary distinctness by a most competent authority, who had unrivalled advantages in access to records, and who doubtless sought example therefrom for his own guidance. This instance, signal though it be, is yet but one among the abundant instances of Chinese individuality. But after two centuries and a half of rule, his dynasty succumbed to the Manchu Tartars, who then founded that dynasty which still sits on the Chinese throne.

The Manchus did not consist, like the Mongols, of mighty hordes; they were a small but valiant tribe inhabiting a romantic valley around Mukden, near the head of the Gulf already mentioned. They claimed descent from the Kins, whose splendid resistance to the Mongol invaders has been already described. They obtained possession of the Chinese kingdom within one generation after their first occupation. This vast success won by a petty tribe in a short time over a kingdom full of power and resource, has been counted by some authorities as one of the marvels of history, It was, however, rendered possible by the misconduct of the Chinese Government itself. Under the Mings, the events which opened for the Manchus an entrance into China, form, perhaps, the most disgraceful episode in Chinese history, and illustrate the weakest points in the Chinese polity.

The Chinese Ming emperor was effete, and in consequence of mismanagement, the usual movements and upheavals were occurring. There were, indeed, still many elements of military and civil strength in the provinces; but the paralysis at the headquarters affected the body politic. Such trains of events had often come about at previous epochs, and yet the kingdom survived. But at this epoch there occurred an insurrection unparalleled, even in this land of movements. In that region of the upper Hoang Ho, which has been already several times mentioned as fatal to China, there arose a robber rebel, who gathered bands of bandits, military deserters, and armed men of all sorts. These bands, under their predatory leader, gained strength, like the snowballs, as they rolled along. First, detachments of royal troops misbehaved, some allowed themselves to be overpowered, others fraternized with the insurgents. Lesser forts opened their gates to those golden keys which insurgents gorged with plunder are able to apply. Then the fortress of Tung Kwan was taken by a *coup-de-main*. Half-hearted armies, under bad commanders, despatched from Peking, yielded to the swelling tide of insurrection. Flushed with easy victory over nominally disciplined troops, the predatory leader with his undisciplined multitudes made a dash for Peking. The garrison were too panic-stricken to resist; the Emperor, after displaying a selfishness and cowardice utterly alien to the Chinese character in extreme danger, committed the usual suicide; and the predatory leader assumed kingly power in the refined, cultured and illustrious capital of China. The city had indeed before been insulted as well as sacked by the Mongols; but after all the Mongols were vast organizers and mighty men of war. But here it was for a while ruled over by a brutish robber, who had nc attributes save his audacious spirit and his mailed hand. Had he remained, and had the Chinese from the provinces been left to deal with him, they would, as usual, have rallied, and displacing him, might have re-established a native sovereign. But another strange event supervened. A competent Chinese commander with some really good troops was stationed near the frontier, to watch the Manchus. He, considering the situation of Peking to be intolerable, resolved to rid the capital of the robber who had usurped the kingly status. To this end he adopted the desperate expedient of inviting the Manchus to join him in liberating Peking. Thus Peking was liberated, and the usurper was hunted to death in his native mountains near the Hoang Ho; but the Manchus were in joint occupation of northern China. The sequel can be imagined; the object for which their intervention had been invited having been effected, they were asked to retire: and of course they refused. As they had been thus admitted to possession, their ejectment was impossible; and they set up in northern China a new kingdom. Their coming to power was merely a question of time: nevertheless, had it not been for the strange concatenation of circumstances, as just described, their invasion would have been long delayed, or else their kingdom would have been restricted to northern China, just as that of the Kins had been. As it was, southern China did resist the Manchus on their advance from northern China; but the scandalous events at Peking must have taken the heart out of Chinese patriotism. Still a respectable contest was carried on over many years, though it was but a pale reflex of the splendid resistance by the Sungs as already described.

It is noteworthy that as the inhabitants of the country round Canton afforded the last standpoint of the Sung, so now they again struggled on behalf of the Ming with the energy of despair. Again, as the Sung resistance was organized by Chinese officers and administrators without personal guidance from their sovereign; so now the final efforts of the Mings were directed by Chinese ministers despite the errors committed by the Ming princes. Hereby is afforded proof of the national virtue which still resided in the nation.

Thus by the year 1650, the Manchus were masters of all China which then, for the second time, fell under a foreign yoke. The Manchus, however, were as rulers, far superior to the former foreign rulers, namely, the Mongols. In reference to that superiority there is an extraordinary circumstance to be noticed. The Manchu chiefs had for many years been studiously qualifying themselves for the administrative task which now devolved upon them. They seem to have previously fixed their resolve to conquer China, and then by good government to retain the conquest. For the work of such government they prepared themselves beforehand, by studying the Chinese language, literature, and institutions. In many parts of China their rule was at once successfully introduced; in other parts there were grave troubles. In south-eastern China there was a predatory insurrection marked with much brutality, and affording an instance similar to the extraordinary case already described. The pirate leaders on the sea coast and the adjacent islands not only succoured and sheltered the last remnant of Chinese patriots, but struck a hard blow inland to recover for China the kingdom which the Manchus had recently won. The growth of piratical power in the Chinese waters at this epoch is worthy of a longer notice than can at this moment be accorded. The organized pirates were then (A.D. 1650 to 1700) the largest maritime power in the eastern seas. Their centre was the island of Formosa; they also held several towns with adjoining districts on the mainland of southern China, and some places near the mouth of the Yang-tsze-Kiang. With a fleet of war vessels they now entered the estuary, and sailing up the great river attacked places of the first importance. This maritime invasion was repelled by the Manchus immediately, but several years elapsed before the pirates were dislodged from their settlements, and a still longer time before their last stronghold in Formosa fell into Manchu hands.

In China proper the Manchu rule was consolidated by the conciliation of the Chinese. The care with which the Manchus at the outset distributed the civil and military patronage between their own people and the Chinese is remarkable. The extent, indeed, to which the Chinese were admitted to a share in the management of their country was one among the chief causes of the success which greeted the new regime. The Manchu rule was distinguished by two long reigns, each lasting more than half a century. Of the two sovereigns, one was among the best rulers, and the other among the grandest monarchs of the age. The reign of the second lasted close up to the beginning of the nineteenth century, which is the limit of time assigned to this historical analysis. Within China proper the administration developed to the utmost all the best characteristics of the Chinese as already described. But it moved in the old grooves, and on lines nearly the same as those which have been already sketched as those existing before A.D. 1200, and before the accession of foreign rulers. Hardly any new principle, political or administrative, was evolved from the busy brains of the Manchus. Once more we see the same centralization, the same constitution, departments, and bureaucracy, the same literary and educational organization, the same official hierarchy, the same provincial subdivisions, as of yore. There is still that sedulous attention to imposing forms, the hollowness of which is attested by the want of result altogether, or by the disappointing character of the result attained. For instance, despite the existence of an enormous statistical machinery, it is impossible to ascertain any large economic fact relating to the empire even during the last century; a financial statement of income and expenditure, provincial and imperial, can hardly be made out; the numbers of the population are returned so badly by census after census that the total cannot be stated within 50,000,000, or, as we might almost say, within a hundred millions.

The influence of several European nations began during this period to be felt on the outskirts of the dominion. The Roman Catholic clergy obtained a locus standi in the midst of the empire. Had it not been for their dissensions they might have converted masses of Chinese from Buddhism and Lao-ism to Christianity. As it was, they shed some lustre on the public service of China, they supplied many corrections to Chinese science and geography, and many noble additions to Chinese historical literature, emulating even the wondrous industry of the natives. Christian converts were made in numbers not enough to constitute a political power, but enough to arouse a spirit of jealous exclusiveness among the Chinese. This spirit, though existing in the earlier ages, was not very active, and its manifestation at this time, the eighteenth century, is a proof that the Chinese were beginning to lose self-confidence in respect to the inroad of foreign thought and intellect. Although the religion of China is essentially tolerant as compared with other Oriental religions, yet the annals of this time began to be marked with instances of fanaticism, even of persecution sometimes ending in Christian martyrdom.

On the whole, the internal order, the growing prosperity, the general contentment, the increase of population, the attachment of the people to their country, proved that the Manchu administration during the eighteenth century was, if not enlightened, at least humane, parental and effective.

But besides consolidating internal order, it essayed an external achievement of which the importance at the time was great, and of which the final consequences cannot even yet be foreseen. For it restored to the Chinese empire the dominion over the central plateau of Asia already described on the map. We may remember that the suzerainty over this wonderful region had been claimed and fitfully exercised by the ancient emperors of China. But before the Mongol era (A.D. 1200) this suzerainty had ceased, and since that era, the Central Plateau had been politically separate from the Chinese kingdom. The re-assertion of this suzerainty, then, in the seventeenth century, and the re-vindication of it during the eighteenth, taken together with its successful retention during the nineteenth, invest the circumstance with cardinal importance in the politics of Asia. The military operations by which this success was won, the marches in the desert, the endurance of extremes of heat and cold, the commissariat supplies in foodless and shelterless regions, the transport arrangements in rugged and precipitous lines of communication, deserve the professional study of soldiers and politicians, as showing what China has done in recent times, and what possibly she may yet do. We may also admire the area on which the comprehensive capacity and genius were displayed. For it extended from the Pamir steppe and the source of the Oxus on the west to the Chinese uplands on the east, from the Altai range and the Siberian confines on the north to the heart of the Himalayas on the south. Indian hill states, now under the political control of England, then sent annual presents to China in acknowledgment of fealty. I have heard the Nepalese warrior Jang Behadur feelingly recount the blows inflicted on Nepal by Chinese armies that had crossed the snowy ranges.

Lastly, one characteristic trait may be mentioned in reference to the mountain dominions. The Manchu sovereigns in the eighteenth century believed that in order to maintain their ruling capacity in the softer climate of China, they must recruit their nervous force by sojourning for a while amidst the mountains every year. It was for this purpose that the royal hunts were a part of Manchu-Chinese statecraft. It is noteworthy that early in the nineteenth century, the successor of the Manchu monarch-statesmen resolved to abandon the royal and national institution of annual exercises amidst the mountains. He thereon issued a proclamation to that effect, and those who read between the lines of that document can perceive the first traces of Manchu degeneracy.

## CHAPTER IV.

### LAKE REGION ON THE FRONTIER OF EASTERN TIBET.

[*Speech delivered before the Royal Geographical Society, in London, February*, 1882.]

**Extraordinary picturesqueness of the Eastern Himalayas — Road from Bengal to the border of East Tibet — Line dividing the empires of England and China — Mountain passes in that quarter — Series of lakes situated there — Beauty of their aspect — Fine scenery around them — Altitude too high for vegetation — Temperature and climate — Forests in lesser altitudes — Snowy mountains within Tibet — Views of remarkable splendour or interest — Geological features.**

I AM about to speak before you upon the subject of "The Lake region on the frontier of Eastern Tibet." My speech will comprise mainly an exposition of the map and of the pictorial illustrations which have been made for this purpose. The map has been prepared specially by our draughtsman, Mr. Turner. The illustrations have been prepared on a large scale by my brother, Lieutenant George Temple, R.N., from water-colour sketches made by myself.

In the first place, I must ask you to observe that the district of Sikkim overlooks from the north the rich province of Bengal, and is situated in the eastern part of the Himalayas; and that a railway runs up from the direction of Calcutta to the foot of the Himalayas. From the base of the mountain, there is a well-engineered road (now superseded by a tramway) up to the hill station of Darjiling, which is the capital of British Sikkim. You will perceive that British Sikkim is marked within the line, which in our maps always indicates British dominion. It originally belonged to the

Rajah of the native State of Sikkim, and was annexed to the British dominions by reason of his misconduct in imprisoning for several days Dr. Campbell, the British Superintendent of Darjiling, and Dr. (now Sir Joseph) Hooker, the Director of Kew Gardens. In punishment for that offence, this district was taken from him and added to British India. Since its annexation to British India, the district has flourished immensely, and has become one of the principal seats of the tea industry of India. It is now dotted and studded with flourishing tea plantations.

From the station of Darjiling you have a view, 45 miles distant, of the celebrated mountain of Kanchanjanga. Now, Kanchanjanga is the principal of a group of mountains upwards of 28,000 feet high (above sea level), and is the second highest mountain in the world. But the celebrated view of Kanchanjanga is not the only claim which Darjiling has upon the attention of the world. This place is the summer residence of the Government of Bengal, and the hill of Darjiling constitutes a remarkable watershed. In the first place, it is a physical watershed, inasmuch as it constitutes the water-parting of the rivers Ganges and Brahmaputra: the water that flows from the south side of the crest, ultimately finding its way into the Ganges, and that on the north side running into the Tista, which is an affluent of the Brahmaputra. But it is also, if I may so call it, a moral and religious watershed, for every man on the south side of the crest is a votary of the Hindu religion, and every man on the north side is a Buddhist. On the south side of the crest, the bell of the Hindu temple calls the faithful to prayer. On the other side begin the Buddhist monasteries and chapels, where the deep-sounding gong summons the votaries to worship. Inasmuch as the Hindu religion numbers nearly 200 millions of people, and the Buddhistic a similarly vast number, the fact that this particular crest should be the boundary line between these two wide-spread religions, constitutes a remarkable circumstance. Moreover, Darjiling has now become the entrepôt and the market of the Eastern Himalayas. At that point are gathered the piece goods the woollens, and other manufactures of England to be exported to Tibet: thither come in exchange the wools, the horns, the various products, the live-stock, the unrivalled sheep and goats of Tibet. So much, then, for British Sikkim.

I must now ask you to leave the British dominions and to cross the red line on the map. We then arrive in Native Sikkim, on the western frontier of which there runs the important line of hills separating that State from Nepal. This range has an average altitude of between 11,000 and 12,000 feet. You may ride along that ridge for 40 or 50 miles almost without a break. On your right hand, travelling northwards, you overlook the State of Sikkim, which is a labyrinth of hills; and on your left you have in view the valley of Nepal. On your right front you see the Kanchanjanga, already described, and on your left front the famous group of snowy mountains, of which the highest is Mount Everest. Now, Mount Everest is about 29,000 feet high—a few feet higher than Kanchanjanga, which is upwards of 28,000 feet high; so from that ridge of hills is obtained the finest view of snow mountains in the world. The vegetation is also very peculiar and beautiful, for besides the fir forests of the mountain slopes, there exist along that ridge the most beautiful rhododendron trees that have ever yet been discovered. The clusters of blossoms may be described in general terms as being as large as a man's hand, and the leaves from 12 to 13 inches long. The colouring of the flower is quite superb, sometimes crimson and sometimes alabaster white. But the most remarkable circumstance is that these splendidly flowering shrubs grow in a climate peculiarly rigorous. The rains and the winds beat on them, the rich tints are soon bleached, and in a few days after, the flower falls. It certainly adds to the extraordinary interest of this floral display to find it thus set forth amid some of the roughest and severest aspects of nature.

Along the centre of Sikkim lies the valley of the Tista, a river which rises in the central backbone ridge of the Himalayas. I am not about to lead you towards the source of the Tista, but I may refer those who are curious upon that subject to the very interesting description of the locality given, firstly, in Sir Joseph Hooker's book entitled 'Himalayan Journals,' and secondly in Mr. Blanford's description of a journey in that region. Both those gentlemen agree in describing the views at the source of the Tista as among the finest they ever beheld, and they are extremely good judges on such a subject, having seen some of the best views in the Himalayas. But the Tista may be regarded as the main artery of Native Sikkim, and all the streams which run through this series of valleys may be considered as veins leading to this main arterial line of drainage.

Now, the interesting point, from a commercial and political point of view, is this: that through Sikkim the British Government is gradually constructing a trade road from northern Bengal to eastern Tibet, more particularly with a view of opening communication with Lhassa, the well-known capital of eastern Tibet. This road is to pass through British Sikkim first, then through Native Sikkim, then on to the Jyelap Pass, which is one of the passes leading over the Chola range of hills, and then into the valley of Chumbi, to which I will allude more particularly presently. This road is to start mainly from Darjiling as the British terminus, and we hope in future generations that it will end at Lhassa as the Tibetan terminus. It is to supersede the old road to eastern Tibet which used to run through the State of Bhûtan, a portion of which you will see indicated on the right-hand side of the map. This old route through Bhûtan is the one that was followed by the early travellers who went upon political missions under the orders of that far-seeing statesman Warren Hastings, then Governor-General of India—such travellers as Turner, Manning, and Bogle. The interesting and instructive journals of Bogle and Manning have been recently published and edited by our talented Secretary, Mr.

Clements Markham, who has prefixed to the work one of those interesting geographical, historical, and political discussions for which he has a special aptitude.

Before we proceed further, I must ask you to look more particularly in the map at the Chola range of mountains, and the Chumbi Valley. You will see that the Chola range lies in the north-east corner of Sikkim, separating that native State of Sikkim from the valley of Chumbi. Now the situation of Chumbi, you will observe, is very peculiar, because it is a portion of Tibet interposed, as it were, like a wedge between Sikkim and Bhûtan. It is a piece of Tibet, and therefore politically a piece of China, protruded in the midst of the Himalayas which pertain to the British empire. To this new road political as well as commercial importance is attached. It leads from Darjiling deep down into the valley of the Tista, where the rich vegetation, the tree ferns, the flowering creepers, the bauhinia and blossoming trees like the magnolia, make you fancy yourself in Bengal and Assam, or even in Ceylon. From the midst of this exuberant vegetation, the proposed road rapidly mounts into altitudes where trees and foliage are seen no more.

After leaving this vegetation, you ascend into the rich pasturages and slopes on the spurs of the Chola range. There it is that the people, dwelling in Chumbi, Tibet and the valleys of Sikkim, bring their flocks and herds for what is called the winter grazing. Beyond the Himalayas the climate is too severe for the flocks in mid-winter, and therefore they are brought to lower altitudes of 10,000 or 12,000 feet (above sea level), where the snow does not lie for more than a few weeks together, and where there is rich herbage. After that you ascend to the Jyelap Pass, at an altitude of about 15,000 feet, and thus you leave Sikkim and enter upon Tibet, which is a part of the Chinese empire. Our engineers have marked the road out, and rendered it available for ordinary traffic as far as the Jyelap Pass, and beyond that it is for our friends in Tibet to continue the line towards Lhassa. As may be imagined, there is a certain amount of reluctance on the part of the Tibetan authorities to construct these roads, because they sometimes believe, justly perhaps, that either commerce follows the flag, or that the flag follows commerce; therefore they think that politics have something to do with trade. Nevertheless, they highly appreciate Darjiling as a commercial depôt. They want money, and they know that they can bring their varied products to the markets there for sale and obtain good British Indian money wherewith to purchase British or Chinese articles. Therefore we hope that they will co-operate with us at last in opening a trade route from India to China.

Next, it must be borne in mind that the crest of the Chola range, and the passes which cross that crest, especially the Jyelap Pass, are sterile in the extreme. The region lies above and beyond the zone of vegetation, and nothing is seen but bare rocks, water, snow and sky.

Thus far I have occupied you chiefly with what may be called the commercial and political portion of my speech; I have not detained you much with descriptions of the picturesque scenery; but before I leave Sikkim proper, I should like to remind you of the extraordinary beauty which belongs to that isolated native state. Sikkim is not remarkable for the industry or the skill of its people; its population involves many ethnological questions which do not appertain to the sphere of the Geographical Society; but its religious condition is in many respects remarkably interesting to all Anglo-Indians, because it is one of the few places where an opportunity is afforded of seeing the living Buddhism, debased in comparison with the original Buddhism as promulgated by Buddha himself many centuries ago. The monasteries and Buddhist chapels in Sikkim are wonderfully interesting structures, and of very peculiar architecture, a mixture of Chinese and Indian; in certain respects it should be called a sort of Hindu-Chinese architecture. But beyond the architecture, there is the extraordinary beauty of the sites on which these buildings are placed.

They are almost always on the crest of rocky and wooded hills, and they have as their background the glorious peaks of Kanchanjanga and the snowy range behind them.

From the altitude of most parts of this region an immense sweep of country is beheld. The deep valleys of the Tista and its affluents, not more than 2000 feet (above the sea level), lie below you, and from their depths you look up straight in one uninterrupted view to the summits of Kanchanjanga; so that, deducting 2000 feet from 28,000, you have in one sweep of the eye 26,000 feet of mountain slope, and that not in one place only, but in many places all over Sikkim. These and other circumstances, combined with the richness of the vegetation and the botanical interest connected therewith, also the many kinds of beautiful birds—this mixture of scientific and picturesque interest—have rendered Sikkim the desire of everybody to behold. The only drawback to travelling there is the severity of the weather. You have really to undergo great hardships. The mist and rain are provoking beyond my power of description. You have to march in the wet, to unpack your tent in the wet, to lie down to sleep in the wet, to pack up again in the wet. For hours, sometimes for days, together you live in the wet; but after enduring all this you are ultimately rewarded, for the rain ceases, the blast subsides, and the mist clears away, and then you behold spectacles such as are imprinted on the tablets of your brain for the rest of your life.

I will now beg of you to follow me on the map along the routes leading to the lakes of Sikkim. The road I have already described was a straight route planned for commerce—the route, as it may be called, of the trader, of the statesman, and the politician, and I am now going to conduct you by what I may call the route of the artist. This route commences with an upper crossing of the Tista on the road leading northward from Darjiling. Here the passage of the river is difficult: I very nearly had my riding ponies drowned at this spot. However, I and my staff succeeded in crossing and then ascended the hills on the way to Tumlong. Thence we farther ascended towards the Chomnaga Valley and the Chola Pass. It was in the Chomnaga Valley that Dr. Campbell and Sir Joseph Hooker were seized, pinioned, and placed in durance vile. I have already explained to you that the finest rhododendrons grow in the western part of Sikkim towards Nepal; but second to those are the splendid blossoms of the Chomnaga Valley. It was there that Hooker collected the seeds of a great number of splendid species and varieties which are now

FIG. 1.—PALACE OF THE RAJAH OF SIKKIM AT TUMLONG.

adorning the public gardens of England; and it is therefore to that scientific journey, taken thirty-five years ago, that we in England owe some part of the pleasure and instruction we now derive in viewing the gardens in this country. Chomnaga lies at the foot of the Chola Pass, from which latter point begins the series of lakes to which our pictorial illustrations relate, and which I will now proceed to describe.

Our first illustration represents the palace of Tumlong. This comparatively humble though picturesque dwelling belongs to the Rajah of Sikkim, and may be regarded as his Winter Palace. During the summer, particularly when the rains descend, he lives, by permission of the Grand Lama of Tibet, in the valley of Chumbi, because Chumbi, being upon the other side of the Chola range, has a climate not affected by the rainy season; but during the winter he lives at this little palace of Tumlong. Humble as the place may be, it is yet the capital of Sikkim. It is situated on a hill, about 5000 feet high, having in the background the north-western end of the Chola range. The mountain indicated in the picture is that known under the name of Gnarean on the maps.

The next picture (2) represents the Chola Pass and Lake. This is one of the old passes by which people used to proceed from Sikkim towards Tibet; but it is much less used now than formerly, since the opening of the commercial route, already described, by the Jyelap Pass. Immediately behind the lake you will observe a rough, rugged, serrated range of hills rising up with its fantastical peaks, something like the jagged edge of a gigantic saw. Now, those are the hills which overlook the valley of Chomnaga—the upper valley where Dr. Hooker and his companions were seized by the Sikkim people. In the distance is Mount Kanchanjanga, viewed in its south-eastern aspect, or that which faces towards Chumbi and Tibet—the very opposite view from that which is ordinarily seen of Kanchanjanga by British visitors at Darjiling, which is really the western view facing towards India. This eastern view is that which is seldom seen by Anglo-Indians, and is, I venture to believe, the finer view of the two. There you see the magnificent expanse of snows, the noble granite formations, and all the glaciers of that frozen world. The height of the Chola Pass and of the Lake may be placed at 15,000 feet above the sea, or very nearly the height of Mont Blanc, the height having been carefully ascertained, first by Sir Joseph Hooker, and afterwards by Mr. Blanford. The geological formation of

FIG. 2.—CHOLA LAKE AND PASS. MOUNT KANCHANJANGA IN THE DISTANCE.

the Chola range, for the most part, consists of gneiss. This, again, has been carefully ascertained by Mr. Blanford. Of course Kanchanjanga, in the distance, is for the most part composed of granite; certainly all the upper part is so composed. The upper part of the Chola range is absolutely sterile; not a tree, not a shrub, grows in the locality—nothing but a few kinds of Alpine grasses and scanty herbage, which are dried up in most seasons of the year.

Our next picture (3) represents the Chokham Lake. Whilst the Chola Lake lies exactly on the boundary between Sikkim and Chumbi, and therefore between the Indian and the Chinese empires, the Chokham Lake is situated a little above it and just within the Chinese or Tibetan border. I say "Chinese or Tibetan," for Tibet is virtually Chinese. The precise relations between the Grand Lama of Tibet and the Emperor of China I need hardly at this moment undertake to explain, but that part of Tibet is thoroughly dominated by China. Tibet has a local government of its own, no doubt, but its affairs are controlled by a Chinese resident supported by Chinese troops, and the Chinese are particularly careful to put boundary marks along the border. They do this in the most jealous and particular manner possible. Wherever I went, my footsteps were dogged by Chinese and Tibetan officials. Even if I stopped to take a sketch, these gentlemen were always considering whether my foot was upon one side of the border or the other. On one side of the wooden boundary-pillars was an inscription written in the Hindi character of British India, and on the other side an inscription in Chinese. When I went up to sketch the Chokham Lake, the Chinese local officers with their Tibetan attendants were very careful to warn me that I had transgressed the limits of my jurisdiction. However, we secured the sketch, and there it is, or at least the copy of it. This is decidedly the finest of all the lakes. I have been reminded by the high authority of our President that I ought not to call these sheets of water "lakes," and that they are more strictly "tarns," because they have no outlets. In some respects they present geological problems; however, you will allow me to use "tarn" or "lake" as interchangeable. If the Chokham Lake is a tarn, it attains to the proportions of a lake, and is the loftiest and largest of the series. I do not know its dimensions, but it comprises an area of several square miles. The colour of the water is superb. The altitude is fully a thousand feet higher than that of the Chola Lake, and therefore must be nearly

FIG. 3.—CHOKHAM LAKE ABOVE CHOLA PASS. MOUNT CHANGU KANG IN THE DISTANCE.

16,000 feet above the level of the sea. We ourselves soon began to find that we were approaching a great altitude, because as we climbed the rocks we became short of breath, and our heads began to ache. However, when we surmounted the rocks we were more than rewarded by the splendour of the spectacle. Emerald, azure, turquoise—all these phrases combined will fail to give you an impression of the indescribable beauty of the water. In the background of our view will be seen a tract of low forest which creeps along the base of the hills overhanging the Chumbi Valley, and beyond the valley rise a series of purple, pinkish mountains. I need not say that, to a spectator on the hills themselves, their colour would be of the dullest and most opaque yellow ochre; but the effect of distance in this clear atmosphere is to throw a sort of etherealised pink-purple over the mountains, which has a lovely effect. Beyond the range of hills rises the snowy mountain of Changu Kang, a sort of pyramid. This Changu Kang is not found on the maps, but is very well known in that locality, and it separates Bhûtan from Tibet.

FIG. 4.—BHEWSA LAKE. MOUNT KANCHANJANGA IN THE DISTANCE.

On the southern spur of the Chola range lies the subject of our next picture (4), the Bhewsa Lake, which is much lower than those which I have been describing. It may be considered as having an altitude of 12,000 feet, being perhaps 4000 feet below the Chokham Lake. In the foreground near that lake, especially on the left-hand side of the picture, you will see indications of vegetation. These represent vast expanses of scrub rhododendron, a sort of rhododendron that grows very low and very thick, and spreads its branches in a tangled mass over the ground. It is a dreadfully difficult scrub for a pedestrian to push through; but it is very valuable to the traveller, because it supplies him with fuel for his fire, which he needs in the cold, and cannot otherwise get, and in the event of extreme want of water it will supply him even with moisture, because its leaves have upon them the hoar frost which can be wiped off, and be made to afford relief to thirsty men, as I and my staff sometimes found out. This scrub is the only vegetation met with in this zone, lying above the limits of trees. The Bhewsa Lake has a purplish-violet colour. I am unable to explain the reason of this variety of colour in the lakes, but the Chola Lake was principally blue, the Chokham Lake a mixture of emerald, azure, and turquoise, and Bhewsa Lake somewhat violet and purple. Behind the Bhewsa Lake, in the middle background, rise the gneiss rocks overhanging the Chomnaga Valley. In our illustration of the Chola Lake these rocks are seen in shadow: here, in this illustration, they are in the full blaze of the setting sun, and beyond them Mount Kanchanjanga overhanging the lake is seen with the same evening effect. Instead of the glittering white in the blaze of the morning sun, it is now tinged with the pink and rosy hues of sunset.

The bad weather, which we generally had, was interspersed with lucid intervals of glorious blue skies, and of course I selected those lucid intervals for making my sketches. Generally speaking, what really happens is this: early in the morning, at sunrise, the weather is quite superb; the sky is unclouded azure, and the mountains are unbroken white. This lasts for some three hours, that is to say, till about 10 o'clock in the day, and that is what we used to call the bloom of the morning. Then, and then only, can you take your sketches. The air is extremely cold—biting cold—and after sketching for a short time your fingers get perfectly numbed, and the only thing to do is to keep a supply of hot water close at hand, into which you can put your fingers, and so get a certain amount of warmth in them, which enables you to preserve their cunning for sketching. After 10 o'clock up come the clouds. You cannot tell how they form themselves. A little bit of vapour, no bigger than a man's hand, expands; fresh men's hands arise and clouds accumulate, till at last the whole atmosphere is clouded over. This lasts till about middle day. Then the clouds seem to turn into snow, and a certain amount of snow falls in the afternoon, which makes you very miserable in the evening, and you sit down to dinner with snow all around you, and your little tent also encrusted with snow. But towards midnight the clouds pass away, and stars come out, and it is a magnificent night. Then you have the sunrise as already described.

Probably the sun when it rises will melt the thin snow during the bloom of the day. With that kind of weather you very seldom get a sunset view; but on that particular evening when I was at the Bhewsa Lake, the clouds somehow were lifted to display the setting sun, literally bathing Kanchanjanga in roseate light; and that happy moment, of course, I seized to make my sketch.

The Bhewsa Lake being comparatively low, we had to ascend from there once more towards the crest of the range, towards the point you will find named on the map as the Yakla Pass. On that ascent we found three very little lakes, for which I will adopt our President's designation of tarns. The first of these is overhung by some very weird, strange-looking rocks, piled one over the other, as it were by Titanic and Cyclopean hands; and in the back the view is not towards Tibet, but towards Darjiling. Leaving this tarn, No. I. (Fig. 5), we get to tarn No. II. (Fig .6). In this latter you will observe a very pointed hill tipped with snow. This is the peak, well-known locally as Dopenti, which geographers will find marked on Stanford's map as Dobendi, another name for the same hill. Dopenti peak is the highest point of the Chola range, and is the same eminence as that called Chola Peak by Sir Joseph Hooker. It really overhangs the Chola Lake; but the lake is so close under the base that the summit is not visible from the banks of the lake. We have now advanced 10 miles to the eastward along the ridge, and thus we obtain a view of the Dopenti Peak which overhangs the Chola Lake and Pass.

We now come to tarn No. III. (Fig. 7), which is exactly at

FIG. 5.—TARN NO. I. ON ASCENT TO YAKLA PASS. DARJILING HILLS IN THE DISTANCE.

the foot of the Yakla Pass. The Yakla Pass is just visible in the illustration, marked by a long saddle in the middle background. The existence of so many of these lakes or tarns—by whichever name they should be called—all at the crest of a lofty range of mountains, presents many geological problems which I will not now discuss; but I may mention in general terms that Mr. Blanford, the best geological authority who has yet visited the country in which they are situated, ascribes

FIG. 6.—TARN NO. II. ON ASCENT TO YAKLA PASS.

them to glacial action. He thinks that in a former geological period immense glaciers have scooped out these hollows in the crest of the mountains. Passing from the tarns, and ascending

FIG. 7.—TARN NO. III. AT FOOT OF YAKLA PASS.

to the saddle, which I have pointed out as indicated on the illustration—a most toilsome ascent—a view is obtained of the Yakla Pass and Lake, and in the distance of Mount Chumalari, all of which you will see depicted in our illustration (8).

This, on the whole, was the most beautiful of all these lovely views. The lakes and the mountains on either side of it, with other mountains in the middle distance, and the graceful

FIG. 8.—YAKLA PASS AND LAKE. MOUNT CHUMALARI IN THE DISTANCE.

obelisk of Chumalari, with the mountain shaped like a double-poled tent on the left of the obelisk—the whole of the features together make up a truly fine group, most difficult to sketch, indeed, because of the extreme, biting cold and the wind in that exposed position. The colour of the lake is an intense blue. In the foreground, on the left-hand side, you will observe indications of a road. The mark of the road is slightly exaggerated in our drawing, in order to make it clear to you from a distance; but it is, of course, an extremely rough mountain pass. It is one of the passes by which the flocks and herds of Tibet descend to British India, as I myself saw. I never beheld such beautiful sheep and goats in my life as those which were coming along that pass at the time of my visit. A Landseer, if he had been present, would have made of these splendid herds a worthy foreground to this dazzling scene. On the other side of the lake are again seen the hills of Chumbi. These hills comprise what is marked on the maps as the district of Phari. In the maps there is a district marked Phari which is a subdivision of the Chumbi Valley, and the hills of Phari are exactly indicated by the middle distance in this picture.

Once more I ask your attention to the peculiar beauty of the top of Chumalari. I have sketched it several times from several points, and on comparing the outlines I always found that they corresponded, so that I am very confident I have got the shape correctly. You will see that on the west side of the mountain there is a beautiful cone, gradually tapering into an obelisk, and on the eastern, or right, side of the mountain there rises a great square mass of snow, which we used to liken to the double-poled tent of the Indian marches.

We are now on the crest of the range, and the altitude of the Yakla Pass is nearly the same as that of the Chola Pass, namely, 15,000 feet. Our route then descends from the pass for several thousand feet, to reach the Nimyetso Lake. *Tso* is a common termination in Tibetan names, meaning water, and is sometimes pronounced *tcho;* in fact, Europeans cannot tell whether natives are saying *tso* or *tcho.* It merely means a lake. Nimyetso is Nimye Lake. And I ought to take this opportunity of mentioning that the termination *la* means a pass, so that Chola, or Cho-la, merely means lake-pass, and Yakla, or Yak-la, is nothing more than the pass of the Yak, the famous Tibetan cow, so well known to geographers and naturalists. These cows are remarkable for the size and beauty of their tails, which constitute an important article of commerce. You have often heard of the long-haired fan being waved by attendants over the heads of emperors and sovereigns on state occasions. These long fans are nothing more than the tails of yaks, and the consequence is they bring thousands and thousands of pounds sterling annually into the pockets of the Tibetans.

After this slight digression, I must ask you to revert to the Nimyetso Lake, as depicted in the illustration (9).

FIG. 9.—NIMYETSO LAKE.

That lake is lower than any of the others which we have been considering. Consequently it is surrounded by forests; fir-woods on one side, and on the other a rich sylvan mass, composed chiefly of chestnut-trees. The lake itself will be admitted to be a true lake, for it has an outlet; situated near to the foreground of our picture. Behind the forests rises the Chola range of hills, from which we have been descending, tipped with snow. On that ridge, on the left-hand side of the picture, is the Yakla

Pass and Lake, which I have just described; and farther on the left, outside the picture, would be the Chola Pass; and out of the picture on the right of that ridge is the Jyelap Lake, to which I am about to introduce you. This Nimyetso Lake is 10,000 feet only above sea-level.

I have now to ask you to ascend with me to the top of the forest-clad hills in the middle distance of our picture, and then to turn off towards the right; you will then be in the immediate neighbourhood of the next scene, which is the Bidantso, what we

FIG. 10.—BIDANTSO LAKE AFTER A SNOWSTORM. MOUNT GIPMOCHI IN THE DISTANCE.

used to call the Blackwater Lake, on account of its unaccountable blackness. This is depicted in the illustration (10). The lake was sketched in a snowstorm, and in the background is Mount Gipmochi. In Sir Joseph Hooker's 'Himalayan Journals' the name Gipmochi is always applied to the mountain which terminates the Chola range. This range you will have observed is the mountain region to which the chief part of my speech this evening has related. At its north-western end rises the Gnarean

Peak behind the Tumlong Palace, and Mount Gipmochi is at its south-eastern end.

Our illustration of the Blackwater Lake, with Gipmochi in the distance, represents the view in a snowstorm. There had been during the afternoon just that sort of snowstorm which I have previously described; but towards evening some puffs of wind came, the mist and cloud lifted, and the snow ceased. Then we beheld a glorious spectacle, slightly represented in the picture before you. The bright and radiant atmosphere of the world below us seemed at that moment to be shining through the mists of these upper regions—mists which resembled a thin veil of transparent gauze. Anything more lovely than this sort of subdued light—dimly illuminating the lake and its snowy adjuncts, with the sombre Gipmochi in the background, and the retreating clouds with the snowstorm still seeming to rest upon the extreme left of the picture—it is hard to conceive. The altitude of Blackwater Lake above the sea-level may be estimated at 12,000 feet, that is to say 2000 feet above the lake which we have last seen, and somewhat higher than the Bhewsa Lake. It also has in the foreground on the left-hand side some of the scrub rhododendrons which I have already described. The leaves of the bushes are represented in our view as encrusted with snow. It was near this Blackwater Lake that we were encamped, and we had to pitch the tents on the only tolerable ground we could find, which was a half-frozen and indurated swamp, so that you may imagine the amount of sneezing and wheezing which troubled me and my followers upon that occasion. After a very snowy afternoon, which was just relieved by this gleam of light at sunset, we spent a rough night on this swamp; but towards midnight the sky cleared, the stars came out, and we were enabled during early dawn to commence the ascent to the Jyelap Pass.

Thus I have conducted you by the artistic route to a junction with the commercial and political route already described.

We ascended to the Jyelap Pass early in the morning, and

once more came upon one of the glorious sunrises of this region. The landscape, as shown in the illustration (11), included not only Chumalari in the background, but also Changu Kang peak, with the Jyelap Lake in the foreground. In the background of our view of the Chokham Lake, Changu Kang only was represented, and in the background of the Yakla Lake, Chumalari only; but here both are seen, forming upon the whole

FIG. 11.—JYELAP PASS AND LAKE. MOUNTS CHUMALARI AND CHANGU KANG IN THE DISTANCE.

the finest background to be found in this region. This Jyelap Lake is a very little one; but behind it, in the middle distance, are once more visible the pink rosy-coloured hills, with Chumbi, combining the district of Chumbi proper and the district of Phari which I have already mentioned. Between this lake and the lower hills there intervenes the valley of Chumbi, one of the deep valleys, which I believe is not more than 3000 feet above the sea. So that in order to arrive at those rosy-coloured hills from the lake, it would be necessary to dip down many thousand feet and re-ascend many thousand feet. Thus it would probably take two days' march to reach those hills. I have already explained to you that the trade route comes from British territory and Darjiling to this Jyelap Pass under British auspices and management; and at the Jyelap Pass we have reached the extreme boundary of Sikkim, and therefore the boundary of the British Empire. Beyond this commences Tibet, and we hope in future ages that the road from India to China will run over those rosy-coloured hills past the western foot of Chumalari. At the left, or western, base of Chumalari in our picture may be seen the point near which this road from India to China is to cross the central line or backbone of the Himalayas. The country beyond has been beheld by very few European eyes, but the road passes on northwards towards Lhassa, and then joins on to the route which was followed by Bogle and Manning, and which has been so well described in the book by Mr. Clements Markham.

Now, gentlemen, I have reached the conclusion of my geographical speech, and also the end of my small picture gallery; and I hope that pictures, maps and exposition together have given you a clear conception of a part of the line which is intermediate between two of the great empires in Asia. I trust that if you have at all followed me through all the travels and hardships of the march, you have also been rewarded in imagination by the splendid spectacles which you have seen; and I trust that when you go forth from this theatre into the streets outside, you will carry away with you bright visions in your inner minds; that you will have, as it were, Chumalari and Kanchanjanga "upon the brain." But I also hope that you will think with patriotic pride of the achievements of your countrymen in that quarter of the globe—achievements scientific, commercial, and political; that you will have a kindly sympathy towards the labours of the many excellent men who have travelled in that region—historic men, as Turner, Bogle and Manning, also Dr. Campbell; and such living travellers as Sir Joseph Hooker, Mr. Blanford, and Mr. Edgar; and that you will take home with you some idea of the peaceable progress of British influence and British power in that quarter of Asia.

## CHAPTER V.

### RAILWAY FROM THE INDUS TOWARDS CANDAHAR.

[*Speech delivered before the Royal Geographical Society, in London, June* 1880.]

Distance from the Indus to Candahar — Natural divisions of the country — The position of Sakkar on the Indus — Construction of the railway through the desert — Gorges and rifts in the hills of Southern Afghanistan — Desolate plain near Quetta — Fine situation of Quetta — Valley of Pishin — Its political importance — Khojak range dividing it from Afghanistan — Dust-storm over Afghan plains — General view of Candahar — Its historic sieges — Garden cultivation around it.

I AM to give you orally what I hope will be found to be a popular explanation of the map and of the pictorial representations which accompany my exposition. The map has been prepared specially by the draughtsman of the Society, Mr. Turner, for this occasion; and in several respects it contains geographical particulars which, although they have been exhibited in India, have never been exhibited before any audience in England.* The pictorial illustrations have been prepared by my brother, Lieutenant George Temple, R.N. These illustrations have been prepared from my own original sketches and under my own supervision, and I can guarantee their correctness. The region on which I am about to dilate

* The map prefixed to this chapter is a reduction, with additions from recent surveys, of the map alluded to here, and the engravings (by Lieut. George Temple) are also reductions of the pictorial illustrations exhibited during the speech.

briefly is fraught with much political interest; but politics constitute a theme upon which I am precluded from entering at the present moment. Still, although all of you are geographers first, you doubtless also sympathize with all the human interest which attaches to these scenes. These are scenes where British soldiers and British people have bled, suffered, and endured. This is a region which many men contemplate with pride, considering the honours they have won; but which many Englishmen meditate upon with anxiety. It is a region also to which many widows and bereaved relations will look back with a life-long regret.

I shall first ask you to look at the map which has been prepared for this occasion. This map relates to the country between the Indus and the Argandab; that is to say, between the town of Sakkar on the Indus and the town of Candahar on the Argandab, a distance of over 400 miles. It is divided for the purposes of this exposition into four divisions, to which I must ask your particular attention.

First, there is the country below the hills; secondly, the country within the hills; thirdly, the valley of Pishin and the Khoja Amran range, which is the boundary between the British territory and Southern Afghanistan; fourthly, the country between the Khoja Amran range and Candahar. Now to each of these divisions I shall have to ask your attention separately.

First, then, as regards the country below the hills, let us begin with the position of Sakkar on the Indus. Near Sakkar there runs up a low range of hills from the south-east towards that town. That range is a remarkable geographical feature, for it determines the course of the Lower Indus. It settles the question whether the Indus shall run through Sind converting it into a lesser Egypt, or whether the Indus shall run towards the east, to the deserts that skirt the western parts of India. Now, the Indus passes by the town of Kusmore, a little above Sakkar. From Kusmore down to Sakkar there is a long line of embankments which constitute a monument of British enterprise and science, and which form one of the largest series of embankments in the world, Holland not excepted. In the neighbourhood of these embankments, that is, under the lee of the protective line, are canals, villages, towns, railway lines, military roads, marts of trade, all nestling in comparative security. But sometimes the Indus breaks through those embankments. Recently it swept over the country and placed an entire district under water. Traffic for the time was suspended, the roads were submerged, and the whole tract was the scene of temporary devastation. These are dangers from which no human skill or foresight can guard us We hope to make these embank-

FIG. 12.—SAKKAR, ON THE INDUS.

ments more safe from time to time; but the Indus constitutes a source of permanent danger. Now, through this piece of country that is marked separately on the map, there runs the line of the new railway from a point near Sakkar towards Candahar, and thus I bring you the first fifty miles of your journey of four hundred miles and upwards.

Before going further, I shall advert to the first of the illustrations (12), which affords a view of Sakkar from Rohri on the left bank of the Indus. Between Rohri and Sakkar, there is a rocky island whereon a fortress was built by preceding dynasties, which is called the fortress of Bakkar.

Our view is looking from Rohri towards Sakkar. In the background you will see the town of Sakkar, on the other side of the Indus, on low hills. Now, between my point of view and Sakkar there is to be carried the bridge of the Indus, by one mighty span from Rohri to Bakkar island, on the suspension principle. Between Bakkar and Sakkar there will be two or three spans. The difficulty is this, that between my point of view and Bakkar the river is so deep and so rapid that no pier could be constructed, and there is nothing for it but to cross this branch of the river with one span of 350 feet on the suspension principle. On the banks of the river at Sakkar you will see in the illustration a number of boats in the Indus. That will be considered the commercial basis of the line between the Indus and Candahar. It is also a military base. From there General Stewart's forces, and the materials of war and all those thousands of camels which you have heard of, were despatched. You will see also, on the river, steamers joining one bank with the other, until the bridge shall be built. Farther you will observe two sets of pillars. Those are the pillars of the electric telegraph, which is carried right across the Indus.

I thus convey you in imagination over the first 50 miles, across the green strip of country. It is entirely cultivated, or else covered with vegetation. After passing this green, you will bid farewell to vegetation for many a long mile.

I now enter upon the second division, namely, the country below the hills, and conduct you into the desert. You will find that tract marked separately in the map. You will perceive that on the left hand of the desert there are strips of cultivation, which is carried on by irrigation from those streams which run from the hills. You will there remark a particular feature in those streams, in that they have sources and courses but have no mouths, because as the irrigation goes on, they are merged in numerous water-channels. Indeed this is the remarkable feature of Central Asia: there are many rivers without mouths. Now the point is, that all these green strips were liable to such floods that we could not well make a temporary railway towards Candahar through such tracts. We were obliged to carry the railway through the very midst of the desert, for there alone could we get ground suitable for the construction of the work. But this ground had a particular disadvantage in that it was waterless. It is light friable soil, the best galloping ground for horsemen that I have ever seen. You can imagine the difficulty we had in getting natives to face this desert. They declared they would die of thirst; but we constructed tanks in the desert, and established a service of water trains by the railway as it progressed, in order to carry the water supply to the people at the works. The people numbered 3500, besides 1500 animals, and water had to be conveyed day after day, sometimes 50 or 60 miles, in order to supply this large number of mouths. Nevertheless the railway was carried on through this desert, at the average rate of two miles a day; sometimes we attained the rate of 2½ miles a day, and one day we made three miles. The construction consisted of earthway two feet deep; besides that there was the laying down of the sleepers and the fastening of the rails. These materials were gathered from great distances in all quarters of India. It has been considered one of the most rapid pieces of work that has been done by any nation— at least out of America; but although I had the general supervision and direction of the works, I make no claim for credit personally. I would rather give the credit to Colonel Lindsay, the engineer-in-chief, and all the staff that worked under me. So I bring you through the desert approaching to Sibi.

I then ask your attention to the picture illustrating the neighbourhood of Sibi (13). You will there see the low hills of Beluchistan beyond Sibi and the hill of Kalipat in the extreme distance; you will perceive, also, a long line of dark trees, the groves of Sibi, the only green trees to be found for many miles around, and on this side of the green trees you will see something that is meant to represent the encampment where the Bombay troops were encamped, which succeeded General

Stewart's forces in Candahar. In the foreground of the picture you will observe the line of the railway, the telegraph posts, and the expanse of desert.

We have now passed through the desert 90 miles in addition to the 50 miles first mentioned, and thus I have brought you 140 miles on the journey which I am asking you to make with me to Candahar. Thus far, we have passed through regions that are familiarly known to many distinguished members of this Society, to such members as Sir Barrow Ellis and Sir William Merewether, who are no doubt present here this evening.

We were, during the first part of my speech, within the British territory: after that, we entered the territory of Khelat.

We are now to enter upon part of the territory that was assigned to us by the recent treaty of Gandamak, called the southern assigned districts of Afghanistan. We are also about to plunge straight into the hills, from which you will not emerge for many miles to come, until I have to direct your attention to the great desert of South-western Afghanistan. So, now, you must make up your minds to quit the plains of India, and to be surrounded by hills for a considerable part of your journey.

As far as Sibi the railway is marked continuously black, which indicates a complete and open line—open at least, if not completed. After that you will find the railway line marked by a dotted line of black on the map, which indicates a railway that is projected; and this railway, you will perceive, follows the line of the Nari river, which passes through a gorge called the Nari Gorge. After that it passes through one or two lines of low hills, and enters upon the Harnai valley at the foot of a mountain called Kalipat. Next it passes through a long cultivated valley until it crosses the Chapar mountain; then it enters a rift or chasm in a great limestone geological formation. It makes use of the river to pass through this otherwise impassable limestone mountain. After that it enters on the upper valley, and so it gets to Gwâl, which lies upon the edge

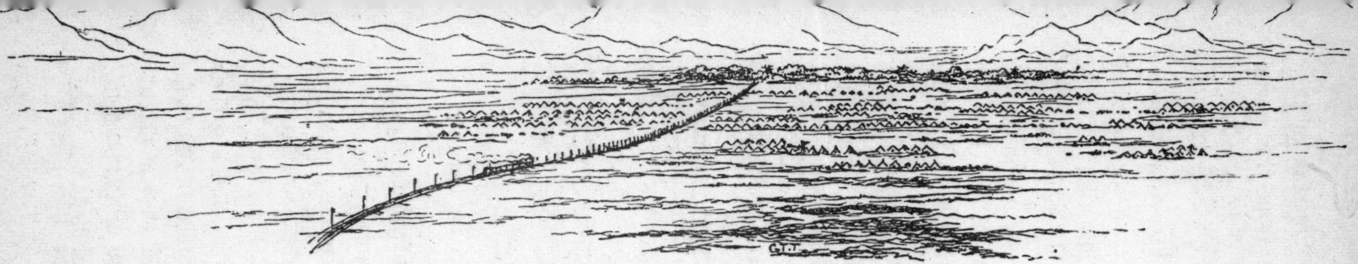


FIG. 13.—APPROACH TO SIBI: THE KACHI DESERT AND RAILWAY.

FIG. 14.—THE NARI GORGE.

of the elevated plateau of Pishin and upon the flank of that range of mountains which separate Pishin from the lower mountains, and constitute the natural defence of the plateau.

I have thus brought you for the moment as far as Gwâl and Pishin, and I must ask your attention to three illustrations of this part of the route. You will first note the picture of the Nari Gorge (14). You will see the low hills we have to pass in the middle distance, light friable rocks in all sorts of fantastic shapes, which are geologically insignificant as compared to the geological formations to which I shall presently call your attention. In the meantime you will

FIG. 15.—THE HARNAI VALLEY: KALIPAT MOUNTAIN IN THE DISTANCE.

understand that these lower hills can be easily blasted with dynamite. They were so being blasted some months ago, when I saw them, and thus the railway can be rapidly constructed.

The next view of the Harnai valley is of interest (15). In the background you have the mountain of Kalipat. Our railway line has now attained the height of 3000 feet above the level of the sea, ascending gradually from Sibi which is reckoned at 700 feet. In the Harnai valley, then, we have attained the height of 3000 feet, and this Kalipat mountain is 11,000 or 12,000 feet. Thus our picture of Kalipat shows some 7000 or 8000 feet of sheer precipitous ascent overhanging this very valley. The mountain is a magnificent limestone formation. Then in the middle distance you will observe a line of towers. They are the defences of the villagers in the valleys against the marauders of the tribes from the hills. These towers are refuges into which the wretched husbandman and his cattle may escape for the moment, while a storm of devastation and plunder sweeps over his fields. You will observe that the towers face the hills whence the marauders come, and behind the towers are the fertile fields. In the extreme left of the picture you will perceive near the heights of Kalipat a slope of limestone formations, and in the left of the picture you will find rifts or chasms, and to these chasms I shall have immediately to conduct you.

For a better understanding of them, I must ask you to look at the next picture (16), which represents what we call the Chapar Rift. We propose to take full advantage of that rift to pass the railway through it. There you see precipitous rocks overhanging the rushing stream, and on the left you will see ledges of rocks over which we desire to conduct the railway. We shall have to construct a viaduct with piers of 100 feet high, in order to approach those ledges. But this is not a difficult work; the foundations are excellent, and we hope to construct the line of the railway within this rift or chasm. The point at which my view is taken is narrow, like the neck of a bottle, but after that the railway passes into the valley opening out like a bottle, and follows the course of the stream, and in that way we make use of the stream for the railway. Thus, almost imperceptibly, we ascend up to Gwâl, which is 5500 feet above the sea (about 2000 feet higher than the Chapar Rift, which may be reckoned at 3500 feet). This incline, with the help of the river, will be effected with comparative ease, considering the railway inclines in other parts of India or of the world.

I have thus conducted you another 100 miles of your journey towards Candahar, and I must now ask you to revert to Sibi. From Sibi you will see there runs on the map a direct line of military road to Dadar, and from there you enter upon the famous Bolan Pass—a pass by which the British invading armies have always passed from India to Afghanistan.

I will now ask you to follow me up the Bolan Pass to a place

FIG. 16.—THE CHAPAR RIFT.

where you will see hills marked on the map somewhat darker than the rest.

Then you should look at the picture of this place (17). In the background you see the high mountains which flank the plateau of Quetta. In the centre you see the line through which the military and commercial traffic has to pass, and in the foreground you see the Bolan river running with branchlets and rivulets under the rocky formations. These rocky formations are geologically insignificant, but the colour of the water is admired by every educated person who sees it. It is the most beautiful mixture of azure and emerald. The stream goes careering over the shingle and sand, and that used to constitute one of the greatest difficulties of the pass. It was in the crossing and recrossing of this stream that everybody got so wet in the cold weather, and that constant failure of health and strength was occasioned. Through the steadiness and industry of the Bombay troops under the direction of General (now Sir Robert) Phayre, who is a brother of Sir Arthur Phayre, a distinguished member of this Society, we managed in a very short time to make a good military road, instead of the steep shingly inclines over which the guns and the military stores used to be laboriously dragged. The pass is now permeated by a road over which officers drive their dog-carts, and over which, when I left India, we were arranging to draw vehicles by horses at five miles an hour. In that way we arrive at the mountains which are exhibited on the background of the Bolan Pass, and so we reach the desolate plain of Beluchistan.

You will see this plain (called Dasht i-bedaulat or desolate plain) indicated on the map. Now this is a plain of which travellers should beware during the winter season, for the most withering blasts sweep over it, sometimes in dust-storms, at other times in snow-storms which chill people to death. I do not know that European lives have been sacrificed, but many natives have fatally succumbed to this benumbing, piercing wind. And so we arrive at the comparatively happy valley of Quetta.

Now the valley of Quetta lies in the bosom of grand mountains. These mountains are about 6000 feet above the altitude of Quetta, and Quetta itself is about 5500 feet above sea-level. Dadar, at the bottom of the pass, is less than 1000 feet above sea-level; but the desolate plain I have just been describing to you is 6000 feet. Thus the mountains near Quetta are from 11,000 to 12,000 feet in height. They are magnificent limestone formations.

All this you will find illustrated by the panoramic view of Quetta (18). On the right hand of the picture you will see the mountain of Mûrdâr. The name signifies "the dead man's mountain," and the natives say that the reason why they call it so is this, that any man who tried to ascend it would be dead before he reached the top. In the distance to the right you will perceive the mountain of Zarghûn, which is remarkable for its forests of juniper, but in this clear atmosphere, in the evening light, so strong is the effulgence of the setting sun that the mountain looks at sunset like one mass of rose-colour. Then midway in the picture you see Takatu mountain, which separates the valley of Quetta from the valley of Pishin. The spurs of Takatu stretch to the left, and through a long gap in the Takatu spurs you see in the distance a line of blue-grey mountains, which form the Khoja Amran range. Between the spurs of Quetta and these blue mountains there lies the valley of Pishin. Farther to the left you will see the mountain of Chihaltan, or "forty persons," so called from a Muhammadan legend about forty saints, with which I need not detain you. In the middle distance you will see the town and mud fort of Quetta. In front of that you will perceive the houses and gardens that constitute the civil and military station of Quetta itself, built for the immediate accommodation of our troops; and farther to the right you will observe the new British bazaar or town. In the foreground you have the road leading from the Bolan Pass towards Quetta, and joining the road near Quetta you will notice a road that comes from the Khelat country. No view I could present, and no colours that I could depict, could give you any idea of the real splendour of this scene. These mountains, 12,000 feet high, with their magnificent rocks, at sunrise, are lighted up with fire, and at sunset they blush with rose-coloured splendour. Down in the valleys, near the little groves, are now carried on our British amusements. There are cricket-matches and lawn-tennis and Badminton, and other games, and on these scenes there look down the proud mountains. I suppose there are few more picturesquely situated play-grounds in the world than those play-grounds of Quetta.

We have thus accomplished another 120 miles of our journey, and I must ask you to look again at the point whither I conducted you on the map near Gwâl. We have now fairly entered the Pishin valley. From the town of Quetta there runs an indication of a military road, which road goes towards the well-known Gazaband Pass, where Generals Stewart and Biddulph passed with their troops towards Pishin. Now that the military road runs into the Pishin valley, and the railway line from Gwâl runs also into that valley, both the military road and the railway will cross the Lora river, which is indicated to you by the map as running through the valley of Pishin. Looking across the valley of Pishin, you see the Khoja Amran range, which is the real boundary of Afghanistan. This range takes its name from the tomb of a saint, Khoja Amran, whose tomb is at the top of the highest peak. But the range is better known to Europeans from the two great military passes that exist within it: one the Khojak Pass and the other the Gwaja Pass, which latter, owing to the project of the railway, is in future likely to become more celebrated.

I must ask you now to look at the next pictorial illustration in our series (19). In the background you will see the Khoja Amran mountains, stretching like an old grey wall. At the foot of the hills you will see an indication of a well-known town, Kala Abdullah, and above that there is the Khojak Pass. In the centre of the range you will notice a peak which is called the Khwaja Amran Peak, and towards the left the town of

Gulistan Karez, which is a pretty place, with water-courses, canals, and fruit-gardens, and above that you will see where the Gwaja Pass is. In the middle distance you will find the partially cultivated plain of Pishin, and the Lora river. This view is taken from where the railway viaduct is to be constructed over the river.

Before I leave Pishin, I may detain you for one or two moments by explaining to you why we wish to take the railway by the Nari river, instead of the old route of the Bolan Pass. Now, a railway by the Bolan route would be vastly better than no railway at all, and would be a great national advantage were

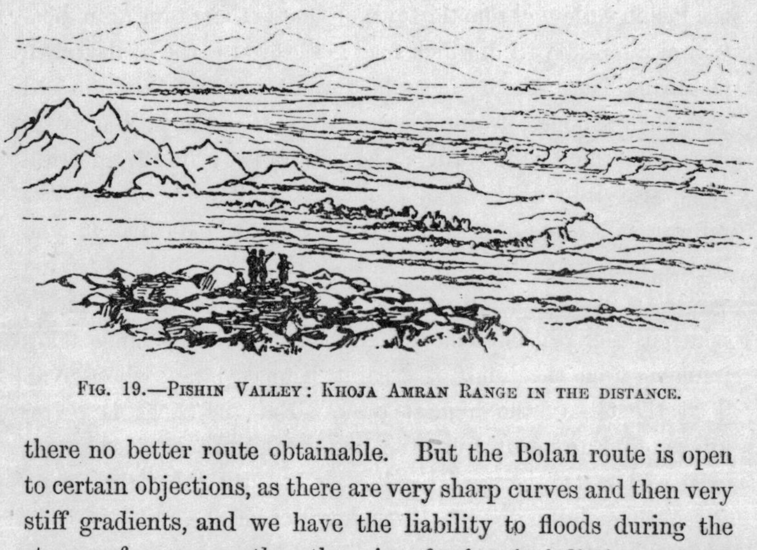

FIG. 19.—PISHIN VALLEY: KHOJA AMRAN RANGE IN THE DISTANCE.

there no better route obtainable. But the Bolan route is open to certain objections, as there are very sharp curves and then very stiff gradients, and we have the liability to floods during the storms of summer; then there is a foreign jurisdiction, namely that of the Khan of Khelat. But the main point was this, whatever might be the expenditure devoted to it, we could not make that railway safe at all seasons, and also there was a rigorous winter, as well as a great want of food supplies all along the line. On the other hand, by the route of the railway I have described to you, by the Nari river, we had much better curves and much easier gradients; we had complete freedom from the floods in summer—that is to say, we are able to take the railway beyond the reach of the floods; we had a much less rigorous climate in winter, and we had supplies along the line, and it will pass entirely through the assigned districts under British administration. Above all, we found with the help of the river a capital engineering line. The difficulty with lines of this kind is that you have to surmount the vast mountain wall which forms the flank of the elevated plateau of Beluchistan, and constitutes the boundary between Beluchistan and India. From some volcanic forces in geological periods, there have been great chasms and rents formed in this wall. Rivers rise in the plateau, which pass through these rents and chasms into the lower valleys. Our engineers took advantage of these rents and chasms, and of these geological circumstances, and that is actually how we have obtained this line.

Thus you ascend minute by minute, and you are hardly conscious that you are ascending at all. In confirmation of this fact I may mention that during November 1879, I, in company with others, marched over a parallel route at a rate of 45 miles a day (or 90 miles in two days), and during that time we were scarcely aware, from any evidence of our senses, that we were ascending at all. Nevertheless on those two days we ascended 5000 feet.

Thus I have conducted you through the lower range of hills on to the valley of Pishin, and to the Khoja Amran range beyond. I have also asked you to remember that the railway is not to ascend the Khoja Amran range by the Khojak Pass, which is the present military road, but is to ascend by the Gwaja Pass farther south. I must, however, ask you to mount with me to the Khojak Pass, 8000 feet above sea-level, and that is the highest point to which I shall have to conduct you this evening. Having arrived in this way at the summit of the Khojak Pass, I must explain to you that the geological features of the range are comparatively insignificant, with the exception of the Gwaja Pass, where good granite formations render the scenery very fine; in the Khojak Pass, where we now are, the scenery is poor.

I must now request your notice to the picture which represents the view (20) from the Khojak summit looking towards Southern Afghanistan. In the distance you will perceive the low hills of Candahar. In the extreme distance beyond that you will also see the hills of Northern or Upper Afghanistan. On the left in the distance you will perceive the desert of Southern Afghanistan, which desert, you will find, is indicated upon the map. In my pictorial illustration you will see it marked by a large dust-storm which is coming up in vast columns. I myself saw that dust-storm rise. It came from 60 miles off, and I saw it rush on with remarkable rapidity. We knew it was coming quick, so we tethered our horses under shelter in the lee of the summit, and we ourselves stood on the summit itself, in order to face the storm. It was as much as we could do to stand. Although we were 3000 feet above that desert the dust blew furiously in our faces, and we could scarcely keep ourselves upright against it. The frequent occurrence of these dust-storms constitutes a noteworthy feature in that desert. In the middle distance you will perceive the military road running towards Candahar, on which line actions have been recently fought, and down at the foot of the range lies the military post of Chaman, and near that is the spot which represents the spring where the only water and the only green thing in the locality can be obtained. In the foreground you will see the place called the "Gun slip." This name "Gun slip" means the operation whereby Stewart's guns were slipped down the precipitous hill-side. The guns had to be passed down by ropes, and the horses were led down. You may have seen this operation depicted in the 'Illustrated London News' of the time. Subsequently our officers have made a good zigzag road down the hill-side, which road you will see represented on the left of the picture.

Such, then, is this remarkable view. Picturesque it may

FIG. 20.—VIEW FROM THE SUMMIT OF THE KHOJAK PASS.

not be, but it is wonderful as being the point from which many heroes and statesmen of the first Afghan war must have looked on Afghanistan, which was to them the promised land—such statesmen as Keene, Macnaghten, and your excellent Vice-President here, Sir Henry Rawlinson, who is now present, and is sitting on my left. Imagine the hope they must have felt when they looked on Afghanistan from this place. And this is the point of view from which the heroes of the last Afghan war must have first gazed at Afghanistan; not only Sir Donald Stewart but Sir Michael Biddulph, who has lectured to you from this very table.

Thus we have accomplished another 60 miles of our journey, and there only remain the last 90 miles of the run. You will observe from the map that the railway is to proceed from the Gwaja Pass at the lower extremity of the Khoja Amran range, and to enter on the southern plains of Afghanistan. It will first take a sweep towards the right, or east, in order to avoid the desert. Then it has to run on the right bank of the Dori river, crossing several tributary streams on its way. It passes by the Mel Pass, where the Afghan Governor of Candahar offered some resistance to the advance of Stewart's forces. After that it passes by the village of Khushab, and so runs on to Candahar. Now, you may ask me why we propose to take the railway on the right bank of the Dori river, when we might have taken it along the left bank, and thus have avoided five tributary streams. To that I have a specific answer, which is—if you went on the left bank of the Dori river you would be much too near the desert. The drifting sands of the desert are very dangerous, and offer difficulties to the engineers; and the desert is one of the dominating features in this part of the country.

It is this desert which mainly contributes to the political importance of the district of Candahar. Everybody who comes and goes either from India towards Central Asia, or from Central Asia towards India, must pass along the elbow of that desert, and rounding its corner must go by Candahar. That is one of the reasons why Candahar has always been deemed so important by all the great commanders and politicians in Asia, from the earliest ages to the present.

Now I come to the last illustration of my pictorial series (21). This illustration shows the first view the traveller obtains as he approaches Candahar. You will see in the extreme distance the hills on the other side of the Argandab river, which are spurs of the Siah Koh range. In the middle distance you have a remarkable series of low hills rising a few hundred feet above the plain of Candahar, which is 3500 feet above the sea-level. Those hills constitute a very interesting series of trap formation. The low hills through which we have just passed near the Mel Pass are gneiss, while some of them are granitic. In front of the hills near Candahar you will see in the right of the picture the modern town of Candahar. To the left, again, you have the ancient city and citadel and fortress of Candahar. They are wonderful ruins; they are not built of stone or brick, but of a hard and indurated earth peculiar to the immediate locality, and I have been told by officers of Artillery that they never saw bastions which would be more difficult to batter down. Immediately above this citadel, on the low range of hills, you will see in the distance some towers. In one of the many sieges to which this old city has been subjected (the new city is not above 150 years old), the enemy, by a striking military *coup*, climbed the hills during the night, took one of these towers by surprise, and so commanded the citadel and town, which had in consequence to surrender. In the midst of the modern city you will see the slightest indication of the tomb of Ahmed Shah, the founder of the Durani dynasty of Afghanistan, that dynasty which performed so important a part in the first Afghan war, and has been superseded by the Barakzai dynasty. In the immediate foreground there runs the military line to Candahar; but that is not the railway line, which will run somewhat towards the right. There is also some indication of the green plain of Candahar, excellently irrigated from running streams, skilfully

FIG. 21.—APPROACH TO CANDAHAR.

cultivated, waving with harvests, and often yielding several crops within the year.

Perhaps this view is imperfectly represented; but it is one of the most interesting and beautiful views I ever saw in my life. It is that view from which people either take their first or their last look of Candahar, and it is a scene that must have been gazed upon with wonderment by many of the most distinguished, or of the most notorious characters in history—by Alexander the Great, by Tamerlane, by the Emperor Baber, by the Great Mogul, by Shah Abbas, by Nadir Shah, and others. All these extraordinary personages must have regarded the scene with as much wonderment as we do; for despite the revolutions of centuries this landscape remains the same.

Now, I have brought you to a distance of more than 400 miles from Sakkar, where I began my speech, and I hope you have not found this journey exceedingly fatiguing or irksome.

I shall conclude by giving you a *résumé* of the distances over which you and I have, in imagination, travelled together. The country below the hills comprised 140 miles; the country within the hills 120 miles; the country in the Pishin valley and the Khoja Amran range 60 miles, and from the Khoja Amran range to Candahar 90 miles, altogether 410 miles. That may be called the military route; but the railway route which I have explained to you is somewhat longer. The railway route we take in this way: Indus to Sibi, 140 miles; Sibi to Gulistan Karez, 170 miles; Gulistan Karez to Gwaja—that is, the southern end of the Khoja Amran range—40 miles; from Khoja Amran range to Candahar, 90 miles. The whole distance by railway line is 440 miles, say 450 miles with a slight margin for detours, and that represents the maximum journey which you have made with me to-night.

I may express the hope, with some diffidence, that the statement I have offered is sufficiently scientific and geographical to satisfy the severe requirements of such a distinguished gentleman as Sir Henry Rawlinson, whose knowledge of these countries is unrivalled, vastly surpassing mine, although mine may be fresher, perhaps. I venture to anticipate that it may also satisfy the requirements of some of the Sind authorities present. I trust it has also been brief and graphic enough for the ladies and gentlemen who are members of the Geographical Society. I further believe that this oral statement, together with the pictorial illustrations, will have the advantage over a written paper, as it will enable you to carry away with you some pictures impressed upon the tablets of your brain and memory, better perhaps than any word-painting can pourtray. I hope that if you do carry away those pictures in your minds to-night, you will also think kindly and sympathetically of the men who have been engaged in these places—of the statesmen, politicians, and commanders who have formed so many great projects for the advancement of British interests in this quarter; of the British soldiers, your own fellow-countrymen, your own flesh and blood, who have sustained your country's cause with a bravery which has never been surpassed, even in the annals of England; of the Native sepoys and soldiers, who have equalled in discipline and endurance their European brethren; of the Native Chiefs who have kept the road and protected our line of march, and who have also escorted many of us, and saved us from ambush and from overt attack, which otherwise would have proved fatal to us; of the men of science, civil and military, who have planned those important public works I have described to you to-night; and lastly, of the patient, enduring, and industrious Native camp followers, who had no particular reward to expect beyond their bare wage, who had no honours, no glory to anticipate, but nevertheless did their duty as men like the rest of us, and who have but too often left their bones to whiten in the localities that have been depicted to you to-night. Remember, ladies and gentlemen, that to whatever class or whatever profession these men belonged, whether the colour of their uniform was black, or red, or blue, whether they were white-skinned or dark-skinned, they were all one in their sentiment of loyalty to the British cause: they were comrades and brethren in arms, in policy, and in administration, for the promotion of those vast interests which are comprised in the British Empire in the East.*

* Since this speech was delivered (June 1880) the political aspect of affairs in these regions has somewhat changed. Candahar was, according to the then intention of the British Government, to be governed by a local Afghan chief under British guardianship; a British garrison was to be maintained there for some time, at least, and a railway was to be constructed thither, to be opened for traffic about the year 1883. It was subsequently decided to withdraw the Britisn garrison from Candahar, and to make over the city with its surrounding districts to the Amîr of Caubul. This step involved among other things the relinquishment of at least that section of the proposed railway which lies between the Khoja Amran Range and Candahar. Then, while the line was kept open for traffic from the Indus to Sibi, it was decided to hold in abeyance the projected line from Sibi to the valley of Pishin, and in consequence the railway works on that section were suspended. But, as Pishin is still under British administration, and as Quetta is still held by a British force, the plan of extending railway communication to those places is under consideration. The alternative line by the Bolan Pass, as discussed in the speech, has been again mooted, and some of the questions regarding it have been re-opened. But I understand that the railway engineers and the local authorities are in favour of the line described in this speech. I myself see no reason to alter the opinion herein expressed, which was the result of the best enquiries that could be made on the spot. At all events, it seems probable that by one line or the other a railway will be made to Quetta and Pishin. Therefore, almost all that is said in this speech is still applicable to current affairs within British borders up to the limit of Southern Afghanistan.—R. T.

# CHAPTER VI.

## LOCAL SELF-GOVERNMENT IN BRITISH INDIA.

[*Reprinted from the 'Contemporary Review' for March* 1883.]

Political importance of teaching Indian natives to manage their own affairs — Former measures relating to local government and taxation in India — Additional measures since 1881 — The elective principle in rural tracts constitutes a new departure — Declaration of principle by the Government of India — District boards to consist of elected members — Local funds to be administered by them — Elections already held in cities and towns — Facilities for holding elections in villages — Electoral qualification ready made — Electors will for the most part be peasant proprietors — Adverse influences likely to arise at first — Still the Government determined that beginning shall be made — Favourable testimony of some among the Provincial Governments in India.

LOCAL self-government for the natives of India is a matter of interest to all thoughtful observers.* Much has been, and is

* Since this article was written the subject has been severely discussed, both in Parliament and in the public prints. The discussion has perhaps been stimulated by dissatisfaction felt in many quarters respecting the project for altering a particular part of the Criminal Law and conferring upon Native magistrates a jurisdiction over European British subjects in lesser criminal trials. That project is, however, wholly distinct from the subject of this article, and there is no real connexion whatever between the two. This subject is for India in some degree equivalent to the new schemes of county government for England. The scheme for India has been deprecated by many authorities as going too far, as being insufficiently fenced with precautions, and as insufficiently providing for European control. It is, doubtless, very advantageous that these and all other objections should be raised beforehand, so that the Government may be able to obviate any of them that appear well founded. Precautions, as suggested by highly competent critics, are indeed necessary. But probably the desired precautions have been, or

being, done by the British Government for its Indian subjects. But it is felt that more than heretofore ought to be done by them for themselves, and that the Government ought to teach them how to do this. The idea that everything should be *for* the people and nothing *by* them, or, in other words, that everything should be effected by the Government and nothing through the agency of the people themselves, is not likely to be approved by the British public. It is well, indeed, to bestow upon them material prosperity, security of rights and property, equitable and moderate taxation, the means both of preserving Oriental scholarship and of acquiring Western knowledge; some insight also into the wonders of modern science. Thus they will look up to the foreign Government as an embodiment of moral as well as political power, and, notwithstanding all that doubting critics may say, they will feel a loyal gratitude in the contemplation of what they have to be grateful for. But it is better still to afford to them that practical education which comes from the actual study of self-government, and that robustness of

---

will be, duly adopted. It is to be remembered that the entrusting of local affairs to elected bodies, though a new departure in rural localities, is yet only an enlargement of a principle which is already carried into effect in the most important centres of the country. The principle, then, is not novel but preexisting. It is justly contended by the critics that the local bodies with elected members must not be left uncontrolled. The Government of India would probably explain in reply that control is provided. If on detailed examination, or after actual experience, the control is found insufficient, it can easily be strengthened. The view that control there must be, is apparently accepted by the Government of India. The proposal that the European district-officers should not sit on the local boards together with the elected Native members, has given rise to an apprehension that European control is to be eliminated, and European authority set aside. If, indeed, such were to be the result, it would be very objectionable. But the Government of India would probably rejoin that this was never contemplated. Certainly, in important issues, European control of the most stringent kind is reserved. The only question would be whether the European district-officer should take part in the deliberations of the local boards. But if he has an effective power of control from without, it is the less necessary that he should interfere in the internal counsels.—R. T.

character which arises from exercise in the discipline of managing their own affairs. Under an administration like that of the British, which, though conducted with a comprehensive legislation and a strict executive, is in many essentials paternal or patriarchal, there is always a fear lest the people should regard themselves as forming an entity separate from the Government. If such should become the state of the public mind, the Government is likely to be *en l'air* as regards sympathy and moral support in the event of a political or military crisis. It is desirable indeed to found institutions intrinsically excellent; but it is yet more desirable to make the people regard themselves as forming a part of such institutions. Then they will begin to feel their corporate existence as being one with the State. England must, no doubt, for an indefinitely long time, rely mainly on her own right arm. Still the popular support, if rendered *ex animo*, would be of priceless value. One of the best and surest means of winning such support is to promote that local self-government which I now propose briefly to consider.

For many years past, indeed almost from the beginning of British rule, there has been in India the germ of what in England is known as "local government and taxation." This germ has been fostered till in some of the principal cities and of the rural towns, and nearly throughout the districts in the interior (which districts correspond very much to English counties), the affairs commonly called local in India, as in other countries, are largely under the management and control of local bodies consisting partly of Europeans (chiefly official) and partly of Natives. These affairs may, for India, be summarized as roads and communications, primary and midle-class education, sanitation and medical work, municipal police. Under this agency much external improvement has been effected, leaving a happy impress on nearly every part of a widely-extended country. The system, such as it is, was further strengthened, in 1872, by a measure introduced and executed by Lord Mayo's Government, officially termed the system of Provincial Services, whereby an increased financial control was conceded by the Supreme Government of India to the several Local Governments in the empire, of various grades, eight in number, respecting the heads of service mentioned above, and some others besides. By legislation also a complete constitution, after the British model, was conferred upon the municipal corporations of the two great cities, Calcutta and Bombay.

Nevertheless, in the interior of the country the position of these local bodies has been uncertain, and their action fitful. The native members were nominated by official authority, and were supposed or intended to be representatives of local interests. Still, not being elected, they have never been representatives in the English sense of the term. Their proceedings have been under an official control, to which there has not been any limitation either by rule or practice. Despite numerous instances of praiseworthy public spirit, there has often been an atmosphere of apathy pervading their conduct. On the whole, their proceedings have been such as might be expected on the part of those who are not stimulated by a sense of real power and responsibility.

Since the middle of 1881, the Government of India, under Lord Ripon, appear to have been earnestly considering the best way of consolidating the position of these local bodies, broadening their basis, augmenting their powers, and investing them with responsibilities corresponding thereto. In September, 1881, the Government issued a Resolution extending further the system of Provincial Services—that is, enlarging the financial powers of the several local Governments in provincial affairs. Then in May of last year (1882), another Resolution was issued regarding the local bodies already described, and for the avowed purpose of promoting the principle of local self-government for the natives.

The language with which the last-named resolution opens is so positive and specific as to deserve quoting, and it runs thus:—

"At the outset the Governor-General in Council must explain

that in advocating the extension of local self-government and in the adoption of this principle in the management of many branches of local affairs, he does not suppose that the work will be, in the first instance, better done than if it remained in the sole hands of the Government district officers. It is not primarily with a view to improvement in administration that this measure is put forward and supported. It is chiefly desirable as an instrument of popular and political education. His Excellency in Council has no doubt that, in course of time, as local knowledge and interest are brought to bear more freely upon local administration, improved efficiency will in fact follow. But at starting there will doubtless be many failures, calculated to discourage exaggerated hopes and even in some cases to cast apparent discredit upon the practice of self-government itself. If, however, the officers of Government only set themselves, as the Governor-General in Council believes they will, to foster sedulously the small beginnings of independent political life; if they accept loyally, and as their own, the policy of the Government; and if they come to realize that the system opens to them a fairer field for the exercise of administrative tact and directive energy than the more autocratic system which it supersedes, then it may be hoped that the period of failures will be short, and that real and substantial progress will very soon become manifest.

"It is not uncommonly asserted that the people of this country are themselves entirely indifferent to the principle of self-government, that they take but little interest in public matters, and that they prefer to have such affairs managed for them by Government officers. The Governor-General in Council does not attach much value to this theory. It represents, no doubt, the point of view which commends itself to many active and well-intentioned district officers; and the people of India are, there can be equally no doubt, remarkably tolerant of existing facts. But as education advances there is rapidly growing up all over the country an intelligent class of public-spirited men whom it is not only bad policy but sheer waste of power to fail to utilise."

This frank and unreserved declaration of principle is followed by directions in detail, of which the prominent points only can be stated here. While the municipal administration in the cities and towns is to be maintained and extended as far as possible, a network of local boards is to be formed in the districts (like the English counties, as already mentioned) into which the country is divided. The area placed under each board is to be small, as an administrative unit; consequently there will be many boards in a district. Each board will have the supervision of a group of villages, following as much as possible the traditional divisions into which the country has from olden times been divided. But ordinarily there will be at the headquarters of the district a central board, having control over the lesser boards. The members of the boards are to be chosen by election, wherever it may, in the opinion of the local governments, be practicable to adopt that system of choice. The qualification of the electors, and other matters pertaining to the elections, are to be determined by the local governments. It is anticipated that, as a consequence, the electoral system throughout the country will present a very diversified appearance. This may prove to be rather convenient than otherwise, as tending to develop the idiosyncrasies of a vast and diverse population. But if there be any inconvenience therefrom, that must be endured, as above all things it is desirable to proceed cautiously, in deference to the sentiments prevailing in widely-scattered localities. The boards are to have as much of independent power as possible, consistently with the control of official authority in two respects—first, the sanction of certain specified acts, such as the raising of loans and the imposition of taxes; and secondly, the power of suspending temporarily a board from its functions in case of any gross and continued neglect of an important duty. Respecting the several branches of local administration already mentioned, the boards are to be entrusted not only with the expenditure of established funds, and of other moneys which may be allotted to them, but also with the management of certain among the Governmental revenues, such as the License Tax.

Thus local funds amounting to several millions sterling annually, roads of many thousands of miles in total length, rustic school-houses numbered by tens of thousands, medical institutions to be counted by hundreds, will be administered by boards elected by electors from the villages of British India, —the total number of the villages being about 400,000. This is of itself a considerable thing, though it is but a fraction of the total Indian administration.

Now, of these instructions the greater part is only an expansion of the existing system. The expansion is, however, remarkable in respect to the number of the boards in each district (*Anglicè* county). Whereas there has heretofore been only one such board in a district, commonly called "the Local Committee," there will in future be several boards. This of itself will ensure a more equitable distribution than heretofore of improvement throughout the whole district, and especially in remote or comparatively neglected tracts. But the real novelty lies in the instruction that, so far as may be practicable, the members of the boards shall be elected. This is a principle heretofore almost unknown practically in the interior of India—that is in the agricultural regions of a country where (in contrast to the proportions existing in England) four-fifths of the population are rural, and only one-fifth urban. According to some calculations, indeed, the urban population may be estimated as less than one-fifth, and nearer to one-tenth. Thus the introduction of the elective principle into the villages, or little townships, of British India may be said to constitute virtually a new departure.

The elective principle is not indeed a novelty among the urban people of India—that is, in the towns, as contradistinguished from the country. In the two capital cities of Calcutta and Bombay it has been in force during several years for municipal administration. Accordingly the municipalities of those two cities, having an aggregate population of 1½ millions and an income of 500,000*l.* annually, are administered by corporations consisting chiefly of members elected by the ratepayers. The citizens of Bombay—which has always been a cosmopolitan seaport readily receptive of fresh ideas—took kindly to the elective system at once, and have behaved uniformly as good electors ought to behave, choosing native candidates for the most part, but giving also their suffrages to some candidates of European nationalities. In Calcutta, the citizens treated it at first with an almost disdainful apathy. But among them there was from the beginning a class of educated natives who appreciated its advantages, and by this time it may be said to have fairly taken root. It has been cautiously and tentatively extended to some other towns, but its introduction into some of them was postponed for political reasons. The measure will now, under the orders of May, 1882, be made to embrace virtually all the towns, large and small (about 1500 in number, for all British India), and ere long it will probably be the fact that the municipal revenues of the country, about 1½ millions sterling in the aggregate, for an urban population of nearly twenty millions, are administered under corporations elected by the ratepayers. In these cases there never has been, nor will be, any difficulty in forming constituencies; the payment of municipal rates is the qualification, and that qualification is possessed by all respectable citizens who thus are the electors; and the wards into which towns and cities are divided become the electoral divisions, each having a municipal representation.

Then comes the question, has the interior of the country, with its large rural population, the necessary facilities for the introduction of this system for the purpose of administering the local affairs already described? Yes, it does possess these facilities in a fair degree. The constituencies, the electoral qualifications, the electors, are all, so to speak, ready made.

In most provinces of India—that is, in Madras, Bombay, the North-Western Provinces, the Panjab, the Central Provinces, British Burma, and Assam, peasant proprietorship largely, and in some parts almost exclusively, prevails, every peasant proprietor cultivating lands with his own hands, and paying land-tax to the Government. Here at once, then, is the electoral qualification, and the peasant proprietors will be the electors. The question will then arise as to whether the qualification should be extended to any of those who cultivate land, but do not own it, nor pay revenue to Government. They are cultivators or tenants, and pay rent to proprietors large or small, even to peasant proprietors. If they are tenants at will only, the qualification will probably be not extended to them. But many of them have tenancy or occupancy rights, and cannot be evicted without cause shown to the satisfaction of a court of justice. These, then, may be regarded as equitably entitled to the electoral qualification. Again, throughout these provinces the village system exists, whereby the proprietors residing in a village, corresponding nearly to an English parish, are grouped together for police arrangements and other administrative purposes. In northern India the bond of union is drawn very close between the proprietors in each village, who thus form a community commonly called a brotherhood. This peculiar constitution will favour the exercise of the electoral franchise. In Oudh large proprietors or landlords prevail; and thus, if proprietors alone were to have the franchise, the number of electors would be comparatively small. But there again a considerable class exists of privileged tenants or occupancy cultivators, many of whom might be selected for the franchise. In the provinces under the Government of Bengal large proprietors are found; but alongside of great estates in many parts of the country there are thousands of small properties. In the aggregate for the whole country, then, the number of electors qualified by the ownership of land will be very considerable. But if the application of the electoral principle is to be equitably distributed in most parts of the country, the representation must include some at least of the tenants—namely, those who have occupancy privileges, especially as they are assessed to various local cesses.

Of all the great classes in India, the agricultural class is the one that can best be trusted with the germ of political privilege, such as electoral representation, for any political purpose, however limited. It is this class that feels most immediately the benefits of British rule, which are seen to be peculiar in an Asiatic country, and in the main its passive loyalty has been proved during times of trial. On the other hand, it is politically deficient in active qualities; and if it is to receive moral education under a civilized and enlightened Government such as ours, it needs the stimulus which will be afforded by an electoral system in local affairs.

That rural electors will, at the outset, prove stolid in appreciating the franchise in local affairs, and will be apathetic in exercising it, is but too probable. But if the European officers shall become convinced that the lesson ought to be learnt, they will ere long succeed in teaching it to the people. Public opinion, too, will by degrees warm to the work. The electors themselves will begin to be interested in the matter when they perceive that the elected representatives have real power and responsibility in local administration. Moreover, although the rural folk have not been habituated to formal elections, in which votes are taken, yet they have from ancient times been accustomed to see affairs of social importance managed by committees nominated by acclamation, and termed "Panchayets."

At the best, however, the elective system for local purposes may probably prove to be a plant of slow growth among the rural population of India. It may even meet with some indirect discouragement. It will be disliked by all those, whether European or Native, who dread reform merely because of its involving a change, forgetting that while some changes, as being for the worse, are to be deprecated, others, as being for the better, are to be encouraged. Some official Europeans, compelled by hard experience to see the darker sides of Oriental character, may be dubious as to the safety of introducing this kind of political privilege. Some non-official Europeans, whose natural instincts would be favourable to the principle, may apprehend that the natives are not yet fitted for such a status, even in respect to local affairs. Many natives of the most respectable station may object to the measure partly because it levels up the classes below them. If such men, on account of their general knowledge and personal character, be consulted by the authorities as to its expediency, they may give a dissuasive answer.

Thus adverse influences may arise to affect in some degree the judgment of the several Local Governments. Consequently, while some of these Governments will be anxious to advance in this direction, others will be disposed to pause and hesitate; though all will be equally animated by a desire to fulfil the behest of the Government of India, so far as they can under the circumstances by which they are surrounded.

The Government of India, though determined that a real beginning shall be made, and that progress shall advance with sure steps, is yet evidently anxious that these steps should be cautious. During 1882 fears were expressed in one important quarter of India lest the proposed reform should prove too subversive of existing arrangements, lest the change should be somewhat too fundamental, the basis of representation too large, the powers confided to the representatives too extensive. Thereon the Government of India lost no time in explaining that its already declared intentions were not really liable to these objections. It stated in a Resolution of last October (1882), that, although the progress of the new system was to be real and substantial, yet a due degree of caution must be observed in connection therewith; that detailed rules of universal application need not be laid down for all the provinces of the empire, a considerable latitude being left to the district authorities; that the several Local Governments might select particular districts for the introduction of the elective principle, on the understanding that the system should prevail generally at last, and in the meantime should be established as widely as possible; that the qualification of the electors and the modes of election would similarly be left to the determination of the several Local Governments, in the expectation that the qualification would in the first instance be ordinarily fixed fairly high; that the District Officer should not be a member of the Local Boards, but should control and supervise their proceedings from without: that the Government would retain all necessary powers for dealing with any Board that failed in its duty, powers ranging from simple remonstrance to absolute, though temporary, supersession of the defaulting body. Thus the political experiment is to be initiated, with a persistent resolve indeed, but in a moderate spirit. The several reservations and safeguards were actually comprised in the Resolution of May, 1882, and have been reiterated in the Resolution of October in the same year. Still, in reference to the judicious distrust with which innovations are regarded in India, and which usually leads to their being carefully considered, it is perhaps fortunate that the objections proceeding from one of the Local Governments should have caused the reiteration of safeguards proving to the world that the Government of India is quite moderate in its intentions.

On the other hand, one of the local Governments, that of the Panjab, has notably accepted the new departure. As being among the youngest of the several local Governments, it might be expected to be the most facile and apt in the management of new improvements. A portion of the language used by it on this occasion is worth quoting. In its Resolution of September last (1882), the following passage occurs:—

"The object of the whole proceeding is to educate the people to manage their own affairs. At the outset it is admitted that amongst the native community the various capacities requisite in public life are for the most part immature; it is precisely for this reason that a period of public and political training is necessary. The value of the policy consists in its tendency to create and develop the capacity for self-help. Placed in new positions of responsibility, the representatives of the people on the local boards will become year by year more intelligent, self-reliant, and independent. But these advantages can be secured only if the local bodies are trusted. Their power and responsibilities must alike be real in proportion; as if there is any pretence or illusion about either the one or the other, there is an obvious possibility that the whole undertaking may degenerate into an officious dislocation of existing arrangements. No such miscarriage of a generous and enlightened policy must be suffered to occur in the Panjab. This risk escaped, the Government anticipating, by wise reforms, those legitimate aspirations which always gain substance and strength with the process of instruction, and providing a career for the people, to open and expand with their growing intelligence and education, will avoid many of the dangers inherent in foreign rule. The scheme, in so far as it can be successfully worked, will tend to educate the country in public life, to relieve the Government of the odium of petty interferences and small unpopular acts; to diminish any sense of antagonism between the people and the Government; to promote better knowledge of the real aims of the governing body; to popularize taxation; to open useful, if not exalted, careers to the native gentry; and to interest leading men in the process of undertakings and the stability of institutions in which they will now have a personal and prominent share."

Such are the high hopes entertained by some at least of the advocates and supporters of the scheme initiated by Lord Ripon and his advisers. In some parts of empire the realization will be early, and in others it will be late.

In the Central Provinces, which have an administration younger even than that of the Panjab, the policy has been put in force by the recent passing of a law which embodies all the principal points in the Resolution of the Government of India of May, 1882, already mentioned.

In general terms, a measure of this nature, if urged by the Government of India, merits the confidence of the British public. For that Government—consisting not only of the Viceroy and Governor-General (as its head), but also of councillors, some men of the best Indian experience, and others drawn from the English professions—possesses both progressive and conservative elements, and usually pursues a line which, though reforming and enlightened, is yet tentative and precautionary.

When the new system shall have taken root in India, and begun to flourish, abuses will doubtless arise similar to those which have arisen in more civilized countries. When seats in the Local Boards shall become objects of strong desire, or of personal ambition, it is to be feared that India will not prove to be free from the petty malpractices with which elections in the United Kingdom have been too often disfigured. For India, however, this objection will not be apparent for some, perhaps many, years to come. By that time perhaps European people will have learnt how to check this evil among themselves. In that case the people of India will doubtless prove teachable in the same direction. The progress of the natives under English education, in all that relates to secular morality, has been happily remarkable. A similar progress will surely become perceptible in their political conduct. Again, if elections are intrinsically good, it is possible to have too much of them as of other good things, as is abundantly illustrated by the example of the United States of America. If, then, ardent reformers, emboldened by success attending the measure now under discussion, were to hastily extend the principle to this, that, and the other branch or department, then a crop of abuses might spring up on the Indian soil, which possesses a signal fertility in this respect. Nevertheless, it must be remembered that the elective principle is essential to that political training which every stable Government (like that of British India) must desire to see possessed by its subjects. Mere discussion, without practical action, will be futile. Hitherto such action has been deprecated by some because the people are unprepared. But the people are not likely to become prepared unless some steps are taken for preparation. Public spirit cannot be created without entrusting the people with a part of their own public business, a part limited at first, but increasing as their fitness shall grow. Unless this be attempted, more and more, there is fear lest the effect of British rule should check such public spirit. A retrospect of the results attained by British rule in India will show what apparent marvels have been accomplished; another marvel now presents itself for accomplishment. Political risk is sometimes apprehended when the British Government undertakes to perform duties which it seems to owe to the people of India. In cases where the duty is clear, some risk must be borne; and on the whole the Government is so strong that it can afford to be trustful in its attitude towards the natives, and may believe that what is just and generous will seldom fail to be safe politically.

# CHAPTER VII.

## RELIGIOUS MISSIONS IN THE EAST.

Futility of objections raised against missions — Satisfactory statistics of mission work — Good character of native Christians — High repute of the missionaries — Large results already attained — The battle with ancient systems — Converts from all classes — Effects of national education — The elevation of Indian women.

## PART I.

"How beautiful are the feet of them that preach the gospel of peace, and bring glad tidings of good things."

[*Speech delivered before the Society for the Propagation of the Gospel in Foreign Parts, at Lincoln, November* 1881.]

I AM much obliged by the kind terms in which your Chairman, the Lord Bishop of Lincoln,* has introduced me to this meeting. Although I am speaking on behalf of the Society for the Propagation of the Gospel, yet I would apply my remarks to the Protestant Missions to India in their entirety. The Society deservedly holds a high place in India as in many other regions in all the four quarters of the world. There are, happily, sister societies belonging to the Church of England. There are also societies belonging to the several Protestant denominations, which zealously preach the Gospel to the heathen.

I have been informed that there are certain objections, originating, apparently, from ladies and gentlemen recently arrived from India, which have a damping effect and a chilling influence upon the hearts and efforts of those in England who are labouring to obtain substantial support for the missions, and

* Bishop Christopher Wordsworth.

are advocating the sacred cause. I am not altogether surprised at hearing these objections here in Lincoln, because in May last I heard very similar objections mentioned in another part of England.

I have therefore reduced the objections, which I understand to be floating about this part of England (Lincolnshire), to writing, and they are as follow:—First, in general terms missions are failures; secondly the missionaries make no converts; thirdly, the converts that are made come from the humblest class, intellectually and socially; fourthly, among the converts many become Christians for the sake of making a livelihood thereby; fifthly, native Christians are not morally better than the heathen, but, on the contrary, worse; sixthly, the missionaries live easy lives and do not exert themselves as much as they might; seventhly, many of the missionaries are deficient in the culture necessary for the performance of their duties; eighthly, missionary reports transmitted to England present over-coloured and misleading views of success in work; ninthly, labour in England for support of missions abroad is not practical, but is little more than romance, whereby good people amuse themselves; tenthly, the delay in attaining missionary success has been so long protracted that people can hardly exert themselves on this account, with so many pressing calls at home.

These objections I have collected and tied together, as it were like a faggot, and if you will bear with me for a few moments I will untie the faggot and dispose of it stick by stick.

The first objection, then, is that missions are failures. I will ask you to consider in what does failure or success consist. What would you consider to be a successful result? What is the actual result? Why, that at this moment there are 390,000 native Christians in India, of whom 100,000 are communicants. Besides these there are 200,000 boys and girls at school, who, though not all of them Christians, are entrusted by heathen parents to the missionaries, and are receiving Christian instruction. Out of these no less than 40,000 are girls. So that, with converts and scholars, there are 590,000 persons, or, in round numbers, 600,000 altogether. Upon these, what with mission funds and educational grants from the State, there are being spent 400,000*l.* a year. That gives an average of less than 15*s.* per head, and I venture to say no Government or State Department could do so grand a work at a cheaper cost.

Statistics, you will remember, are furnished by missionaries, and the objectors may not altogether accept missionary figures. My figures, however, are taken not only from the missionary reports, but are verified from the official reports of the Government of India,—and are particularly confirmed by the returns of the census which is periodically taken in India. Besides that, the statistics of the scholars are attested by the fact that all the mission schools are receiving grants in aid which necessitate the schools being inspected, the scholars numbered, and their attendances tested by Government inspectors. But besides the general report of the Government we have the testimony of witnesses of the very highest consequence and quality, statesmen whose utterances upon all other subjects are generally listened to by their countrymen, received by their Sovereign, and accepted by Parliament; statesmen whose proceedings in all other departments are received with confidence.

Such men are my witnesses, whose honoured words I am prepared to produce this evening, if only time permitted. But the great results of mission work are matters of general notoriety; the half-million of people constitute a fact which cannot possibly be overlooked, and regarding which there is no room nor ground for being mistaken. You may ask any European magistrate, or any tax-gatherer, every traveller, every European merchant, or any one who is engaged in industrial enterprise in that quarter. Really the fact of the greatness of the result of missions is as well attested as the fact that Lincoln Cathedral stands upon the neighbouring hill.

The second objection is that missionaries make no converts.

Well, now I suppose that objection comes from the circumstance that the missionaries are largely engaged in educational work, which work concerns natives who are not necessarily Christian. How stand the facts about converts? Let me remind you that those figures of 390,000 have been gradually rising. In 1850 there were 92,000, in 1860 138,000, in 1870 230,000, and now there are 390,000, so you see that in those thirty years there has been a vast increase. How has that result been brought about unless the missionaries have made converts? The facts that I have mentioned cannot be gainsaid, for they are derived from official reports. There is no doubt some natural increase of the native Christian population, as happily that population has existed for two or more generations; still it cannot have been so prolific as to have produced all this increase, which must be in a great part due to accessions from without by conversion.

The third objection is that the converts that are made come from the humblest class, intellectually and socially. I must say that this is not a very Christian objection, because we have divine authority for specially attending to this class, and one of the distinguishing marks of our religion is that it has to be preached to the poor, the degraded, and the miserable. But let us take the objection as it stands. You must bear in mind that in India the high-class people are to the lower class as one to ten. In other words, out of every ten in the population nine would be of the lower class and but one of the high; therefore if Christians were equally divided over the population we should expect to find nine men of the lower classes to one man of the high.

Now, inasmuch as when natives become Christians they no longer keep any record of their caste, I cannot tell you how many native Christians were originally high or low caste, but I can affirm, as a notorious fact, that a considerable proportion of the most influential among the native Christians have been high-caste men. You may look on the roll of all the native

Christians who have done good work and you will find that the greater portion of them were originally high-caste men. If I were to give you a list of men, natives, who have done honour to the Christian profession, the list would be so long that I should keep you all the evening while reading it. I may remind you of the fortunate fact that in India out of 200 million British subjects (exclusive of native states) 18 millions are of aboriginal races, and 9 millions of no caste at all. Thus 27 (18 + 9) millions are beyond the pale of the principal Oriental religions, and their minds present a *tabula rasa* on which Christianity may work. Accordingly in India there are no less than 27 millions of people whose destiny the Christian missionaries may carve out for this life and the life to come. But it is not a fact that the high-caste people have been behindhand. On the contrary, of all the native Christians, the men who have borne the utmost persecution and have sustained all the moral anguish and torture that could be inflicted, are the high-caste men; and the natives who have helped to uphold Christianity in India have been for the most part men of that class.

Besides this, you have doubtless heard that the most intellectual class of natives in India are those who belong to the Brahmo sect, and many of them are almost persuaded to be Christians. Some of their ministers actually preach sermons from texts taken from the Bible, and they have declared that the British Government may be the secular ruler of England, but the supreme ruler is no less than Christ the Lord. These are extraordinary expressions to be used by men who do not actually profess the Christian religion, but at all events they show that men of high education, high caste, and high social position in India, have at least a regard for Christian principle.

The fourth objection is that among the converts many become Christians for the sake of making a livelihood thereby. You will kindly bear in mind that all the principal missionaries in India are Europeans—necessarily so, and that being the case most of the good salaries, the loaves and fishes that might be in the missionary service, necessarily go to our own countrymen and not to the native Christians at all.

Still there are 4500 natives in the service of the missions; and the converts, taken altogether, number about 400,000. So out of 400,000 Christians, the number employed is only 4500, or just one in ninety. But say the 400,000 includes the families, divide it by half and take the males only, 200,000, and divide by 4500. You will find that it gives them about one in 45, or that out of every 45 males who are native Christians in India one receives service under the missionaries and 44 do not. Where, then, is the strong temptation for the natives to embrace Christianity for the sake of earning a livelihood? The Government itself scrupulously abstains from offering service to Christians because they are Christians, and there is nothing to be gained in that way by adopting Christianity. Therefore you will see the worthlessness of this objection also.

The fifth objection is that native Christians are not morally better than heathens, but, on the contrary, worse. I am afraid that idea comes from reports that are spread about sometimes by ladies and gentlemen returning from India regarding the conduct of natives who have been domestic servants. Conceive the idea of judging a great community, numbering hundreds of thousands, by the isolated conduct of some domestic servant! Why, English servants are largely in service on the Continent, and suppose a Russian, because he was disappointed with one or two of his English servants, were to say that the English were a worthless nation. Yet that is the way in which you are asked to judge of native Indian Christianity. But as a matter of fact there are very few native Christians employed in the service of Europeans. For if an English master has a native Christian servant, while all the other servants are heathen, you can readily believe that the latter would make the place too hot for him. But I will suggest to you a better way of considering this question. The conduct of native Christians should be observed in their homes, in their villages extending over whole tracts of country. Thus viewed in the mass, they are found to be good and respectable people. The civil authorities may be appealed to for confirmation of this. Scandals there have been upon the name of Christianity, but these have seldom or never come from the native Christians. They never apostatise, and never relapse into heathen practices. They maintain the faith from generation to generation, and are regular in having their children baptized. They attend church and holy communion, and now have begun to support the native ministry and general organisation of the native Church. Although they are poor people as a rule, nevertheless their subscriptions amounted, for the organisation of their Church, to 10,000*l.* a year some time ago, and now to no less than 20,000*l.* annually. I am sure the objection does not come from those who have any real knowledge of what goes on in native society, especially of the proceedings which are too common in the precincts of native temples or places of public worship. Although the theory of the religion of the natives may be in some respects pure, nevertheless there is much in their semi-religious practices which could scarcely be mentioned in public. Take all these things, and ask yourselves whether you have so little confidence in the efficacy of Christian morality, as taught from English mouths and English books, as to suppose that it could fail to benefit those minds which have been originally nurtured under such heathen influences as those which I have just mentioned.

The next objection is that the missionaries lead easy lives, and do not exert themselves as much as they might. Now, pray consider what is the work of the missionaries. We have but 500 European missionaries in India, but we have no fewer than 493 mission stations; a mission station meaning, generally, a cluster of native Christian parishes, so you will see that there is little more than one man to each mission station. Then you should look at the number of scholars in the schools—200,000 boys and girls. That will give one missionary to every forty scholars, even supposing that they were all employed in education, but you know that they are not. You know that in all the various parishes into which the native Christian population is divided, the missionaries have all the ordinary parochial work—also the work of evangelisation and preaching in the highways. This is in public, and there is no possibility of mistake as to the fact of the work going on. Then there is the preparation of young men for the University examinations (at Calcutta, Madras, and Bombay), regarding the reality of which there is no doubt.

Besides this, consider the work the missionaries have done in writing and translating the Scriptures into twenty vernacular languages. You may remember also that in times of public danger, in seasons of famine and distress, the missionaries have always been to the front with their services. Indeed, fault has actually been found with them for interfering too zealously on behalf of their flocks in secular affairs. It shows that they have not led easy lives when they are actually charged by their opponents with undue activity.

Amongst missionaries of the past there have been some who were illustrious British men in the highest sense. The present missionaries may or may not be thought to possess equal genius—as genius is a quality not to be reckoned upon with certainty. But is it likely, do you think, that the missionary of the future will be inferior to missionaries of the past, considering that the missionary body of the present is better educated technically and more completely organised? There is the College of St. Augustine's at Canterbury, and the Church Missionary Society has a training institution at Islington. You should therefore consider whether there is likely to be any failure in the supply of missionaries for the future. Our Society, the S.P.G., has now such names as Kay, Skelton, Winter, and Crowfoot, who was once at Delhi; and you may be glad to think of the name of Logsdail, son of one of your most meritorious citizens, who has just gone out to India, where

I am sure that he will bring fresh credit to the name of Lincoln. Last, and greatest of all, I may mention Caldwell, the Bishop, who is now in failing health, and the most cheering message that you could send to him is the assurance that you appreciate his efforts, and that you regard as baseless everything that is said against missionary enterprise. Alfred Cane may also be mentioned, who rendered good service during the war in Afghanistan.

The next objection is that many of the missionaries are deficient in the culture necessary for the performance of their duties. I presume that this objection means that there are two classes of missionaries; one for practical and parochial work, and the other for controversial work among the highly educated natives. Now those are two distinct branches of duty. The first branch does not require a peculiar degree of culture. It is necessary that there should be practical zeal and energy, with a capacity for managing a vast amount of trivial business, business which becomes difficult because of its quantity. Now for that sort of work you may readily understand that we require missionaries of one stamp. But for arguing, and reasoning, and philosophising, highly cultured missionaries are required—missionaries of another stamp, such as some of those whose names have been already mentioned, and the younger men who are furnished by Cambridge to our Society's old Mission at Delhi, or by the Oxford mission to Calcutta. Thus you will readily see it is not the fact that any of the missionaries are unsuited to the duties which they have to perform. Those who are required for parish work receive proper training, and those who require higher culture obtain it at institutions like those just mentioned, and in connection with Oxford and Cambridge.

The eighth objection is that missionary reports transmitted to England present over-coloured and misleading views of success in work. It may be that those reports abound too much in anecdotes, which however illustrative do not afford proof, any more than two or three swallows make a summer. But the real, perhaps the only, fault of the missionary reports is that they generally fail to give an adequate idea of the magnitude of the work, and do not take quite so comprehensive a survey of the facts and figures as they might. You will see then that the reports are thus in some respects actually under-coloured.

The ninth objection is that labour in England for the support of missions abroad is not practical, but is little more than a romance, whereby good people amuse themselves. For one instant let me remind you of the result deducible from the facts which I will venture to marshal out for your consideration. The romance, if it be a romance, consists greatly, I might say sublimely, of the following array of figures. We have 400,000*l.* of annual expenditure, 432 mission stations, 500 European missionaries, and 3 missionary bishops, 4500 native assistants, 300 native ordained clergy, 85 training schools, and 4 normal institutions, from which are turned out 3000 students annually. We raise 20,000*l.* a year from poor native Christians. We have 24 mission presses, from which there issue three-quarters of a million of religious books annually, which are sold to the native public for a sum of 3800*l.* a year. We have 400,000 native Christians, and 200,000 boys and girls at school, of whom 1700 have at different times entered the universities established by law in India, and of whom again 700 have passed on to the taking of degrees. There are 40,000 girls at school and 1300 classes for the Zenana Missions in the apartments of the native ladies, and those classes are attended by 3000 lady students. I feel in giving those figures as if I were reading the record of some great State Department, and not of private enterprise such as this really is. I will say that it is truly honourable to British people and to the zeal of the Protestant Church. You must remember that it is a work which, if not done by our societies, cannot be done at all. It is a work from which Government are bound to abstain. I have always felt in India that the Government which I served might be able to make war with energy or conclude "peace with honour," or they might cover the country with a network of railways and canals, foster a world-wide commerce, spread industry and enterprise over the land, preserve order, dispense justice, diffuse secular education, and give ethical instruction; but with all those things there is one thing which the Government cannot give, and that is the light of Christian religion and morality. That sacred lamp it is for us to light and to carry aloft in distant regions. Believe me it is no romance, but is a stern and magnificent reality, one of which the English nation may be proud. If Englishmen do not appreciate this, other nations will. The Roman Catholics will admit that its magnitude equals the mediæval successes of Xavier and others. The Germans will point to the many men of their nation who have served with the British missions. The Americans will claim a share in the credit, as they also have sent Protestant missions to India.

Then comes the tenth and last objection, which is that the delay in attaining missionary success has been so long protracted that people can hardly exert themselves on that account with so many pressing calls at home. I have shown you that success has already been vouchsafed. The Right Reverend Chairman has eloquently alluded to the great missionary Henry Martyn, a century ago. I wonder whether our forefathers foresaw the greatness of the success which a hundred years would produce. You will remember, too, that the result has been attained by an increase of 50 per cent. in each decade during the last thirty years, or one generation of man. If a similar result goes on, and we prosper equally during the generation upon which we are now entering, then the present number of converts will have increased by the end of that generation from 400,000 to 1,350,000, and the scholars to 625,000, total, 1,945,000, or, in round numbers, two millions. During the coming generation the result is likely to be even greater, because the work is now backed up, not only by European energy and the zeal of the Protestant Church, but also by the influence which education on the part of the State is producing throughout the land and amongst all classes of the people. Thus India is like a mighty bastion which is being battered by heavy artillery. We have given blow after blow, and thud after thud, and the effect is not at first very remarkable; but at last with a crash the mighty structure will come toppling down, and it is our hope that some day the heathen religions of India will in like manner succumb.

To conclude, I told you at the outset that I would take the bundle or faggot of objections stick by stick, and it is for you to judge whether I have succeeded in breaking each of those sticks in detail.

Those objections, you will have seen, crumble to the touch of fact, and wither in the sunlight of criticism. Now you see how futile such objections are, amounting to nothing more than excuses for indifference and arguments for the old object of how not to do it. The reverend gentlemen around me who are leaders of public opinion in respect to missions, may believe me, that we are not fighting an uphill battle. If it were an uphill battle, we would still no doubt fight it, because we believe in the ultimate fulfilment of our Divine Master's promise. Still our hearts are but human, and therefore we must be depressed if we really were to think that we were labouring without hope of any present success. But we are not chasing a shadow, we are not rolling a Sisyphean stone, we are not ascending an inaccessible hill; or, if we are going up hill, it is that sort of ascent which soon leads to a summit, from which we shall survey the promised land. And when we reach the top what prospect shall we see? We shall see churches in India raising up their spires towards heaven, Christian villages extending over whole tracts of country, churches crowded with dusky congregations and dusky communicants at the altar tables. We shall hear the native girls singing hymns in the vernacular, and see boys trooping to school or studying for the universities under missionary auspices. Those things, and many others, I have seen, and would to God I could fix them on the minds of my audience as they are fixed upon my own. But at all events I feel that by answering these objections I have brought out the whole missionary case, according to my view of it, and I have stated all the best arguments that have occurred to me on behalf of missions. Therefore, I trust that I have performed my task in a manner which will be acceptable to you as labourers in the vineyard of Christ, and which may do some little good towards the help of that great Missionary Society on whose behalf I have the honour and pleasure to appear before this meeting.

---

## PART II.

[*Speech delivered before the Board of Foreign Missions of the Presbyterian Church in the United States, at New York, November* 1882.]

I TAKE pleasure in meeting your Missionary Board on this occasion, and in giving my testimony to the value of Christian missions in India.

And in what I have to say I would speak of Protestant missions in their totality. While we trust that the Church of England will be found to have taken her full share in the missionary operations, yet we fully appreciate the great work done by the Presbyterian Church, and especially by the Free Church of Scotland, which I regard as having done as much, in proportion to its numbers and resources, for the cause of missions in India as any community in Christendom. We regard with gratitude and respect the assistance obtained through the piety and generosity of the several Protestant churches of America. Certainly the American missions of all denominations in India are working thoroughly well. That I can testify, having seen them. At the same time I would give full credit to the Roman

Catholic missionaries in India, who certainly are earnest labourers, and have devoted themselves to the heathen. Indeed, they show their best side when labouring as missionaries in India. I would not desire to disparage them, and yet even they cannot keep pace with Protestant missions so far as the result can be gauged by statistics. I apply my remarks then to Protestant missions in their integrity, their totality, in which the Presbyterian Church, on both sides of the Atlantic, has borne a prominent share.

In the first place I would allude to the disparaging reports often made by travellers with regard to the missionary work in India, which reports are but too current in England, and have, I am sorry to hear, found their way to America. Some gentlemen, and ladies too, returning from India after travelling or residing in the country, deride the results of missions. Now, statements like these are made either by persons who never took the trouble to obtain information, perhaps never enjoyed the opportunity of obtaining it, or by those who have no interest in religion, and no care for religious work. You well understand how difficult it would be for a person passing through your great city (New York) to form a just estimate of its various institutions of charity and public beneficence. How imperfect is the knowledge of one just residing only for a time in city or country! How much more does this hold good of the observations by European travellers or temporary residents in a country so vast as India. The work of missions does not strike the casual observer. You have to inquire and investigate, not only at the great centres, but in the interior of the country. You must not suppose that because a lady or gentleman has happened to reside or travel in India, he or she must necessarily know all about the missionary work going on in that land.

Those who undervalue missions will belong to one or other of two categories, either persons who do not care for religion, or persons who, while caring for religion, are not experienced in the interior in India. On the other hand, those who have examined the work are those who give a favourable testimony. The favourable witnesses are not mere casual or superficial observers, but men of the highest character, statesmen, civilians, politicians, and soldiers, men on whose judgment their government and the civilised world depend with confidence on other subjects, and whose opinion may be safely trusted on this great subject of missions.

The evidence depends, moreover, not on mere personal statements and impressions, but on statistics and facts, liable to be checked by witnesses with local knowledge, and subject to verification in many collateral respects by official men who are not likely to deceive themselves.

In the next place objectors are fond of saying, What after all is the actual success of missions? Have they done anything in India? The answer to this must come from well-verified figures and facts. No argument is so potent on this subject as that drawn from the official documents. I have not my papers and figures with me, while travelling in America, but I could give you an array of facts of which all Christendom would be proud.* They sound like the statistics of some great governmental undertaking, but they really constitute the result of private enterprise undertaken in the most sacred of causes. The fear is not that we shall be discouraged by the small result already attained, but that the result is becoming so great, and increasing with such rapid growth as might be well styled, in view of the rapid development of your great country, an *American* growth, that it may ere long so grow on your hands that you cannot cope with it. It is now advancing fifty per cent. every ten years during the generation (thirty years) ending with the year 1880. If it goes on at that rate, during the present generation there will be by the year 1910 about 2,000,000 of native Christians on your hands, and any organisation you can make with European agency will be inadequate to deal with them. Your only hope will be in organising a native church.

* See figures given in pp. 132, 140, and 141.

And this work is already receiving due consideration. Natives of acknowledged ability and piety are entering the Christian ministry, and the Government have already had to sanction, in conjunction with the English missionary societies, three additional bishops to examine and ordain the native ministers and deacons. There are now in India three hundred native ministers with five hundred European missionaries, and we hope that ere long the natives will outnumber the foreign missionaries.

But for a long time to come the prime movers in these operations must continue to be European. And we hope that a great Christian, and if we may use the term, ecclesiastical army will be raised, the rank and file consisting of natives, while the captains and generals are highly qualified Europeans.

Again, you are, I am informed, sometimes asked by objectors, Is there any chance for Christianity to make headway against these antiquated systems of false religion?

With regard to Buddhism, that religion is not extensively prevalent in India, but it is met with in the mountainous regions of the eastern Himalayas. In its inception it was lofty and pure. But however excellent and attractive the poetic accounts of Buddhism, as given in the well-known poem, 'The Light of Asia,' the actual Buddhism of India (Himalayan) and Tibet is as degraded and degrading as can well be imagined. It is liberal toward other faiths, but when you have said that, you have exhausted the catalogue of its merits. It is very picturesque to the fancy in its ceremonial rites, but is far otherwise in doctrine and discipline.

Then, as to Muhammadanism, it is a much more formidable adversary. Yet converts have been made from among the Muhammadans, and these converts are among the best yet made in India. Muhammadanism presents us a nut which is hard to crack, having had the advantage of Christianity in coming after it, and having borrowed many of its teachings. The Muhammadans say willingly that they revere "the Book" as they style the Bible. They have the idea of God, of one God. No uninspired book has so fully formulated the attributes of Deity as the Muhammadan writings in the Arabic language, and that is perhaps the most elaborately constructed language ever known. Many noble and impressive dicta, also, may be culled from their sacred books.

Yet as a religion Muhammadanism establishes a narrow exclusive character. It withers human character as with a blight, warps all the feelings and sentiments, crystalises everything which it touches, and rivets all customs and opinions in a groove. Though it inculcates the duty of almsgiving, it is in several respects uncharitable. It is utterly intolerant. Anything more sanguinary than the fanaticism, cherished by some of its members, cannot be imagined. Benevolence towards those who differ from us, love to our neighbour, and charity in the Christian sense of that most noble term, are wholly alien to the Muhammadan religion. I know the Muhammadans well, from long and familiar acquaintance, and desire to do justice to their many virtues. But their peculiar character convinces me of the necessity for giving them the freedom of Christianity.

Then as to Hinduism. The Hindus number one hundred and fifty millions of souls, about two-thirds of the population of India.

Do not suppose because you hear and read of the pristine purity of the early Vedic faith that this is the Hinduism of the nineteenth century. The Hindus who strive in our day to purify their faith are thinking themselves out of Hinduism. Though the educated classes are soaring toward the light, yet the masses of the people to-day are as devoted to a corrupt religion as in the darkest ages of the East. I cannot give you an exact idea of the vicious orgies which occur constantly in the Hindu temples. There is a considerable amount of immorality, which is practically the outcome of the religion; though, on the other hand, there are many domestic virtues practised by the people, showing how much of goodness would be produced, if the religion were purer. The practical instruction given by Hinduism to the young is defective. The ideas of truth and honour are not always inculcated. The parent in training a child does not say, Never tell an untruth, but rather says, in effect, Do the best you can in the circumstances, thus teaching expediency, not morality. When contemplating the Hindus you recall the absurdity of their superstitions, and the immorality of many among their practices, you will see the need of carrying on missionary work in India.

I have heard in England and even in this country (America), that many think there is not much need for Christianity in India, and even if there were need, that there is no chance for its success. There is the need as seen by the character of the three great religions of the land, and that there is a chance of success is abundantly proved by statistics of the work already done.

Again I have been asked what is really the character of your missionaries in India. I have heard at times, on the other side of the Atlantic as well as here, the remark that the missionaries of our day are far from being of the apostolic type, that they go to distant regions only to earn a living and draw salaries without zeal for doing good, and with little hope of accomplishing anything. Now all these insinuations are incorrect. They are the careless and thoughtless remarks of men who do not know the qualifications and idiosyncrasies of the missionaries now becoming an extensive body of men. I have, during my life in India, been the local governor of 105,000,000 of people in different provinces. Many hundreds of Europeans have served under me, and I ought to know something of the value and the character of men. I have also been acquainted with the missionary stations throughont the length and breadth of the country. I believe that a more talented, zealous, and able body of men than the missionaries does not exist in India. In a country abounding in talent and learning they fully hold their own.

But it is said, The present missionaries are not equal to those of former years. Now, is it likely that the present and future missionaries will be less able than the past, when they profit by all the experience of that past, and besides have professional and technical instruction to give them especial preparation for their work, thus possessing advantages which their earliest predecessors never enjoyed ? In England we have excellent missionary training schools at Islington, and at St. Augustine, under the very shadow of Canterbury Cathedral, and at other places. Of course genius is not to be evoked by examinations, and whether some of the historic originators of the missionary work will, as individuals, be equalled by their successors, we cannot say. But, with the means of preparation now in use, I can promise confidently that the average missionary in the future will be equal to if not better than the past. I have seen the missionaries in every province, from Cape Comorin to the Himalayas, and I know their high character. I do not say that there are no failures; but the percentage of failures is as small as in any other department of the public service.

Pray remember that you want two kinds of missionaries. In the first place, you need practical "parish priests," to do the work of visiting and directing several thousands of simple-minded people, namely, native Christian peasants—missionaries always prompt, thoughtful, patient, able to despatch details rapidly, and all this in a work not requiring the highest intellectual exercise. A man highly qualified intellectually might not succeed in this labour. Next, you need men of another kind thoroughly versed not only in the religion, but also in the literature, philosophy, and poetry of India, to enter into the subtle fallacies and twistings of Oriental reasoning, and also versed in religious dialectics and trained in Christian theology.

Just as in an army there must be men of all arms, cavalry, infantry, and artillery, so here in this Christian warfare, we need men of varied gifts and culture. In the country which you kindly call "the mother land" there are the Oxford Mission to Calcutta and the Cambridge Mission to Delhi, which are organised to train missionaries of this higher kind. These efforts are specially connected with the two ancient Universities of England.

Inquiry is naturally made regarding the character of native converts. It is often carelessly said that they are no better after than before their conversion. These taunts may have come from some lady or gentleman who at some time has been deceived by a native Christian in the capacity of a domestic servant or a camp follower. But the native converts in India must not, as a whole, be judged by the casual misconduct of individuals. Those who attempt to apply such a test should remember that the efficacy of Christianity even among ourselves would be discredited by the application of so unreasonable a standard. The native Christians are no longer obscure and unknown, scattered here and there like "Rari nantes in gurgite vasto," but they are numbered by tens of thousands, and occupy whole tracts and districts of country. You should see them in their rural homes, but such a visitation takes time and trouble, and is seldom undertaken by those who disparage missions. You would then find these Christian communities remarkably well conducted. I do not claim for them any unusual display of Christian graces, but they behave as well on the average as Christians in any land. If you appeal to the magistrates in India, they will give the native Christians everywhere a good character. These Christians are obedient to their religious guides; attend faithfully the ordinances of religion, the services of the Church, the Holy Communion and Confirmation; and send their children to school during the week, and to the Sunday-school on the Sabbath. It would be well, if all of us white Christians contributed as much relatively as the native Christians do for the support of the Gospel, and of their religious institutions. In their villages you see the rustic chapels and the little schools which they have reared by their own contributions.

Again, they have never scandalised their Christianity nor put their religion to open shame. We must admit that India, like other countries, has had scandals reflecting unfavourably on

Christianity. But unhappily these scandals which have been brought on the faith have been chiefly from white men calling themselves Christians. We trust that the native Christians will judge of our religion by the admirable conduct of the good white Christians who abound in India as in other lands. We do not hear of apostates among the native Christians. When the Sepoy revolt with the consequent war spread over the land, and many were tempted to apostatise, were threatened, and exposed to danger, yet they stood firm to their faith, and there was no noteworthy instance of apostasy whatever.

You sometimes hear that the Christians in India have become so for pecuniary gain. They have been called "rice Christians," as if they became Christians in order to be fed with rice. They are rice Christians no doubt, but in a different sense from what the term was intended to convey. Truly, they are rice Christians, because they work industriously and produce the finest rice crops for themselves! They are largely of the peasant class, peasant proprietors who cultivate the land they own and hand it down to their children. They are by nature attached to everything ancestral; and those whose families have been Christian for more than one generation, begin to feel an hereditary attachment to Christianity. Everything hereditary is by them stedfastly cherished. I have often heard the native Christians speak affectionately of the missionaries who first instructed their fathers in the Christian faith.

Again, it is said that the Christian converts are only the humble classes. "Show us one of the higher class!" I accept that challenge. Let us go through the list of the native ministry and we shall find that most of the able preachers, who have done the best in vindicating Christianity, have been of the high caste.

Yet we should remember that the mass of the people belong to the humbler castes, and that the majority of the Christians *must* be of the lower caste if Christianity be diffused as it ought to be among all castes equably. The humblest people are, after all, the most needy and most appeal to our Christian sympathies. We believe that their souls are as valuable as ours, and we should gladly labour for their salvation.

Then there is a body of men in India who belong to no caste at all. They are regarded by all others as out of caste. They are the aborigines and the Pariahs. They number, according to the census, twenty-three millions of souls, and it may be encouraging to recollect that while in a large part of India you encounter caste, priestcraft, and bigoted hostility, yet among these you have a clean surface on which to write; hearts unsullied by guile and superstition, on which you may inscribe the doctrines of eternal truth. Here, then, you have a field in which may be won an encouraging success.

Believing in the inviolability of the Divine command to "preach the Gospel to every creature," you would doubtless persevere even in the absence of present success, trusting in the ultimate fulfilment of the Scriptural promises. Yet we cannot but feel our energies stimulated if we see success attending our labours. Now you have in India a sure success before you, which will be certainly augmented in proportion to the labours put forth, and to the resources brought into play.

It will occur to you to ask what effect is the system of public instruction to have on the temper and disposition of the Indian people? You will be told it is producing disloyalty, discontent, and irreligion, taking away from the people the religion of their forefathers, and giving them nothing in return.

As to loyalty or disloyalty, England will do her duty without fear. I believe education will produce loyalty. But, be the political consequence what it may, we must be just and fear not, and give India the education in those arts and sciences which have made England herself what she is. Even if a certain sort of disloyalty were to be the consequence, we must persevere, for we could not consent to keep the people ignorant in order to keep them loyal.

As regards religion, the Government has to be very careful

not to mix religion with the State education. But we give the same educational grants of State aid to the schools of all communities alike, and the missionaries come in for their share, the pecuniary assistance being given on the well-known system of "payment by results." Thus indirectly the missionaries obtain a modicum of public aid which they win in open competition.

Irreligion might be the consequence of the secular teaching under the State, but the contrary is the case. The highly-educated Hindoos almost invariably break away from their heathen religion. I do not say this is true of Muhammadans, but the Hindus on receiving western education do, with scarcely any exception, cease to believe in the ancestral faith. They do not, however, become atheists or materialists. They rather become theists, believing in the immortality of the soul and in human accountability to a supreme judge for deeds done in this life. If you look at the sermons of the Hindu religious reformers, styling themselves the Brahmo Somaj, and the addresses of welcome lately given by them to the missionaries of the Oxford Mission to Calcutta, you can judge whether they are not on the high road to Christianity. Then if you can send out missionaries intellectually able to cope with these men, a rich harvest may be reaped.

I must now say a few words regarding female education; the importance of this is acknowledged by the British Government in India. We encourage the opening of female schools in every direction. Formerly females were kept in degradation and seclusion, yet there have been manifold instances of female heroism and genius in Indian history. Even to this day, widows would be quite ready to burn themselves on the funeral pyres of their husbands, were they not prevented by the strong hand of the British Government. They certainly are not lacking in what we call grit of character. Hence we may infer that a great future is in store for the women of India, when properly educated. Both the high and the humble are anxious to go to school. But the daughters of the rich and noble do not attend school, as they cannot break the bar of public opinion which prevents girls of more than eleven or twelve years from appearing in public. Hence you must teach them in their homes, in the Zenanas or female apartments. For this reason, European ladies of special training are becoming teachers in the households of the wealthy and the great. I suggest to you that American gentlemen cannot do better than advise some of the young ladies now being educated in the ladies' colleges and the normal institutions of the United States, to go out as teachers to the daughters of the great Indian houses, and so carry western enlightenment into recesses heretofore secluded from the light. Female education is already advancing in India. I know hundreds of educated natives whose grandmothers could not read at all, whose mothers could read but slightly, and whose wives can read and write imperfectly. But their daughters are being brought up with an education conducted upon the western models.

In conclusion, then, gentlemen, the result thus far in India is relatively inconsiderable, though absolutely it may be large. But the smallness of its proportion arises from the vastness of the country and the immense population, a consideration likely to be fully appreciated by Americans. Still there is every ground for encouragement. A shining goal invites your Christian efforts. Such efforts are not indeed put forth with a view to political effect. Still, as a matter of fact, the political effect of the Christian missions in India is excellent. The spectacle of private enterprise undertaken in this disinterested manner, does not render the natives jealous, but rather edifies them. The natives are but too apt to imagine that British policy is governed by political ambition or national aggrandisement. Let them see in our missions something higher and nobler, a benevolence disinterested and pure, a sunny spot with no shadows or earth-born cloud to rest upon it.

The result of missions thus far is nationally and politically good. We Englishmen feel our responsibility. We thankfully acknowledge the aid sent from the religious world in the United States with a truly disinterested liberality, and we cordially welcome the co-operation of our American kinsmen in this noble work.

---

## PART III.

[*Speech delivered before the Baptist Missionary Society, in London, April* 1883.]

I HAVE felt it my peculiar duty to be present on this occasion because, as Lieutenant-Governor of Bengal, I have been specially acquainted with the Baptist missions in that province. The names of Carey, and Ward, and Marshman, which you read about, are to me living memories, and not only to me, but to thousands of my fellow-countrymen in the East, and what is more, to many millions of natives. These are memories of men who were the pioneers of civilisation and of humane refinement, the earliest propagators of Christian literature amongst the heathen. The results, indeed, of their work are to be counted among the peaceful glories of England and a portion of that national heritage which is splendid in the highest sense of the term. Again, the Serampore College, which you see mentioned in the earlier publications of the Society, and in the later reports of this session, is to me a familiar sight—a place where I have distributed prizes, and where I have addressed meetings, not so great as this meeting, but still meetings inspired with equal enthusiasm. I have further thought it my duty to appear at the meeting, because of all the Protestant denominations in the East there is not one that, according to its means, its numbers, and its opportunities, does more than the Baptist denomination. Of all the Protestant denominations the Free Church of Scotland is equalled by few and surpassed by none; but there is one by which it is equalled, and that is the Baptist denomination. In reference to your numbers and your wealth in this country, you, the Baptists, must indeed be possessed with a real zeal for religion—for consider not only your stations in Asia and in the East, but also in every part of the world. Look at the map of the world, and you will see your stations dotted from hemisphere to hemisphere, from one quarter of the globe to another, with little bright spots which are indeed the focuses of religious light. This meeting, too, which is so influentially and so numerously attended, is an earnest of the zeal which animates the community. I have seen many missionary meetings in all the chief cities of the north and west of England held on behalf of the Church of England and of other Protestant denominations, but nowhere have I seen a meeting which showed greater signs of real earnestness than the meeting which I have now the honour to address.

Now, India presents the greatest of all fields for missionary exertion, greater even than China, for the reduction recently made in Chinese population statistics shows that India may be nearly equal to China as regards numbers of population. Then, in respect to our moral responsibilities before God and man, India is a country which of all others we are bound to enlighten with eternal truth. It is a happy thing that in India all the various Protestant denominations are acting together in brotherly sympathy. All their little difficulties about church organisation and the like are sunk before the heathen in the presence of the sovereign truths of the Gospel, and, happily, we may say that our spears are spiritual lances all pointed in one direction.

I have just returned from a pilgrimage in Palestine; and, toiling laboriously, from sunrise to sunset, among the rocky paths of that mountainous region, I have seen the very landscape upon which the Divine eyes of the Saviour gazed, the very roads which His sacred feet trod, and the very rocks which re-echoed His words of more than mortal eloquence. And I ask you, my brother Christians, whether, of all the commands which He issued to us, there is any command more explicit than this, that we should preach the Gospel to all the world? If you believe in the Bible, if you are resolved to obey its ennobling dictates, then I ask you whether you are not bound, collectively and individually, to do your utmost to spread over the world, into its very utmost regions and among its most degraded tribes and classes, that light which emanated from Palestine? Look round and see whether there are any of the nations of the earth upon whom that responsibility more obviously and manifestly rests than upon the people of the United Kingdom. For we are proud of our empire, of our fleets, mercantile and naval, which cover the seas. We not only administer, in India, a vast empire directly, but over the Chinese empire we exercise almost commercial supremacy. We take Asiatic Turkey under our protection; we have now spread our benign sway over Egypt. We dispute with other Powers the valley of the Congo and the island of Madagascar. We have establishments on the Niger. We take the South African tribes—the Zulus, Basutos, Kaffirs, the Bechuanas of the Transvaal frontier—under our protection. We establish a new East India Company, so to speak, in the Island of Borneo, and now we discuss the prospect of taking over New Guinea. We are extended over various islands in the Pacific Ocean. We foster emigration from British India to the West Indian Islands and to Guiana. We are carrying communications right across North America from the Atlantic to the Pacific, which I have recently visited. We do these various things. You will have your own opinions, politically, as to whether all this is right or wrong, but it is done; and I ask you, do you believe that the Providence which permits us to do this, allows it merely for our national, our temporal, our secular aggrandisement? Can you believe it is permitted for any purpose but one—namely, the ultimate spread of the enlightenment of truth? And, as Christians, we believe that all ultimate truth must consist in religious truth. I press this argument not for the purpose of exciting imperial ideas in your mind, but merely for the purpose of enforcing upon your consciences the religious obligations under which you lie.

Remember, too, that while we do these things, no doubt partly for our material benefit, or for the benefit, as we should say, of our labouring classes in this country—while we seek new fields for investment of capital, new markets for our manufactures, new communications for our commerce—we also, I am thankful to say, as a nation, remember that these imperial advantages carry with them imperial obligations. For certainly, wherever our influence extends, whether it be secured peacefully or in a warlike manner, there is no doubt as to the ultimate result for the good government and the worldly prosperity of the tribes or nations that come under our charge. What is more, while the Government does its part in these matters, the Christian public never fails in doing its part—namely, in the spread of the truth which the Government, owing to its political obligations, is unable to diffuse. Therefore, looking abroad over our foreign interests throughout the world, you also look upon growing and increasing fields for our missionary exertions. Remember that every island, every valley, every continent which we occupy politically we are bound to enlighten morally and spiritually. It should be a matter of thankfulness to us that, whereas you so often see in human history the grandest qualities of humanity devoted to profitless wars and to various political combinations, of which there is either no result or a disappointing result, or in which among the actual results the harm preponderates over the good—yet in the British Empire you gladly perceive, from ordinary observation, that the results of our domination are material progress and civilisation, followed by moral and spiritual enlightenment. Therefore, it is a matter of thankfulness to us to find that the British qualities, the valour and genius, the statecraft and policy, are, under Providence, overruled for the good of the human race. And of that good, I venture to think, as a man of the world, as a politician, that one of the most potent instruments consists of those missionary exertions which we are here assembled to advocate and to encourage.

Without troubling you at this moment with statistics of the wonderful progress of missionary operations in the world, I would refer you, first, to the decennial report that was published ten years ago in India, and now to the still more interesting report recently published of the proceedings to the end of 1882. You will see from such reports a mighty progress, to be measured by hundreds of thousands of persons gathered into the fold of Christ. Progress such as that is found in India. I know that these reports are true, that entire efficiency is secured in India from one end to the other for the missionary cause; and further I infer, with the utmost confidence, that similar results are also secured for you in China, in the West Indies, in Africa, in Australasia, and in whatever region may be reached by your missionaries.

Very often among Protestant denominations, doubts are cast upon the utility of missions, and many people, who ought to know better, come back from the East and bring disparaging reports. I am thankful to hear that these doubts do not exist among the Baptists, and that, at all events, our Baptist countrymen who come back from the East bring true reports. And these reports being true, I know myself that they must necessarily and inevitably be favourable. But may I remind you now of one or two points of a practical character which will confirm your faith and strengthen your resolve to do your duty? The religions in India—the old-established religions—are each of them waning and declining towards their ultimate fall. Buddhism is effete. Hinduism is gradually breaking up, like the clouds before the advancing sun. Muhammadanism, no doubt, will hold out much longer for this reason—that it has a much more rational foundation than either Buddhism or Hinduism. Now-a-days, the practice of Buddhism is a miserable superstition. The humane and comparatively sound doctrine of the original belief of Buddha has become utterly overlaid by the most wretched, the most degrading superstition. Hinduism is still the religion of the million, no doubt, but only of the uneducated million. It is no longer the religion of the educated Hindu. It is no longer the religion of those who have either theoretical enlightenment or practical knowledge. It is being gradually dissipated, like the mist, before the science of the nineteenth century—that science which is being freely distributed amongst the people through the agency of the Government. Caste, no doubt, still holds its rule over the masses of India. But with some it no longer exists as a religious institution; with them it is purely a political institution. It binds them with iron fetters still, no doubt, but these fetters are secular rather than religious. But what is most important to you friends of missions, is this—that there is a large population of aborigines, a people who are outside caste, who do not belong to any old-established religions, who are not under the influence of bigoted and hereditary superstition. These aborigines by their mind and conscience offer a surface like clean paper, upon which the missionaries may make a mark. Although they are humble people, no doubt, still they are brave, resolute, faithful, and truth-telling people. If they are attached, as they rapidly may be, to Christianity, they will form a nucleus round which British power and influence may gather. Remember, too, that Hinduism, although it is dying, yet has force, and endeavours to proselytise amongst these people; and such tribes, if not converted to Christianity, may be perverted to Hinduism.

The character of your missionaries is everything, permit me to assure you, everything that you could reasonably desire. Perhaps people will say, Where is the genius of Carey and of Marshman now? Well, individual genius is an exceptional thing in all departments of public and of private life, as well as in missionary life; but in all probability the average of Protestant missionaries in India is improving year by year. I do not mean to say that there is greater zeal now than there was in the last generation. The piety of the present may not exceed the piety of the past. One important thing, however, is gained nowadays, namely, the technical, the professional training for the missionary work. Every denomination has now training colleges for the missionaries, and not only that, but there are missionaries of two kinds—those that have the superior training to argue dialectically with the principal classes of Hindus, and those that have the practical and administrative training to look after the large and growing congregations in various parts of the empire. The relations of the missionaries with the natives of India are satisfactory. The missionaries are looked upon not only as angels of light, but as ministers of benevolence. When natives are in trouble or difficulty they send to the neighbouring missionary, and in times of pestilence and famine it is the missionaries that have always marched in the very van of beneficence and of relief.

The character of the native Christians is also satisfactory, and worthy of the care that has been bestowed upon them. For I say, and there are hundreds of magistrates and of merchants and other independent witnesses who will bear me out in my assertion, that the native Christians are thoroughly well behaved, and are all the better in every walk of life for the Christian education and training that they have received. You will ask, In what does this goodness consist? It consists in this: that they, without exception, educate their children, and that the children so educated receive enlightened education in the sharpest contrast to the morally unhealthy and the degrading education in which the heathen children are brought up. Remember that it is a difficult thing in any country, even in our European countries, to induce every man, down to the poorest, to send his children to school. The native Christians in India, now to be numbered by hundreds of thousands—and, ere long, to be numbered by millions—send their children to school without any exception whatsoever. In the attendance upon their churches the native Christian congregations are not surpassed in regularity of attendance by any congregations in Europe. You will also find statistically that the proportion of communicants is very considerable. You will further find that these native Christians are not, as some people will have told you, mere hangers-on upon the skirts of the missions, or only persons who live from hand to mouth. They are industrious peasant proprietors, owning their own little bits of land which they cultivate in their villages. They hold their Christian faith in hereditary tenure, as it were, from generation to generation. They have been often tried in times of mutiny and rebellion, but have never apostatised. Take them all in all, these humble and unpretending people set an example worthy of consideration by their Christian brethren in Europe. They support their ministry, each and all. Though they are poor, yet they are industrious. They are people who never drink, who never run into any excess, who have their small savings. They have not the advantage of the organisation of friendly societies like we have in England, yet, nevertheless, every man saves a little; and of that little he gives to the support of his minister, to the building of his chapel, and to the organisation of his church in the broadest sense of the word. Remember, please, all this when measuring your opportunity and your responsibility.

Likewise the system of State education, as carried on by the Government, aids wondrously in India in enlightening the people; the missionaries themselves following the example, or, perhaps, the Government are following their example, to educate largely. The fact that so many tens of thousands of natives who do not profess Christianity, nevertheless, without the slightest hesitation, intrust their children to the Christian missionaries, while all the time there are Government schools open to them, speaks volumes for the confidence our missionaries have inspired amongst the masses of the people. This education not only spreads amongst the masses of the population, but it is working wonders among the upper and middle classes. It is leading men to look towards a religion of the monotheistic or theistic kind. It is inducing them to abjure the faith of their fathers, if I may call it faith—or rather, the superstition of their fathers. It is leading men to open their consciences, their intellects, their faculties to the revelation of Divine truth. There is a sect called the Hindu Theistic Reformers. I shall not trouble you with the vernacular names which this sect has in different parts of the country, but, as its operations now are extending among all the educated class, they constitute a most important moral and religious movement. It is for you, my Christian brethren, to exert yourselves to attract that movement in the direction of Christianity. There is difficulty in attracting it, because these people have considerable intellect. They are not easily reasoned with. They cannot possibly be talked over. They must be convinced by the power of Christian argument, and, we should say, by the still greater power of Divine grace.

While there is this vast spread of enlightenment amongst the men, the young men, and the boys, on the other hand the women and the girls of all ages, who once remained in darkness and in seclusion, are now gradually but rapidly emerging and striding into the light. For female education by the State has made not only a beginning, but a considerable progress. There are now thousands of girls' schools scattered over the country, attended by tens of thousands of female children, and within the next generation, no doubt, the great moral movement, the great instalment of progress to be expected, is the spread of female education, and that is a matter which ought to command the sympathies of every lady present. Remember it is a difficult thing to get schoolmistresses in India, because of the social prejudices, and because of the early age at which the girls are married. But there are, we grieve to think, large numbers of widows who, according to the Hindu system, must lead a thoroughly miserable life without hope or occupation in the world, and for them the honoured profession of schoolmistress opens an excellent career. But, ladies, especially ladies present, I particularly commend to your increasing attention the cause of the Zenana Mission. The schools of which I have been speaking have been for the humbler kinds of girls; but the operations for which I venture to bespeak your best exertions, are those of the Zenana Missions, which are carried on, not in the villages, nor in the busy streets of the towns, but in the houses, in the apartments, of the middle classes and of the wealthy. It is most important that the enlightenment should spread among the upper classes of the women, in order that it may be the leaven to affect the whole mass of female education throughout British India. But these benevolent operations in the inner apartments of the women necessarily demand a peculiarly delicate organisation —a sort of organisation which cannot be roughly attempted by us plain, practical administrators, as it requires all the gentle and patient thought which the educated women of England are peculiarly qualified to exercise. You cannot do better for the cause of Christianity than to continue these exertions on behalf of your Eastern sisters, in the full confidence that such educational enlightenment must be necessarily followed by the propagation of Christianity.

I shall conclude by reminding you that, as patriotic people, you may be confident that the missions in India are doing a work which strengthens the imperial foundations of British power, and raises our national repute in the eyes of the many millions of people committed to our charge. You may be also confident that the results are fully commensurate with the expenditure. As an old Finance Minister of India, I ought to know, if anybody does, when the money's worth is got by any operation; and myself having also administered, from first to last, provinces which comprise nearly half British India—I say that, of all the departments I have ever administered, I never saw one more efficient than the missionary department, and of all the hundreds of officers I had under my command,

European officers and gentlemen, I have never seen a better body of men than the Protestant missionaries. Of all the departments I have administered, I have never known one in which a more complete result was obtained than in the department—the grand department—which is represented by the Protestant missions. You may say that you ought to have not only statistics and reports to convince you, but that you ought to have corroboration of all the fine things that are told you. Now, for most of the statistics that are published by the missionaries you have absolute official verification. The census of the native Christians of India is as trustworthy as the census of the Europeans of British India itself. The main facts upon which you rely when you give your subscriptions to the missionary cause are as certain as any financial, or commercial, or political, or administrative fact whatever. As regards the evidence, you have that of some among the greatest administrators, the bravest soldiers, and the most skilful politicians that have ever adorned the annals of the East. I wish that some of them could be present upon this platform to bear witness of what they have seen and known. They are men accustomed to make responsible statements which shall command the trust of their countrymen, and even the reliance of the Government itself. They are not men likely to be misled by prejudice or by enthusiasm; on the contrary, they are cool, calculating men. Would that they were here to bear evidence to-night. But, having administered the finances of India for several years, having governed in succession some of her largest provinces, having also by fate been cast among the troubles and difficulties of almost every part of British India, from north to south, from east to west —I have thought it my duty, without claiming any credit whatever for myself, to stand before you, to give my personal testimony, and to add to that testimony whatever weight I could by presiding over your deliberations this evening.

# CHAPTER VIII.

## EFFECT OF RELIGIOUS THOUGHT AMONG INDIAN NATIVES.

[*Reprinted from the 'Fortnightly Review' for January* 1883.]

Intellectual and spiritual crisis impending in India—Opportunity thus offered to Christendom—Men looking retrospectively towards a golden age—The old-fashioned style of natives — The new style of educated men — Their national aspirations — Germ of representative institutions — Muhammadan expectation of an earthly Messiah — Brahmoism a new religion — Prospect of Christianity in India — Theological mysticism arising — Jealousy between rival creeds — Ideal of native existence — Tendency of religious sentiment.

As the material conditions—some favourable, others unfavourable—affecting India become better understood in England, so the mental and moral phases through which the population, composed of many diverse nationalities, is passing, seem to be attracting increased public attention. There has just appeared an interesting volume by Sir Alfred Lyall (now Lieutenant-Governor of the North-western Provinces of India), entitled 'Asiatic Studies.'* It consists of a series of essays, the chief of which are entitled: 'The Origin of Divine Myths in India,' 'The Influence upon Religion of a Rise in Morality,' 'Witchcraft and non-Christian Religions,' 'Missionary and non-Missionary Religions,' 'Islam in India,' 'Our Religious Policy in India,' 'The Religious Situation in India.' By these essays the reader is introduced into a part at least of the penetralia of the

* 'Asiatic Studies, Religious and Social.' By Sir Alfred C. Lyall, K.C.B., C.I.E. London: John Murray, 1882.

Indian mind, and into some among the recesses of the native heart. Thus an insight is gained into the spiritual nature of Orientals; its birth and growth in primitive ages; its expansion during the course of national history; its survival even under the crushing depression of conquest and the iron heel of revolution; its stagnation under the early influences of British rule; and its new development as Western knowledge is diffused by education. Those circumstances which tell in favour of, and those which militate against, the effective power of the Hindu religion are analysed. The reader is reminded that, although Hinduism is involuntarily loosening its grasp on some of the best classes, it is winning a fresh dominion—social and religious—over the aboriginal races to be numbered by millions. The temper of our Indian Mussulmans is examined with judgment and discrimination. It is shown that, notwithstanding fanaticism and bigotry, there is much sensible moderation and sound fidelity in this important section of the people. The position of the British Government, as a Christian power ruling over divers religious communities, is circumspectly considered, and a befitting attitude, during the intellectual and spiritual changes of the immediate future, is indicated.

The situation is well set forth in the following quotation from the last of these able essays:—

"We (the English) have now established reasonable personal security and free communications; we are giving to the Indians leisure and education, the scientific method and the critical spirit.

* * * * * *

"It is not easy to conceive any more interesting subject for historical speculation than the probable effect upon India, and consequently upon the civilisation of all India, of the English dominion; for though it would be most presumptuous to attempt any kind of prediction as to the nature or bent of India's religious future, yet we may look forward to a wide and rapid transformation in two or three generations if England's rule only be as durable as it has every appearance of being. It seems possible that the old gods of Hinduism will die in their new elements of intellectual light and air as quickly as a netful of fish lifted up out of the water. . . . . . Their primitive forms will fade and disappear suddenly, as witchcraft vanished from Europe. In the movement itself there is nothing new, but in India it promises to go on with a speed and intensity unprecedented; and herein lies the peculiar interest, perhaps the danger, of the Indian situation."

Surely it is a matter of duty as well as of interest for British people to enter into this speculation calmly and perseveringly, so that, by taking thought beforehand, the British Government may be prepared to guide the people of India aright through the intellectual and spiritual crisis which is already impending. After all, in England, an instructed and enlightened public opinion must ever be a powerful force in moulding the action of the State respecting India. In the formation of such an opinion this volume of Sir Alfred Lyall's will be a valuable help. He is known to be a thoughtful student and a deep observer as well as a man of action. His works in verse as well as in prose have been instinct with knowledge of native sentiment and imagination. He is well qualified to inform his countrymen regarding the thoughts which are surging in the breasts of Orientals, although no trace of the inward movement may be betrayed by their impassive aspect. His present volume invites the study of those who would govern India aright, and who would attend not only to her economic conditions but also to her mental phenomena.

One more passage from this volume may be cited as having interest for those concerned in the welfare of Christian missions:—

"Some may think that Christianity will, a second time in the world's history, step into the vacancy created by a great territorial empire, and occupy the tracts laid open by the upheaval of a whole continent to a new intellectual level. But the state of thought in Western Europe hardly encourages conjecture that India will receive from that quarter any such decisive impulse as that which overturned the decaying paganism of Greece and Rome."

Here is impartial testimony to the greatness of the opportunity which presents itself to Christendom, if only the state of thought among Christians themselves shall be favourable to the diffusion of Christianity among the heathen whose natural spiritualism is being moved by Western civilisation; if only there be in the Western Christians enough of faith, fervour, zeal, and earnestness. But if those qualities shall in any degree fail, then full use will not be made of this momentous opportunity. In view of these facts a brief inquiry into what may be compendiously described as the under-current of native thought in India can scarcely fail to be useful, and to that I now propose to address myself.

At first sight many observers might be of opinion that among the mass of the native population no such under-currents, as have just been spoken of, exist, that the minds of the vast majority of natives are quite superficial, being absorbed by the commonest affairs of life, and that such people scarcely think at all. There may no doubt be some *primâ facie* ground for such an opinion. The common folk do not at all exercise their minds in public affairs; nevertheless regarding the matters of their humble society, their caste, their festivals, their priests, they think for themselves as much as the corresponding classes do in civilised countries. But further, they are apt to follow the thoughts of various classes among their countrymen who think very much, and who constantly ponder over problems moral, social, and political. In fact, notwithstanding any appearances to the contrary, there are under-currents of thought perpetually moving in the native mind. The case may be likened to the well-known condition of the water in the Lower Ganges and its affluents. The surface, though always in swift and noiseless motion, is smooth to the eye, but underneath there are unseen currents of extraordinary potency. We may hope, however, that the analogy ends here; for these under-currents in the Ganges waters are notoriously dangerous; whereas, perhaps, on examination it may be found that, with good management on the British side, the under-currents in the native mind may be kept free from political peril.

It is difficult to summarise concisely what two hundred and fifty millions of people are presumably saying to themselves every day. But probably the sum of their thoughts amounts to this, that they are, by the will of an inscrutable fate, living under foreign rule; that they are ineffably better, nicer, pleasanter people than their rulers; that they have a purity of descent, a grandeur of tradition, an antiquity of system with which an European nation has nothing to compare; that despite their union, socially and morally, they cannot hold together politically; that consequently they have fallen under the control, first of Turks or Mongols who had force alone, and now of the British who have both force and sagacity; that great care must be taken lest the unavoidable contact with white people in business and in affairs should lead to social intercourse where the gulf of separation ought to be preserved; that British rule cannot last for ever, and meanwhile its advantages must be accepted with scanty thanks or recognition; that doubtless on some great day there will be successors to the heroes of old who may bring back the "golden age" (in eastern phrase); that this prospect, however, being wrapt in the haze of sunshine, is too dim to be within the practical domain of hope.

This turn of thought is quite compatible with a material contentment and a satisfaction respecting the external results of British rule. The vast majority think favourably of the British Government and wish it well; they find fault with it in several ways, but do not condemn it generally—on the contrary, they fully admit that it is good on the whole; they regard it, too, as an emanation from a mighty power across the sea, at the head of which power is a sovereign; in their minds the attributes of royalty are supremely august, and these attributes they accord to the British Queen. It is all this which people mean when they affirm that in the main the natives are loyal. But, notwithstanding all this, the natives never forget that British rule has the necessarily inherent defect of being foreign. For it, then, they seldom feel patriotic sentiments in the English sense of that term.

In the earlier days of British rule, say two generations ago, the contrast between order and disorder, between the reign of law and the reign of plunder, between peaceful industry and revolutionary tumult, was strongly felt. Such phrases as "the blessings of British rule" meant something palpable and tangible. Every one had a standard, present in his own mind, whereby to measure the merits of that rule by comparing it with what had gone before. The sense of relief after suffering and anxiety was so great as to overpower any reflection as to whether the new rule was foreign or indigenous, or whether it had angularities incompatible with native genius and feeling. It had one overwhelming merit, in that it answered for order. This merit, like Aaron's rod, swallowed up all other considerations. But, in the same manner as other good things, it wears away with time. Other generations grow up that have never personally tasted the misrule which their fathers used to compare with the British administration. Paternal or ancestral traditions are very lasting with them, and doubtless they have a shrewd idea of what used to happen in the evil days. But this idea cannot have a tithe of the vividness with which the memory of these things was seared and branded upon the minds of their forefathers. They had indeed a flavour and a *soupçon* of this during the war of the mutinies twenty-five years ago. Thus their eyes were opened as to what might happen if British rule were to be withdrawn. Still their apprehensions are comparatively sluggish. In this way the British Government, not through its own default, but actually by reason of its long-sustained merits, is actually losing one of the pristine elements of its popularity. Thus, too, a new difficulty has set in from the time that the empire was thoroughly well established. The natives criticise and criticise; no government can be fully proof against criticism, much less a foreign one. Together with captious fault-finding no adequate allowance is made for the cardinal virtues of the system.

Many remarkable individuals, in number limited, still exist, who are really interesting as examples of feeling or of thought, which will pass away with their death. They have proved fitting subjects for descriptive poetry: and it is historically important to have a literary photograph of them while they are still in the land of the living. Their minds, however, dwell on the past, not on the immediate future, hardly even on the present. Thus they do not constitute a class which has to be reckoned with seriously.

The foregoing description is applicable to what may be termed the old style of natives.

But there has sprung up among the natives a new style which is produced by the Western education under British rule. These men hold, though with less of intensity and tenacity, most of the views summarised above. They are beginning to entertain in addition some peculiar views of their own. They hope to improve themselves by means of Western science and knowledge. This improvement of theirs, however, is to take the form of self-development, not of self-change. They are not thereby to be Europeanised but are to remain Asiatics. They will conscientiously search for abstract truth, sternly rejecting the rubbish with which, in recent ages, Hinduism has been cumbered, but fondly gazing retrospectively upon the records of primitive times. That there must be much of crudity in their speculations is shown by the fact that men claiming to walk by the light of Western civilisation should persist in looking back towards hoar antiquity, as if therefrom the art of true progress could be learnt. But their candour, their intellectual honesty, their moral worth, are indisputable. In regard to the tightness with which the social yoke is fixed on the necks of the people, the rigour with which the tyranny of caste is enforced, the moral torture which can be inflicted on those whose nature is extraordinarily sensitive to the displeasure of relatives, the pains of ostracism—these men must have braved much that to them was terrible, and suffered much that to them was acutely distressful. But, having made up their minds to break off from the superstitions of their fathers, they never look back. They reject palpable error without any hesitation, they repudiate the religious efficacy of caste, even though they retain its social distinctions, they believe in the innate superiority of their race over the European races, they wonder at the obscuration of their star, but hope that its brightness will yet be restored. It is paradoxical on their part to imagine that Western enlightenment can be made the means of vindicating the dictum *ex oriente lux*, but such is the substratum of their thoughts. Though willing to learn what they can from Europe, they yet look upon such learning as a means of recovering the intellectual heritage of their ancestors. Though quite alive to the wonders of physical science, they probably think that such science is subordinate to some higher and occult purposes of abstract truth.

Several sects under various local designations hold views of this nature, differing in particulars, but generally alike. This philosophy (if such it can be termed) is spreading fast, and seems likely to embrace the majority of the educated classes throughout India.

These under-currents of native thought unquestionably portend that the British Government, in order to preserve a moderate and essential degree of popularity with the natives, must rest its case on something more than the establishment of external order, and the increase of material prosperity. As education spreads, the natives will not only criticise, but also carp and cavil. In so far as the criticism is just, it must be met by reforms. Therefore fresh departures administratively must from time to time be taken. While primary education is not valued as much as we desire, while disappointment is felt respecting the attitude of the masses in this matter—superior education is eagerly desired by the middle classes. Why is the Government urged to apply its resources to this superior education, why are sacrifices made by parents to secure it, why are donations and subscriptions given in aid of it by the wealthy? Because the natives hope thereby to win for themselves a larger share than heretofore in the administration of their own country, and to acquire some of the advantages hitherto enjoyed almost exclusively by Europeans. In justice it must be admitted that this hope is a reasonable one.

There is also portended a desire for what may be termed political privileges culminating in something like representative institutions. There is already a vague hankering for such privileges; although in respect to political "representation," the natives have not yet conceived any definite notions, yet their thoughts are tending in that direction, even though they may be unaware of that tendency

Thus, though the natives are very far from aspiring to autonomy, they always have thought much of their nationality, and are thinking more and more of that as education spreads. These thoughts of theirs are growing into a moral force which the British Government must recognise. The significance of these thoughts is proved in most (though by no means in all) of the lesser outbreaks or disturbances which occur from time to time in India, and which it would be tedious to particularise. The strongest example, however, is to be drawn from the War of the Mutinies during three terrible years, 1857 to 1859. One among the lessons learnt by Anglo-Indian statesmen from those grave events was this, that when once a spirit of fanaticism and of national ambition shall arise, once a resolution to have done with foreign masters shall be formed, considerations of material advantage, of regularly received emoluments, of security to agriculture, trade and industry, are flung to the winds.

Although men are much wiser after these events, yet if before those events they had questioned themselves regarding the probability of such occurrences, the answer would have been that surely natives had become too deeply interested in the continuance of peace, too sensible of the benefits thereby acquired, too timid of risking their prosperity, to think of insurrection. This was true indeed of the mass of voiceless easy-going people, but not at all true of many classes whose influence would for the moment determine the course of events. With such classes the benefit from British rule was counted as dross in comparison with the pleasure of reasserting Indian nationality. The bearing of the Brahmans in Benares, of the territorial classes in Oude and Behar, of the Mahrattas in Western India, of the Muhammadans almost everywhere, of the Sikhs after (though not during) the crisis—attests what was to us a melancholy truth.

The next question to be asked and answered is—Have the natives in their inner minds any religious convictions which make them believe in a future when an earthly messiah shall have made them the lords of the land they live in? In order to answer this question, the population must be divided into three categories, namely the Muhammadans, the Hindus, and those who acknowledge neither Islam nor Hinduism. The Muhammadans in India comprise about one-fifth of the whole population, and have a full share of whatever resolution, capacity, or vivacity may pertain to the people at large. They certainly have religious convictions of the most definite character. They believe in God, in a future state, in a judgment for blessing or for condemnation, in Muhammad as the prophet of God, in the Korân as a divine revelation, in the Caliphs as successors of the Prophet, and in many saints. They believe, too, in the coming of an earthly Messiah, in the person of the Imâm Mehdî, who is to be the seventh and last of the Imâms, six having already appeared in historic times. The Imâm Mehdî is to inaugurate an era when Islam now militant is to be finally triumphant, not only in India, but in other regions besides. This belief is an active principle, and allusion is made to it periodically whenever any trouble is in the air. It is bruited abroad explicitly on the average once, perhaps twice, in every decade; and in a less explicit manner it is mentioned frequently. According to that religious conviction, the Indian Muhammadans would be their own masters, and would be lords of the land they live in.

But this view cannot be gratifying or satisfactory to the Hindus, who comprise full three-fifths of the population. For it assumes that they are to accept the Muhammadan faith, or else be utterly subject to Muhammadan rule until they shall be converted to Islam. But they do not trouble themselves regarding this idea, which is regarded by them as impossible of realisation, or as a harmless lucubration.

It is hard to say whether the Hindus in the mass have that which could properly be called religious conviction. Many pious and philosophic individuals, some learned classes, even some ascetics, doubtless have convictions worthy of the name. But for the mass of Hindus the religion, or in fact the superstition, is so grossly absurd, the multifarious deities are so grotesquely imaged, participation in divine attributes is so largely allowed to a great caste of Brahmins, who are very human indeed, that the sentiments of the worshippers can scarcely be dignified with the name of religious convictions. The conception of divinity, too, is so sensuous as to debase and corrupt any sentiments that may gather round it. Still the ordinary Hindu of to-day has a vague impression that after death he will be absorbed body and soul into a supreme being who is beyond all the gods and goddesses. But his notion of a blessed reward for virtue, or of a future punishment for sin, is so shadowy as to be almost evanescent. Many observers have thought that it is this want of active belief in a judgment to come which causes the natives to face inevitable death with such stoic calmness. The Hindus have indeed a moral code binding on their conscience and conduct; they seldom or never ask themselves whether this code is an emanation from the supreme being; if pressed they would doubtless acknowledge that, originally, it must have so emanated.

The Hindus have no definite expectation of an earthly messiah visiting India to rehabilitate the Hindu religion and to re-establish Hindu domination. Still a vague idea of this description does sometimes float across their minds. Some of their chief gods are deified princes; and there are mythical heroes of more than mortal prowess (Pandus), the mention of whom has an exhilarating effect on a Hindu audience. Allusion to such persons is sometimes made in proclamations, or other notices privately circulated, for raising political excitement. In short, the Hindus have a transcendental notion of the afflatus which rested on their progenitors in a remote antiquity. They trust that hereafter this ancestral spirit will descend upon some heroes, who shall restore all that has been lost to the Hindu race during many ages. But they do not pretend to discern any way in which the fulfilment of such a hope can happen.

Allusion has been made to the new school which is the product of Western civilisation. The natives of this school have many religious convictions of a negative kind, but less of a positive nature. The Indian name assumed by the most prominent among them is "Brahmo;" some of them have adopted, apparently from Transatlantic quarters, the designation of Theosophist—and by the best English authority they are termed the Hindu religious reformers. The originator was Ram-Mohan-Roy, and the best expounder now living is Keshab Chander Sen, both of Calcutta. But ramifications of this sect, and kindred sects moving in a parallel direction, have spread throughout the three Presidencies of Bengal, Madras, and Bombay. The intellectual tendencies of these sects have been just described, and inquirers will ask whether the religion of these people is at all likely to be the religion of the future in India.

On its negative side this religion renounces superstition,

paganism, monstrosities, and absurdities of all sorts. It abjures atheism and materialism. It repudiates Muhammadanism, Buddhism, and Hinduism. It regards Christianity not as a religion to be adopted, but as one of several ways leading towards pure and abstract truth. It looks towards the Vedas and other ancient writings, handed down from the Aryan Hindus, as constituting another of these ways. It holds the minds of its adherents as open mirrors ready to catch the rays of truth whencesoever coming. It fails to find that this truth has anywhere been finally and definitely revealed. Then, on its positive side, it is theism, including faith in a Supreme Being, in the abstract principles of right and wrong, in the immortality of the soul, in the accountability of mankind during a future state for good or evil done during this life. The dictates of the conscience, the power of the moral sense are fully acknowledged. But there hangs about all the tenets much of haziness, dreaminess and mysticism generally. This faith is likely to become the religion of the immediate future among the educated classes of Hindus, but will hardly supplant Hinduism among the masses for a long time to come.

Christianity has not as yet spread sufficiently to become an actual power in the country. It hardly possesses half a million of native adherents, but that number may, at an ordinary rate of progress, from conversion and natural increment, be augmented within a generation to something between one and two millions. Whether there will be any extraordinary accession from the ranks of the Hindu theists it is impossible to hazard a prediction.

Then there arises the question, if this theological mysticism exists, has it any political meaning? Does it, or does it not, foreshadow danger to British rule? It will have been seen from the foregoing observations that this theological mysticism does exist. For the present, and for the immediate future, it does not foreshadow danger to British rule. On the contrary its political tendency is favourable to the existing centre of power and adverse to any disturbance. It is not hostile to the Christian religion; on the contrary it admires Christianity in the main, as supplying a pattern for human conduct. It assumes the continuance of Western enlightenment and the progress of education after the Western model, and this assumption is essential. Without the maintenance of British rule for a long time to come, these advantages are manifestly unobtainable; it is never pretended that they can be had without British aid. The educated natives hope that, possessing these advantages, they will peacefully win the desired improvement in their status. They have no thought of winning this by violent or revolutionary means. They know too, that this could never be won by relapsing into the old native system. They have learnt to look at public affairs through Western spectacles, and to think in Western phrase. Thus they are disposed to cling to the Western ideal. Their political conclusion then is to preserve the existing status.

For the distant future, however, this new religion clearly has a political meaning, which is this, that the Indian nation, emancipated from British leading-strings, should govern itself. But avowedly this meaning refers to a time so far ahead as to be beyond the region of practical politics. It therefore does not foreshadow anything which could be termed danger to British rule. But existing alongside of, or in combination with, other movements, it will have a political force to be borne in mind by Anglo-Indian statesmen.

There are, indeed, some educated natives who may be not unreasonably suspected of disloyalty, or at least of hostility to British institutions and dislike to the British nation—though it is hoped that such cases are somewhat exceptional and abnormal. It will be found, however, that this hostility on the part of individuals does not arise from their Western education. It arises from the old prejudices and the old sentiments of nationality, which that education has not subdued. Many, perhaps most, educated natives cease to be politically Hindus. Others, despite their Western education, remain as Hindus of the old school, and of these some are apt to become disloyal. It is the sight of such occasional disloyalty that causes some observers to apprehend political mischief as a consequence of education. This view, however, is superficial, for the mischief exists not by reason of the education but in spite of it. Without the education it would have existed in a worse degree.

It may next be asked, how far does jealousy between the different creeds in India paralyse their activity for any united purpose in hostility to their British rulers? Now the Hindus do indirectly proselytize among Indians who are outside caste, or who, being aborigines, are supposed to be without any formal religion. But they have not ordinarily any thought of making proselytes among other races that have settled religious systems. According to their principle, a Hindu is born in rather than admitted to Hinduism, *nascitur non fit.* They would not dream, if they had supreme power, of making converts among Indian Muhammadans. On the other hand, the Muhammadans, if they were in the ascendant, would undoubtedly seek to make converts among the Hindus by persuasion if possible, or failing that, by force. Their absolutism in this respect would be tempered only by the probability of resistance. The jealousy then, if it were ever evoked, would be on the part of the Muhammadans and not of the Hindus. But while both are under the British Government, as a common master, the sense of religious difference is suppressed. When political excitement arises, the enemies of the British Government always appeal to Hindus and Muhammadans together. Many instances have occurred of seditious or treasonable notices being expressly addressed to both alike. Doubtless the foreign government gains something from the fact of there being these two religions, and from the diversity of interest, sentiment, and sympathy, which thus arises. Still jealousy between the different creeds might somewhat affect, but would not paralyse, their activity for an united purpose in hostility to their British rulers. The British Government might simultaneously have enemies both among Hindus and Muhammadans. These hostile elements would combine, without any hindrance what ever on account of difference in religion. If they were to be victorious then they might begin to quarrel, owing to religious difference among other reasons; but until victory were secured they would sink such difference. If then political conjunctures were to arise, in any way compromising or threatening the safety of British dominion, no reliance whatever could be placed in the religious differences between Hindus and Muhammadans as weakening hostile combinations among the natives.

Finally, let us see whether there is any esoteric or spiritual propaganda which may at any moment find expression in an exoteric and material form, dangerous to the empire of India, as now existing, or to the ascendancy of any Western nation.

The answers to the preceding questions have implied that there is an ideal of native existence towards which some people are yearning. But the ideal is too dim for the yearning to be very strong. Then it will, from these answers, have been seen that there is an esoteric and spiritual propaganda limited in extent at present, but growing steadily if not rapidly. This propaganda does find exoteric expression in a marked manner. It has induced the legislature to enact laws for the performance of marriages between those who do not belong to Hinduism, Buddhism, or Muhammadanism. In as much as it possesses an organization, appoints office bearers, reckons its open and avowed adherents by tens of thousands, causes chapels to be built in which congregations worship, it must be held to have assumed a material form. But as yet this form is not dangerous to British rule and Western ascendancy, nor are the tendencies of the movement objectionable politically. This answer then is virtually a summary of a portion of what has already been set forth.

If the British suppressed, or even discouraged the movement, the results might be different; but on the contrary, the freest play and the fullest scope are accorded to it. If the Government refused to concede anything, then discontent might accrue. Concessions, however, are made, not indeed sufficient to produce plenary contentment, but still enough to make people hope for more than what they already have. It is this hopefulness which produces loyalty.

On the other hand, this spirit induces men to find fault with the Government for not moving faster in the direction of beneficence; it urges them to demand that positions of responsibility and importance shall be more and more entrusted to natives, that on the one hand taxation shall be revised and the State income thereby diminished, and that simultaneously improvements shall be introduced augmenting the expenditure,—often forgetting the impossibility of all these things being done at once. It is this apparent disregard of practicability, administrative or financial, that imparts to many British observers an unfavourable impression regarding the native character. This effect is heightened when they see that native writers and speakers support their recommendations by means of statements which unjustly vilify everything British in India. The natives fail to see how greatly they damage their cause by this style of argument. Still, if the argument be examined by Englishmen who can "read between the lines," it will be found that there is an obverse and a reverse; on the one side the merits of British rule are depicted, on the other side the demerits. The description both of merits and demerits is worked up with Oriental hyperbole. As a counterfoil to undue laudation there is undeserved disparagement. The contrast thus produced is like a picture wherein the lights are too white, the shades too black, and the colours crudely vivid. The real object of the vilification, however, is to make the most of existing defects in order to incite the Government to reform and improvement. This method is frequently adopted by natives who are manifestly bound to the British connection in almost every possible way, and who cannot mean really to be disloyal. On the other hand, such fault-finding may verge, and has sometimes verged, upon treason; in that case it should of course be dealt with according to law. But so long as it remains within the largest latitude allowable for criticism, as it generally does, it releases mental steam and prevents disloyalty arising.

In fine, the tendency of sentiment, moral and religious, among the educated natives, appears to be beneficial politically. It might indeed become dangerous if the Government were unreforming and unprogressive. But it is an element of safety, as the Government is both reforming and progressive, walking in the light of the age. It stimulates improvement, produces hopefulness, counteracts bigotry, weakens fanaticism. It depends on Western enlightenment, which postulates the continuance of the existing administration. Thus, on the whole, the political effect of religious thought in India is favourable to British rule.

# CHAPTER IX.

## THE DUTY OF BRITISH PEOPLE TOWARDS INDIA.

[*Speech delivered before the East India Association, in London, March* 1882.]

Past services of the East India Association in England — Its independent and impartial attitude — The material objects to which its attention is directed — The moral and social improvements which it advocates — The application of British capital to railways and canals in India — Sanitation, forestry, agriculture and emigration — Educational efforts by the State — Superior instruction and primary education — Honorary offices and the elective principle for the natives — Kindness to natives visiting England.

It now devolves upon me to deliver to you an inaugural speech upon my assuming the honourable office of President of the East India Association. One reason which caused me to accept the office was that the Association has now existed for more than fifteen years, during which period it has carried some weight in influencing public opinion in this country. It has won the support and confidence of the natives of India; its representations have been listened to by some of the highest authorities; and it has had many great men connected with it. I had the less hesitation in accepting the Presidency when I understood that my immediate predecessor was Sir Laurence Peel—a name honoured and respected by the whole of the Anglo-Indian community. I also saw that connected with the Association there was a nobleman who has done so much for the cause of humanity all over the world—I mean the venerable Earl of Shaftesbury—so distinguished a statesman as the Marquis of Salisbury, and three men so well known for everything that relates to the welfare of the people of India, as Sir Bartle Frere, Sir Charles Trevelyan, and Sir Henry Rawlinson, the last of whom I may call an Asiatic statesman. It now devolves upon me to explain to you what, according to my humble comprehension, are the duties, the purposes, and the functions of this Association.

In the first place, we should remember that our Association consists, firstly, of Anglo-Indians who have retired from active life in India, either official or unofficial; and, secondly, of natives of India who are resident in England; besides those many excellent members, European and Native, who reside in India. Then our duties seem to me to divide themselves into two main parts—viz., first, to enlighten and inform English opinion, as much as possible, upon all matters relating to India; secondly, to make, from time to time, to the India Office or the authorities in this country (England) such representations as may seem desirable upon the current course of affairs. Therefore we must induce men of original and independent minds, men of suggestive thought, as well as large experience, to come here, and deliver addresses and lectures to us from time to time. But if we are to have men of such independent minds, they will be sure to hold strong and divergent opinions, and they will be apt to have ideas directed to, or focussed, as it were, on one particular point, and, consequently, in the lectures and addresses there will be various matters which will not command absolute assent. Therefore, I think, in the first place, we must be vigilant not to adopt entirely the theories, crotchets, and hobbies—if I may so express myself—which will be from time to time presented to us. We desire to have the advantage of the hobbies; only we must not, we cannot, undertake to ride them ourselves. We desire also to hear the crotchets, as they may prove instructive and interesting; only we, as an Association, do not undertake to retail them as pure metal, with our own hall-mark—as I may call it—attached to them.

Another thing to be guarded against is this. We have many accomplished and learned native gentlemen in this Association. With all deference to our native fellow-subjects in this country, I must say that they occasionally make speeches in public which are really, as efforts of oratory or rhetoric, honourable to them, but which nevertheless teem with exaggeration. The native gentleman, speaking in England, is apt to state his case with a good deal of Eastern imagination and Oriental imagery, which may elicit a passing cheer, but which ends in distorting the subject, so that, after all, we have, not a picture, but a caricature. Now, I would warn my Indian fellow-subjects that the English people are, above all things, plain-judging, accurate, and discriminating; and although any exaggeration may, for the moment, evoke applause, nevertheless, in the end, it will prevent the speaker carrying the weight to which his statements would otherwise entitle him. A further source of danger is the running into the extreme of what is nowadays called pessimism. There is the other extreme—optimism—of course; but, on the whole, optimism is a safer thing than pessimism, because pessimism is apt to make the people of Britain despair regarding the future of India, and begin to ask themselves, "If the country is in such a wretched state, if agriculture is being carried on at a loss, and the people are too thick upon the land, and are gradually starving, what is the use of taking any interest in such a declining Empire?" We who know India, are well aware that there is a better and brighter side of the national picture. So, if we countenanced such pessimist representations, our Association would soon lose its hold upon public opinion, and we should be roughly contradicted by a reference to the plainest facts of the day. Nevertheless we need not be thought to discourage any pessimist members who may honour us by delivering addresses here, because no doubt they do good in warning the Government and the public of the dangers which environ the paths of even the wariest administrators.

One more word regarding the dangers to which we are subject. I understand that some of the native gentlemen who are resident in this country are apt to fall into some of the atheistic ways that may be current in the present age. Now, we may admit that there are many temptations to this path; nevertheless I hold that we should really, as Christians and as Englishmen, warn our native fellow-subjects in this country that the British people will, in the mass, give no countenance to what passes for "free-thought" or atheism in their Indian fellow-subjects. They will not, indeed, press the natives to become Christians, as the adoption of Christianity must be the result of private conviction. They will even acknowledge thankfully the religious sentiment which pervades many of the new sects among the Hindus which are rising into prominence, the Brahmos and others. They will sympathize with the moral, intellectual, and spiritual views, the religious aspirations and difficulties of their Asiatic fellow-subjects; but to anything like atheism they can never lend their countenance. Our native fellow-subjects may be certain that, despite all the alleged tendencies of the nineteenth century, there is as much religious earnestness now in Britain as in any preceding century, and in many important respects much more than there ever has been, enough to justify the assertion that in the main the British are a religious and God-fearing people.

I hope I may be excused for having so unreservedly stated the dangers that beset an Association like this; and now I proceed, in the briefest and most rapid manner, to recapitulate some important matters to which our attention should be constantly directed, and upon which our gaze should ever be fixed. These subjects are, first, material, and, secondly, moral and social.

Now, among the many objects of material importance to India, the first appears to me to be the application of British capital to the development of the resources of the country. This application of capital will be partly private and partly public (that is, expended some by individuals or corporations, and some by the Government), and it should be our endeavour to gather up the threads of all valuable information which may be interesting to the individual capitalist and to the moneyed classes who are likely to invest some of their accumulated savings in the improvement of India. One great application of capital will be that on the part of the Government. The Government capital will be utilized largely for purposes of irrigation; and we who have lived in India can never do wrong in keeping the claims of irrigation constantly before the public of England and the Government of India, more particularly as experience shows that this is a matter which the private capitalist cannot conveniently compass. Several Irrigation Companies have tried, and have not succeeded; and thus the most important means for the material improvement of India, if attended to at all, must be taken in hand by the Government.

Then as regards railways, we are assured that much has been done by the State and much more by those justly honoured and now historic Guaranteed Companies. This matter of railways offers a field to which private capital may be greatly attracted, provided only the branch railways which remain to be made in the future shall be constructed in a cheap and economical style; in the fashion of what may be called temporary railways, which can be worked to the benefit of the country, and at the same time shall be sufficiently good to pay interest to the private capitalists who may invest in them.

Another matter which we cannot too earnestly impress on the attention of all concerned is sanitation. This is a matter to be advocated from Britain through British opinion. There is no matter which more entirely concerns the physical welfare of the Indian people; nevertheless, there is no matter regarding which the natives of India show so little thought, and so little appreciation. That being the case, it becomes the more incumbent upon us, as civilized foreigners, to press this matter first upon our native fellow-subjects, and, secondly, upon public opinion, in the conviction that what England thinks to-day India will think to-morrow, or, at least, the day after.

Further, a matter upon which opinion in India is as yet uninstructed both among natives and Europeans, is the subject of forestry. I rejoice that this most important matter—which nearly concerns the future climatic condition of India, and which partly explains the sequence of droughts and famines, and the like—is being earnestly taken up by the Society of Arts in London, and by the Scottish Arboricultural Society of Edinburgh.

Then there is the use of manure. The great desideratum for Indian agriculture is manure of various sorts. The soil is becoming exhausted, slowly and imperceptibly perhaps, but still surely, owing to the non-application of manure for its proper purpose. What should be used as manure is largely used for fuel, because there is no wood-supply available; the absence of a wood-supply arises from there being no adequate system of forestry; and that, again, is ascribable to the want of education of public opinion in this most essential matter.

As regards the land, there are two or three points to which I think we should diligently attend. First, there is the extension of tenant-right. The rights of landlords, great and small, the status of peasant proprietors, of occupancy cultivators and of sub-proprietors, are, on the whole, well arranged throughout India; but there still remains much to be done regarding a class which numbers many millions—the ordinary cultivators and tenants-at-will. Here, I say, very much remains to be accomplished; and I earnestly hope that the advocacy of this Association will never be wanting towards that end. Another matter nearly concerning the welfare of the great peasant proprietary, who form the very backbone of the country and people, is a reform in the law of debtor and creditor. Indeed, the peasant indebtedness, in spite of our good administration and the improvements in property in land, is one of the curses of the country. Although I think most highly of our enlightened legislation, as a rule, and regard it as pregnant with blessings to the people, it is very defective in this respect.

Another matter regarding which this Association might exercise an influence for good, is emigration. There is no doubt that, although India can well sustain all the 250,000,000 of people who stand upon its surface, although she has much waste land available, there are, notwithstanding, many districts which are utterly over-populated, and in which the population considerably increases every decade. These districts may well send forth hundreds of thousands to create new Indias in the Tropics, or to colonize in Madagascar, the West Indies, or South America. This is a matter in which our Association may exercise a beneficial influence. We may constantly obtain information regarding the condition of those classes who may be prepared to send forth labourers; that information we may constantly communicate to those classes in this country who are interested in our colonies. All those colonies which I have mentioned, and several others, have representatives in this country—representatives who are always inquiring about the supply of cheap labour from India. Let us help to keep them thoroughly informed on that point.

Then, again, from time to time, it may be well for us to say something about opium. That is a matter upon which there is a great divergency of opinion. I, for one, wholly differ from those benevolent and excellent people who are raising an agitation on the subject in this country; and, having observed the use and abuse of the drug, and knowing what actually are the habits of the Asiatic populations, whether Indian or Chinese, I am prepared to justify our present position. One item of Indian revenue is from opium, and it is as legitimate a revenue as that of the English Government from the excise or customs on wines and spirits. Again, the Chinese themselves grow the opium poppy more largely than the Indians. If, then, we believe that opium in moderation is no more harmful to the Chinese than wine and beer are to the English people; if we believe that the taxation levied by the Indian Government on opium, instead of encouraging consumption, rather checks it by making the drug dear; if we believe that nothing but harm can come to the Chinese themselves from the destruction of that revenue—which revenue really renders the drug expensive—then, I say, it is our duty to lend our weight and our support to the authorities, and to make such representations as shall bring conviction to the minds of those classes in England who are ready to be convinced when good reason is given them.

Trusting that you will excuse my running so rapidly over the subjects, I will at once turn to the second division of my theme; namely, the moral and social improvements in which our advocacy may be beneficial to the people of India. The first of these, of course, is education; and education is, of all others, the most legitimate subject for our deliberations. You hear a great deal about high education *versus* primary education; and there are many people who will speak disparagingly before the British public regarding the results of high education in India. Let me assure you, as one who has but recently returned from that country, that the high education afforded mainly by the Government and partly by private institutions, chiefly missionary, has been fraught with blessings to the upper and middle classes of the people of India. It is not alone that the intellects of the men, thus highly educated, have been improved, but their moral tone has been raised, and they have become trustworthy gentlemen. In fact, the improvement in character, the mental and moral elevation, which have resulted are greater than anything I ever expected to live to see. That being the case, we should not countenance those who would disparage the high education merely because it is wished to advocate primary education. People in this, as in other things, look at only one side; they perceive the benefits of primary education, and have all their mental rays concentrated upon it, and so they fail to perceive the benefit of high education. This superior education is, as I have said, carried on mainly by the

Government, but partly by private agencies. Some people think that the private agencies, which chiefly consist of missionary institutions, could be left to undertake all that is necessary in respect of high education. Now, having been myself an earnest advocate of Missions, and being necessarily very well acquainted with all the operations of the great Missionary Societies in India, I venture to affirm that the Missionary Societies have done already their utmost in respect of high education, and have not the means to do essentially more than they are doing in this respect. If high education were left to them alone, they would not prove equal to the task: and, therefore, if high education is to be adequately afforded, the Indian Government must do a great deal. It may be that the Government operations could be improved; it may be that their assistance is more needed in the interior of the country than in the Presidency towns. In the interior of the country you find very few men well educated; and the only chance of increasing the number of the colleges in the interior of the country is by the intervention of the Government. It is most important that Government should not compete injuriously with private institutions; and Government does not do so. On the contrary, the fees of the Government colleges are higher than those of the missionary colleges, and perhaps as high as the people can afford to pay. Throughout India the rule has been that Government shall give one-half, and the people one-half; and that rule, on the whole, is carried out from the top to the bottom of our educational system. You will find that those who receive a high education pay half of the cost. We should be glad if they could be made to pay more; but if you make high education too expensive in India, you will restrict it to the well-to-do and the rich, and that, I am sure, no Indian philanthropist would wish to do. We desire to raise up any natives of talent to whatever class they belong, and it would be hopeless for such men—youths of genius and of high moral qualifications—to obtain superior education if they have the misfortune to be born of poor parents; and, therefore, if the fees must be kept high, we must agitate for a large number of scholarships to be constantly offered by the Government for competition by the best youths throughout the whole Empire of India, with the effect that the youth who wins a scholarship gets his education almost gratuitously, and that, in order to win this, he must have capacity and character above his compeers. Nevertheless, I quite admit that the development of the grant-in-aid system deserves constant attention on the part of the Government and of the public.

Now, as regards primary education, no doubt that is the crying want of India; for although there are as many as 2,000,000 of students in the schools, which may sound very fine, yet after all it is a very small number relatively to the number of people in India. What are 2,000,000 among 250,000,000? You have 3,000,000 of children at school in Great Britain, where the population is not one-ninth as large as in India; so that there is a great distinction between the development of education in Britain and in India. Primary education is the *crux* of Indian administration; you will find it a most difficult problem that awaits solution. We are doing our best to induce the peasants to send their children to school; still the total result is insufficient. I fear that before long we shall have to come to compulsory education in some mild shape for the rural districts. It has been accepted absolutely by every great nation of continental Europe, and now is at work in a gentler form among the English people. Though I do not recommend that compulsion should be attempted universally in India, I do not forget that the students —boys—come chiefly from the artisan class, and very little from the agricultural class, and it is the agricultural class which is most important, and which most needs education. I am sure, then, there are many sections of the agricultural class to whom a certain sort of compulsion might be applied, if the Government had the moral courage to do so. It is by an

Association such as ours investigating these matters, and making due representations to the public and to the Government, that an effect will be produced on the Legislature, and something will be done to compel the proprietary and landed classes, at least, in India to educate their children. Much, too, must be done towards the encouragement of vernacular literature. One of the most important problems we originally had to solve in India was that we found no vernacular literature worth mentioning. But within fifty years we have created a vernacular literature, which, though it may not be fully understood by ourselves, has been pronounced by scholars in France and Germany to be among the greatest of the many glories of England in the East; but much remains to be done before all the 60,000 schools which exist in India are properly supplied with class-books. This is a matter upon which we can offer not only information, but also great encouragement, to many persons in this country who may be disposed to assist the natives of India in the direction of improving their vernacular literature; and though the Society for Promoting Christian Vernacular Education has, no doubt, a religious object, with which we shall sympathize, but which we cannot directly promote, it still must be conceded that the Society is doing yeoman's work in the extension of the vernacular literature of India.

Before I quit the subject of education, I must remind you that the best opinions now concur in this,—that hitherto our education has been too exclusively literary and philosophic, and not sufficiently practical and scientific. We are doing much in one or two great branches of applied science—in medicine and in civil engineering—but there are still important fields in which much remains to be done, especially in those sciences —like chemistry, botany, mineralogy, geology, and physical geography—which have an obvious practical value. Above all, there is agriculture. I suppose there is no matter so important for the future welfare of India as the diffusion of agricultural education; and if we are to apply anything like compulsion upon the agricultural classes, in respect to having their children educated, we must take care that the primary instruction shall be of a practical character; and if so, above all things, it must be agricultural. Nothing would exert so powerful an effect as a reason for our having to take any stringent or compulsory measures as the certainty that agriculture was the first and foremost subject of the national education.

Further, we may do much as regards rendering the industrial arts of India popular, and respected by our fellow-countrymen in England. There was a danger at one time lest, while exhibiting to the natives the fruits of European art and culture, we should choke and stifle their own. That danger, however, has been overpassed, and now the real merits of Indian art are beginning to be appreciated in England. It is even recognised that, despite all the advantages which our Western civilisation has given us, we are really, as artists, not equal, nationally, to the Indians, the Chinese, or the Japanese; setting aside, of course, the individual artists of genius who may be among us. This is a field in which our Association may still do much to gradually enlighten our English fellow-countrymen respecting the artistic tendency of the natives hereditarily transmitted among them from generation to generation, and respecting the many beautiful fabrics of India.

Lastly, I should like to remind you that whatever progress we have made as regards the instruction of boys and men, the progress is extremely small as regards women and girls. But while I am not very sanguine of our making much additional way and further progress with men and boys without compulsion, yet I am very sanguine of great voluntary progress among the girls and women of India. That is one of the things in which I believe we shall see a great change in the next generation; and English ladies may exercise a graceful and beneficial influence in that direction. This is a matter in which the first spring and impulse must be given from England, and among the many important needs of India, none is more important than this. It is quite within the power of the ladies of England to exercise a direct and powerful influence in the education of their Indian sisters; and if we, as an Association, constantly urge the claims of this subject upon the attention of the many benevolent and highly-educated ladies in England who are willing and anxious to do some good and work some benefit for humanity, we shall have an increasing number of ladies going out to India to carry the influences of education into the homes of Indian ladies—that is the Zenanas where the ordinary schoolmistress, and, still less the schoolmaster, can hardly ever reach.

In connection with education, there is still a subject of great importance. Although religion is a matter in which we can undertake no direct interposition, nevertheless, I can assure you that while Christian Missions are distinctly religious, and have avowedly a Christian character, they are, on the whole, thoroughly popular with the natives of India; and this seems to teach us that the more we advocate the claims of our own religion, the more we show ourselves determined to abide by its dictates, the more we are respected as a nation by the millions of people whom Providence has committed to our charge. While religious matters, however, are beyond our province as an Association, yet the social, moral, and political effects of the Missions have great claims on our advocacy.

Another subject of importance is the improvement of the arrangements for the admission of natives into the Covenanted Civil Service; and this is a matter which will have the sympathy of members of the Association. It has been too much accepted as an axiom in India that the natives, when highly educated, are fitted for the judicial service, but not for the administrative, or the highest branches of administration. Our object should be to render the natives fit to be administrators; and we shall not, in my opinion, have done our duty until we make them so fit. We have already turned out completely educated natives in some branches of natural philosophy and law. Especially in law have we succeeded: we have made them effective advocates, and upright, discriminating judges. We have remaining the duty of rendering them able magistrates and first-rate collectors; and, I repeat, we shall not have done our duty by them until we have made them administrators. This is a point on which our rule compares unfavourably with native rule. Somehow native rule elicited the administrative genius which exists among the natives, and we may hope so to arrange our education as to produce similar results and train up native statesmen. Another thing of importance is to encourage, as much as possible, the assignment of honorary public offices to native gentlemen. The idea of a benevolent despotism—that everything shall be done for the people, and nothing by the people—is not the object of such a Government as ours. Everything, indeed, should be done for the people, but we should induce the people to do as much as possible for themselves, and make them feel their responsibility for it. And that can best be effected by constantly inducing natives of character to undertake honorary offices—to serve as honorary magistrates, as judges of conciliation courts, as jurymen, and the like; to sit on school and road committees, and to be municipal commissioners. The more we do in that direction the more we shall be carrying out the true principles of moral education, which not only seeks to discipline the intellect, but also to form the character. Above all things in respect to honorary offices, we should encourage what may be called the principle of the elective franchise, and provide that candidates be elected by the vote of their countrymen. That principle has long obtained in the municipality of Bombay; and, seeing that, some years ago I determined to carry it out in Calcutta. There was much opposition at the time, but the elective system has triumphed, the object being to make the educated Bengalese of the middle classes take an interest in the affairs of the capital city, and elect men of character and independence to fill the honourable office of municipal commissioner. And the more we carry out that principle in every part of the country the better it will be for us and for India. I rejoice to observe it stated that the Government of India, in connection with the development of provincial finance, will encourage the Local Governments to associate with themselves, in the work of local financial administration, native gentlemen elected by the voice of their fellow-countrymen. It would be, I believe, a desirable thing for men to be elected in the same way to seats in the Legislative Councils, instead of being appointed as they are now. The difficulty would be to find constituencies, but this might be arranged. Men thus elected would have a greater interest in their work, and would speak with greater weight in the Councils. There could be no danger in this, because it does not follow that you need give any majority to them. Government may still retain, as now—and it must do so for a long time to come—an absolute majority in the Legislature for its own officers; but there is no reason why there should not be an influential minority composed of native gentlemen of first-rate character and status, elected by their countrymen.

Before I conclude let me mention one thing which we should avoid. Nothing is so dangerous to the welfare of India as that our dealings with our Indian fellow-subjects should become matters of party strife in England. Formerly these matters were quite free from such strife; but within the last ten years there seems to have been a great and regretable deterioration in that respect—so much so, indeed, that it is difficult to find important Indian matters which have not become more or less tinged with the kaleidoscope of party. I hope the Association will keep its non-political character, and continue to advise the natives of India not to allow their affairs to be mixed up with either of the contending parties in English politics; for if they espouse one party, they are apt to be discredited with the party they do not espouse. They should remember, amid the ebbing and flowing, the surging and falling, of the tide of English opinion, that their object should be, to remain on friendly terms with both parties, in the trust that, whatever party is in power, that party will be doing its utmost, as it has hitherto done, for the general welfare of the Indian people.

In conclusion, there is one duty we should constantly perform; that is to hold out the hand of fellowship to every native gentleman who visits this country. There are already in London, Oxford, and elsewhere some clubs and institutes which offer them a home, such as the Northbrook Institute in London, established under Lord Northbrook's auspices, and the Institute at Oxford, organized by the exertions of our friend Professor Monier Williams,—both which institutions were inaugurated by H.R.H. the Prince of Wales. It should be our pride and duty to offer information to our native visitors, and to place at their disposal the results of our knowledge; for such knowledge must be regarded in connection with the best interests of India. We should strive, by these and other means, to create a favourable impression on the minds of our Indian fellow-subjects, who visit our shores, by making their associations with England happy, so that they may carry back with them to India pleasing recollections of English people and things. We shall thus produce impressions which will be favourable to us as a nation, and tend to render us popular in the Eastern Empire. I am sure that those of us who have spent many of their best days in that distant country still look back to it with fond recollections; and though, while we were in the country, we saw the faults as well as the merits of our native fellow-subjects, now that we have left the country, the memory of the faults has faded, while the remembrance of the merits and virtues becomes brighter and stronger.

# CHAPTER X.

## POLITICAL ECONOMY OF THE INDIAN EMPIRE.

State of Indian finance — Public debt — Works of material improvement — Their remunerative character — Condition of the people — Absence of Poor-laws — Physique of the peasantry — Dangers always threatening India — Impossibility of European colonization in India — Nevertheless large field for employment of Europeans — Practical instruction needed for them — Landed estates held by them in the interior — Industries under their direction — Tea, coffee, sugar, wheat, rice, cinchona, tobacco, malt liquor, jute, flax, hemp, coir, silk, indigo, vegetable and mineral oils, skins and horns — Working of coal and iron — Doubtful prospect of gold-mines — Forest produce — Competition to be expected from natives in trade and industry — Purchasing power of the rupee — Rise of prices and of wages simultaneously — Capacity of the empire to absorb new capital — Railways, canals, and staple industries — The directions in which new capital will probably be required — Annual drawing of capital from England to India.

### Part I.

[*Speech delivered before the Royal Colonial Institute, in London, December* 1880.]

I HAVE the honour at this moment of speaking before a large number of gentlemen who have been taking part in the Government of the various Colonies and possessions which make up the British Empire in the world; also many gentlemen who have been or still are engaged in the numerous affairs and various kinds of businesses in which the British Empire is concerned. Well, then, gentlemen who have governed our dependencies, gentlemen also who have taken part in the concerns commercial and industrial of those dependencies, you are, as I understand, anxious to hear something regarding the Government, and the affairs, industrial and commercial, of what I venture to think is the greatest dependency of them all, in fact, perhaps the greatest foreign empire which has ever been seen in ancient or modern times. But we sometimes hear in these days that this splendid dependency is verging upon insolvency. I am far—and those who think with me are far—from complaining when gentlemen in this country,—learned and accomplished both in statistics, economy, finance, and administration—make observations of this character, because such observations constitute warnings of the dangers which lie before an Empire—a distant alien Empire like that of India—and warnings also against the pitfalls into which the administrators of that Empire are likely to be betrayed. But still the effect of such observations is to throw us back, as it were, upon our haunches, and make us consider whether the finances of India are sound or not. Now, in the first place, let me assure you that they are sound.

You hear of deficits, annual deficits, year after year. But these are technical nominal deficits, and are hardly deficits at all in the proper sense of the word. These merely arise because the sums spent by the Government upon the improvement of the country, upon canals and railways, are included in the ordinary finances. But, in no other country in the world are such charges included in the ordinary finances; on the contrary, they are excluded; and that being so, there is in India no deficit whatever; on the contrary, there is an exact equilibrium established between income and expenditure. Upon the finances of the last twelve years there has been actually a slight surplus; and thus it goes on, a little deficit one year with a little surplus another; and, when you come to draw out the threads of a series of years, there comes out a slight surplus. Then the revenues are said to be inelastic; well they are inelastic as compared with the elastic revenues of England; but, nevertheless, they are growing and increasing. The incidence of taxation is excessively low, when you take it per head of population, it is as low as taxation can possibly be, if there is to be any taxation at all. Then, the army expenditure is not excessive; it does not amount to above one-quarter of the annual receipts. Or it may be said to bear a proportion of about one-fourth or one-third, accordingly as you choose to take the total of the revenues proper or the total receipts of all kinds. It does not exceed the proportion which the defensive expenses of any one of the great Powers of Europe bear to the general finance of that Power. Therefore the army in India costs about as much as it costs in all other civilised countries—that, and no more. The civil expenses are not outrunning the constable; they are kept well in hand, and, while they are rather diminished in all those respects which affect Europeans, they are slightly increased in other respects, but merely for the sake of giving the natives better pay and better preferment. But even then, so correct has been the management, there has been no real increase on the whole, savings being balanced against augmentations. Then public works have, no doubt, been carried out to a great extent; the Government has invested 125,000,000*l.* sterling upon railways, of which about 93,000,000*l.* have been expended by guaranteed companies, and the rest directly by the State.* Upon the whole of that concern taken together—some railways paying more and some paying less—upon the whole they are paying about 5 per cent., and this notwithstanding the many new railways which have just been opened, or are not quite completed, and which have not yet got their traffic developed. You hear much about canals. Well, we have the finest irrigation canal system to be seen in the world. Whether it is equalled by the canal system of the Babylonians in the days of Nebuchadnezzar, or of Alexander the Great, I hardly know; but even

* These figures have, of course, risen somewhat during the three years which have elapsed since this speech was delivered.

in Mesopotamia there could hardly have been canals to surpass the canals now to be seen in India. There have been 20,000,000*l.* sterling spent upon them, and upon that six per cent. is being paid now; and if that is so now, you can judge what will be obtained a few years hence.

Then you will ask, how about the Public, or National Debt? The Debt stands at about 150,000,000*l.* sterling.* But that includes all that has been spent upon the State railways which I have been describing, and also upon the canals; it likewise includes large sums of money which have been spent for the relief of the recent famines. So that if you deduct this sum, and take the debt which has really been spent upon actual war, upon military operations, and the like, which corresponds to the Public Debt of the European Powers, the Indian Debt is just about equal to two years' revenue. That is not an excessive incumbrance; that will not sink the Imperial boat, nor drag the Empire into ruin. Further, what is the condition of that debt? The rates of interest have been repeatedly reduced of late years. They have been reduced from five to four-and-a-half, and even four per cent., and the Fours once rose to 105, or five per cent. premium, though they have since fallen. The Fours and a Half, however, still command a premium; and, altogether, if you look at the quotations—the financial quotations of the world—you will find that the Indian Government is now borrowing at a rate which is the most favourable in the world—next after that of England itself. Well, then, you hear also that this Public Debt is not raised locally—not in the country, not from the natives, but in England. It is perfectly true that the debt for the guaranteed railway was entirely raised in this country, but exclude that and exclude also the public debt that has been raised in this country, then you will find that of the remaining debt, which has been raised in India, of which the interest is payable there, and which amounts to about 60,000,000*l.*

* This is exclusive of the 93,000,000*l.* mentioned above, as expended on guaranteed railways.

sterling, one-third is held by natives. Thus a sum of about 20,000,000*l.* sterling is invested by the natives of India in British securities—that is, securities of the Indian Government. That is not a bad sum for the natives to have invested; and they would have invested much more if it had not been that the Government have been constantly reducing the rates of interest on account of the increase of competition. The natives used to lend us money at five or five and a half per cent., but, as you know, money can be raised at four and four and a half per cent. in London, and therefore the Government raise it there. Otherwise the natives would have held still more stock than they hold now. Still they have subscribed about 20,000,000*l.* sterling, and are still lending us about 2,000,000*l.* a year on an average for carrying on our public works; and the other day when a sum of 2,000,000*l.* was wanted for the service of the year, no less than 23,000,000*l* were tendered—that is to say people offered to lend us 23,000,000*l.* when we only wanted 2,000,000*l.*; and out of that 23,000,000*l.*, 9,000,000*l.* were offered by the natives of India. Then, you are told that we must add to that 150,000,000*l.*, which I mentioned as the Public Debt of India, the debt for the guaranteed railways. Well, add that, and it makes another 93,000,000*l.* But what is the effect? The effect you will find to be, that upon the total of what I may call the debt thus consolidated, the interest would not be above two and a half per cent. upon the whole. I should like to know whether there is any other Government upon earth that is paying so little as two and a half per cent. on its National Debt. Perhaps the Dutch Government is not paying more than this, but its debt is limited. So that, on the whole, if you take the debt in that way it is in one of the most favourable positions in the world, if not actually the most favourable. Well, then, so much for the finances. If these propositions which I have stated are correct—and I say you will find that they are absolutely correct in all essentials (I have recently verified them all)—then you can judge for yourselves, gentlemen, regarding the great dependency of India, as to whether its finances are in a sound state or not.

Then perhaps you would like to know next the condition of the people of India. It is said sometimes that they are gradually starving, and are gradually becoming poorer and poorer every day. Well, of course they are poor upon an average of the entire population. But the wealth of India is vast in the abstract; relatively it is not vast, because the population itself is so vast. The trade is in one sense great, but it is not really so very great; indeed, relatively to the mighty population it is somewhat small. Nevertheless, the progress of the nation can only be measured or gauged by a reasonable comparison of the people at one time in reference to another—at one age or one era in reference to another age or another era. Then, according to that standard, I say the people are advancing. The population is being, no doubt, at times reduced by famine; nevertheless, after making abatements for that, the population will be found to be increasing. The people are increasing and the cultivation is increasing. The trade is increasing immensely, both in the foreign or external trade, and the domestic or internal trade. The dwellings of the people are being improved; the interior of their homes is being made brighter and their condition happier. The people have better houses—better built cottages—better furniture, and better domestic utensils than formerly. Their industries—their ancient industries—are, despite some losses, on the whole on a par with the industries of the palmiest days of the Mogul Empire; on the other hand, a number of new industries never known before are being introduced by the aid of steam and machinery. Their property is secured to them in a degree never seen previously. Formerly there was doubt whether the land belonged to the people or not. It was generally considered to belong to the Government; but now a proprietary title, from one end of India to the other over this vast area of the country, has been created or recognised for their benefit by the British Government. Justice is administered in such a manner that every man feels secure of reaping what he has sown, and of enjoying the fruits ot his labour, and a sense of moral independence is growing up among the people. The food supply is said to be sometimes deficient; but it is impossible to understand an abstract proposition of that nature in face of the known facts that people are storing food to the extent of millions of tons annually for their sustenance in time of drought; and, besides that, are exporting hundreds of thousands of tons annually to Europe and to the Colonies. Wages are rising. There are no doubt many poor; there are many beggars pursuing mendicancy as a profession, I am sorry to say, in India, and statistically it is known that there is, at least, a million of them, taking the whole empire together. Still they are all sustained without any poor-rate or any poor-law organisation for that purpose; and in that respect India sets a good example to even the most civilised nation. Then, as to the people being starved or impoverished, would you be surprised to hear that there are many millions of them that are on an average taller if not stouter than we are? There are many millions also who are somewhat gaunt, somewhat thin; and there are some hundreds of thousands that are stunted in growth. I want to know whether that description does not apply also to some of the most strong and robust nations of Europe. And remember, pray, that the Government of India—if you take military inches in the ranks as at all a test of the stature of the people—could be backed to put into the field more tall battalions, as regards inches if not chest measurement, probably than any other Government under the sun. If all these economic facts are demonstrable, as I conceive they are, then on the whole the material condition of the people is tolerably satisfactory. I am far from saying it is perfect or all that we should desire; but I say that the state of the people is as good as can reasonably be expected considering their past history, their climate, and their physical surroundings.

Now I do not pretend to give you a rose-coloured picture.

I admit that notwithstanding these considerations there are at least four or five dangers which always overhang us, and which we see no immediate chance of removing. First, no doubt, and foremost of these difficulties is the periodical recurrence of famines. Beyond question we do have famines at least once in every decade. Secondly, there is a constant liability to financial derangement by reason of the exchanges. Silver, as you know, fluctuates in value considerably. Just now it is very low as compared to gold; that is a great trouble to the Indian Government, which has to make large payments to England in silver which is measured by a gold standard. This fact does seriously derange the calculations of Indian financiers, and we cannot help it. Thirdly, with respect to the death-rate of the Indian population, it is no doubt high—there is no denying that. That is to say, if 2 per cent. or 2½ per cent. or something under 3 per cent. of population is to be considered a favourable or a normal death-rate according to the statistics of the most civilised countries, then it must be admitted that the death-rate of India is something over 3 per cent. I say something over—I know it is over 3 per cent.—but how much no one can tell, because our vital statistics are imperfect, and therefore I can only say that the death-rate is over 3 per cent. There is no doubt that the surroundings of the people are insanitary, that there is a great deal of infantile mortality, and a great many diseases amongst the adults. There is no question that impure drinking water and want of proper sanitary arrangements near their dwellings do affect the health of the people. Fourthly, there is the constant political agitation and ultimate financial disturbance caused by the war cloud which is always rolling from the direction of Eastern Europe towards our Afghanistan frontier. Until that cloud shall disappear, if it ever shall—but I must not enter into that subject now—but until that disappears we have constant danger or trouble from that quarter. Fifthly, in a foreign country, and an alien and a distant Empire like India, you must expect that there are elements of political danger. The mass of the people, I state without hesitation, are contented and loyal. I cannot say anything too good of the people of India in that respect. Considering that they are aliens, and that we are foreigners, I do not think any other people on earth would behave as well as they do in this respect. Nevertheless, I do not want to land you—I was going to say in a fool's paradise—I do not want to land you in what the natives call "a green garden," which is an expression that is equivalent to the château in Spain. I do not want you to suppose that there is no danger at all; on the contrary, there are many dangers. We, by our system of education which we have introduced, and our Western ideas, and various other influences of the nineteenth century, are indirectly causing the popular religion to be undermined, and that of course sets the ancient priesthood against us. There is an old feudal aristocracy which flourished in the days of war and revolution, which cannot get on and flourish equally well under a settled and civilized Government like ours. So there is another class against us. Thus, in our own British Indian territory, we have several classes against us. There are next the Native States. I am not alluding to them as being in any way disloyal; on the contrary, India is an Empire—in the sense in which Rome was—that is to say, there are vast British territories, and there are a number of feudatories and native allies scattered throughout the Empire which are loyal to the backbone; and it was partly owing to that fact that we got through the war of the Mutiny (in 1857) as well as we did. We owe our victory—under Providence—at that time to our strong right arm, no doubt; but even the British bayonets would not have been finally efficacious if there had not been a great conservative party in the country, which mainly centered in the Native States.

Thus I have now put that part of the case fully before you. You can see the dangers, you hear the objections, and you hear the answers to them, you also perceive what are the elements of security. So much for my brief discourse, addressed to those who have been concerned in government and administration.

I will now offer a few remarks to the gentlemen—my Colonial fellow-countrymen—who are concerned in industry and commerce. You will naturally ask me to give you some idea of the products, the industries, and the commerce of India; also some idea as to what sort of field they offer for the employment of young Englishmen. I take it that one of the burning questions of the day to British fathers is, What are we to do with our sons? I say that India will help very much if the subject is approached in the right way.

First, let me remind you that you cannot colonise India in the way you have colonised Australia, South Africa, North America, and the like. If you say, granted, you cannot colonise the plains of India, but you can the Himalayas—I am afraid not. A certain experience shows that the European race will not survive more than two or three generations in these eastern longitudes, or in these southern latitudes, whichever way you like to look at them. It is the latitude and the longitude together that produce certain climatic effects which are absolutely fatal and inimical to our Anglo-Saxon race; and therefore, if you were to send father and mother and family to India, or a number of families constituting a small population of that kind, in the course of two or three generations that race would become nearly extinct. That is a physical fact in the first place; and secondly, even if that were otherwise, it is quite impossible in such a climate for a European as a labouring man to compete with the natives, because he would be undersold and underbid in every way, and in the end he would find nothing to do. Therefore you cannot colonise in that sense; but in another and equally good sense you can settle in the country. You must no doubt come home to Europe from India during the evening of life, and, above all things, a man, woman, boy, or girl, must spend the morning of life in this European climate. But the middle of life may be spent perfectly well in India, and you may bear the brunt and the heat of the day, and come back tolerably fresh to your country and address your countrymen as I address you this evening.

Although a man cannot work with his hands alone, I may remind you, to make the subject clear, that some men work with their hands and others work with their heads, and others work with both together. An European man cannot work with his hands alone in India; but he can work to a great extent with his hands and head together as a skilled labourer. More particularly he can work well with his head, can direct, control, and exert authority. He can exercise over the natives in industry and commercial pursuits that power of command which has never failed an Englishman in any exigency where it has been tried. But in order to do that his habit of mind must be suited for his business. He must, as a European, if he is to live in India at all, live more or less as a gentleman, but he cannot afford to live as a prince. His habits must not be grand, but simple—that is to say, he must manage to live cheaply and economically. That you will think is a truism. But it is no truism at all; it is a sad warning which has to be given. No doubt hundreds of commercial and industrial enterprises have failed because our young friends have forgotten that principle. They have gone out—having been brought up in simple homes in this country, where they were taught economical habits, and to work—they have gone out to India where they think they are to live entirely as gentlemen. They build fine houses, or the firms out there build the houses for them. Thus great personal expenses are incurred, and then, of course, the concern is found not to pay. But it would have paid right enough if it had been administered in the frugal manner in which similar concerns are administered at home.

Then the education of these young men must be good, of course; but still it must be practical. I do not disparage classical, literary, and artistic education; it is the only education I ever received myself, and I am duly thankful for it. But something besides that is wanted for the affairs with which I am now dealing. For, in future, in these lines of life, every man's education must be technical and practical; and he must not only be taught the theory of a business or trade, but must learn something of the working of it in this country before he proceeds to India. You may think that this also is a truism; but it is no truism at all. It is a solemn fact that scores of concerns have failed simply because men have thought it required no particular training or professional education to become a planter of tea, coffee, or indigo. Afterwards it is found that the tea does not fetch a good price because it has not been properly prepared for market. The coffee similarly fails, or the plants wither. But why, simply because gentlemen went out from this country to undertake those difficult businesses without any previous proper training, or without that sort of education which would qualify them for such kinds of trade. Thus you understand that a man who has had merely a general education, would not have had that education which enables him to take to agriculture in India as a planter. Thus, the sort of man to go out to India is he who has had plain practical industrial instruction besides general education.

Now, as regards the general trade of the country, as you probably know, it is very considerable. So rapid is the increase of trade in Australia that you would not be surprised to hear that the trade of India is computed to exceed 100 millions sterling in value per annum; one year it got up to 120 millions;* but in good average years it has been 105 to 110 millions, and the greater part of that trade might be in the hands of Europeans, as it was once in their hands. This is the trade which belonged to the East India Company; but it is fast falling into the hands of natives. They are outdoing us, no doubt, in economy of management. They are becoming better educated; they are establishing their branches in London, in New York, and many other cities; and they are gradually getting their share of the

* In a subsequent year it has amounted to 140 millions.

trade. Still there is a great opening for young Britons, a much larger opening than they avail themselves of, for employment in the general business of commerce. I say almost the whole of this great trade which I have described to you might be in the hands of Europeans if they could only manage to outstrip the natives in the competition. It is rather, perhaps, an extraordinary thing to hear that natives are so rapidly competing with us in this respect. Remember I am not talking of manual industries, but of regular mercantile business, and of natives who establish themselves at the centres of trade at the principal marts of the Presidential towns, exactly in the same way as Englishmen might settle themselves down. The natives organise, buy produce up country, arrange for its being brought down to the coast, and for its being sent to England. All this class of business is now done immensely by the natives, and year by year in an increasing degree. So that if this is a fact, and I say it is a demonstrable fact, you will see there is a great opening for young Englishmen to compete in that branch of business.

Then, with regard to the productions; they are enormous, as you are aware. The natural products of the woods and forests and the wilds of India are multiform and various. The agricultural produce is some of the most extensive in the world. The manufactured produce is also very considerable. We are justly proud of the pre-eminence of Great Britain in manufactures. Would you be astonished to hear that there are scores of articles which India makes and exports to other countries? Now, I deliberately say, without exception, that there is not one of these things in which the management and direction might not fall into the hands of Europeans if they were qualified; and that, in every instance where the European got the command, there would be an improvement in the staple and in the manufacture. Nevertheless, almost the whole of this trade, or a greater portion of it, is in the hands of the natives. The trade, also, is not only very extensive externally, but it is most extensive internally. Why, the railways alone carry backwards and forwards 8,000,000 of tons of produce annually from one part of the country to the other. The boat traffic, the river navigation of the interior of India, rivals that of China, and is perhaps the most extensive in the world. The boats are to be numbered, not only by tens, but even by hundreds, of thousands. It is excessively difficult to state the number of boats as they go backwards and forwards from one station to another up and down the rivers. But the river kingdom of Eastern Bengal, and the navigation of the great rivers Ganges, Brahmaputra, and the like, is superior, I believe, to that of any other river in the world, the Mississippi and the Yangtsze Kiang hardly excepted. Therefore, you see what an important field there must be in all this for the employment of Europeans if they would set to work and win the position which they might assume in that country.

Land holding might be attempted by Europeans to a limited extent only, because the natives are like the Irish in one respect, in that they cling very much to their homes, and it is difficult to find any land to be purchased. But, even then, land might sometimes be purchased to a considerable extent, provided always that this were done in an economic spirit. I have known many estates in Bengal which have been held by Europeans, and, afterwards, the European families have fallen into poor circumstances, and their property has passed into other hands. But it is due to the old complaint. They begin by building fine houses, large enough for English noblemen, with very nice parks, and all that sort of thing; and then the estates will not pay for all that. But if they had lived as small squires do in England, their estates would have kept them in tolerably easy circumstances.

But let us turn for a moment to some of the great products of India. In the Eastern Himalayas, in Eastern Bengal, in Assam, in the Panjab, and in other places, you will see beautiful tea-gardens picturesquely situated, the houses high up and well placed; although the gardens are low down and in rather hot valleys, still the houses are nice and cool up above. They are charming places in every sense of the word. Hundreds of your countrymen are following the profession of tea planters there; and these gardens may yet be indefinitely multiplied. There are upwards of half a million of acres growing tea now in those regions, and the export of tea alone is thirty-four million pounds (lbs.) annually, and all that has been the work of only the last few years. You see, therefore, what an opening there is for young men, provided they learn their work and practise their profession. Then, let me ask you to turn your eyes to the Western mountains on the Malabar Coast, down towards the lower part of the Indian Peninsula, especially to the southern part of that range, including the hilly district of Wynaad, the mountains of the Nilgiris, and the hills of Cûrg and Mysore. There you will find what are now almost the finest coffee-gardens in the world. Perhaps I may hardly say the finest in the world, because they are equalled by those of Ceylon, but still as fine as any in the world, producing a coffee which has superseded the old Mocha coffee of Arabia, and affording spheres of labour to young Englishmen. But here, again, the number of tea and coffee companies that have gone into liquidation and been broken up, with hopes blasted and fortunes wrecked, is something painful to contemplate, and the reason is that men have sometimes undertaken to manage these affairs who have no proper professional education for the work. Before I pass from that I may remind our Australian friends that many of the Indian coffee planters believe that they will before long be emigrating to Australia, and they will make fresh coffee plantations there; and as regards tea, it is the hope of all the tea-planting interest of India that they will have a great market for tea in Australia.

Now, another industry is that of sugar. The sugar of India, if well refined, would be inferior to no sugar in the world; but the cultivation is not all that it might be. The manufacture, and the refining especially, of the sugar is anything but good. Nevertheless, some European firms have established themselves in India, and do a very prosperous business by sugar refining. There, again, is an opening for young men.

Well, we hear a great deal of the wheat of India, which is large in the total quantity produced. Take the produce of the United Kingdom at 10,000,000 quarters—well, then, the wheat crop of India is not less than 40,000,000 quarters; and in good years it is as much as 50,000,000 quarters—five times the yield of the United Kingdom. Then the quality is extremely good; the upper valley of the Ganges, the valley of the Nerbadda river, in the centre of India, are wheat producing countries, and the export is rapidly developing itself.*

Then there is rice, as a staple produce of India, and more particularly a staple of British Burmah, since the annexation of that country within the last twenty years, and the delta of the Irawady, where the rice trade has sprung up wonderfully. That is almost entirely at present in the hands of Europeans. But it is to be apprehended in the course of a short time that the old story will be repeated—the natives will find out the ways and the habits of the trade, and will begin to elbow the Europeans out of it; but at present the Europeans have got it nearly all their own way.

Next, there is the chinchona, that produces the famous febrifuge. Considering you have an immense population of 250,000,000 living in a generally feverish and malarious country, you can imagine what a market is opening for the consumption of the bark which is a prophylactic against fever. The Government has established plantations among the Nilgiri hills in the South, and among the Himalayas in the North—beautiful plantations, and in most picturesque localities, all requiring European management.

Tobacco in India is extensively grown; but again the old story is repeated—it is inferior to that of Manilla and South

* This was said at the end of 1880; since then the exportation has increased in the most satisfactory manner.

America, because it is not skilfully cultivated in India nor properly prepared. That manufacture really awaits the entry of Europeans into the business. The Government itself is so alive to this that it has been making experiments, and subsidising one or two European firms, in order to see what they can effect in this matter.

So, again, with malt liquors, we flatter ourselves that we are one of the best beer-producing communities in the world; but would you be surprised to hear that barley is sent from this country to India, turned into malt out there, the yeast being obtained locally, and the beer manufactured in the Himalayas?

Then carry your minds for a moment right up to the north-eastern portion of India, and bear in mind the boat traffic which I have described to you in the upper valleys, where is produced the *Corchorus capsularis*, as botanists call it, commonly called jute. Thence it is sent down in boats throughout these great arterial rivers and their branches right down to Calcutta. There it is manufactured along the banks of the Hughly at Calcutta: where you may see rows and rows of factory chimneys towering into the skies like forests on both banks of the river, for the manufacture of the jute. Formerly the jute used to go to Dundee to be manufactured, now it is largely manufactured at Calcutta. Lately the Indians have begun to get a share of the manufactures into their own hands; but in the main the companies, directors, managers, and foremen are Europeans. And the concerns may continue to be guided by Europeans unless the natives acquire knowledge of the business, and thus virtually carry off the chief prize in the competition. Now, where is this jute going to? Why, to Australia, to Eastern Asia, to Siam, to China, but more particularly to Australia; and what is most interesting of all, going to the United States of America. It is sent now past China and Japan, right across the Pacific to California and to San Francisco. At this time there is probably no foreign name more familiar to the inhabitants of Calcutta than San Francisco. So much for jute. The same may be said of flax. India is essentially a flax-producing country, that is to say, it produces the linseed plant. But this plant, which yields the flax, is grown almost entirely for the sake of the seed, not for the sake of the stem or the fibre, because it requires a great deal of culture and management and manufacturing skill to arrange all that; and there is no European in the business; but if Europeans do take to the business, there is nothing to prevent India competing with Russia and other flax-producing countries. Exactly the same story may be told of hemp and coir, which latter is a most important fibre, and makes the very strongest cables and most unbreakable sort of rope; and there is no country that can compete with India in that respect, for this reason—the fibre is got from the husk of the cocoa-nut. Ceylon, no doubt, produces cocoa-nut, but nothing surpasses the cocoa-nut of the delta of the Ganges and the coast of Malabar, and the quantity is immense.

Next, silk is produced from two kinds of worms; one feeds on the mulberry which is the best kind; the other feeds upon various other trees which grow wild in the forest. The mulberry-fed silkworm was the worm which was most esteemed in Bengal in the days of the East India Company, but latterly China has successfully competed with us in India; and so has, until recently, Italy. Our silk exportation mainly depends upon the question whether there has been a good crop in China and Italy; whenever there is a failure of crops in those two countries we have a good export trade of silk from India. At present, then, our Indian silk trade is somewhat precarious. But there is a new silk trade coming up—viz., that of the silk produced by the worms which feed upon the trees that grow wild in the forest, which is called "tusser"; and there is no country which can compete with India in that respect. There are specimens of it being made and sent to Paris and other principal centres of art and industry in Europe, and it is found to produce beautiful fabrics at a cheap cost; and if this should succeed, there will be another industry opened out for young men from England.

Well, leaving the fibrous substances which I have touched upon, and the agricultural produce also, may I say a word or two upon the dyes? Let me ask you to carry your imagination back for a moment to the fine estates and properties belonging to your countrymen in Behar. Formerly, indigo was produced from Bengal; and it has been ruined there for the last twenty years, because it could not be produced at prices which would prove remunerative in Europe. You see all sorts of chemical blues are being discovered in Europe—beautiful blues of course, but not very lasting—whereas nothing in the world equals in richness and in durability the blue of the Indian indigo. Well, this competition of what I may call these meretricious chemical blues kept down the price of the indigo. Then the prices of rice and the like rose. So the cultivators of Bengal refused to cultivate indigo at unremunerative prices, and the indigo planters could not afford to give better, and discontinued the business; thus in the course of half a dozen years there fell to the ground what was once a great European industry. The indigo of Behar, however, still thrives, and scores of young Englishmen may continue to find employment in it, provided that such concerns be economically conducted. But if the indigo planters are to be like fine country gentlemen of the olden time, and are to have estates with country seats and the like, then the indigo may not suffice to maintain their position.

In order to avoid fatiguing you, I must run rapidly over the remaining products. The subject is extensive and interesting. There is the oil, the common oil of India, that will not employ Europeans: but the cocoa-nut oil of India is largely exported to Europe, and I believe when it arrives there it is called olive oil! But the mineral oils of India may largely employ Europeans, if what I hear is correct regarding the mineral oils of America, which are said to be on the decline. Then up jumps the kerosene oil of India. Thus there are mineral oils springing up in Assam and Burmah, of course under European direction.

One word regarding the cattle of India. Notwithstanding

what may be said about their destruction by famine, there are still untold numbers of cattle in India, and the consequence is that there is a trade in horns and skins, of which enormous quantities are exported abroad. Then comes the question of curing the skins, which is one of the things that Europeans will understand better than the natives, and which Europeans might teach natives to do. Consequently there rise up tanning concerns in Northern India, employing Europeans, and so a great leather trade springs up. At present, you perhaps imagine that England is the only country that can make harness properly. Would you be astonished to hear that the harness for the cavalry and artillery is now being made by Indians from Indian leather, of course under European direction? Then the wool of India is not of course a large article of export, as we in England get our foreign wool from Australia. But there, again, is a trade in which Europeans may be most advantageously employed. Certain wools in India can only be produced there: they are the peculiarly fine and soft kinds from the Himalayas and the great uplands of Central Asia. That wool trade ought to be in the hands of Europeans. So with camel's hair; that is an article in which hardly any country, except Arabia, can compete with us; an article also which might afford excellent employment for Europeans.

Then you come to minerals. I have not time to mention to you all the coal mines, but you are aware that there are extensive coal mines in India now—not indeed having a great output, like those of the collieries of England, but still extensive coal mines—up to which railways are being made in the western parts of Bengal, in the Panjab, in the Nerbadda valley, in the Nagpur province—all those countries produce coal; and here an extensive number of natives are employed, of course under European direction. Then the iron trade of India. The iron manufactures are extensive: and now that European companies are being formed for the carrying on of iron works, that business is beginning to prosper.

I must briefly allude to gold. Great hopes are, of course, entertained by many people about that, but I do not wish to lead you to entertain expectations in that respect which may not be realised. There are most interesting gold formations which have been discovered on the western or Malabar coasts, and the survey reports have been extremely favourable. But the superficially accessible metal has been apparently extracted already in former ages, by mining operations of which traces are extant; and so the cream, as it were, may have been previously skimmed off. Then it has to be seen whether the gold which yet remains is in great quantities, or whether it can be extracted in a manner that will make it pay. There is reason to fear that it will not be extracted easily, and there will not be gold diggings as there were in Australia in the manner which you understand. The extracting of the gold will be done, if done at all, by a comparatively delicate process, which requires a good deal of capital. There will also be many difficult questions regarding the royalty and the rights in respect to these minerals. There will be much trouble and negotiation and the like, so that, one thing taken together with another, it is, as yet, extremely doubtful whether these gold discoveries will come to much.* Of course, every one in India hopes they will lead to success—a matter of great importance to the country, as it might affect favourably the difficulty about silver.

Then I might say a word about chemicals. Saltpetre is one of the most important. That is produced extensively all over India; and I believe nearly all the saltpetre used in this country comes from India; and you will see that this is a matter in which Europeans might be employed. Borax, also, can be got as well from the Himalayas or the countries beyond as it can from Italy.

Further, there is forest produce; and I believe, if any of our naval friends were present, they would say that the teak of

* This unfavourable anticipation has been confirmed by subsequent events.

the Indian forests is not to be surpassed by any wood anywhere, and that will be confirmed by the highest authority—namely, the British Admiralty. There are the sandal wood and the ebony of India, which are also among the best in the world. We have the nuts called Myrobalans, which are most useful in commerce, and are largely produced in the forests of India. There, again, are fields for the employment of Europeans. The india-rubber of India is probably superior to that of any other country; it is very imperfectly developed, merely from the want of such skill as Europeans can bring into play.

Lastly, the art products are most numerous, such as shawls, carpets, pottery, inlaid wood, together with horn, ivory, and the like. The opinion has been gaining ground in Europe, especially since the last Exhibition at Paris, that nothing can be made in Europe that exceeds in beauty and real merit these art products of India. Then, if these sorts of products are to find their way into all the markets of Europe, manifestly there ought to be Europeans in the business; and young Britons, before going to India to join such business, ought to be posted up in all these things, in order to discern what are the best articles of the kind in India, and send them thence to the markets of the world.

In addition, a word might be said about model farms, only time does not permit. Agricultural education is amongst the burning questions of India, and as soon as such education spreads there will be model farms everywhere under European direction. Wherever European skill has been applied to cattle breeding in India, under the direction of Government, marked success has been obtained, as might be expected from the aptitude which Englishmen always show in this work. Horse breeding I am afraid we shall not make much of in India, for the conviction is gaining ground that we cannot compete with the beautiful horses which are coming by many hundreds every year from Australia, Persia, and Arabia.

I have not said anything about cotton, there is hardly time;

but you are well aware that there are cotton factories for cleaning, weaving, and spinning; and that these Indian-made cotton fabrics are, in some ways — not in all respects, but in a limited respect—competing with the fabrics of England. Here, of course, is much employment for Europeans.

As to the mechanical arts, why imagine all the different factories I have described; imagine, also, all the various workshops which exist—the workshops for the railways, the workshops for the canals and the public works for the Government. Imagine, further, that there are many hundreds of locomotive engines in India, and there are many thousands of wagons and trucks, and the like. All these require repairing or putting together, or making up, and such things give employment to large numbers of Europeans. Then, with regard to public works, we have 10,000 miles of railways open; we have 8000 or 9000 miles of principal canals, with branches, making up in all, 15,000 miles of canals. Take those two kinds of works alone. Consider the number of roads, and bridges, and barracks, and public buildings, and all the magnificent structures arising up in the Presidential towns and the like; and imagine what important public works are springing up in India, the whole of which must give employment to European engineers, assistant engineers, overseers, artisans, and mechanics. True there has been a sudden reduction of establishments which have thrown some young men—I will not say thrown them out of employment—but induced the Government to retire many officers, and that, no doubt, has cast rather a damper upon the spirits of engineers. Nevertheless, we have an excellent college at Cooper's Hill, near London, for training civil engineers for India; and it is not likely that this great profession will be seriously diminished in India; for, no sooner has the Government discharged some of its engineers, than fresh requirements arise, and it begins to regret having discharged them; so that, the fact is, there is and always will be a great demand for European engineers in India.

I may be asked to specify the sources of information to which young men intending to go to India might resort. I am afraid, at this late hour, it would be impossible for me to go into that question, for I should have to give an analysis of what is a very extensive literature. There really are publications, official, and non-official, upon every one of the subjects on which I have touched. Volumes have been written by private individuals, and reports without end have been published by the Government. I might explain, if time permitted, that there are public bodies, non-official bodies. I speak of them as public, for they are in the nature of Corporations, although they are non-official, consisting of private gentlemen. I allude to the Chambers of Commerce in India, and especially the Chambers of Commerce of Calcutta and Bombay, which are among the most important Chambers of Commerce of the world. They are second to none in their knowledge, in their intelligence, and in the vast store of information at their command. But, besides that, there are extensive Trade Associations both at Calcutta and Bombay. If time had permitted I might have alluded to the European tradesmen class of India. I mean tradesmen in the same sense in which tradesmen are mentioned in England. The European tradesmen in India are so numerous that they form associations and give annual dinners, which are, in a small way, like the civic feasts of London. They entertain there the principal officials. Annual speeches are made by the highest officers in the country, which correspond to speeches made by Ministers in London. So that these associations have the very best information, which they would be happy to place at the disposal of young men visiting the country. From what can be given by these associations and the literature of India, I imagine no man would have any difficulty in learning all that he could be expected to learn in England.

In reference to the remarks adverse to India made by some of my friends, what I have to say is this, that if you bear in mind all they say you will find that it comes to matter of opinion; their opinion is very able and valuable, and the opinion of native friends, whom they consult, is also valuable; but after all they are but opinions which may differ from ours, and you don't expect every Englishman and Native to agree about the affairs of India any more than you can expect Englishmen to agree about the aspect and condition of England. I hope, however, that my address has consisted of facts rather than opinion. I have stated to you a body of facts; every financial and economic statement I made is a fact; bear that in mind kindly, gentlemen. They are facts irrefragable, indisputable, demonstrable, unquestionable. And if these are the facts, it is for you to judge whether there is prosperity or not, and whether the country is in a safe, sound condition or not. Having stated those facts, I leave you to judge whether they are consistent with the adverse opinions of the gentlemen whom I have mentioned. I will not attempt to recapitulate the points; I only ask you, as you go away home, to remember that I claim for my statement an absolute foundation of fact, and you will draw your own conclusions.

To conclude, you see now in all these various respects—and I daresay I might multiply instances—but I have given you as many instances as your attention can bear this evening—you can see what an immense field there is for industrial persons, which has been open, is open, and will yet open for young Britons in India. But, in conclusion, remember there is this competition of the natives. There is a great system of State education going on in India. I have not time to touch upon the moral progress and the mental advancement of the natives, though there I might also show as favourable a picture as I have shown regarding the finances and the material condition of the country. But, irrespective of the moral progress of the natives, their intellectual and mental progress is considerable. They are becoming clever, handy fellows, and are beginning to learn the arts and industries which have made England as great as she is. That very science which has placed Britain in the van of the nations of the world, we are offering to the natives, not only offering, but pressing upon them. We are indeed making them adopt the ways of science and civilisation. So you must expect—if any of my young friends are present who are thinking of going to India—you must be prepared for competition from the natives, and you must be ready to meet them on their own ground, otherwise you cannot possibly succeed. There will be a cry raised of India for the Indians. Well, you would not wish a counter cry to be raised of India for the British. The true cry, which cry alone the Government will follow, is this—India both for the Indians and the British alike. Let them run a race which is to be won by the swiftest, and let them fight the battle of emulation in which the victory will go to the strongest—not the strongest physically, but the strongest intellectually and morally. There is no fear that the result of such competition will do any harm to the natives; it may do good to the British —God grant that it may! But if it does good to the British, that good will, in return, benefit the natives; for, invariably, experience has proved in India that wherever Europeans have gone and settled and flourished, those are the places where the natives have also prospered and flourished the most. So that in going to India, and following all the industrial and commercial pursuits I have indicated, you will not only be benefiting yourselves, and raising the status of your country, but you will also, by the blessing of Providence, be the indirect means of helping those who, although they are not your fellow-countrymen, are your fellow-subjects, and, like you, live under the shadow of the gracious sway of our Sovereign Lady the Queen-Empress of India.*

* At pp. 202–203 the preeminence of Indian Canals relates to irrigation. The Swedish canal works are magnificent, but they are for navigation.

## PART II.

[*Speech delivered before the Institute of Bankers, in London, March* 1882.]

THE somewhat difficult questions which have been propounded to me are—first, "The purchasing power of the rupee relative to labour, produce, &c., in various parts of the Empire;" secondly, "The capacity of the Empire to absorb new capital, and the direction in which new capital will most probably be required."

The first point is the purchasing power of the rupee. Now, this sounds a formidable question, but it really refers to the rise of prices of all the necessaries of life and corresponding rise of wages. It also refers to the point as to whether, since the depreciation of the rupee about ten years ago, there has been any special rise either of price or of wages. In the first place, it is a notorious fact that the prices of almost all articles in India have greatly risen. This rise, however, began in the time of Lord Dalhousie, before the great war of the mutinies, when tens of millions sterling of British capital began to be expended in the country. The rise, both of prices and of wages, was not at all arrested by the war of the mutinies, but continued rather at an increased ratio during the period of disturbance. When the disturbances were over, capital began to be expended more rapidly than ever, and prices went on rising. Not only were railways pushed on at an unexampled rate of speed, but also many new industries under European guidance, and with the resources of European capital, were introduced into the country, so that by the time of the viceroyalty of Sir John Lawrence, afterwards Lord Lawrence, the rates both of prices and of wages reached their culminating point. Since that time both the high rate of prices and the high rate of wages have been maintained, but not more than maintained. The rupee, as you know, has been depreciated, but still it seems to have at least the same purchasing power as it had before the depreciation set in. I need not detain you as to the causes of that depreciation, but these causes certainly set in immediately after the termination of the Franco-German War. The payment of the French indemnity to Germany, the accumulation of silver in Germany, and the rapid demonetization of silver were among the causes. There are also other causes which you know have been so well set forth in the report of Mr. Goschen's Committee. The particular point to which this question refers, however, amounts to this: Has the rise of prices and of wages increased, since say the year 1870 or 1871? Well, gentlemen, this is a matter of fact, and there is no time this evening for me to prove it to you; but I can assure you, on the whole, the best opinions in India are to the effect that there has been no particular rise since that time. Prices no doubt vary very much in India. For instance, all the necessary articles of food are almost always dear in Western India, and somewhat dear in Southern India, and much cheaper in Northern India and in the Panjab, and particularly also in a part of Bengal; but Bombay is the centre of the area of dearness. With all these fluctuations wages rise, and have risen in a corresponding degree, though with respect to the wages there has been no particular rise since the year 1870. But the wages that have risen are generally those which are earned by the most skilled and industrious classes of native labourers. In the interior of the country and in many of the villages the wages are still lamentably low. But with the poorer classes of labourers throughout the Empire of India wages are largely paid in kind. Thus although the rates of wages may appear to be very low, and, on the other hand, the prices of food may appear to be high, nevertheless, the poorest and most helpless classes of labourers are paid in grain, so that they at all events do not feel specially the rise of prices. No doubt those who are paid in cash would feel the rise of prices; but their wages are much higher now than before. If generally the price of food has doubled, so has the rate of wages doubled for all skilled labourers. As for all the poorest and helpless labourers it is fortunate that they are paid in kind, for if they were not paid in kind they would be much more pinched in these days than ever they were before. That perhaps is as much of a general answer as it is possible for me to give to this difficult question in the short space of time allotted to me, especially as I must hasten on, with your permission, to the, perhaps, more interesting question which follows.

This question relates to "the capacity of the Empire to absorb new capital, and the direction in which new capital will most probably be required." Upon this question I must ask you to remember that capital in India will be of two kinds: first, that which belongs to the Natives; secondly, that which belongs to the Europeans. Now, there have been as regards native capital, writers in this country who labour to prove that Indian capital is decreasing under British rule, but this view is not for a moment accepted by statisticians and economists in India. On the contrary, we allege that, although the outward and visible signs of native wealth may not be so remarkable as they were in former times, yet there are many strong salient facts which prove that native capital must have been accumulating and must still be increasing rapidly. For instance, there is the fact of the increase of foreign trade, the increase of the internal trade, and the increase of the coasting trade; there is the fact of a great many industries in the presidency towns in which natives are largely engaged; there is the painfully notorious fact of the growth—the undue growth—in wealth and influence of the money-lending class which I described to you in my other address,* and although it is a class which must be spoken of with all due respect before an audience like this, nevertheless there has been a fear lest that class should become too powerful relatively among other classes of their native countrymen. All these circumstances

* See the address comprised in Chapter XII.

go to prove that native capital is increasing largely. Then there is the fact of 20 millions sterling invested by the natives in Government securities; there is the fact of the rates of interest having diminished a great deal within the last generation or two, probably diminished from a rate of 20 per cent. to a rate of something between 6 per cent. and 12 per cent. All this seems to show that money is becoming more plentiful, and consequently cheaper.

However, it must be at once admitted that if the Empire is to be developed in the future it must be mainly through the agency of European capital. This European capital will be laid out—first, by the Government, and, secondly, by private bodies or individuals. But, remember, that if the capital is laid out by the Government, that capital will in the main come from England. State outlay in India means the outlay of British capital. I beg you to bear that point prominently in mind. For instance, taking the whole public debt of India together—unproductive war debt and productive debt, which represents the outlay upon remunerative works—taking that at 250 millions sterling, out of that less than 25 millions is owned by natives, so that natives at the best have not more than 10 per cent. out of the total investments. Clearly, if the outlay of capital by the Government is to continue, that outlay must be based upon a thoroughly safe and sound national finance, and, upon an occasion like this it seems desirable that I should recapitulate to you the main grounds upon which the safety of Indian finances rest.

More than a year ago—the last time I had the honour of expounding to the English public the finances of India—the case I had to make out was this:* that upon a period of twenty years the income of the Government and the ordinary expenditure were upon a safe equilibrium, supported by a small surplus; that taking one year with another upon that twenty years there was a surplus of 1½ million. It was very important to make that

* This alludes to the book entitled 'India in 1880' Chapter XXVII.

point good, because at that time there were several public writers, able and well-meaning, who had been trying to make out that India was rapidly sinking into a state of insolvency. But insolvency was not at all to be imputed; on the contrary, there was really a small surplus. This surplus was obtained after the Government had paid 15 millions sterling out of its Treasury for the relief of India from the famine. Two years have elapsed, and what is the present state of the case? I ought to mention, that the payment of the expenses of the Afghan war was just commencing two years ago: the payment is now almost completed. Well, up to the close of the current official year, the cost of that war was 19 millions sterling. Now, the whole of that 19 millions has been defrayed without any borrowing. I think that is a remarkable fact. How has it been paid? Why, in the first place India paid 9½ millions out of her cash balances for the three years ending 1880–81. Besides that, she reduced her ordinary cash balances by another 4½ millions which makes up just 14 millions, and in addition she received a grant of 5 millions from the English Treasury. That makes up the 19 millions. You may have heard much of the Government of India having appropriated certain money for the payment of the war-expenses, which money had been raised for protective works against famines. And in the urgency of the moment no doubt money was advanced from the Treasury for the purposes of the war. But within a couple of years the whole of that was repaid to the famine account—as soon as the grant was made from the English Treasury. Thus it is the fact that towards the expenses of this war India contributed 14 millions sterling out of her current revenues, and though she had in the urgency of the time to appropriate quite temporarily the famine insurance money, she repaid every farthing of that the moment she got the promised subsidy from the English Government. So you see she really has a surplus, and there is still some expense remaining to be paid for the Afghan war; but after the favourable Budget of which we have just received notice from

India,* one cannot doubt that the expense of the war will be defrayed in the same sound financial manner as it has hitherto been. Thus, at the present moment Indian finances stand in the satisfactory position that they have still a small surplus, notwithstanding that they have defrayed 15 millions for famine and 14 millions for war; so that this heavy war expense has been entirely defrayed without borrowing. Now all this constitutes a satisfactory basis upon which a Government may proceed when it begins to lay out capital upon productive works for the improvement of the country.

Well, as I have just explained to you, the public debt of India really represents a large outlay of British capital. In round numbers that debt amounts to 250 millions sterling. Out of that about 100 millions represent payments for wars in times past, and may be classed as non-productive debt. Of the remaining 150 millions, in round figures, 50 millions have been spent upon State railways and canals of irrigation, and the remaining 100 millions have been laid out by guaranteed railway companies. The guaranteed railways and State railways together are now paying interest at the rate of 5 per cent., and the canals are paying interest at the rate of 6 per cent. Out of the 50 millions you may say that a little more than half has been spent upon railways, and a little less than half upon canals. The railways, State and guaranteed together, are moving about 10 millions of tons of produce per annum, which you will admit represents a great accommodation to the Indian public. The profits upon these works are so considerable—that is to say, the railways, both State and guaranteed, and canals—that although the capital amount of the debt has been increasing during many years past, nevertheless the interest charges are gradually diminishing, that is to say, the net charges. The Government on the one hand has to pay the interest upon the debt; on the other hand it receives the net receipts from the works. These

* This was the Indian Budget for 1882-3 with revised estimates for 1881-2.

net receipts give an income, and as they increase the interest charges diminish. Thus you may now say, that although the interest on the debt is 4 per cent., nevertheless, owing to the receipts on the other side, the real charge upon the estate is not more than 3 per cent.; and if you take in the guaranteed railways, then, according to the least favourable calculation, the interest charge is not more than 2 per cent., and the most favourable calculations make it out to be not more than 1½ per cent. So that you see upon the debt proper of about 150 millions sterling the Government is, owing to its productive public works, paying interest at the rate of about 3 per cent.; and upon the total debt of 250 millions, which includes the amount of the guaranteed railways, the Government is paying from 1½ to 2 per cent. I think you will admit that if these figures are substantiated the result is very encouraging. It will come to this, that before long, in another generation, the Government will be paying no interest upon its debt, or, in other words, the interest charges will have been recovered by net receipts, and ultimately there will be a considerable profit. Even now, according to some very able calculations put forward the other day by Sir John Strachey, it would appear that upon this capital of the debt which I have just explained to you, about 11 millions sterling nominally are being paid by the Government to the capitalists who lend the money, which capitalists are mainly Europeans. Out of that sum, three millions may be set down as the amount due on account of the non-productive debt, which leaves eight millions. This amount is paid by India to the British capitalists without any burden being put upon her, while she on the contrary reaps an immense benefit from the works themselves—a benefit as regards her trade, her cultivation and her irrigation.

Such being the general outline of a rather large subject, namely, the outlay of capital by the State upon India, it is desirable that I should explain to you how far this outlay is likely to extend in the future. Now, in the first place, you probably are aware that the guaranteed railways system is not likely to be extended. The next point is that of the State railways. The State railways in India mean railways constructed by the State out of borrowed capital. This system is undoubtedly likely to be much extended. We have now 10,000 miles open of what may be called first-class railways—Guaranteed lines and State lines taken together. By the most limited calculation 10,000 miles are still required. Whether that 10,000 miles will be constructed speedily or gradually must greatly depend upon the cost per mile. You are aware that with all their immense merits and with all the vast services they render to the country, the guaranteed companies certainly did incur a very liberal outlay. Their railways cost 14,000*l*. a mile on the average, and in many instances they cost much more. The State railways have been also somewhat liberal in the same way, and have not been essentially cheaper than the others. Then comes the question of broad gauge and narrow gauge. Financial people desire to have the narrow gauge, because it is likely to be cheaper, but the great railway interest, especially the engineers and contractors and many other professional gentlemen, were much opposed to that view, and the military authorities joined in with them, so ultimately the broad gauge prevailed. Still there are many instances which have lately occurred of short lines of railway, both broad and narrow gauge, being made for sums less than 5,000*l*. a mile.

An interesting question to you is the chance of railways being made by private companies. There are several instances of that. First of all, you are aware of the company which, under the auspices of the Portuguese Government, is making a railway from the sea-port of Goa to the south-west part of India. You will remember that a company which has started under a very able chairman, my friend General Dickens, is making railways in Bengal. There are several branch lines also being made by private companies. However, the success of such undertakings will greatly depend upon the practicability of making the railways cheaply. The fact is that, once the Government with its officers and its engineers shall grasp the fact that railways can be made easily and cheaply, not in first-rate professional style, but good enough for practical purposes, then there is no limit to the extension of railway enterprise in India. What are ten, or twenty, or fifty thousand miles of railway in such a country as India, with an area of one and a half million square miles and a population of 253 millions of souls, while the subsidiary lines of road are not less than 20,000 miles? If you take the railway mileage of any great country in Europe—to say nothing of the United States of America—and compare it with India, then India ought to have something between 50,000 and 100,000 miles of railway, and I am sure she very much needs even that mileage. If, as I say, our engineers would only condescend to make lines cheaply and practically useful for the purpose of Indian trade and Indian passenger traffic, then every road almost may be a basis, first as a tramway, and then, when worked by the steam-engine, the tramway becomes a cheap railroad. There are many instances of the success of this plan. During the famine in Behar we wanted a temporary railway to carry the Government grain to the famishing people. However contrary these light and cheap constructions might be to professional views, we said, "It must be done;" and owing to the urgency of the case, it was done, and was opened. It has remained open ever since, greatly to the benefit of the country. The same principle was applied during the Bombay famine. There again we constructed what is called a chord line, between two great lines, for the sake of the urgent traffic in food grains. That was done cheaply, and it remained open for nine months out of the twelve each year; that is to say, in the three months of the flood season and during the height of the rains the line was closed; but for nine months in the year it did yeoman's service for the good of the country; and it was constructed cheaply. In the same way almost every macadamized road, through the length and breadth of the land, might be gradually utilised; and if this were done, we should have the commencement of a thorough railway system all over the country. There is also the case of a native statesman, the Minister of the Gaekwar of Baroda, who declared there were no materials in his country for the making of roads,—in fact, there was no material for metalling; so he determined to have a railway made—which was called a "baby railway," and which was a very cheap line, with a very narrow gauge of 2 feet 4 inches or 2 feet 6 inches. It was made so cheaply that some critics laughed at it; but it did a vast amount of business, and carried passengers and goods cheaply, easily and quickly; and its cost was within the means of the Native State. And really, if once the Government were to begin and work in that way, and make its engineers apply their professional talents to that sort of business, there is no limit to the vista of railway enterprise which opens itself before the imagination in India.

I must turn now to the canals. The canals of irrigation will probably continue to be made by the Government. No doubt it is greatly to be desired that this beneficent work should be done by private companies. You are aware of the great canal companies that were set on foot in Orissa, under Sir Arthur Cotton, and in Southern India; but from various causes, which I must not detain you by recapitulating, neither of these companies proved quite successful, so they ultimately had to be bought up by Government, and the works are now carried on entirely under Government auspices. Still there are some enterprising gentlemen endeavouring to start companies for this purpose both in Sind and the Panjab, and we may wish them every possible success; but still there is a fear that even when the works are done there will be some difficulty with respect to the payment for the water. The payment for water for irrigation enters greatly into the landed and agricultural systems of the country and gets mixed up with questions of land revenue, so that it is the opinion of the best authorities on irrigation that this is one of those matters which must be managed by Government. But, even if this is done by Government, still it is the London money market which has to supply the capital. Then, you are aware, we have already a magnificent canal system. It could be proved statistically to be simply the finest the world has ever seen. All other irrigation canal systems, whether ancient or modern, sink into insignificance when compared with the canals of India. That being the case, many of the best sites have been taken up, and the waters of many classic rivers—the Ganges and others (I mean with reference to sources of supply)—have been monopolised already for the purpose of irrigation; nevertheless there are many other noble fields for irrigation enterprise. On the east coast several magnificent deltas are already occupied with a reticulation or network of canals; nevertheless there are two deltas remaining there. On the west coast, north of Bombay, two or more deltas also remain. Out of the five Panjab rivers two only have been utilised for irrigation, and three remain awaiting utilisation. The Lower Indus, that now makes Sind a lesser Egypt, and the Upper Indus have yielded up their waters to the irrigation engineer. But there are several important rivers in Oude from which canals may be taken. In fact, in every part of the country there are still giant rivers which await the invasion of the engineer. Thus on the whole, you may hope that from time to time there will be a constant extension of irrigation, and for that the funds will be supplied from England. It is to be hoped that the profits upon that capital outlay will be as great as the profits which I have been just mentioning to you with regard to the past.

Now, I have been asked whether there is any chance of capital being laid out upon the roads. I may at once say "absolutely none whatever." It has been determined that the expenditure upon roads shall be incurred from the State revenue. There would be, really, no means of securing anything like a return for private capital invested for such a purpose, because experience has shown that with the habits of the natives it is impossible to levy tolls, and one does not therefore see how returns are to be realised.

You will ask me upon what other things has capital been, or is being, or will be, laid out? Pray remember that there are many valuable and interesting products upon which British capital may be expended. In the first place there is tea. You are probably aware that within this generation the export of tea from India has risen from nothing to 40,000,000 lbs. annually. The tea crop of India is worth now between 4,000,000*l.* and 5,000,000*l.* annually. The area under tea gardens is perhaps now 200,000 acres. If you will look at the returns you will find that several hundred thousand acres have been allotted to various tea planters and companies; but the proposed plantations have not yet been all cultivated, although the Eastern Himalayas, the valley of Assam, and the upper part of the valley of the Brahmaputra are remarkably well fitted for tea gardens. There are vast tracts also between Bengal and Burmah fit for tea-culture which have yet to be cultivated: thus you may look forward for a large field there for the outlay of capital. Then there is coffee, which grows in the south-west of India. I am not sure that there is any likelihood of so great an expansion with reference to coffee as there is in regard to the tea plant. Then there is cinchona. That at present is a culture which is undertaken by Government, and once the Government shall succeed in this culture the febrifuge will be popular. There are many parts of India where cinchona might be grown to a vast extent and so afford quinine, or something like quinine, for many of the millions of the people. Then there is rice, which already largely employs European capital. At all the great ports there are many European firms entirely engaged in the rice trade; and at a time when some writers were statistically proving to the satisfaction, or dissatisfaction, of the British public that India was gradually starving. India, nevertheless, gave a most practical refutation by persisting in exporting, even in years of scarcity, tens of thousands of tons of rice to all parts of Europe. Now the wheat cultivation has begun to develop itself extraordinarily, there are some persons even beginning to say it is not American competition that we have to fear—it will be Indian competition. Certainly within the last two or three years the manner in which the wheat cultivation has increased is startling. The quantities have increased from 392,000 qrs. in 1879, to 1,300,000 qrs. in 1880, and to 3,742,000 qrs. in 1881; while in value the amount has risen from less than 1,000,000*l.* in 1879, to 7,750,000*l.* in 1881. Next, there is the product of indigo. That used to take up a great deal of European capital; but the production is declining, because it cannot be carried on profitably by the natives now as the price of all other articles of produce have risen so much.

Then we have the whole class of articles named fibres. There is cotton, regarding which I need not trouble you with details; but jute has become a great article, not only of domestic manufacture, but of exportation abroad, and it is probable if native capital is not invested American will be, because a great deal of jute from Calcutta goes to San Francisco and California. Then there is the article of hemp, a fabric about which I cannot go into details. But I may remind you of the textile fabrics. The value of cotton manufactures imported into India from England now amounts to the large sum of 26 millions sterling annually. There has been much discussion as to whether Manchester is, or is not, succeeding in clothing the people of India; whether she is supplying half, or one-third, or two-thirds, of the clothing for this vast population. I am not sure I can undertake to give you a positive opinion as to the extent to which Manchester is obtaining the Indian custom, but the best opinion is that Manchester has got a large part of the Indian custom. Still a large part yet remains for her to win, and it is likely that she will win it now the import duties have been taken off by the Government of India. Whether Manchester has or has not obtained a great part of the custom with regard to cotton manufactures, she has got but little with regard to woollen; but she has acquired some hold on the market, and when once the use of English woollens begins to increase there is a limitless field for private enterprise. The people of India, even the poorest of them, have their blankets; and the day will be a great day when all the blankets for this vast population shall be furnished from England.

Then there is a whole set of mining products—coal mines and iron mines. The coal mines are already pretty well worked. The iron mines were once well worked by the natives, but have fallen away; but recently private companies have been started for working them. Formerly there were copper mines being worked all over the country, of which many remains are to be seen in every district. Gold mines more readily recur to your recollection. On former occasions I have ventured to speak only with great caution regarding the prospects of the gold mines; and I am afraid my gloomy anticipations have been unfortunately fulfilled, for these mines are not doing much. It seems that there is yet gold, but it is deep down and cannot be brought to the surface at a remunerative price.

There are other things also. New companies have been started for making paper from bamboos. There is a considerable interest in the tanning of hides for leather, and making every kind of article with leather. There is a company formed for producing petroleum in various parts of Burmah. Recently orders have been given by the Government of India, with the approval of the Government in England, for the purchase on the spot of all stores necessary for the public service in India. Again, there are the interesting works of art in which natives excel, such as pottery, the various fabrics in gold and silver embroidery, and rich or beautiful stuffs. British capital may be employed in importing all these articles into the United Kingdom and introducing them to the public. To conclude the list of those miscellaneous articles I should mention machinery. The use of machinery will greatly depend upon technical education among the people of India. I am afraid education has been defective in this respect in all parts of the British Empire. But now that England herself is waking to the necessity of technical education, no doubt this kind of education will soon spread to India, and when it does, in a generation or two, there will be a great demand for every sort of implement and machine, and if that should be the case, you will see what bright prospects open for the mechanical profession. The same with agricultural education. It has been most defective in India, and that is, no doubt, one of the defects the Government will remedy during the next generation. Scientific agriculture in India will cause an importation of any amount of agricultural implements from England.

Before I conclude I must ask you to think of the probable absorption of capital in the future. Well, you see that for State purposes there will be a constant drawing, a requirement of capital of several millions annually. All these other industries which I have mentioned will also require several millions of capital, so we may hope there will be a drawing of British capital to the East of some millions annually. I am not attempting to give you an estimate of the amount of capital required on each one of them. It will be no use giving you an estimate without supporting it in detail, and it would be impossible for me in one evening, to give matters of detail necessary to support my estimate. But you will readily understand that there is a great probability of increased power of production arising in the country, because after all, what are the 250 millions sterling already mentioned in comparison with so vast a country as India? What is even the trade? Much is said of the foreign trade of India, and it has wonderfully increased. In this generation it has risen from 40 millions in value to 140 millions sterling annually. Perhaps 100 millions of increase in one generation is as much as could be expected. Still the total amount of the trade is very small for so vast a country. Besides the trade with foreign countries there are 60 millions' value of coasting trade, and the vast internal trade represented by the railways. But after all what is 60 millions' worth of trade for such an extensive coast? The coast itself, dotted with harbours from point to point, is upwards of 1000 miles in extent. And, after all, what are 10,000 miles of railways for the area I have described?

May I mention in conclusion one or two articles, which will illustrate to you the rapid rate of increase which has been going on within the last 25 years? Take the period of the war of the mutinies, 25 years ago, and think of the increase in several important articles! At that time the English cotton manufactures imported to India were valued at six millions yearly, and they are now valued at 26 millions sterling. The British metals, then, imported into India were valued at 1½ millions, and they are now valued at 3¾ millions sterling. Grain of all kinds, wheat, rice, and pulses (all food grains) were then valued at three millions sterling. They are now valued at 13 millions. The shipping at that time was stated at 2,800,000 tons, and is now at 6½ million tons. These are the imports and exports of India, but there is one more article I may mention, namely, the export of cotton. That is supposed to have declined in India since the American civil war, but at the time of the war of the mutinies—25 years ago—it was valued at 3 millions sterling annually, and now it is valued at 13 millions. Thus you see upon every one of these very important articles there has been a very rapid increase within the last 25 years.

Such, then, are the facts of various sorts, which I venture to mention to you as constituting an earnest of hope for the future, and I trust that the prospect will be satisfactory to you, gentlemen, as men of business in London, the greatest commercial centre of the world.

# CHAPTER XI.

## INDIAN FORESTRY.

Services rendered by the Society of Arts in England — Sylvan glories of India — The cedars, cypresses, rhododendrons, and other trees of the mountains — The palms, bamboos, and other trees of the plains — Use of forests for economic purposes — Their climatic value — Past destruction of Indian forests — Their conservation at the present time — Large operations of the Indian Forest Department — Good work done by European foresters in India — Services rendered by the Scottish Arboricultural Society — Methods of scientific forestry — Reservation of rights pertaining to the Natives — Services rendered to India by British arboriculturists and foresters.

### PART I.

[*Speech delivered before the Society of Arts, in London, January* 1881.]

I ESTEEM it an honour to be asked to speak before the Society of Arts, remembering as I do, in common with all Englishmen, the historical and distinguished part which the Society has played in the educational and industrial history of England during the nineteenth century. Not only has the Society effected much for the fine arts, of which we see traces in the room in which we are assembled, but more especially has it done great things in the application of science to all the varied industries of England. It has also effected more, probably, than any other corporation in England, for the advancement of technical education; and in the remarks I shall make to you regarding forests, you will find a signal proof of the mischief which has been wrought, mainly, from the want of technical and professional knowledge on the part of our own countrymen in

India regarding forestry. I feel, however, much encouragement in addressing you this evening, when I look back on the names of the great men who have guided the deliberations of this Society, such men as the Duke of Norfolk in the last century, H.R.H. the Duke of Sussex, H.R.H. Prince Albert, and now H.R.H. the Prince of Wales. We have also had and have now on the Council of the Society men whose names are really the property of the nation, such men as Wentworth Dilke, Lubbock, Leighton, Siemens, Brassey and Galton. But more especially we have had on the Council many men who have contributed much to develop the industries of India in particular, such men as Cole, Sykes, Birdwood, Alcock, and Cunliffe-Owen. Well then, looking to these names of men, some departed, and others still present among us, we ought all of us, those who speak and those who listen, to feel the responsibility which attaches to us while assisting in the deliberations and proceedings of such a corporation as the Society of Arts. Among its many educational and scientific operations, arboriculture was one of the earliest.

As a remarkable instance, I may remind you that it is now nearly 130 years since this Society began to pay attention to forestry, an attention which remains undiminished up to the present moment. It was soon after 1760, as you will perceive from the history of London, written by Charles Knight, and Davenport's history of our Society, that gold and silver medals, presented by this Society for planting firs and cedars, were won by such distinguished persons as the Dukes of Bedford and Beaufort, Lord Paget, Earls Winterton, Ossory, Mansfield, and Wilton, the Bishop of Llandaff, and the Marquis of Tichfield. There were also men in those days whose names have been handed down in the history of British agriculture as well as arboriculture, namely, Curwen of Windermere, Morse and John Hutton, of Yorkshire, and Bucknall. These men originally showed what could be done in the way of tree plantation in Great Britain, and it is to be hoped that they may prove to be the ancestors of a long line of Englishmen, who from generation to generation, will distinguish themselves in arboriculture in all parts of the British Empire throughout the world.

From this brief preface I will pass straight to the subject of the evening, namely, Indian forestry. Now India, of course, is not the only country in which questions regarding forestry are becoming prominent. The mischief which has been wrought by the destruction of forests is patent on the face of Western Europe. The destructive floods which have occurred in many parts of France, are directly due to the denudation of the Swiss hills. In many parts of Russia the same sort of mischief is seen by every traveller to be going on. Similar questions are being raised in South Africa, and we hear even of injury being feared in the United States of America. But in Scandinavia I have witnessed with admiration the forest conservancy established, and fine area of forests preserved by the Government of Sweden and Norway. The forest preserves in Germany, too, afford us a capital example.

Now, in India the destruction has been vast. The traditions of the forests in India show how the land was once clothed with sylvan and other vegetation, but every time in olden days a city had to be formed or a palace erected, or in modern days a railway to be constructed or barracks to be built, there has been a ruthless destruction of forests. Of course forests were made for the use of man, but they may be so cut as to leave something for reproduction. Instead of that they have been swept away as clean as if they had been shaven by a razor—I speak figuratively. Well, notwithstanding this destruction, some forests remain, though they can be hardly said to be more than the remnants of what once were the forests of India. You will say, perhaps, why did not the Government and its officers stop this devastation? They did not stop it, simply because they were none of them properly instructed in matters regarding forests. Such ignorance is not to be wondered at, considering the ignorance which has prevailed in Europe and in other parts of the world. I know that twenty or thirty years ago, when we were young men in India, we, none of us, heard of any principles regarding forest conservancy. The consequence was that forests, being remote and difficult of access, not easy to visit or to understand, and we ourselves being ignorant of everything regarding forestry, we paid no attention whatever to the subject. Consequently, whenever wood was wanted, forests were cut down by persons who had nothing to do except to make as much profit as they could at the present moment, without regard to the future, and so forests have been destroyed in the most thoughtless and merciless manner. Still, there are great mountain ranges, for instance, the Western Ghats, which form a mountainous wall on the western coast; the Eastern Ghats, which form a similar range, although not so regular, on the eastern coast; two great ranges, the Satpura and Vindhya, which unite in the direction of Bengal, and form one broad mountainous region; the mountain ranges on the east of Bengal, separating Bengal from Burmah; and, lastly, the great Himalayan range itself. I do not now speak of the mountain range on the west of the Indus, because that was originally a region mainly destitute of vegetation, and whatever vegetation there was has long been swept away by the action of man; so that really the great range which separates India from Afghanistan counts for nothing, in the language of forestry. The ranges, with which forestry in India has to do, are the Western Ghats, the Eastern Ghats, the Satpura and Vindhya, the Eastern Bengal ranges, and the mighty Himalaya.

In these mountain ranges, there are numerous kinds of trees which constitute a forest flora in themselves. It is quite impossible for me, within the time at our disposal, to even enumerate, much less describe to you, the various kinds of trees which exist in the Indian forests; still I may mention, by way of recapitulation, some of the most striking and interesting trees which we have. The trees of India must be divided mainly into two main divisions, the Himalayan division, and the division of the plains as contra-distinguished from the Himalayan region, which latter division comprises the whole of India proper.

Now, the Himalayan trees are allied mainly to the trees of Europe and other temperate regions. The *coniferæ*, including the great genera of firs, pines, and the like, are found all over the Himalayas. Amongst them the queen is the cedar. Nowhere in the world are such fine cedar forests to be seen as in the Himalayas. You have some idea, in England, from the lawns of our principal country seats, of what beautiful shape and colour the foliage of the cedar is; then imagine trees much grander, much finer in trunk, branch, and foliage, with a background of everlasting snow; imagine them, too, standing in the midst of rugged situations, and with the most glorious surroundings. There is a further interest attaching to them, from the way in which they are felled, and the mode in which the logs, when felled, are transported to market. The value of a cedar forest depends on its situation. If the trees stand upon precipitous sites, overhanging rivers, they are felled to great advantage. The tree is felled, and the log is shot down the precipice into the roaring, cataract-like, torrent of the river. The river itself acts as a carrier, and whirls log after log down to the plains. And as the river, laden with all this freight of cedar logs, emerges from the Himalayas, skilful native swimmers are stationed on the bank, who dart forth and catch the logs as they descend the stream.

Similar remarks apply to the *Pinus longifolia*, which is, next after the cedar, the most valuable timber tree in the Himalayas. In fact, in Northern India, most of the great public buildings of the British Government, and most of the palaces of the native princes, are largely constructed with the timber of cedar and pine. As a matter of interest, I should not omit to mention the cypress. But the cypress of the Himalayas is not the funereal sort of tree which you read of, or see depicted, as constituting a great feature in the cemeteries and burial-grounds of the Levant or Constantinople, but is a truly magnificent tree, growing, too, in the very midst of limestone formations. There appear to be certain chemical elements in the limestone which favour the growth of the tree, and the consequence is, that the cypress may be seen fringing limestone precipices, where you would suppose that no vegetation could possibly grow—in places, indeed, where the only vegetation perceptible consists of these cypress trees, springing, as it were, out of the very crevices of the rocks. But as regards funereal aspect, the most mournful looking tree in the Himalayas is the fir, which is named the *Abies Smithiana.* That, indeed, has long, pendent foliage, of a very weeping, pensive appearance, but still impressive and picturesque, especially when combined with other foliage, and more particularly, perhaps, when it is adorned by the golden red of the Virginia creeper. Imagine the bright scarlet leaves of the creeper winding about amongst the dark-coloured, mournful-looking foliage of the fir, and you have a delightful picture.

Then another tree, most beautiful in the Himalayas, is the yew. It does not grow there singly, as it does in this country, but in a few spots among the Himalayas it grows in a dense forest, limited in size, but extremely thick; and nothing can surpass, from an artistic point of view, the beautiful forms of these dependent branches and the foliage of these yews. The beautiful lines of Wordsworth are applicable to these yew forests—

> "Joined in one solemn and capacious grove
> Huge trunks, and each particular trunk a growth
> Of intertwisted fibres serpentine;
> Nor uninformed with phantasy, and looks
> That threaten the profane—a pillared shade.
> Upon whose grassless floor of red-brown hue
> By sheddings from the pining umbrage tinged
> Perennially. . . . Ghostly shapes
> May meet at noon-tide."

Lastly, I should mention the juniper. This tree is extremely fine in the Himalayas; and when I mentioned to you just now that the trans-Indus range, near Afghanistan, was almost treeless, I ought to have made one exception in favour of the juniper. We hear now much of the Bolan Pass, and of Quettah, but the only valuable timber you have near Quettah consists of juniper forests, that grow near the summits of the limestone formations, 10,000 or 12,000 feet above the sea, which overlook those valleys, now so interesting to us from a political point of view.

Then, passing from this great natural order of *coniferæ,* we come to the other trees which are very familiar to us all in this country, the ilex, the oak, and the walnut, which are found in great abundance at Simla, where, as you know, is the residence of the Governor-General and his Council in the summer months. Near Simla, there grows the holly. In that locality it is not a shrub, as it is in this country, but a very fine tree of fifty to sixty feet high. I ought also to mention the plane tree. The plane tree is a great ornament of the so-called happy—at all events the world-wide celebrated—valley of Cashmir. The scenes of the poem, Lalla Rookh, were laid in the midst of plane groves. Plane trees formed the ornament of the gardens of the great Mogul on the margin of the beautiful lake of Cashmir. The famous wooded island which stands in the midst of the lake is adorned with plane trees; in fact, in Cashmir, the plane is the crown and glory of the valley. In the eastern part of Himalayas, near Darjiling, we have the maple; also the magnolia, which is brilliant with masses of white flower, so that it looks in the midst of summer as if it were sprinkled with fresh snow. The laurel grows there to a great height, not like the shrub as we see it here, but as a great tree seventy to eighty feet high. The tree-fern is probably the most graceful member of the vegetable kingdom to be seen anywhere—the tree-fern of the eastern Himalayas. No word-painting of mine can give you any idea of the minutely graceful character of its foliage, especially, too, as it is generally seen with the distant background of the highest snow mountains in the world.

Before we leave the Himalayas, I must say one word about the rhododendrons. The discovery of the Himalayan rhododendrons is mainly due to Sir Joseph Hooker, the distinguished director of the Botanic Garden at Kew. With great toil, hardship and exertion, he discovered and brought to England specimens of most of the finest species of rhododendrons. The tree does not grow there in shrubs as you see in this country, but attains a height of twenty to thirty feet. Its flowers, seen in its native habitat, are almost as large as a man's head. The leaves found on the trees there are twelve to thirteen inches long. The branches and the trunk are permeated with a sort of red colouring matter, so that the whole of the tree seems ready to burst out with red; anything more magnificent, in the botanic kingdom, than the appearance of this tree cannot be imagined. It is generally found in the midst of very rocky scenery: it flowers with great abundance, at altitudes of 12,000 to 13,000 feet, and that generally at a season in May and June, when the long winter of those regions has hardly passed away, so that the rich flowers are faded and bleached, in a day or two after blooming, by the masses of fog and driving rain, and sometimes even of sleet, to which they are exposed.

So much, then, for the trees of the Himalayas. I regret that time does not admit of my dilating more fully upon them.

I must pass rapidly on to the trees of the plains. The first I shall mention of course is the teak, or *Tectona grandis*, which is the queen of trees in the plains, just as the cedar is the queen of trees in the mountains. The teak is said by enthusiastic foresters to possess every virtue of which wood is capable. It is good underground, it is good in the water, it is good in the burning sun, it is good everywhere, and under all cirumstances. It carves well; it is light, it is durable; it will stand wet, and is seldom affected even by insects. It is used, as you know, largely by the British Admiralty. Its appearance always attracts the eye of the observer, on account of the arrowy manner in which it shoots up. Even the young tree, which is hardly a foot or two above the ground, always looks like an infant giant, or a young Hercules, amongst trees, by the striking manner in which it rises from the ground and seems to aspire upwards.

Then there is the sāl, or *Shorea robusta*, which has been called the iron-hearted Sāl, on account of the great strength and durability of the wood; but it has not nearly so many virtues as the teak, especially in that it is very heavy. But its appearance is fine, with a tall, straight trunk, and branching head. It is to be found in the greatest perfection near the source of the Nerbadda, near the point where the two ranges of the Satpuras and Vindhyas unite. Next I should mention the two finest kinds of the natural order of the *Terminalia*. First, the *arjuna*, or anjun, is remarkable for the beauty of its trunk, which can only be likened to a great marble pillar. The trunk is absolutely white, bright and smooth, generally growing amidst rocks, on the margin of streams, and in a very hot climate. The trees I have hitherto been describing grow in the cool, but this tree grows in the midst of the greatest heat. The other kind of terminalia is the *Pentaptera tomentosa*, or sāj. That is the very opposite in appearance. Instead of having a white and smooth trunk, it has a black and rough bark, and, as the two trees often grow in juxtaposition, the effect is as though you saw a pillar of smooth white marble and a pillar of black rough stone placed close together. Then there is the *Pterocarpus marsupium*, or bije sāl, also a tree with a black-looking bark. In contradistinction to them, I may mention the salai, or *Boswellia thurifera*, commonly called the frankincense-tree. I have just mentioned the bije sāl, which has a rough, black bark, and, in contrast to that, I mention the salai. Instead of black bark, it has white bark; instead of a straight trunk, it has a winding, bending, straggling trunk, with branches thrown out in a kind of weird, wayward manner.

The salai, in the hot weather, when the leaves are off, may be called the ghost which haunts the forests of India.

The trees which I have just mentioned grow always on the lesser mountain ranges of British India, as contra-distinguished from the Himalayas; but I must now mention some of those which grow in the plains proper.

First of all there is the babul, or *Acacia arabica.* That is the one tree which is universal in India, and is used almost for every purpose that can be useful in the daily lives of the natives. Then there is the mango-tree, which is known, of course, on account of its fruit, and which furnishes a staple article of food to the mass of the people. But it is also valuable for timber. It is found in fine avenues on the side of the roads, and in sacred groves near to the Hindu temples. Then we have the sundar tree. You have often heard of the Sunderbunds, that great, semi-marine forest which grows on the low, sandy region near the mouth of the Ganges. They are called the Sunderbunds, but that name is really derived from the sundar, which is the principal tree in that part of the forest, extending for thousands of square miles. In that forest, the most remarkable tree is the sundar, from which most of the country boats of Bengal are made. As you may have heard, the river traffic in Eastern Bengal is, perhaps, the most extensive thing of the kind in the world. The network of rivers are navigated by hundreds of thousands of boats. The boats there are to the inhabitants what carts and wagons are to the inhabitants of other countries; and nearly all these countless boats are made from the sundar tree, which grows in the forest, near the mouth of the Ganges.

Next we have the different kinds of fig tree, or *Ficus.* There is, first of all, the ordinary *Ficus,* which is known popularly throughout the world as the banyan tree. That is the tree under the shades of which whole regiments have been occasionally encamped. It is the tree which you have read of in Milton, and the works of several modern poets. Its beauty consists in the manner whereby it throws down tendrils from its branches, which take root in the earth and form fresh trunks; so that a finely-developed banyan tree looks like the interior of a great Gothic structure. The tree has its colonnade, its arches, its aisles, its naves, and its transepts. Its roof consists of the densest foliage, so that the perspective view, taken in the interior of one of these great banyan trees, is, perhaps, the finest sylvan subject which the artist can possibly have for his brush or his pencil. Then there is the pipal, which is called *Ficus religiosa*, and is to be found near every Hindu temple. It is remarkable for the manner in which its branches entwine themselves amidst the masonry. You know the old song—

> "Creeping where no life is seen,
> A rare old plant is the ivy green."

Similar to this is the *Ficus religiosa*. It is always to be found in the midst of ruins; in fact, it is one of the causes of old buildings becoming ruins, for once it insinuates itself into the building, it gradually works its branches and its tendrils through all the interstices of the masonry, until possibly the whole structure is embraced in its fatal grasp. The building then becomes like a human being seized by a boa constrictor, or like the Laocoon encircled in the folds of the Python. Lastly, there is the *Ficus elastica*, or india-rubber tree, which many ardent foresters believe will, ere long, more than rival the india-rubber trees of South America.

Then there is the bamboo, the beautiful feathery bamboo, which affords the means of constructing almost all the huts, cottages, and villages of the inhabitants of Bengal. But, besides what may be called the domesticated bamboo, there is the wild bamboo of the forests of Central India, which is truly a lovely tree. A single shoot of wild bamboo has been shown at an exhibition, to the height of 80 or 90 feet, with a little flag at the top. These bamboos, too, generally overhang the pools of rivers, so that taking these tall, beautiful, graceful bamboos, bending over the stream, and the reflection in the stream—together forming almost an arch in appearance—a more picturesque object can hardly be conceived.

Lastly, we come to the palm. The first of the palms to be mentioned is the date-palm, that is the kind which is known to poetry as the feathery palm. Our Indian date-palms are, no doubt, not so fine as those of the valley of the Nile, or those on the banks of the Tigris and Euphrates, which run into the Persian Gulf. Still, next after these, our Indian palms are the finest to be found. Sometimes they grow singly, but often they are to be found in great clusters, and often in long, straight avenues. Then we have the Palmyra palm, with broad fan-like leaves, just like a human hand stretched out. It is, perhaps, more noxious than beneficial, for from it some of the strongest spirits in India are distilled. I shall conclude my mention of trees by describing the cocoa-nut. Now, the cocoa-nut, probably taking it all in all, is the most useful tree of all the trees in India, for it is commonly said—and truly said—that the cocoa-nut will provide everything which a human being needs physically. It will give him the most nutritious food, slightly oleaginous, perhaps, but still very strengthening; it will also give him the sweetest and most delicious drink; it will afford him everything that he can require for clothing; it will furnish him with roofing for his house; and it will give him not only the roofing, but the rafters. It will supply timber for the pillars upon which the edifice rests, and it will also give him the best material for rope. Thus there is hardly a want of man in the vegetable world which is not supplied by the cocoa-nut, and the cocoa-nut of India is second only to that of Ceylon, if, indeed, it is second. It grows in the greatest abundance all along the Malabar coast of India. There the cocoa-nut tree constitutes a little freehold, a distinct property, for actually the land revenue in some districts is based upon the cocoa-nut trees. That is to say, a man and his family get their living and pay their revenue out of a few cocoa-nut trees, so valuable is each tree.

Now, I wish I could dwell much longer on all these beautiful, interesting, and useful kinds of trees in India. I have hoped to induce you to feel an affectionate interest in them, to love the forests, so that they may live in your imaginations as they are living in mine. But I must pass on to the question of how all this vast national wealth should be preserved.

Before doing so, I must first say something as to the reasons why the trees are valuable. They are valuable for two main purposes, one economic, and the other climatic, and I will touch upon each of these subjects separately.

First I will allude to the economic purpose. Now, the preservation of forests is desirable for the sake of conserving the great wealth with which Nature has endowed India for the use of man. There are no less than 37,000,000 of inhabited houses in British India, and I need not say that for every one of those houses wood is required. The majority of these 37,000,000 houses are constructed mainly of wood, so you can imagine from that what an enormous demand there must be, in the vast British Indian population of 200,000,000 persons, for timber for house building alone; besides, there are 50,000,000 of inhabitants of Native States. Again, most of the domestic implements of the people are made of wood. No doubt, implements of various metals are being substituted for implements of wood, but, still, wood enters more largely into the consumption of the Indian population than that of most populations in the world for domestic implements. Among agricultural implements, take ploughs for instance, there is no accurate return of the number of ploughs in British India, but the best returns show at least 8,000,000 of ploughs. That, probably, is much below the mark. If you consider that there are not less than half a million villages, if there are 10 ploughs to a village, that would give 5,000,000; if there are 20 ploughs to a village, that would give 10,000,000; and if, which is much more likely, there are 30 ploughs to a village, that would give, perhaps, 15,000,000. From these facts you can judge what an enormous demand there is for wood, even for implements of agriculture. Then there are the carts. It is almost impossible to give any idea of the number of carts. There is no proper return of them, but they must be counted also by many millions; and as for the boats, in some parts of the empire they are also to be numbered by hundreds of thousands. Then, also, there is the consumption of fuel. Now, to meet the demand for all the purposes I have been hitherto mentioning, wood is somehow found from the forests; but, for fuel, there is, in most parts of India, an absolute want of wood, and the consequence is that the people use for fuel the cow-dung which ought to be used for manure. You hear very much in India of the gradual exhaustion of the soil. I hope (and that is all we can say) that the exhaustion is very gradual. It certainly does appear, from many proofs, to be very slow. But, at all events, the gradual exhaustion of soil is to be feared, unless the people can find some better means than they have at present for obtaining manure. At present, much of the natural manure of the country is being used for burning, and you can thence understand what a grave disadvantage is inflicted upon a country from the want of forest conservancy. In fact, the agriculture of the country is suffering greatly from this cause.

You will readily perceive how numerous and extensive the markets must be for timber and fuel, how difficult it is to keep them adequately supplied, and yet how fatal to the country it would be if they were to become depleted. Without a system of State conservancy, the forests would shrink and shrink, while population increases; materials in wood and timber would become scarcer and scarcer; the price of fuel would rise, so as to press heavily upon the poorer classes.

But there are other purposes, namely, the climatic. Many people think the droughts with which India is periodically visited arise from the destruction of forests. Too much, perhaps, must not be made of that cause. There is a certain amount of evaporation from the Indian Ocean, there are masses of clouds, and they must condense somewhere, so the total rainfall of the continent of India cannot possibly be affected by forests; but the distribution of the rainfall is probably very much affected. The clouds pass over the dry plains, and go straight on to the mountains. They arise in the Indian Ocean; the first obstruction they meet with is from the wall of hills along the western coast, but, passing over this wall of hills, they sweep over the dry plains of India, and then they meet with the Satpura and Vindhya ranges which I have described. They are stopped there; they condense on these ranges, and then cause torrents of rushing streams to arise and swell the rivers. Thus the clouds return back to the plains in the shape of floods, sweep away the railway viaducts, carry roadways to destruction, and so effect numerous damages. Now, a great deal of these floods might have been avoided, had the clouds been arrested in their course over the plains, and this arresting can only be brought about, in the opinion of the best judges, by the preservation of the forests. If the forests exist, a cool surface is presented to the clouds, which causes them to stop and condense into rain, and drop fatness on the earth. If there are no forests, the clouds pass on in the upper stratum of the air, until they are stopped by the hills.

The same description applies to Bengal; the vapours arise from the Bay of Bengal, are swept over the plains of Bengal, and are stopped by the great mountain ranges which divide Bengal from Burmah; or, again, they pass over the upper valley of the Ganges and Jumna, until they are checked by the Himalaya.

Time does not admit of my properly entering into this meteorological subject, but you will see, from these main facts, how very probable it is that the existence or non-existence of forests may greatly affect the distribution of the rainfall. If there are no forests, the probability is that at one time there will be droughts, and at another time immoderate rains, for a period of floods almost always follows, according to past experience, a period of drought. Thus it is to the forests we must partly look for being blessed with the early and the latter rains in due season.

I proceed to another point with regard to climatic influences, viz., the retention of moisture. There is no doubt that forests produce this result very considerably. If the vegetation is destroyed, the streams run dry unseasonably, and the wells have but a scanty supply of water. If the vegetation is preserved, the excessive moisture of the rainy season is stored by a natural process, for the use of man during the dry season. More especially is this important in those parts of India where canals have been constructed. Some of the canals of India are drawn from rivers which have their source amidst the Himalayas, in the perpetual snow, and for them forests are not of great importance. But many of the canals of India are drawn from rivers which rise in the mountain ranges of India itself, and if these mountain ranges are denuded of vegetation, the streams which feed these precious canals will all run dry in seasons of drought. If, then, we are to maintain our great canal system in full efficiency, we must preserve the forests near the sources of those rivers.

One more point with reference to climatic considerations, and that is the preservation of pasturage. The cattle in India have too much food at some seasons, and too little food at other seasons, and the consequence is that the animals, which have been suffering from depletion or inanition during the dry months, are apt to surfeit themselves as soon as the vegetation bursts forth into life upon the commencement of the annual rains. Now, the object is, by preserving forests, to preserve also the grass during the dry seasons. If there is a certain amount of vegetation, the grass is sheltered from the burning sun, and will thrive and afford fodder for cattle, whereas, if all the vegetation is swept away, grass will not thrive. For that reason, many experienced men think that more ought to be done in the plains of India for the establishment of what are called communal forests, and that every village, or cluster and circle of villages, should be induced or compelled to organize itself or to combine themselves for the establishment of communal forests, which shall afford a certain amount of timber and fuel, and shall also preserve the grass for the cattle.

These are the main reasons, in brief, why the preservation of forests is a matter of such vital importance and national concern in India.

I then come to the measures to be taken for preserving these forests. I have sorrowfully admitted to you the neglect on this subject, which has prevailed in former years. Nobody is more zealous than I am in vindicating the character and conduct of our Government and officers in India, but I must admit that in respect of the preservation of forests, we have not, until within the last twenty years, done as much as it behoved us to do. I attribute that not to any wilful neglect, but simply to the fact which I stated at the outset of my speech, namely, a want of knowledge. It is the deficiency of technical education on this subject which has caused the partial destruction of these great sources of national wealth—a wealth too, which, as you see, is essential to the well-being of the country. But, of late, we have been mending our ways in that respect, and we have established a highly organised department of forestry. We now have a large staff of trained forest officers. I wish I could add that they had been trained in this country (Great Britain). You may have seen lately that there is a project for establishing a forest school in England, in connection with the forest of Epping; and now we hope to have a forestry class attached to the College of Civil Engineering at Cooper's Hill. Hitherto, however, our British forest officers have been trained, not in their native country, but in France and Germany; and we must acknowledge the great debt we owe to our gallant neighbours, the French, for the excellent forest school of Nancy, which has given us many English officers for the benefit of the Indian forests. Still, there is no reason why forestry should not be taught in England or Scotland as well as anywhere else. You do not require a very large or extensive wild forest, in order to learn the principles of forestry. Any of the numerous woods and covers which adorn the undulating valleys of England would do perfectly well for instructing Englishmen in the art of forestry, to say nothing of the woods which may be found in Scotland or Wales. But, at all events, it matters not so much where the men are instructed, as that they should be well instructed somewhere; and I am happy to state that we have now a Forest Department of India which, in respect of scientific, technical, and practical knowledge, is second to no similar department in any country.

Now, you will ask, what exactly does this great department do? In the first place, the remaining forests—I must call them remaining forests, because you see how the ancient forests of the country have been destroyed—are divided into two great categories. They are divided by law (for the matter has received careful attention from the Indian Legislature) into two classes; firstly, "reserves," or the forests which are absolutely guarded; and, secondly, "protected" forests, which are imperfectly guarded and preserved. To give you any idea of the extent of these forests, I must mention to you the area in square miles, and you will find that at first sight this area does present a respectable aggregate or total. In the Panjab there are now 4000 square miles; in the North-West Provinces, 3000; in Bengal, 9000; in Assam, 7000; in the Central Provinces, comprising the Satpura and Vindhya ranges, which I have mentioned several times, 20,000; in Berar, 5000; in several miscellaneous districts, 1000; in British Burmah, 2000; and the Burmese forests are probably the best in the empire. All these make up, for the Bengal Presidency, a total of 51,000 square miles. To this you must add 13,000 square miles for Bombay, and 5000 for Madras, which make up a grand total of 69,000 square miles, or, say in round numbers, 70,000. This sum total will, ere long, be augmented, because there are many thousand square miles yet to be marked off in British Burmah, and, I believe, there are some thousands of square miles also to be marked off in southern India, within the limits of the Madras Presidency, so that, I dare say, within a few years, we shall have not less than 100,000 square miles of forest in India, which is a figure worthy of being mentioned before a distinguished Society like this. But it were vain, if I were to lead you to believe that the whole of this area, of 70,000 square miles, is properly protected; I am afraid that the greater portion of it is imperfectly protected; but still, nearly half is really well preserved; and the Famine Commission, in the very careful report they have recently made on the resources of India, say that 25,000 square miles are thoroughly guarded and preserved; but at all events, the whole of this great area is, more or less, under some protection and supervision.

The Forest Department, as above described, manages directly all the forests technically described by law as "reserved," and supervises the management by the ordinary civil officers of the forests technically described as "protected." From these forests, the markets for timber and fuel are largely supplied. The proceeds for all British India amount to about three-quarters of a million sterling annually, and the expenses to half a million.* Thus, the department defrays all the charges for the conservancy, and yields a small revenue to the State. Many articles of wild forest produce, such as gall-nut and sandal-wood, are sent to the great marts for exportation abroad.

Besides the area of forests, as above set forth, there are extensive areas of jungle of equal, probably more than equal extent, left in the hands of the people, under the terms of the Land Revenue Settlement. From these jungles most of the local wants of the country, as above mentioned, are supplied.

The first-class timber markets are, however, supplied from the "reserved" forests, and the second-class timber markets from the "protected." From both kinds of forests excellent fuel is obtained.

The railways were at first worked with wood fuel; but coal

* Since this speech was delivered these amounts have increased by 20 per cent.

is largely used, now that the mines are being opened. With a good conservancy system, however, there ought not to be any apprehension on account of wood being consumed by the railways. For forests could, in many places, be formed all along the lines of railway, and would supply fuel, while improving the country.

Then the question arises as to what does this preservation and guarding consist of, and to what intents and purposes are the forests protected? They are first protected as to the matter of wood-cutting. Timber is intended for the use of man, and the object is not to preserve the trees for ornament, but for utility. As soon as a tree has attained its utmost development, and grown to its full height, it is fit to be cut, and ought to be cut; and in many cases the trees grow so thickly together that thinning of them is a positive benefit to the vegetation of the forest. So, then, the restrictions upon wood-cutting are not made absolute, but are instituted in order to insure that a certain number of trees shall always be left for reproduction.

The next point is to regulate the practice of what is called "rab." Now, rab means this, that the new shoots and sprigs of the trees are burnt, and their ashes are used for manure. You will readily understand that such ashes contain many of those chemical constituents which are needed for manure, especially where much of the natural manure of the country, viz., the cow-dung, has been used for fuel. Now, this practice of cutting the sprigs of trees, and burning them to ashes for manure, is a practice which, if not regulated, will cause great damage to the forests; but, nevertheless, to a certain extent it is necessary.

Then another matter is the prevention of the jungle fires. These fires are partly accidental and partly intentional. When they are accidental they present some of the most magnificent spectacles you can possibly figure to yourselves. I, myself, and many other people in India, have been sometimes out at night in the midst of these fires, and you then see some of the grandest, if not, perhaps, the most alarming sights you ever witnessed. The way in which the devouring element rushes over the country, travelling sometimes at the rate of several miles an hour—the wild animals fleeing before it in terror, the native inhabitants of the forests sometimes even being caught in the flames and being burned to death, poor men, and occasionally even mounted Europeans having to gallop away to escape from the vast rushing conflagration—all these things constitute a wonderful sight. Then the burning trunks of the trees form as it were pillars of fire, the clumps of bamboos rattle and crackle just like the roll of musketry, the sound of the falling forest, and the roar of the flames is not unlike the resonances of artillery or the thunder of Heaven. Again, the manner in which some of the trees smoulder is quite wonderful. Stories are told of trees sometimes burning for many months together, and one I heard of, or rather read of, as having burned for three years consecutively. First, the trunk smouldered, then the fire got to the roots, and gradually burned through the radicles for months and months together.

Now, you will readily imagine what mischief is caused by such conflagrations as these spreading over many square miles. Yet the cause of the accident is often trifling, a wayfarer lighting his pipe, a labourer cooking his dinner (after the Oriental fashion) in the open air. With a system of conservancy, these accidents are minimised, or almost prevented altogether. Without such a system, they become terribly frequent.

But the fires are also intentional, and are lighted up every year to insure the plentiful growth of fresh green grass for the grazing of the cattle. Of course, to some extent, that is permissible, and the hills at the back of Bombay, in the months of April and May, are lighted up at night with a splendid illumination. In fact, so popular is the practice, that, whenever there is any political disturbance anticipated, the natives say "the fire will be out on the hills," and from that figure of speech we understand that a disturbance is brewing.

There is another way in which the burning of the fires is intentional, namely, this, there are many wild hill tribes who carry on their agriculture, not by means of ploughing, but by means of burning trees, and letting the ashes lie on the ground until the rains come. Then the rains descend on the virgin soil, which, fertilised by the ashes of the burnt forest, produces abundant crops without any further labour whatever. This, of course, is an utterly barbarous practice. No doubt the localities are often very steep, and it is not so easy to plough as it would be in the plains, with these sharp gradients. Nevertheless, the practice arises from ignorance on the part of the people and from their want of agricultural capital. The object of the British Government is to wean these poor people from the barbarous practice, to reclaim them from the habits of agricultural savagery, and to make small advances of money to them for purchasing ploughs and plough-cattle, and so teach them to depend on settled agriculture rather than on these wasteful destructive fires.

Then, another purpose to which the forest conservancy is directed is the preservation of the grazing. If the cattle are allowed to wander unchecked in the jungle, they will eat a little and destroy very much; that is to say, they will tread down and trample and destroy uselessly ten times as much as they consume for food. The object, therefore, is to restrict the grazing by means of a sort of block system, that is to say, to allow the cattle to graze in certain blocks or areas of forest range, and to prevent them grazing in others. The block or area is protected from grazing for a few years; and afterwards when its vegetation has grown up, then the cattle may be admitted to graze safely. Of course cattle must have pasturage, and the object should be to provide pasturage ground sufficient for their real consumption, but to prevent them from needlessly destroying the vegetation.

It is this useless destruction of the pasturage, from want of conservancy, that renders the country so destitute of fodder whenever drought occurs. It is essential to husband the spontaneous fodder of the country, as a resource to be available in time of need.

In all these matters you may readily perceive that questions arise regarding the restriction of the rights of the people, and there is, to some extent, a slight contest always going on between the forest officers and the ordinary civil officers of the Government. The forest officers, of course, are zealous for preserving the forests, and the civil officers naturally protect the rights of the people. The object is to maintain a judicious compromise. The people who sparsely inhabit the forests have been accustomed to cut, burn, and destroy somewhat recklessly, and they cannot speedily be reclaimed from these evil habits. This can only be done by degrees. But while, on the one hand, their reasonable rights are protected, on the other hand, they must not be allowed to destroy forests altogether, otherwise there will be no *corpus*, as the lawyers say, on which any rights are to be founded; the whole property of the country will be destroyed, the natural wealth will vanish, and there will be nothing for anybody to have rights in at all. So that, in a judicious gradual and conciliatory manner, forests must be preserved, while a fair and equitable consideration is given to the well-established customs of the country, notwithstanding that these customs are, to some extent, objectionable.

The "reserved" and "protected" forests, technically described above, have been adjudicated, after inquiry, to be the property of the Government. Full provision is made by law for determining disputes between the people and the Government authorities regarding the ownership of the forests, and the boundaries are defined of the jungles which belong to the State and to the natives respectively. An ample quantity of the jungle has everywhere been marked off as belonging to the people, and within that area no restrictions are placed upon the natives. The restrictions exist only in those forests which from time immemorial have belonged to Government under native dynasties as well as under British rule. Within some of the Government forests, especially in the technically "protected" forests, subordinate rights are found to pertain to the natives, under the Government as lord of the manor. These rights are also investigated under the law, and defined.

Thus no just cause of complaint whatever is allowed to exist on the part of the people against the forest system, though there is no disguising the fact that many would desire to cut down the State forests at their will for immediate gain, without any care for the future.

There are certain things which in all countries are recognised as pertaining to the business of the State, or rather public authority, such as the coinage, the post-office, the electric telegraph, besides the important departments of sanitation, education, and the like. In some great branches, the State, if it does not directly undertake the management, does yet interfere considerably, notably in the case of railways. Now, in India at least, forest conservancy is to be classed in this category. There are many things in which private enterprise is better than State action, but forest conservancy is not one of these. The saddest experience has shown that if forests are left to private action unrestricted, they will be destroyed. Hundreds of tracts are to be seen in India, now bare and barren, where forests and vegetation once abounded, and might again abound under a proper system of conservancy. Hundreds more of tracts exist where the denudation has occurred within the present generation. Sadder still, in many places the mischief is irreparable, because the soil has been, after the loss of its vegetation, washed away by the action of rain. If left to themselves, the people would work out the forests to destruction, just as a spendthrift lives on his capital; in homely phrase, they would kill the goose which lays the precious eggs. The true object of conservancy is to preserve the forests as an inestimably valuable capital with which Nature has endowed us, and to draw from these, for the use of the people, interest, in the shape of timber, fuel and other produce judiciously cut or felled, and grass or fodder grazed according to a scientific system. It is this which is now being done effectually, though but too tardily, in India. If forests are worked without any State supervision, they are exhausted, and nothing is left for reproduction. If they are worked by the State, then some trees are always left to keep up the vegetation.

I have now touched on the nature of the forests, on their value, climatic and economic, upon the means which should be provided by the legislature and the executive for preserving them, and the objects to which that preservation is directed. Before resuming my seat, I would desire to re-call to the grateful recollection of patriotic Englishmen, the names of some of our countrymen who have most distinguished themselves in respect of forest conservancy in India, but I must first mention two distinguished Germans. It has always been the pride of the Indian Government to attract to its service eminent men of other nations, and amongst its best servants is Dr. Dietrich Brandis, who has done more for forest conservancy than any other person who could be named; for not only has he organised a system which is scientific and practical, but he has also contributed much to the botanical science in India, and is the author of an excellent work, entitled, "The Forest Flora." Next after him I would mention his distinguished countryman, Dr. Schlich, who, for a long time, was Conservator of the forests of Bengal and Assam. I would mention Dr. Cleghorn, Dr. Stewart, Mr. Beddome, and Maj. Campbell Walker, all in Madras; the late Dr. Dalzell of Bombay; Col. Pearson and Capt. Forsyth, of the Central Provinces. Capt. Forsyth was one of the men who worked so hard in the forests, that I may say he almost laid down his life for their sake, and has left, as the memorial of his labours, one of the most charming books on forestry that has ever been written. In Burmah, the forest department has been well represented by Messrs. Seaton and Ribbenthorp. Then I may mention the two zealous officers who are now carrying on forest conservancy under great difficulty in the

Bombay Presidency. These are Mr. Shuttleworth and Col. Peyton. Lastly, I would particularly mention a member of the Covenanted Civil Service, Mr. Baden Powell, in the Panjab. These are the men who have struggled to preserve our forests through evil report and good report, with a considerable measure of success, and who have, from their sense of public duty, from their regard to the welfare of India, and from their love of the forests, borne much hardship, endured many toils, and risked their health. Some even have lost their lives in the service of the forests of India.

It is a cause of thankfulness that scientific and practical forestry is taking a hold upon the public mind in India. The European civil officers of the Government are beginning to understand the subject, and to co-operate with the regular forest officers. Schools of forestry for the natives are being established.

In conclusion, this subject is worthy the best attention of such a body as the Society of Arts. The Society has influenced Englishmen in many directions, and there are few directions in which the influence of so learned, influential, and practical a body can be more beneficially exercised than in furthering the interests of forest conservancy in India.

---

## PART II.

[*Speech delivered before the Scottish Arboricultural Society, at Edinburgh, October* 1881.]

I HAVE great pleasure in speaking before this Society at this meeting under the presidency of Mr. Hutchison of Carlowrie, a gentleman who, by promoting the objects of this association, has rendered, I venture to say, a national service to Scotland and to the Empire, and who has by many instructive and interesting writings illustrated its proceedings. I am proud also to think that among the members of this association is Professor Balfour, a man who is venerated in all botanical circles throughout the British Empire, and whose books are read, not only in his native country, but also in the far distant region of India, sometimes by foresters amidst the snows of the Himalaya, and sometimes in the torrid zones of central and southern India. But, gentlemen, I have another reason for pride in addressing this association, because, in common with many other visitors, I have been delighted to observe the progress it is making within the last twenty years. It appears to have risen in numbers from 200 members to now nearly 800 members, and even this very day upwards of fifty new members have been admitted. Now these growing numbers afford a proof of the interest which has been taken in Scotland respecting the subject of arboriculture, and I am sure that your influence must spread with advantage throughout the Empire. But, gentlemen, Scotland is a country that has long been in the van of improvement in this respect. In the last century such distinguished names as Athole, Belhaven, Haddington, and Sir James Hall of Dunglass, illustrated the history of forestry in North Britain; and in the nineteenth century we have first of all among arboriculturists the illustrious name of Prince Albert, whose august example has been followed largely by the nobility of Scotland, among whose honoured names may be mentioned Breadalbane, Mansfield, Fife, Sutherland, Seafield, Stair, and lastly, the lamented name of Airlie, who was mentioned to you by our noble president (the Marquis of Lothian) at our meeting this day. In fact, it may be said that the nobility of Scotland, have been in the very van of practical improvement in this respect. But besides the nobility we have distinguished commoners such as Mactier of Durris, Gordon-Cumming, Macpherson Grant, Menzies, Mathieson, Fletcher, Duncan of Benmore, Fowler of Braemore, and many others. Lastly, you have the lamented name of Adam of Blairadam. His death, his untimely death, in the midst of a career of usefulness, was lamentable in many departments, but to none was it more lamentable than to that of forestry, because there is no part of India, let me assure you, where there remains so much to be done in this respect as in southern India comprised within the Madras Presidency. And there was a hope that Mr. Adam would have taken to Madras that practical knowledge which he acquired on his own estates. I myself recollect the interest with which some years ago I went round with him the noble woods he and his forefathers had planted at Blairadam. It is to be hoped that his successor—Mr. Grant Duff—who as a good Scotchman must be imbued with Scotch ideas regarding forestry—will follow the example begun to be set by Mr. Adam—an example too early closed. But in conjunction with these gentlemen we should remember, and the general public should remember, the names of good sound practical foresters who have managed the woods on the great estates of the Scottish noblemen—such names as McCorquodale on the Mansfield estates, McGregor of Ladywell, Grant Thomson on the Seafield estates, David Scott on the Moray estates, Dewar on the Lovat estates, Dunn on the Buccleuch estates, and France on the estates of Sir George Clerk of Penicuik. These gentlemen possess many of the qualifications required for the work of forestry in India, and it is to be hoped that some systematic instruction in forestry, both for Great Britain herself and for her numerous dependencies, may be set on foot.

Thus I venture to hope that an important and extensive public opinion is growing up, at least in North Britain, in favour of the preservation of forests, not only in Scotland, but in the colonies, and more especially in India. For let me assure you it is always the case in India that light is shed on the Empire by public opinion in the United Kingdom. It is public opinion which is wanted to stir up the minds of our legislators and our statesmen in this most important respect. Forestry, recollect, is a subject comparatively novel. A few years ago it was but little understood, and even now, you well know, as practical men, that a great deal has to be learned by us all, and more especially by the governing classes. And therefore it is to be hoped that a substantial support will be given by public opinion in this country to the government of India in overcoming all obstacles that still lie in the path of improvement in forestry. I congratulate myself on having this opportunity of bearing testimony before such an important body as the Scottish Arboricultural Society in behalf of these forests, in which, as a well-wisher of India, I take a deep interest. And I do hope that your action, in its moral effects, will produce a reflex action upon the authorities of these far distant regions to which I am about to invite your attention.

Now, gentlemen, after this brief preface, let me remind you that the forests of India are varied and extensive. I doubt not that you bear in mind, as educated Scotchmen, the general outlines of the geography of that vast continent. Remember that it is usually compared to an inverted triangle, of which two sides are bounded by the sea, and the base by the Himalaya, the apex being near Ceylon. Well, then, in the first place the forests of India lie in the Himalaya. But in the vast continental triangle that lies below that unrivalled range of Himalayan mountains, there are several subordinate ranges. So bear in mind that in the centre of India there lies a great mountain mass, consisting of two main ranges—the Vindhya and the Satpura hills. And next, down the western coast of the triangle, there extends one long line of mountains called the Western Ghats; and on the eastern coast a lesser line of mountains, called the Eastern Ghats. Kindly keep in your memory these five ranges of mountains—the Himalaya, the Vindhya, the Satpura, the Western and the Eastern Ghats —and you will have a sufficient idea in your own minds of the forests of India.

Remember, too, that the forests of India were once almost co-extensive with the country itself. But they have been destroyed through many centuries—first by the natives of the country. It is a most unhappy fact that, with but few exceptions, the natives have no feeling of affection for trees and forests. They seem to look upon them as common enemies almost to be destroyed. They are indeed very fond of planting trees in their own court and backyards, or in the immediate neighbourhood of their villages. They also plant groves for sacred purposes, and preserve them with religious care from century to century. They likewise plant a few other groves for fruit-bearing and the like, and in this respect many of the groves are justly celebrated. But the natives of India are a non-foresting people, and they will not only fail to take care of forests, but will destroy them, believing in a certain stupid way, that they are thereby benefiting the land. That is a great difficulty with which we have to contend. But we British people have been very much at fault also, in respect to these Indian forests. During the early days of British rule we rivalled—quite unintentionally—but still we rivalled the natives in our destructive power. We allowed forests to be cut down and swept away as clean as if the country had been shaved with a razor. We did not do this ourselves, but quietly allowed, in our carelessness, every kind of contractor, native or European, to commit this destruction. Well, then, after a time, perhaps first of all in the enlightened reign of the great Lord Dalhousie, some efforts were made for forest conservancy. If there was any Governor-General who was the originator of forest conservancy more than another, it was that distinguished statesman. But after his time there came the convulsion of the Indian Mutiny, and the era of the construction of railways. And then I must confess that we did sin, even in the light of knowledge, for we allowed European contractors to commit the same destruction that native contractors had, for so many generations, committed. Thus again, many square miles of splendid forests of teak and sāl were swept clean away with the besom of destruction. New brooms, indeed, sweep clean, and the new broom in this case was the railway contractor; so once more these splendid forests continued to be destroyed. After the Mutinies, Lord Canning's administration had hardly time to do much for the forests, nor had Lord Elgin's. It was reserved for my old master, John Lawrence (afterwards Lord Lawrence), to take up the work which had been begun by Lord Dalhousie; and from that day to this there has been no Governor-General who has not done much for the forest conservancy of India. But remember that the fatal phrase "too late" must be inscribed over many of the preservative and conservative measures which we are now undertaking. A vast amount of mischief has been done which cannot be remedied for several generations to come. Still a large field remains in which the beneficial influence of forest conservancy can be practically exerted, and there much is being done.

You may ask, "How comes it I have such a sorry story to tell regarding the interests of forest conservancy in India?" I yield to no man in the pride and satisfaction with which I look back on the achievements of my countrymen in the East, and few persons can have a higher estimation than I have of the condition and the progress of the Indian administration. But I am bound in conscience to admit before every assembly of my countrymen, that in respect of forest conservancy we have lagged behind, and that our failures and shortcomings in that respect do constitute one of the few blots upon the past history of the British rule in India. And what is the cause of this? It is simply ignorance. It is want of instruction and education in these matters; and also the sluggishness which accompanies uninstructed public opinion. But this fault is now being remedied. When I went to India, I had never heard of forest conservancy, and no kind of instruction or preparation was given to me in that respect. Whatever I have learned regarding the forests of India, I had to acquire for myself, despite every obstacle and discouragement. And that was the case with all my brother officers of that period, and it is still too much the case with regard to many officers sent forth to the East. You can understand that if the rulers have no proper idea as to the value of forest conservancy, they are not likely to overcome the obstacles which stand like lions in the way of all improvement. Every prejudice which an Asiatic population feels in this matter has to be encountered. That is a very grave affair which we must deal with considerately, for fear we should create popular discontent. But, although that is a very important thing, still it must be faced for the sake of an object sufficiently important, and by judiciously considered measures it must be gradually overcome. Unless, however, the rulers feel in their own mind a due sense of the importance of the matter, they will not have a vivid apprehension of these affairs, nor will they deal with difficulties with becoming energy. It is owing to the want of instruction on these subjects that the grievous national losses, to which I have referred, have been inflicted indirectly upon India. Therefore it is that I hail most heartily the formation of your important Association in Scotland, through whose means instruction will gradually permeate all the influential classes here, and from them will reach the equally influential classes abroad.

May I remind you for a moment, as practical men, what are the consequences which have arisen, and will continue to arise for some time to come, from the destruction of forests. In the first place timber and fuel are scarce in a country which needs those articles to a peculiar extent. The scantiness and dearness of these most necessary articles affect the prices generally of all the necessaries which are required by the poor, and consequently their normal poverty is aggravated. Wood is an article which, in the absence of iron, is peculiarly necessary in a country like India. In the north of India, indeed, the native houses and cottages can be constructed of earth; and there, wood is not so much necessary. But in the east, west, and south, wood and timber are absolutely necessary for house-building. And I need hardly add, that in every part of the country it is required for boats, carts, ploughs, and a hundred domestic, agricultural, or commercial uses. But, what is more important still, a vast people requires a mass of fuel for fires to warm their houses in the winter time, and at all seasons for cooking purposes. That is a simple thing to say. No doubt, there are scientific men who tell us that in the future our meals are to be cooked and our firesides warmed by electricity. Well, gentlemen, that sort of millennium may be reached in Scotland or in England in our day. Yet it will be centuries, or generations at the least, before anything of the kind will be reached in India. Therefore, the people must have some fuel with which to cook the countless numbers of meals which have to smoke every day for so vast a population as is contained in India; and if they cannot get wood for fuel, they must use something else. And what is that something else? Why, nothing less than the manure. The dung of cattle is in most parts of India extensively used for fuel. As Scotch agriculturists you readily see what a great detriment that is to agriculture. You hear that the soil is being gradually exhausted. I hope that it is not being rapidly exhausted, but I think the proof is undeniable that some process of exhaustion, however imperceptible, is setting in, and if it does set in, the main cause must be the want of manure. Now, under these circumstances, and with a vast population to be fed by indigenous agriculture, is it not ten thousand pities that the people should be obliged to use for fuel that which is wanted for manure, simply because our enlightened government has for several generations failed to preserve those beautiful forests, with which a gracious Providence once endowed India?

But, there are economic reasons in connection with the forest conservancy affecting the wealth of the people, and these reasons are more particularly felt in the northern and eastern, than in other parts of India. It is for the sake of these economic reasons affecting the national wealth, that forests are wanted to be preserved in northern and eastern

India. But there are climatic reasons as well as economic reasons, and these climatic reasons are severely felt in southern, central, and western India. These exist in those parts of the continent, in addition to the general economic reasons applicable, more or less, to the whole of India. I need not detain you as a body, consisting partly of scientific men, and partly of experts, by any very long description of the scientific theories whereby forests are considered to affect the climate. I don't suppose that in a country like India the existence or non-existence of forests can possibly affect the total rainfall of that vast continent. You can imagine that in islands like our own the existence or non-existence of forests may possibly affect the total rainfall. The clouds from the Atlantic, if not arrested in their course by forests in Great Britain, may pass over to Scandinavia. But you understand that nothing of that kind can possibly happen in India. There the vapours come from the southern ocean, and if they are not arrested in their aërial course somewhere over the continent, they pass on to the Himalaya, and there they must stop. That stupendous range of mountain peaks is a real barrier to their progress; if not condensed previously, they must stop there, and in the shape of floods return to the plains; so that the total condensation and precipitation of vapour cannot possibly be affected. But it does not follow from this, that the forests have no effect. Because if the clouds are not condensed in the Himalaya, they must be condensed somewhere else on the continent. And the somewhere else may, for the convenience and happiness of man, largely depend upon the forests. More particularly too, the season of condensation may be affected by the forests. If you have forests in abundance, you may hope to have the early and the latter rains in due season. If you have not, you may have drought, to be followed by unseasonable rain; so that in the words of the prayer-book, you will be "plagued with immoderate rain."

We hear much of the earth being modified by human action.

We may humbly believe that a good Providence arranged all terrestrial conditions rightly and for the best; but we, in our short-sightedness, grievously interfere with all the arrangements of Nature. Can we wonder, therefore, if we are punished by alternations of drought and inundation?

That meteorological theory as to Indian seasons has been greatly discussed. There is a department at Bombay of scientific men who have given guarded utterance upon this subject. You know that scientific opinion as a rule is very judicial. But still when the scientific men in Bombay have explained to us their theory on these matters, the result has always been that in their own phraseology and terminology, they have given us an explanation which comes to much the same result as that which I have given you. You have present to-night, I believe, a great meteorological authority, your excellent and distinguished member Mr. Buchan, and I am sanguine if you ask him he will corroborate—perhaps in different terms and in much better language than I have used—the general theory which I have ventured to propound, which is certainly believed by many scientific authorities in India, and which is confirmed by everyday experience. We see these two things invariably linked together, on the one hand deforesting and drought, on the other hand forests and abundant rainfall. Now, when you see things chained together, or following each other in unvarying sequence by some unseen mysterious force, you naturally fall back on the theory of cause and effect. Thus we in India, in common with all other nations, maintain that forests do affect the rainfall, although we endeavour to avoid attributing any undue effect to this or to any one particular cause. But surely our experience in India is borne out by the experience of every other country in the world. I need not recapitulate all that the best authorities in Great Britain have said regarding the effect of forests, even on the climate of Scotland. The injury done to the climate of the south of Europe by the cutting down of the forests is a matter of notoriety. Every Spaniard, Italian, and southern Frenchman will tell you the same story.* We hear the same tale, again, from Cyprus. What—under centuries of misrule now, as we hope, to be remedied by British administration—has ruined the fertility of that classic isle, once the gem of the Mediterranean? The destruction of the forests first by felling and then the injury to young trees by the unrestricted browsing of goats. Then in the East it is notorious that many of those famous lands, which once maintained mighty nations, are now almost uninhabitable or incapable of maintaining more than the scantiest average of population per square mile. What has become of the regions of Nebuchadnezzar, of Cyrus, of Alexander, and all those other persons of sacred writ or classic story? Everybody now sees that no such population, no such wealth could possibly be sustained in these lands at the present day as in the times when they arose to historic fame. And without attributing an excessive causation to forests, one cannot doubt that the deforesting of these once richly-wooded regions has had much to do with the destruction which we see so widespread to-day. Every mountain-range in these regions is as bare as the bones at which the lions have been tearing. Similar experience has been brought to us from South Africa and from Australia; and now, although North America possessed the finest forests in the world, we are beginning to hear a similar tale from that continent also. In Canada the deforesting is

* For instance, see the following quotation, extracted from Murray's 'Handbook of France:'—"After crossing a high ridge the road descends by a gradual sweep into the valley of the Durance, which it reaches by zigzags at the foot of a precipitous mountain, *le Morgon* (7632 ft.). The valley hereabouts is a scene of desolation: the turbulent river rolls along a furious flood of muddy water, undermining the loose shaly rocks composing its sides, strewing the bottom with rubbish, and constantly forcing its banks. The road is frequently swept away by inundations, and for some distance is carried along temporary causeways. All this waste and ruin has been caused by the reckless cutting down of the forests on the high mountains. The Government have come to the rescue, and have taken measures at great outlay to regulate the torrents, avert the landslips, and replant the forests. Such works may be seen near Embrun."

causing public anxiety, and forestry associations are being formed there. I say, then, that as reasonable men you will not doubt that the forests, or rather the want of forests, must be affecting the climate of India.

But irrespective of this, there are other effects produced by the destruction, or, on the other hand, by the preservation of forests. In the first place, the air is kept comparatively moist by the presence of woods, by the vast expanse of foliage which is presented by the forests. That again acts upon the clouds, and surely it must be the cause of condensation. Then what is even more important, the moisture which does exist in the country is retained by means of forests. You cannot doubt that the streams and the rivers have their fountain heads kept moist by the trees, which fountain heads will be gradually dried up if the trees be destroyed. The sources of streams and rivers have in India a significance of which we have hardly a practical idea in Great Britain or even in Europe. Because recollect we are in India dependent greatly on artificial irrigation. We have an ancient system of canals, which system has been mightily developed by the British Government. Some of the canals derive their water from the Himalaya, or from streams which are fed by the everlasting snows of the mountains. No doubt these canals are comparatively independent of the forest. But with these exceptions all the great canals of India, which give life to so many millions of people, are really dependent on streams which have their sources in the hills, which must be clad with forests, if these sources are to be preserved. If you allow the woods, the forests, the vegetation to be destroyed, then the sources of these streams which feed the canals will be subjected in a mitigated degree to the very uncertainties of climate which we have been deploring. There is, therefore, a most potent, cogent, and peculiar reason in India for preserving the forests, which are the sources of our streams.

Then if we do not preserve the forests, there is another evil which happens. I have shown you how the clouds, if they are not condensed, pass over the plains and become condensed on the hills. What follows? Violent rain falls in buckets-full, in tremendous torrents, and thus awful inundations occur. Down come the floods, sweeping away not only the precious soil which would have sustained vegetation and cultivation, but also tearing up the works of man—such as bridges, buildings, dykes, and the like. Not only are enormous volumes of water wasted by rolling along to the sea, but with the water is carried *débris* which had formed part of the resources of nature and of the useful works of man. All these terrible consequences arise from our shortsightedness in respect to the preserving of vegetation. There is yet another evil, namely that of denudation. In many parts of India the country is mountainous, or at least undulating. The hill-sides consist of the precious humus or rich soil overlying masses of rock. The trees with their network of roots form a great binding agency to keep the soil together and prevent it being swept away from the rocky surface. If these trees are destroyed, the torrents fall and carry away the humus. The sides of the hills become perfectly bare, barren, and inhospitable. Still a further evil happens; sometimes great artificial lakes are fed by streams that come down from the hills. If the forests are preserved these streams roll down their waters in a gradual measure, the tanks are kept filled, there is no silting up, and no inundations to destroy the dams, dykes, and embankments. If the forests are destroyed, down rush the streams in destructive floods, carrying away a mass of earth and *débris*, causing a dreadful silting up of the tanks, and sometimes even bursting dykes and embankments altogether. The list of evils is yet not exhausted. In a dry country like India a plentiful supply of water is wanted, not only for drinking, but for the purposes of washing and ablution. If we have little vegetation, there will be a corresponding diminution of the water supply; and of all causes which produce cholera, epidemic sicknesses, and destructive ailments of that kind in India, the deficiency of the water supply is not only the greatest, but is perhaps equal to all the other causes put together. Now that water supply, so vitally important, is largely dependent on these forests—whose cause I am pleading before you.

Then there is another matter—that of pasturage. You have heard of the countless herds and flocks on a thousand hills in India. Whenever drought threatens, mortality first shows itself in the cattle. The destruction that happens from devastating murrains is deplorable. All this arises from a deficiency of pasturage. The natives as a rule, are very unwilling to restrict the pasturage of their herds. Nevertheless, if the herds are allowed to wander at their will over the grazing-grounds, they will destroy and trample down much more than they eat. Unless something is done to restrict the grazing—not in its total quantity, but to restrict it in such a way as to prevent the cattle grazing in particular places until vegetation has grown up—following, in fact, the block system—the pasturage will be destroyed. The block system means this, that in a given area a certain number of cattle are allowed to graze, and when they have cropped the herbage on one block they are taken to the next. Young trees are thus preserved from the browsing of goats and cattle. If this system were carried out, there would be plenty of grazing for all the cattle that exist, and double their number, while young plantations would be permitted to grow up undisturbed. If something is not done in this direction, there will be a perpetual want of proper sustenance in ordinary times, and an utter want of food in seasons of drought, so that the cattle will be always thin and out of condition, even in good years, and emaciated well-nigh to death in every year of drought.

These are the grounds on which I venture to urge that a proper system of forest conservancy is absolutely necessary. Let me point out to what extent that necessity has been recognised by the Government in India. Your excellent Chairman, Mr. Hutchison, was kind enough to tell you that the Indian system of forestry was the best in the Empire. I am afraid that is a too generous recognition of what we have been able to do. I fear it is far from being so good as Mr. Hutchison has been led to suppose. Nevertheless it is considerable. For, in the first place, we have now 25,000 square miles of forests in India that are regularly preserved, and about 50,000 square miles of forest which are imperfectly preserved, total, 75,000 square miles. Now, gentlemen, in Scotland I believe that you reckon your forests by acres, but the forest area in India is so vast, that to reckon it in acres, would lead us to very tall figures indeed, and therefore we are obliged to reckon it by the square mile. But observe that British India (exclusive of the Native States) has an area of one million square miles, and the 75,000 square miles of forest represent just 7½ per cent. of that area. Or if you choose to reckon only the 25,000 square miles that are properly preserved, that will give 2½ per cent. on the total area of one million square miles. Or if you like to take it in acres, according to the Scotch plan, then you have forty-eight millions of acres preserved, of which sixteen millions are perfectly preserved, even in the manner which might be approved by those practical Scotch foresters whom I have been mentioning to you this evening. Let us compare, for one instant, these figures, with the results which have been mentioned with so much pride and satisfaction by your Chairman in some of his admirable addresses. Mr. Hutchison makes out, that though there has been a regrettable falling off in the forest area of Scotland within recent years, that is, as against 900,000 acres of wood forty or fifty years ago, we have 750,000 acres, or three-quarters of a million acres under wood. Now that gives 3½ per cent. upon the total area of twenty million acres in Scotland. I have taken these twenty millions from the last edition of the Statesman's Year Book; so that on the whole India compares favourably with Scotland as regards the total area of forests, taking together the forests perfectly and imperfectly preserved, but compares unfavourably with Scotland in respect to the area of perfect preservation.

But such a large total as 75,000 square miles, or forty-eight millions of acres will appear to you extraordinary, and you may say, "Just give us one or two details of these enormous figures, and let us see how you get them." Well, let me explain to you how this area is obtained province by province. You are doubtless aware that India is an Empire divided into many provinces, under several separate local governments and administrations. Here are the figures for each. In the Panjab there are 4000 square miles of forest; in the North-West Provinces 3000; in Bengal 9000; in Assam 7000; in the Central Provinces 20,000; in Berar 5000; and miscellaneous 1000; in Burmah, which comprises probably the best forests in all Asia, 2000; total 51,000 square miles. You have to add 13,000 for Bombay, 10,000 for Southern India and the Madras Presidency, and so you get the large total of 75,000 square miles or forty-eight millions of acres. Besides these, there is a vast extent of what are called local forests which are not preserved, but which are left by the Land Revenue Settlement in the hands of the people. And from the description I have given you of the habits of the natives, you can imagine how these are treated. They are indeed battered and knocked about. Of course some trees do yet survive in these local forests, and on the Darwinian principle of the survival of the fittest, they do exist in a precarious sort of way.

With this large area, you, as practical men, will ask me, "of what does the conservancy consist?" The conservancy is of two kinds, general and special. The general conservancy, which is applicable to all kinds of forests, consists in guarding against fires. These fires are of two kinds, accidental and intentional. The accidental fires are truly tremendous. The commonest form of accident arises from a man lighting his pipe and dropping some sparks. Once the conflagration is set up, then many of the wonderful and thrilling incidents which you have read in books of travel in regard to the firing of the American prairies, are applicable to these Indian forest fires. I was out in one of them during the dead of night, and it was only owing to the fleetness of my horse that I escaped. The wonderful noises, the crackling of the dry bark of the trees sounding like musketry, and the flight of all kinds of animals from the swift rush of destruction, form a wonderful experience. But there are intentional fires which are quite as destructive as the accidental ones. Nothing is so common as for the natives to burn the tall grass at certain seasons, in order to promote the growth of the young herbage. And then the whole hill-sides are lighted up, affording a glorious spectacle from the point of view of the ordinary spectator, but saddening to the forester. There is another thing: in many hill regions the lazy people, sooner than plough their cleared land, cut down the forests, burn the wood on the spot, and then spread the ashes all over the surface. Then as soon as the rain falls, they cast the seed over the soil, and so they are saved the trouble of cultivation. Another way is this: in many parts of the country the people cut off all the young shoots from the trees and burn them for the manure. If you remonstrate with them, and tell them that if they will cut off branches, they should leave the young wood and prune the older branches, you are told that the young shoots are the richest—it being meant thereby, that these are filled with all the chemical constituents necessary for fertilisation. Thus they obviate the necessity of using any more expensive manure. It is against all these kinds of destruction that the forest officers have to wage war as best they can, with the support of the magistrates and the civil authorities. Of course there is a general guardianship against illicit cutting and the like, on which I need not detain you. But there are also the special operations of conservancy.

Now let me assure you, practical experts, that each and all of the measures you adopt in Scotland are adopted in the specially protected forests of India. Think for a moment, Scotch foresters, what are your ordinary operations? I believe they are first enclosing, fencing, and draining the land for planting; second, planting; third, thinning and pruning; fourth, utilising limbs and branches for crate wood and the like; fifth, felling;

sixth, barking; seventh, leaving some standard trees for reproduction; eighth, gathering the produce, fruit, cones, seeds, nuts; ninth, sawing and manufacturing; tenth, rearing and propagating in the nurseries. There may be possibly some other operations which suggest themselves to experts, but I believe I have enumerated the principal of your operations. Now let me assure you, gentlemen, that every one of these things is done, and done over that area of 25,000 square miles or sixteen millions of acres. The special conservancy which I have just described to you, is carried on in what are called the *reserved* forests, and the general protection which I have sketched to you in what are technically called the *protected* forests. The names "reserved" and "protected" are technical, and are embodied in the forest legislation for these special purposes. Thus you see our system has a sound legislative basis and a positive legal sanction.

There is one remark I have to make in regard to planting. I know that in Scotland great importance is attached to it. Some importance is attached to it in India also. We have some splendid plantations of teak in Burmah and Malabar. These plantations have an immense value. I observe in one of Mr. Hutchison's reports that the woods on Lord Mansfield's estates are estimated at a quarter of a million sterling. You can infer from that what would be the capital value of our great teak plantations in India. No doubt it is not so much planting we look to, as preserving the natural forests and the spontaneous vegetation of the country. The area is too vast to be affected materially by anything we can do in the way of planting. Therefore our national object is to preserve that which we have already. Still, as a matter of public policy, and as a valuable investment of capital, we have got plantations also. But there is one particular kind of plantation which we hope to establish, especially in northern India, and that is what we hope to call the communal plantation connected with every village. I have explained to you that the cattle suffer from scantiness of herbage in the hot weather. If such communal plantations can be established in every parish, there will be some preservation of the vegetation for the grazing of the cattle during the hot season.

One word more, mainly on the preservation of what are called popular rights. The existence of these popular rights has proved a considerable obstacle towards the proper conservancy of forests. We know how justly jealous the British Government is of everything that pertains to the rights of its native subjects. Still I am sanguine that by the equitable arrangement that has been made under the laws passed for forest conservancy, the rights of the people are being respected—not indeed so much as they themselves would demand, but as much as reason and justice can properly require. You must understand that the natives themselves are ignorant and prejudiced on this subject. They hate everything new, and they are but too much disposed to regard the efforts which Government makes for preserving the forests as against their interests. Nevertheless, it is the duty of the civil officers to thoroughly explain these matters and overcome the dissatisfaction and reluctance which the people feel in obeying the forest laws; because we must remember that the people, if left to themselves, would simply work out their own destruction. What is the use of talking to them so much about their rights in the forest, when really their destructive habits will sweep away what the lawyers call the corpus of the case, that is to say, the property involved in the case will become so valueless that it will not be worth disputing about? So then we must, in a considerate manner, satisfy them in regard to the importance of the measures which we are undertaking; and I am sure that if our civil officers are properly instructed in all matters connected with forests, and have a due appreciation of the importance of the subject, they will, in all instances, be able to make a satisfactory compromise with the people—preserving the popular rights on the one hand, and on the other, those national interests which are essential to the very existence of the country.

I must ask you to recollect that the area of 75,000 square miles above stated is the property of Government, and has been adjudged to be so by formal proceedings. Over and above this area, the local forests have been adjudged to be private property. But in some of the forests which are Government property, various privileges are recognised as pertaining to the people, and in other Government forests even rights have been adjudged to them; while many of the best forests are absolutely in the hands of the Forest Department.

One word as to the financial results. You will be happy to hear that already the Government of India is deriving a considerable income from these forests. The gross proceeds amount to 750,000*l.*, say three-quarters of a million sterling per annum; and the expenditure amounts to half a million, giving a net return of 250,000*l.* to the public treasury. So that after all the forests of India do even more than pay their own way.

Now I have concluded this exposition of the forest policy of India and some of its results. Allow me to refer to some of the good men and true, Scotch countrymen of yours, by whom these results have been achieved. You must not be nationally jealous, when I assure you that the man to whom, if any one is to bear it, must be accorded the proud title of the father of Indian forestry, is not a Briton at all but a Prussian, and that man is Dr. Brandis. Another man, Dr. Schlich, a countryman of Dr. Brandis, is second only to him in the successful efforts he has made for Indian forest conservancy. We are always glad to welcome these foreign gentlemen into the British service. We have, as a nation, a wonderful faculty for assimilating all these foreign elements into the body politic—on this one condition that they do something for the glory and greatness of Great Britain. I will not detain you by giving you a list of the Englishmen or Irishmen who have done something for Indian forests, but I will do myself the pleasure of mentioning to you the names of some distinguished Scotchmen. And first of all I commend to your grateful recollection the honoured name of Dr. Cleghorn. Having done service for many years to the forests of India, he has returned to Scotland to plead their cause before his countrymen; and he has also been among the most learned, intelligent, and practical supporters of the Scottish Arboricultural Society. Besides him I will mention Dr. Stewart and Mr. Dalzell, Captain Forsyth, and Major Campbell-Walker, all good Scotchmen. I may mention to you Dr. Brandis' work on the "Forest Flora of India" as instructive for your leisure hours, and I would commend Captain Forsyth's charming book from which you will learn all about the camp life in India, and receive a striking narrative as to the wild sports of the East. I may also mention two practical foresters who deserve a place in the Indian forest valhallah, namely, Ferguson of Malabar and Ballantyne of Berar.

Recollect, in conclusion, that this policy of forest conservancy really is vitally important to India in the sense in which it is hardly so vitally important to any other nation. If in Great Britain you do not choose to preserve your forests, if you think they do not pay you, you can deforest, and nothing very dreadful will happen to your favoured lands; for you have still your insular position; you have still got that mysterious agency, the Gulf Stream of the Atlantic, which moderates your climate, and keeps it comparatively temperate. If you have no wood at home you may get it from other places, from Scandinavia, from Finland, from Germany, or from a country still more important, namely Canada. If you don't choose to preserve your forests at home, other nations will preserve wood for you. If you think conservancy does not pay you, they know that it pays them to conserve for you. That is all very well for you in Europe, but you cannot follow out a policy of that kind in India. For remember you have an enormous population there—now upwards of 250 millions of people. You cannot find wood and fuel for these people unless you preserve your indigenous forests in India. If India does not preserve wood for herself, whence is she to import it? Is she to import it from those great central regions in Africa which Livingstone explored? The cost of transport effectually forbids that. Is she to import it from

Arabia? Why, Arabia has not a stick to support herself with except palm-trees, which she wants for food. Persia has no forests except those which were judiciously alluded to to-day by your noble president (the Marquis of Lothian), namely the forests on the hills which face the Caspian, and which are so far inland that the hope of getting them to the Oceanic coast, or to any sea except the Caspian, is out of the question. Central Asia is equally destitute. China has an enormous population, and more than plenty to do with all the wood she can produce. So, then, you have nothing to fall back upon except Burmah, Assam, and Cochin-China. These countries would afford you some wood, but it would be very expensive, and when got it would prove utterly insufficient for the wants of India. Remember that there are 37 millions of inhabited houses in India, the greater part of which are constructed of wood. There are perhaps 15 millions of ploughs, all made of wood. The number of carts I cannot give you, but they would amount to several millions. And as for boats—the inland navigation of India is, next after the Southern States of North America, among the greatest in the world. I have no time to give you any idea of the magnitude of that navigation, but it depends upon hundreds of thousands of boats, the building of which has to be maintained by the indigenous forests of the country. So that unless India preserves her own forests, she must suffer, sooner or later, a national misfortune. I trust that from any such direful consequence as this she will be preserved by the Government of India, with the support of a national and instructed public opinion in Great Britain.

In conclusion, India has great claims on the British nation, and these claims are rapidly increasing. From the last census it appears that she has added $1\frac{1}{4}$ million every year to her population, or 12 to 13 millions every decade of industrious subjects to the Empire of Queen Victoria. And of all sections of the British nation there is none on whom she has greater claims than on the Scotch. There are more old Anglo-

Indians residing in Scotland than in any other part of Great Britain, and I am sure that Scotland will remain in the very front in all that relates to the welfare of the Indian people. I am likewise sure that if by means of this Association and the general advocacy and agitation of these subjects, she shall succeed in placing forest conservancy in India on a sound moral basis—I mean that basis which results from enlightened public opinion—she will add one more leaf to that laurel wreath which encircles her brow.

# CHAPTER XII.

## MONETARY PRACTICE AMONGST THE NATIVES OF INDIA.

[*Speech delivered before the Institute of Bankers, in London, May,* 1881.]

Ancient gold-mines of India — Hindu currency originally in gold — Silver currency of the Muhammadans — Extraordinary number of native mints — Variety of native coins — Double standard in India up to 1835 — Single standard in silver subsequently — Hoarding in specie by the natives — Capital consisting of precious stones — Primitive barter still going on — Payment in kind — Circulation of cowrie shells — Probable amount of silver circulating in India — Probable amount of gold — Importance of native bankers as forming a class — Native Bills of Exchange — Savings-banks — Want of life insurance.

I HAVE been asked to speak before you regarding the general monetary practice amongst the natives of India, with some estimate of the use and probable future absorption of silver as coin; also to give an account of such practices amongst the natives as have a banking character, and lead up to the larger banking operations of the country.

This comprehensive question divides itself naturally into three parts. The limited time at our disposal, and the largeness of the subject, prevent my dilating upon many of the graphic, picturesque, and almost poetical details which I should have liked to indulge myself in and you also. If I should linger on the picturesque portion I should not have time to dwell upon the solid facts which I am bound to bring under the notice of a body of experts such as the members of this Institute. Therefore, bespeaking your indulgence so far, if I seem to pass hastily over details, I shall at once proceed to the subject matter of my address. I will begin by treating of the first of the three parts into which it divides itself.

### "*The* GENERAL MONETARY PRACTICE *amongst the* NATIVES *of* INDIA."

Now you will doubtless be aware that the ancient coins and numismatics of India form an historical record of priceless value, and have rescued from oblivion many dynasties and long lines of kings, which would otherwise have been forgotten. But passing by that interesting and brilliant topic of the numismatics of India, I may remind you that among the original Hindus in the southern part of India coinage was in gold, because in the south of India they had gold mines—the very gold mines, indeed, about which in recent days we have heard so much, Indeed, the reason why there is so much uncertainty as to the profit to be derived from the re-opening as it were of these gold mines, is because the ancient Hindus worked out for their gold coinage all the accessible veins of precious metal, leaving the more deeply sunk veins to be worked with the assistance of our modern mining engineers. The Hindus in the north of India had gold as well, but there they had a silver coinage also, because they obtained silver from Central Asia, across the Himalayas, and in the Himalayas themselves. When the Muhammadan sovereigns came to power they developed the silver coinage and retained the gold coinage, and they further paid great attention to copper coinage.

According to English laws one metal is legal tender to any amount, and another metal is legal tender to only a limited sum. In ancient and mediæval India the relative value of coins of each metal was fixed by the State, and all were legal tender virtually without any formal limitation. Each Native ruler in India, upon his accession to the throne, instituted a new coinage, recalling as much as he could the coinage of his predecessors, and charging some discount called "*batta*" upon the new coinage. There were a great number and variety of mints in mediæval India. Each Native State had several mints, and, as there were some hundreds of States, if I said there were a thousand mints I should not be far wrong. Equally there was a great variety of coins, and looking at an old table of coins the other day, I counted a hundred coins of gold, 300 of silver, and 50 of copper. The money-changers used this multifarious currency for their own benefit. Moreover, there was a practice whereby the money-changers became the contractors in the Native States for the mint, thereby acquiring the entire control over the mintage of the country. Thus they were able to have frequently a fresh coinage, actually yearly, again charging the old "*batta*" or discount. The troubles to which the public were thus exposed under the later dynasties of Native rule, before the appearance of the British Government, were indescribable and endless. These troubles continued during the early part of British rule until, by the celebrated regulation of 1793, the East India Company put an end to the legal currency of the multiform Native coinage. They then instituted the gold mohur and the sikka rupees. These were practically legal tender to an unlimited amount, their relative value being fixed by law. This system lasted until 1835, when silver was declared to be the sole legal tender to an unlimited amount.

Therefore it may be interesting to recall the fact, that under every Native monarch, and also after the establishment of British rule, until the year 1835, India had what was practically a double standard. But in the year 1835 silver was declared sole legal tender to an unlimited amount, and thenceforward gold pieces were coined only for the purpose of general convenience, without being a legal tender at all. The Government, however, made a concession in favour of the gold coins, to the effect that they should be received in the public treasuries in payment of revenue; and with certain modifications the arrangement has lasted up to the present time. In the year 1865, about the time of the crisis of the American Civil War, proposals were made for making gold the sole legal tender to an unlimited amount, and practically demonetising silver. These proposals were originated before the well-known depreciation of silver set in. This depreciation has placed all proposals of that character out of court. The recent tendency among some thinkers in India is again towards the bi-metallism of former times. But this tendency has not found favour with the Government. Before leaving this part of the subject, I should remind you that the many hundreds of native mints were abolished by British rule, and the British mints have since been reduced, first to three and now to two, so we have now only two mints in the whole of British India.

The possibility of a political revolution occurring is always present to the monetary and financial mind of the people of India. The consequence is, that their coinage is used partly for purposes of circulation and partly for hoarding. I think, as you will see presently, that silver is hoarded almost entirely in specie, and gold is hoarded partly in specie but chiefly in bullion. The reason of hoarding in specie is that the man, who hoards, considers that the stamp, image and superscription upon the coin constitute a certificate of its value. The amount of unused capital thus existing in India is almost melancholy to contemplate. Then the natives of India have many other uses for gold and silver besides circulation and hoarding. I wish time permitted me to give you many of the graphic and interesting details which might be given regarding the manner in which these humble natives use gold and silver for domestic purposes, ornamentation, and personal decoration. The hoarding is not, however, confined to the precious metals. The natives of India are very fond of using precious stones for hoarding, and a man considers his little fortune locked up in so many diamonds and emeralds. It is to be borne in mind that they import jewels but little into India, and that some of the best diamond mines are in India, and perhaps the finest ruby mine in the world is in Burmah, while the Indian waters have some of the largest pearl-fisheries on the face of the globe. The necessity for precious metals for circulation is but slightly diminished by the use on the part of the natives of the Government paper-currency, represented by fourteen million pounds sterling. The natives of India, however, do invest largely in Government securities. They hold 20,000,000*l*. of that class of stock; and it is remarkable that both the larger kind of Government notes and Government securities, that is to say, scrip-paper, are used to some extent for the further purpose of hoarding.

Then, in some respects, the necessity for circulation in specie is reduced by the primitive barter, which is very common in the country. I admit that there are no recognised standards of barter in India such as there have been among some aboriginal races. Nevertheless there is an immense extent of this barter going on—that is to say, the poor people in villages take little articles, which they make with their own hands, to the rustic fairs, and therewith purchase food and grain. In ancient India, again, a great deal of business was done in kind. The land revenue was collected in kind; the rent was paid to the landlord in kind; the wages of the agricultural labourer were given again in kind. This system of course reduces the necessity of gold, silver, or paper for circulation. In many British districts, however, it is ceasing altogether, and is lessening in the Native States.

Lastly, there is a medium of circulation represented by cowrie shells, which are imported to India from the Bay of Bengal. 3200 go to the shilling, and 266 to the penny; so you can imagine the extent to which this shell circulation supersedes copper. You will remember that the natives are a poor people and are very thrifty, looking to the narrowest margin of profit and loss. These shells have a very large circulation. Nevertheless, the British Government has succeeded in introducing a successful copper coinage, though its circulation is somewhat impeded by the various customs which I have just mentioned. I have now said as much as time will permit in regard to the monetary practices of the natives of India.

### "*Some* ESTIMATE *of the* USE *and* PROBABLE FUTURE ABSORPTION *of* SILVER *as* COIN."

I thus come to the most difficult and important part of the question, and I must preface my answer by reminding you of a few salient, statistical, and economical facts relating to India. First, the Indian national income, assessable to income-tax, somewhat on the same principle as that which exists in England, amounts to not more than a hundred millions sterling. You doubtless remember, as I am addressing experts, that in the United Kingdom 570 millions sterling of income are assessable to income-tax, and the rest of the income of the nation is conjectured at 700 millions more, making a total of 1270 millions. Apply that principle to India and you will get 100 millions assessable to income-tax, and say 150 millions pertaining to the humbler classes, and that will give 250 millions in all. The external trade of India with foreign countries amounts, on the average, to 125 millions sterling a year, with a tendency to increase considerably. The value of the internal trade is probably greater still, but I regret to say that in this respect the statistical department in India is not sufficiently advanced to be able to furnish the value in figures. The State revenue amounts to about 65 millions sterling a year, of which 43 millions only represent the actual taxation, and of that amount six millions (net) are paid by the Chinese for opium. The ordinary expenditure is about the same in amount. The Government now keeps a cash balance in its treasury of 13 to 16 millions sterling. When I was finance minister the cash balance used to be from 17 to 22 millions sterling. The greater part of that is hard cash, kept under lock and key in the Government treasuries of the country, but a portion of it is in the three Presidency Banks. The population of India numbers 203 millions in British territory and 50 millions in the Native States—253 millions altogether.

Now, in such a country under these general economic conditions, what may we believe to be the amount of silver coin in actual circulation? The best opinions in 1850 put this circulation at 150 millions sterling, and the best opinions now, in 1881, would put it at 200 millions. As a check upon these calculations, I have ascertained that the coin issued from the Indian mints during a period of thirty-five years averaged eleven rupees per head of the whole population, which amounts to just 220 millions sterling. You may ask me why I do not put that as the total circulation? Now, nobody believes that the silver circulation is really 220 millions, and we account for the difference between the 200 millions circulation and the 220 millions coinage, by putting it down as part of the vast amount which is known to be hoarded by the people of India.

Remember that gold does not help the circulation. Gold coins, as I shall show you presently, are, indeed, issued from the mint. They are not circulated, they are only hoarded. Copper also does not help much. We have only got four millions sterling worth of that coin. The Government note circulation to some extent supplies the place of precious metals, but the total amount of notes in circulation is only 14 millions. It will at once suggest itself to you that Native bills of exchange supply the place of circulating medium. I shall presently show you that these bills of exchange, though their total cannot be accurately stated, must be vast in amount.

With such a circulation the question arises, what is the amount of precious metals which India possesses? Now, I think, that India has at least 333 millions of silver, and 122 millions of gold—total of precious metals, 455 millions sterling. Of this amount I shall presently show you that 255 millions sterling of silver have been coined, and three millions of gold, by British coinage from the British mints—total, 258 millions coined. Thus you will perceive that while on the one hand this coinage of 258 millions exceeds by 58 millions the highest estimated amount of circulation, namely, 200 millions, it is, nevertheless, 197 millions less than the quantity of precious metals which is possessed by the people of India.

You will ask how do I make this out—333 millions of silver and 122 millions of gold. I must trouble you with a few details of calculation under these headings. The silver imported into India is partly fine and partly specie, or coins of other nations. Since 1835, which you remember is the year of silver being declared the sole legal tender, 237 millions sterling of silver have been imported, that is to say net, less export, and 255 millions have been coined, and that is an excess of 18 millions. How are these 18 millions supplied? Why, they are taken from the former British coinage anterior to 1835. We know that 22 millions of that coinage have been re-coined. That is more than enough to account for the difference. Of the former British coinage, from 1793 to 1835, the amount was 70 millions. Deduct 22 millions re-coinage, and there are 48 millions of that coin still out in the hands of the people. But in 1793, 70 millions could not possibly have represented the total circulation in silver, which must have been at least 100 millions; therefore, 30 millions of that amount must still be out. Thus we have 255 millions of silver new coinage, 48 millions of former British coinage, and at least 30 millions of old native coin still out—total 333 millions. Besides this there is a balance of old silver importations, of which no one can give any estimate.

During this century there has been a great importation of gold into India. The gold imported from 1793 to 1835 amounted to 8 millions, and from 1835 up to the present time to no less than 104 millions, that is to say, the total importations amount to 112 millions. The coinage from 1793 to 1835 amounted to 13 millions, and from 1835 to 1880 to 3 millions—total 16 millions. This being deducted from 112 millions leaves 96 millions of gold uncoined in the hands of the people. Or, if you take the British period since 1835, there will be 104 millions imported, 3 millions only coined, leaving 101 millions of that in the hands of the people, which is either uncoined altogether or is coined in the Native States. Then you should allow for the old gold coin current in India before 1793. There must be at least 10 millions of that still out in the hands of the people. Thus, 112 millions, plus 10 millions, brings you to the total of 122 millions. Besides this, there is a balance of old importations, of which no estimate can be given.

It was fully explained in the report of Mr. Goschen's Commission on the Depreciation of Silver, that the purchase of bills of the Secretary of State for India in this country does *pro tanto* diminish the remittances of silver to the East. Two hundred and twenty-six millions sterling have been obtained in this country by these bills, or Council drafts as they are called, and they would have been much greater if it had not been for the raising of 97 millions in England for the construction of the guaranteed railways.

In regard to the question of the "probable future absorption of silver as coin" in India, you will find that the amount coined —255 millions sterling—in the last forty-five years just gives an average of 5⅓ millions annually. In quiet years the coinage amounted to from 2 to 3 millions, and in brisk years to from 10 to 15 millions—such as in the brisk years of the war of the mutinies, of the cotton famine, and the American Civil War. The variations from the slack years to the troubled years have been tolerably uniform. Thus, you can believe that if things remain quiet in the country, India will absorb about three millions sterling worth of silver per annum; but if there should arise wars or famines, or if some article which is much wanted in England and is obtained from other countries, should suddenly fail, and India could supply that, then she will draw silver to the East to the amount perhaps of ten or fifteen millions per annum.

Such, in brief, is my answer to that difficult question about the probable absorption of silver in India.

"*An* ACCOUNT *of such* PRACTICES *amongst the* NATIVES *of* INDIA *as have a* BANKING CHARACTER, *and lead up to the larger* BANKING OPERATIONS *of the* COUNTRY."

I come now to the third and last part. In the first place, among the Natives of India there are no banks of deposit as you understand them, where depositors place their money and upon which they draw cheques. The natives, as a rule, never draw cheques of this kind. It may perhaps be regarded as an instance of mutual distrust between man and man. But the native bankers do an enormous business in advancing money in large and small sums upon the security of landed property. This system is among the necessary consequences of the property in land that has been recognised and virtually created by the British Government. Hence, however, arises that indebtedness among the peasant proprietors of India of which you have heard so much, and which has caused considerable trouble. Also the natives have a great banking business in connection with general trade and agricultural produce. In this country, as we all know, every tenant-farmer has his accommodation from the county bank; but in India every landlord and every peasant proprietor, and almost every cultivator hypothecates some of the standing crops to the village bankers, and receives accommodation thereon, and if he clears his account in the year he is free, but if the account runs on at usurious interest he becomes considerably indebted. This being the nature of the business, how many people should you suppose are concerned in it? There are no less than 3½ millions of adult males engaged in commerce in British India. out of whom 118,000 adult males are bankers proper, 110,000 are money lenders, and 21,000 are money changers—total,

249,000. Deducting the money changers, that leaves about 225,000, or a quarter of a million adult male bankers, which constitutes banking as a large profession. There are at least half a million villages in India, and that is giving about two bankers to every village or parish. You will ask at once how in the world are 225,000 adult male bankers to find business? These, at the rate of an hundred customers each, would require 25 millions of customers, that is to say 25 millions of accounts. This seems to be a large number of accounts; but you will find that the numbers of people always run so high in India, that even this great number seems to be not at all improbable. There are 33 millions of adult males engaged in agriculture, of whom there are 7 million proprietors, and 26 million cultivators. Thus you will see there are plenty of customers for the quarter of a million of bankers. Besides there is a large residue from among the 3½ millions of adult males engaged in commerce.

I should add here that the rates of interest upon loans used to be in India very usurious, chiefly owing to the badness of the security, and ranged at from fifteen to twenty-five per cent. Now, under British rule, with good security, they range much lower, that is, only from six to twelve per cent.

It remains for me to explain to you some of the practices of the Native bankers in respect to the general trade.

Native bankers have a system of bills of exchange which are known locally by the name of *hundy*. These *hundys* are written not only in a distinct language of their own, but have also a distinct character, that is distinct letters of their own, so that the chances of forgery or any malpractices are greatly diminished. They have a system of technical terms almost exactly corresponding with those with which you are all familiar; and, in order to prove to you that it is no imagination of mine, I may mention some of the technical terms. For instance "Darshani" means "at sight," "Khokha" means "first of three copies of bills of exchange;" "Pênth" means "second bill;" "Parpênth" means "third copy of bill of exchange:" "Jawabi

Hundy" means "a letter of credit;" "Anth" means "discount;" and "Arath" means "credit." These *hundys*, I assure you, circulate from one end of India to the other, that is, from the Himalayas down to Ceylon, and some Native merchants can give you a draft upon any place in the world, upon Constantinople, upon the Levant, upon London, and now, I almost regret to say, upon New York,* and they have long been able to do so upon San Francisco. Of course, the total amount of these *hundys* depends upon the internal trade, the value of which, as I have before said, cannot be exactly estimated; but if I were to say that an amount of from fifty to an hundred millions sterling worth of these *hundys* must be in circulation in India at one time, I should hardly be guilty of any exaggeration.

Thus, you see that if I am asked whether this part of the question at all leads up to the idea that there is great room for development of banking in India, then I am afraid I must answer in the negative, because the Native system is so ramified and extended, that there does not appear to me to be much room for European banking as generally understood. There are savings-banks in India established by the Government, and, although only 4 per cent. interest is allowed, there are already three millions sterling of deposits, mainly Native, which amount is likely to increase. The amount of each single deposit is limited, otherwise the total would be vastly greater than it is. There are several European exchange banks in the country, and the shareholders are almost entirely European. There are also three Presidency banks in India, and in them many of the shareholders are natives. The Presidency banks keep the cash reserves of the other banks, in the same way as the Bank of England keeps the cash reserves of all the other banks in the country.

* That is to say, some of the Indian trade, which used to be arranged through England as an entrepôt, is now being done directly between India and the Continent of Europe, or the United States.

With regard to the native bankers, these form generally an entirely separate class. No doubt, in most instances, their business is managed with skill and ability. As a rule, bankers and money-lenders of India form separate guilds from generation to generation. Hitherto they have borne, I must say, an excellent character as regards commercial honour and credit, though they certainly have the reputation of being grasping and usurious in dealing with the humbler classes of their fellow-countrymen. Formerly they used to be remarkably free from speculative tendencies, but since we have carried to India the blessings of civilization, they have in some instances taken to speculation, and some of the most desperate gamblers in the market of speculation are to be found among the natives of Western India.

I have one word only to add here, namely this; you often hear that benevolent persons have propounded schemes whereby savings-banks might be established by the State, which banks might also grant advances to peasant proprietors and cultivators, and the prospect has, at first sight, a practically beneficent aspect. But I may tell you at once, after much inquiry, that we have found all these schemes to be futile. It would not be in the least possible for Government to undertake such a business. We have even inquired of European banks in the country, and they have refused to undertake it. This, then, concludes my answer to the third and last part of this question.

I am conscious that I have given you but a very small and imperfect reply to searching and comprehensive queries, and I shall conclude by urging just a few measures upon you, in which an Institute like this might beneficially influence public opinion. I would recommend you to encourage, as much as in you lies, the improvement in India of the law of debtor and creditor, the extension of savings-banks, the permission for natives to subscribe even very small sums to State loans, on the model of the French Government, and after the model which virtually has been introduced by the present Postmaster-General, Mr. Fawcett. I would urge the extension of the system of money orders, whereby the natives may be induced to use the British Post Office and other public departments for remitting their money. Also I would recommend that the system of life assurance by the State should be instituted. This will not at all interfere with private insurance companies in India, who chiefly have business either among Europeans or among Anglicised natives. Still, if the natives at large are to take to life insuring they will trust nothing short of the Government itself, and considering the priceless benefit of the habit of thrift which would thus be introduced, I think it is one of those things which the State might fairly undertake. By urging these and other kindred measures, you will not only produce a good monetary and financial effect, but you will also bind the natives by new ties to the British Government, and you will give them a substantial stake in the permanence and stability of British rule.

# CHAPTER XIII.

## COOPER'S HILL COLLEGE OF ENGINEERING.

Beauty of landscape around Cooper's Hill — Establishment there of College for Civil Engineering — Enlargement of the original design — Adapted both for England and India — National advantage of technical education in civil engineering — Peculiar advantages offered by a college of this description — Character of professional instruction afforded therein.

I DESIRE to include in this collection of essays a brief description of the Royal Indian Engineering College at Cooper's Hill, inasmuch as I have special facilities for doing so, being Chairman of the Board of Visitors appointed by the Government to supervise the course of study pursued there, and to advise regarding the internal management.

The situation of Cooper's Hill is both beautiful and interesting. The place stands on high ground about 200 feet above the valley of the Thames, overlooking the right bank of the river, about twenty miles from London, and four miles from the stone at Staines, which marks the limits of the old jurisdiction of London City over the Thames. The name is derived from the Cooper's Company, one of the historic Livery Companies of London, and the almshouses of the Company still exist in the neighbourhood. Within a reasonable distance are situated many spots of classic interest in English annals. There are, St. Anne's Hill commanding a famous prospect, and the retreat of Charles James Fox—the churchyard, with its old yews, where Gray composed his elegy—the spot where Herschel erected his 40-foot reflector—the monastic remains of Old Windsor—the spot where

Falstaff is supposed to have been thrown into the river—the Bells of Ouseley, mentioned in the 'Merry Wives of Windsor'—King John's hunting lodge—the beautiful Burnham beeches—the village of Horton, where Milton's mother lived, and where the poet composed some of his immortal works. Windsor itself is only five miles distant, and the nearest entrance to the Great Park is close at hand. The royal Castle forms a conspicuous object in the view. More particularly the college site directly overhangs the plain of Runnymead and Longmead, almost level with the river, where the king and the barons were encamped before Magna Charta was signed. Amid-stream is the island called after that event, having a house wherein there still stands the stone table on which the king's signature was affixed to the Charta.

Besides the historic there are also literary associations. In the seventeenth century Sir John Denham spoke of Cooper's Hill as the Parnassus of England. His verses received high commendation from Dryden; and from among them the following lines may be quoted:

> "My eye descending from the hill, surveys
> Where Thames among the wanton valleys strays.
> * * * * * *
> O, could I flow like thee, and make thy stream
> My great example, as it is my theme,
> Though deep yet clear, though gentle yet not dull,
> Strong without rage, without o'erflowing full."

Pope also in his 'Windsor Forest' wrote,—

> "On Cooper's Hill eternal wreaths shall grow
> While lasts the mountain, or while Thames shall flow."

Whether the poet's vision of future glory for Cooper's Hill was ever realized, certainly wreaths of which he little dreamed are gathering around this classic spot. For here has been established a college which affords the best example yet seen in the

United Kingdom of a comprehensive effort in the cause of technical education in civil engineering. If this effort shall prove successful, a living fame will accrue to this spot such as will surpass all its previous associations and traditions.

It is generally assumed that, as compared with the nations of continental Europe, perhaps even with the United States of America, England is backward in technical education. In this assumption it is probable that allowance is not sufficiently made for the technical instruction that is afforded in most of the private establishments at the industrial centres of England. If a *résumé* were made (and it would prove extremely interesting) of these efforts on the part of individuals, of firms, and of corporations, the sum total would represent a national effort that might astonish those who are ready to pass a hasty condemnation on English progress. Much excellent instruction in engineering is also given at the universities, the colleges, and other educational institutions of the kingdom both old and new. Still at these institutions engineering is taught in combination with other subjects. The whole strength of the establishment is not bent upon engineering exclusively, nor is the student obliged to devote himself to that alone. Doubtless the engineering instruction which he receives is excellent so far as it goes, but there remains doubt whether it will send him forth as a complete engineer theoretically at least, and fully equipped professionally all round. Again, if it be admitted that the instruction given in numerous private establishments is equivalent to what would on the continent of Europe be termed sound second class instruction, still it is hardly possible for private firms to organize technical colleges of the superior class. For such an organization a large expense is needed, and a concentration of effort, such as can be compassed either by a great association like an university, or by the State itself acting on behalf of the nation. It is by such means that the famous college of practical science, which exists largely for engineering but for other branches besides, namely, the Polytechnicum at Zurich, has been organized and maintained for Switzerland, and that similar institutions have been established in France, Belgium, and Germany. This, too, is the principle present to the minds of those who have sustained the English college at Cooper's Hill.

The idea of this college originated with the Government of India, which in 1871 set up the institution for training young civil engineers for the department of public works in India only. This purpose was well fulfilled for several years. But it was found that owing to reduction in the Indian establishments, the demand for India alone would hardly suffice for maintaining the college in full vigour. The Government therefore decided, in 1880, to throw the institution open to all comers. By this arrangement all qualified applicants would be admitted as students. It was expected that some of these would proceed thereafter to India according to the requirements of the public service in that country, and some would follow the profession of a civil engineer in the United Kingdom or in the colonies, or in foreign countries of Europe and America.

In order that the collegiate system might be rendered fully suitable to the requirements of the profession at large, a Board of Visitors was appointed by the Government to consider and report upon this matter. Upon this Board there sit the President and past Presidents of the Institute of Civil Engineers, together with eminent officers who have served in the Public Works Department of India, such as General Richard Strachey, Colonel Henry Yule, and General Dickens, or in the general administration, as Sir Barrow Ellis. To these has been added one whose name will command the confidence of the scientific world, Sir William Siemens. The Board has within the last two years carefully examined every branch of the collegiate instruction, the descriptive engineering, the architecture, the surveying, the applied mechanics, the experimental physics, the chemistry. It advised the Government to strengthen the instruction in the purely scientific branches, the physics and the chemistry especially, by an augmentation of the practical instruction in the laboratory. It also supported the College authorities in asking for increased accommodation for geometrical drawing and for testing machinery. The object was to render the students thoroughly acquainted with the forces of nature and with the substances that are essential to material undertakings. These several recommendations were accepted by the Government, and the education is as good as the Board can for the present make it, though the highly qualified members will doubtless from time to time suggest further improvements.

As the college must be self-supporting the fees have been so regulated as to cover the educational expenses. The Government indeed advances the funds, but does not expect ultimately to incur any loss. Nor does it contemplate setting up this college in unreasonable competition with other institutions by means of State funds. As the college is to be strictly self-supporting, whatever competition it produces will be reasonable and healthy. At the same time the fee for each student, 175*l.* to 180*l.* per annum for a course lasting three years, does not seem unduly high in comparison with the average cost in England of professional education. The income thus accruing from a complement of 120 to 150 students will cover the expenses which have been carefully calculated.

The Government have been wise in their selection of the men who are to be at the head of the College. The first President was Colonel Chesney, R.E., well known in India as an able engineer in the field, and in England as an author of graphic power. After him came Sir Alexander Taylor, whose name is inscribed in the proudest roll of those who by science and valour helped to wrest Delhi from the grasp of the mutineers in 1857.

As yet the yearly applications for admission are satisfactorily numerous. At present it is understood that many of the best young men contemplate proceeding to India if they can obtain appointments there—probably because engineering employment is at present somewhat slack in Europe.

The point, then, of real novelty and interest is to observe how many young men go to the college who have no thought of India, but contemplate working in England or elsewhere. If young men thus disposed are to resort in satisfactory numbers to the college, it must be that they expect to reap advantages therefrom during their future career in the profession at home. The question then for them or for their friends to ask themselves is, whether the professional education in the college is better than that which can be obtained elsewhere? The value of technical education, during the most receptive time of life, say from eighteen to twenty-one years of age for such a profession as that of civil engineering, will not be doubted, and is too obvious to need exposition. The real questions are whether the instruction at the college is of a first-rate kind, and whether equal advantages can be obtained elsewhere? Now let the points be recapitulated.

Here is a college founded and started under generous auspices with a liberal outlay of State capital. The British Government of India has colossal interests at stake in its public works. It has therefore the strongest incentive to secure well-educated engineers. It possesses immense resources for so arranging its plans that this object shall be secured. It has accordingly deemed that this college does answer this purpose. It bears favourable testimony to the ability evinced on actual service by the men who have received their training there. Consequently there is the weightiest authority to attest the actual efficiency of the institution. The college authorities, the president, and the professors, are sure to be persons of the most competent stamp. The course of study has been revised by a board of visitors of whom the majority are scientific men. The technical instruction has been reviewed, in reference to professional requirements, by the Board, among whose members there are gentlemen of the first standing in the engineering profession of the United Kingdom. This instruction may prove to be yet susceptible of improvement, but presumably it is the very best that can now be devised. To the prosecution of this course three years must be exclusively devoted by the students. Nor is the intellectual training alone regarded. The moral training, the discipline, the thoughtful tuition, which so greatly conduce to forming the character of youths, fitting them to achieve victorious success, whether in the engineering profession or in any walk of life, are here secured. The traditions of the place, though happy, are also salutary; its influences, though encouraging and exhilarating, have a steadying and sobering effect. These in brief are the advantages which this college, primarily designed for the sake of India, incidentally offers to the youths who are destined for the engineering profession at home.

It is for the young men and their friends to reflect whether these advantages are not, in the United Kingdom at least, unique. Much excellent instruction in engineering is given at the universities, the colleges, and other institutions in the kingdom, both old and new. Much training, theoretical and practical, is afforded in private establishments. But those who are interested in these matters may be asked to consider where else, in the United Kingdom, does an institution exist which is designed exclusively for civil engineering, and what other college has such a course of study as Cooper's Hill, to which course the whole time of the students must be devoted for three years? Upon the answer which the public voice may give to these vitally important questions must the success of this college depend. The students who do not proceed to India must, after leaving the college, doubtless seek employment in the many private establishments of the United Kingdom. If they prove to be better trained professionally than other young men, they may have a chance of obtaining more favourable terms than might otherwise have been obtainable, and they will be more likely to become immediately useful. There must yet remain the question whether the Cooper's Hill system will render them thus qualified. This can be decided by the future only. All that we can now say is this, that the system probably will have such an effect, having been expressly designed for that purpose by some of the most competent persons in the country.

# CHAPTER XIV.

## PAN ISLAMISM OR POLITICAL MUHAMMADANISM.

[*Reprinted from the 'Evening News,' London, July* 1882.]

Predominance of England in the Muhammadan world — Number of her Muhammadan subjects as compared with those of Muhammadan Powers — Character and disposition of Muhammadans generally — Muhammadans in British India — In Afghanistan — In Central Asia — In China — In Persia — In Arabia — In Turkey — In Egypt — Attitude of England towards the Muhammadans, first, as a Christian Power — Secondly, as a civilizing Power.

THERE has been for some years past, and there still is, a stir among the Muhammadan nations of the world. It is called "Pan-islamism" by Europeans: the word "islam" meaning the Muhammadan religion. As is well known, the Slavs of Europe, or their political leaders, have recently been writing and speaking of "Panslavism." This implies a general union among the Slavs living in Russia, in Austria, in European Turkey. In the same way "Pan-islamism" implies a general union among Muhammadans dwelling in the various countries of Asia and in some parts of Africa. This Pan-islamism, then, is a real movement, though perhaps it has not gone very far as yet. But no man can say to what lengths it may go. At all events, it deserves the watchful attention of Englishmen. For England, herself a Christian Power, has now more Muhammadan subjects than any Muhammadan Power in the world. Englishmen may perhaps be surprised to hear that, but it is the case. While Britain has been busy with her fields and her factories, her trade, her ships, and her colonies,—her sons have, within the last generation, raised up for her a dominion among the Asiatic Muhammadans. In the presence of that Anglo-Muhammadan dominion, the Sultan of Turkey, the Shah of Persia, the Grand Sherif of Mecca, must droop their flags. There are in India, Ceylon, and other British possessions, 50 millions of Muhammadan subjects or feudatories of the British Queen. In Afghanistan, Beluchistan, and other places there are 10 millions more under the political control of England. On the whole, then, the Anglo-Muhammadan dominion includes about 60 millions of souls. As compared with that, the other Muhammadan Powers of Asia have altogether only 32 millions. This is exclusive of China, which has a body of Muhammadan subjects whose numbers are not exactly known. In Egypt and the rest of Africa there may be several millions of Muhammadans.

But it may be said that the mere numbers of the population prove little. What is the power and wealth of the Anglo-Muhammadan dominion as compared with that of the other Muhammadans? Well, as regards power, it is impossible to distinguish the Anglo-Muhammadan power from that of Britain herself. To describe the effective might of such a power, as compared with other nations, might savour of national vanity. We need not, therefore, dwell upon that. But as regards wealth we may remark that the agriculture of the Muhammadan peasantry of India, the navigation in the hands of her Muhammadan sailors and boatmen, the trade conducted by her Muhammadan traders, greatly exceed anything that can be shown by any other Muhammadan nation—indeed, by all other Muhammadan nations together.

Moreover, the Anglo-Muhammadan population is increasing fast, whereas in Turkey and Persia it is understood to be decreasing.

In all the counsels of political Muhammadanism, then, the British Sovereign is entitled to a place in the very first rank, as representing the dominion over the largest and richest Muhammadan population in the world.

In India the mass of the Muhammadans are peaceful, industrious, and loyal. It is well that Englishmen should realise this great fact. But it is also necessary for them to remember that among these generally sober-minded Muhammadans there are many persons of a different stamp. These are bigoted, even desperate; and nothing that we can offer will pacify them. Therefore Muhammadan troubles have from time to time arisen in India. The assassination of Chief Justice Norman at Calcutta, and of Lord Mayo at Port Blair in 1872–73, are instances fresh in the public memory. Bad as these events were, even worse things might possibly happen if England were to fall asleep. But if she remains wakeful they may, under Providence, be prevented.

It may then be asked, Why are the Muhammadans bestirring themselves in these days, and what is it that they are thinking about?

Well, outside India, they feel that they are politically decaying. They are generally disposed to shut their eyes to that which is disagreeable. But they can no longer help seeing the strides which the Christian nations are making in wealth, power, and civilization. Thus they dread the advance of Christendom. The leaders among them look back wistfully to the great days when the Crescent drove back or bore down the Cross in many of the fairest and holiest regions of the earth. When the Cross rallied under Christian warriors, such as Charles Martel of France and John Sobieski of Poland, and stopped the Crescent in its career, they comforted themselves with the thought that South-Eastern Europe, Northern Africa, and a goodly part of Asia still remained to Islam. They perceive, however, that within the last hundred years the Christian power has been making inroads upon Muhammadanism in all directions. Yet some of them have been trusting that Allah and their prophet Muhammad would somehow draw once more the flashing scimitar to scatter the unbelievers. Others of them, again, who do not rely upon divine interference, have been dreaming that destiny (Kismet) would at last set all things right. Now, however, they are becoming aroused by the idea that Christian influence and authority are drawing so near as to threaten the very existence of Islam itself. The alarm is gradually growing in their minds. This alarm refers in the first place to their political power, but in the second place to their religion also. Possibly they might view with some sort of patience the loss of mere earthly dominion. But in their minds worldly power cannot be quite separated from religion. They all, from the highest to the humblest, revere their faith as pure and lofty. In fact, like many other faiths, it has in practice been often clouded over with mummery and superstition. Still there remains something of grandeur about it. In the hearts of its followers it is associated with splendid and glorious memories. Its triumphs of war, in politics, and in art, its efforts even in the cause of science, are well known to the upper classes, and are dimly understood by the multitude. It was skilfully contrived by Muhammad, its founder, to appeal forcibly to the notions and sentiments of hot-blooded races dwelling in sunny climes. Though it is really opposed to human progress, though it blights the prospects of civilization, and stunts the growth of society—yet it reigns in the affections of many millions of bright-eyed and strong-handed men. Such men will turn out to fight for it, and in the excitement of action will face death on its behalf. They used in former times to make converts by the sword; indeed, no religion has ever spread itself so much by force and indirect pressure as theirs. Strangely enough they continue to gain men over (though by gentler means) to their faith in Africa and in Eastern Asia.

The question then arises as to whether the Muhammadans have anything like a policy, while raising this movement of Pan-islamism. Is this stir merely a breeze ruffling the surface of the political waters, or does it portend a real storm? The answer depends, no doubt, largely on the conduct of the Western Powers. The Muhammadans have certainly got a general policy, which is this, to resist the further encroachments of the Christian States, to hold at least their own, and to keep what remains to them of the broad regions that submitted to the Prophet of Arabia. We must acknowledge, too, that this is reasonable in theory. In practice, however, a great power, such as theirs once was, does not yield to dangers from without so long as it is solid and prosperous within. It is the canker eating into the vitals of the State that makes them yield to foreign pressure. The Muhammadans probably are well aware of this also. They know that somehow their body politic is becoming feeble; that their lands are becoming less productive, that their cultivation is shrinking, that their flocks and herds are lessening. They see that famines come and decimate the people sadly, and that afterwards the population does not recover. They feel that there is something fatally the matter with them, but cannot make out exactly what it is. The feeling is aggravated by the sight of neighbouring nations in blooming health and vigorous life. All this is enough to make them despair, and at times they must be somewhat downhearted. But at bottom they are brave; and, while preserving an apathetic appearance, they have an enthusiasm burning within them. If common sense were joined to this enthusiasm, they would soon learn to set their social house in order, to give light and liberty to the people, to secure to every man the fruits of his toil whether of brain or of hands, and to spread abroad that sort of useful knowledge which makes people thrifty, self-reliant, and intelligent. If this lesson did not come to them by inspiration, they might gather it from the example of several among the Christian nations. They would doubtless wish to do this if they could, but they do not know how to set about it. So they drift on towards political ruin. Meanwhile they are becoming very uneasy under the prospect, and are thinking that some plunging struggle must be tried. Instead of looking their misfortune quietly in the face, and devising really workable remedies, they seem to believe that the first thing needful is to restore the energies of their religion. Reformations of sorts are thus undertaken. The Wahhabi revival in Arabia, of which the public has heard much, was an attempt of this nature. It is likely that similar movements may arise in various quarters; indeed, they are springing up already.

There might, then, be a rising in the Muhammadan world, outside the Anglo-Muhammadan dominion above described. Such a combined movement would manifestly affect British interests. It would of itself be serious indeed; still England is quite mighty enough to withstand or overcome it, if only she were left to herself. But would she be let alone? Obviously not. Other Christian powers would be naturally jealous of her acting singly. They would lift up their voices and put in their claims. Thus political complications would arise. In the midst of such complications any rash proceedings on the part of one or other of the Christian Powers might bring on a deadly quarrel within Christendom itself about the affairs of the Muhammadan world. That would indeed be an unseemly spectacle to be exhibited by Christianity in the presence of the heathen.

Such is the outline of political Muhammadanism on the whole, or "Pan-islamism," as it is beginning to be called. This outline touches on the broad features of Muhammadanism as it exists in Asia and Africa. I now propose to deal somewhat more in detail with Muhammadanism in each of the principal countries where it prevails.

First let us take that division of the Muhammadans which is numerically the largest of them all, namely, the Indian. Under British rule these Indian Muhammadans have been beaten in the intellectual race by their Hindu fellow-subjects. For the first generation or so after the introduction of British rule the Muhammadans got on well in the public service, having more of readiness and vigour than the Hindus. In the next generation there came a system of national education and competitive examinations. Then the Hindu youth, being more patient and studious, had altogether the best of it. Thus the Muhammadans found themselves to be fast slipping out of the position they had so long enjoyed in the administration of the country. Seeing this, they have begun to exert themselves more than formerly respecting their schools and colleges. Still they have much way to make up before they can come abreast of the Hindus. In the larger operations of commerce they never have been equal to the Hindu caste which combines the functions of money-lender and traders. But in the lesser business of trade, and especially in retail dealing, they always excel. They are probably among the best pedlars in all Asia. For agriculture they effect but little in most parts of the country. But in some parts, as in the Panjab, they do something considerable. In eastern and northern Bengal, too, they do very much indeed. Englishmen, perhaps, do not ordinarily realise that many articles coming from that quarter to Europe, such as jute, safflower, rice, are produced by Muhammadan hands. This Muhammadan peasantry is rising in a humble but solid prosperity, and is growing in numbers more rapidly than the population of any other part of the Empire. Their temper, though generally good, is excitable. I have known them listen to the voice of agrarian agitators, threaten their landlords, demand a general lowering of rent, surround with angry crowds the offices of the land agents and the like. But with promptitude and firmness on the part of the Government such movements are always kept within bounds. As boatmen on inland waters, too, these Bengali Muhammadans are excellent, and the traffic which they thus conduct is enormous. As seamen, on the coasts or on the ocean, they are the principal class employed. They supply the crews to the vessels of steam navigation companies. If ever England decided to have some ships of war with European officers and native crews (for service in Eastern waters), the Muhammadans of the Bengal and Bombay coasts would be the men for this work.

In regard to religion, the Indian Muhammadans preserve their faith despite all the efforts of the Christian missionaries. Some few converts are made from Muhammadanism. But the great numbers of native Christians, in whom Christendom thankfully rejoices, belongs to tribes other than Muhammadan. One reason of this, no doubt, is the comparative purity and simplicity of the doctrines of Islam. The Muhammadan priesthood continues to be thoroughly organized, although the British Government stands quite aloof from the organization. Most of the religious endowments, granted by former Muhammadan Sovereigns, are respected and maintained by the British. Still, the priestly classes are fanatical and often fierce. We must hope that a kindly policy will conciliate many of them. Nevertheless, we must be prepared to find that some of them are implacable, and will not accept us on any terms whatsoever.

Politically, the Muhammadan peasantry are for the most part well affected. Among the upper classes some are singularly loyal, and play a truly honourable part towards us. Others, again, are in quite the opposite way. Among these last there are at least a few very dangerous characters indeed. They stir up mischief of the worst kind on every opportunity. A religious revival in Arabia—a war in Turkey—a rumour of a war in Europe—a trouble in Africa—will give the cue. Hardly a year passes without small conspiracies of sorts being hatched in some part or other of the Indian Empire. The British authorities, being accustomed to the thing, take it coolly, adopt their precautions, and say nothing about it. Thus the Government pursues its course of national improvement, quite unmoved.

It is fair, perhaps, to add that the Muhammadans are not alone in this kind of mischief. Other Indian tribes occasionally try their hand at it also.

The Indian Muhammadans will probably be found to entertain a profound veneration and a keen sympathy for the Sultan of Turkey. They do not care equally for the Afghans. On the contrary, they thought that in the last war the Amir of Caubul turned rather against the Sultan and leaned towards Russia. They were displeased at seeing the Sultan's envoy go from Constantinople to Caubul and return without being able to arrange any alliance with the Amir.

They still trust that England must, for her own sake, if not for any other account, continue to sustain the Sultan. Their spirits will droop if this hope shall be shaken.

Let us next glance at the Afghans. They have been said by some authorities to be democratic, whatever that may mean. They certainly hate authority of any kind. They cannot hang together for any purpose of politics or of war. They form little societies among themselves like clans. Then every clan will insist on being a law to itself and of doing as it likes. What they all like best is this—to quarrel, kill, and plunder, according to the impulse of the time. Such a people is never formidable politically of itself. But it may be as a double-edged sword, as a sharp-pointed lance, for a temporary purpose in the hands of a designing and organising Power. Why this people has such a strange character we cannot now pause to inquire. But obviously the rugged and isolated nature of the country is one of the reasons. Meanwhile, this people is ungovernable—indeed, untameable for the most part. It may be kept with difficulty in a loose union under one Amir as head. Yet it will always be trying to split itself up into several petty States. But though untameable in most parts, it is tameable in some. For instance, had the British Government seen fit to hold Southern Afghanistan, the measure could have been accomplished in the end with firmness and patience. Trouble here and there would have arisen at first, but success would have rewarded perseverance. Trade would have grown, and cultivation would have spread. Regions which were once gardens, but are now half-desolate, would have been re-peopled gradually.

With all his bloodthirstiness and general naughtiness, the Afghan as a farmer and cultivator is second to few in the world. As a fruit-grower on a large and varied scale he will not be beaten by any European. If a jury of British farmers were deputed to inspect the irrigated fields near Caubul and Candahar, they would be amazed at the number of crops that are raised on the land during the year, and the manner in which the powers of the soil are kept up under all this cropping without exhaustion.

Next we may note how Russia fares with her new dominions in Central Asia. Remembering their own troubles in Afghanistan, Englishmen at first imagined that Russia was unconsciously preparing for herself a hornet's nest in Central Asia, that is, in Kokhand, Bokhara, and Khiva. But she apparently escapes being stung. She thoroughly understands, in these regions at least, the lesson of religious toleration. She pays some attention to education. She overawes with military force all disturbers of the internal peace. This force costs her much more than the revenue of the territory can afford. Yet she is consolidating a real dominion in this quarter. Politicians will justly dread the possibility of such a dominion being made a basis of movements hostile to England. Nevertheless, humanity will rejoice at the civilization which is gradually replacing barbarism there.

The same remarks may be applied with still greater force to the most recent acquisitions of Russia in the Turkoman country under Skobeleff. The conduct of these Turkomans, who dwell near the north-eastern border of Persia, has long been a disgrace not only to Muhammadanism, but also to humanity in the nineteenth century. To describe the horrors of the slavery practised by these Turkomans would require the tongue and pen of Wilberforce or of Brougham. Doubtless the evil will be checked, if not finally stopped, by the Russian domination. We may well wish that England had insisted on taking her share in this good work. Many will think that it was as much the concern of England as of Russia. There may, indeed, have been political or ambitious motives at work. Yet we must acknowledge that the prevention of Turkoman misdeeds will be a boon conferred upon humanity by Russia.

There are many Muhammadan subjects of China dwelling at Yarkand and elsewhere in Central Asia. They shook off the Chinese yoke for a time. Then the British Government made a commercial treaty with them, in order to support them in their independence. But shortly afterwards China re-asserted herself, and after a sharp and sanguinary fight brought them back into her fold, where they now are. Within China proper there is a considerable Muhammadan population. Their real character is not certainly known. But the best opinion seems to be that they are not politically important and not likely to join in Muhammadan movements.

We have now to turn for a moment towards Persia. The Shah of Persia must be rolling his anxious eyes first in this direction and then in that. Northwards he looks to Russia, southwards to England. The success of Russia in the Turkoman country must have deepened his impressions regarding Russian ambition. The Persians as Shiahs form a great religious sect, and cling with superstitious devotion to their tenets. Still they are regarded by the Muhammadan world at large as sectarians, perhaps even as heretics. This affects the cordiality of their relations with Turkey. Thus one may wonder how Persia can really join in Pan-islamism; also, how Pan-islamism can practically work while so large a member as Persia is left out. By all accounts the Persian population is declining. The authentic stories of the late famine are quite heartrending. The administration is feeble, and the public treasury is too poor to afford material enterprises. But without such undertakings no nation can in this age either make its way or hold its own. From the north under Russian auspices, and from the south under English auspices, Persia might be traversed by roads and railways; irrigation works might be renewed in various districts; gradually the forests (long since destroyed) and the hill vegetation might be restored. With all this, the independence of the Persian State and Sovereign might be reasonably preserved. Meanwhile, however, poor Persia remains land-locked, unimproved, and stagnant. In a progressive age like this, nothing is more dangerous nationally than stagnation.

The dangers which threaten un-improved Persia do not affect Arabia, to which we must next allude. Arabia is, from the nature of its territory, isolated. It may, therefore, go on for a long time without improvement in the modern sense of the term. In this generation, at least, the Arabians have given up dreaming of foreign dominion. Their Wahhabi reformers did indeed not long ago imagine that the faith, as handed down fresh by the Prophet, might be revived. With such a revival, the old sovereignty was to be re-established, as they thought. The Wahhabi State, however, contents itself at present with managing the central uplands of Arabia. According to the best evidence this plateau is flourishing. Mecca and Medina are thronged with pilgrims from India and Persia, who take advantage of the British shipping which navigates the Indian Ocean, the Persian Gulf, and the Red Sea. Thus the British name becomes indirectly popular with pious Muhammadans. The Arab tribes near Aden are disposed to fall under British protection. Thousands of Arabs, too, enter the military service of some of the Native States of India.

Regarding the Turks there have been doubts in the English mind as to whether these people are good or not. Well, they are really good. All accounts agree respecting the merits of the ordinary Turk. He is brave, patient, enduring, truthful, and honest. In bodily strength he is surpassed by few races on earth. But he is lazy in mind and un-enterprising. Under superior leadership he might become formidable politically, but not otherwise. Such leadership is not likely to be supplied from his own nation. The official Turks are, owing to a vicious system, exposed to much temptation. They have generally an indifferent, and often an evil, repute. Among the upper class, or Pashas, there are some men of a patriotic stamp, who are personally trustworthy, and would not stoop to corruption. Such men, however, are sometimes narrow-minded and impracticable. They seem to think that Turkey is declining, not because she cannot march with the age, but because she has strayed too far into European ways. Such persons would think that the only chance for saving the State is to revert to the practices and institutions of past centuries. The priestly classes, though much more tolerant than they once were of other religions, are yet bigoted at heart. They feel dread lest the light of modern civilization should be brought to bear on their system. They have the control of the national education, which they render as unscientific as they can. Being, of all Muhammadans, the nearest to Europe, they apparently believe that European freedom will never agree with the principles of Islam. This belief is shared by the Turkish nobility. The Sultan is the head of the Faith in Turkey. Many Turks would like to see him made the head of the whole religious community of the Muhammadan world. Thus he would become a sort of Vicar of the Prophet upon earth. Such men do not wish the Sultan to be supreme and absolute as a ruler. They that think he ought to be hedged in by powerful advisers, priests and nobles. The State being thus composed should, in their ideas, have absolute authority over the people. They set their faces against every sort of reform, fearing lest it should lead to representative institutions after the European model. Some of them are actuated by sordid motives, and support the old system for their own gain. Thus the prospect of reform in Turkey is quite clouded over. Meanwhile, the unreformed state of the country is dangerous to the stability of the Turkish Empire.

There remains but one Muhammadan country to be mentioned, and that is Egypt. Whatever may be the faults of the upper classes, or the wickedness of the mob, the Egyptian peasantry are quiet, industrious, and law-abiding. They were, under Anglo-French influence, in a fair way to flourish abundantly. That prospect is not impaired, is even improved under the British control now existing in their country. Next after the Muhammadans of Bengal, already mentioned, the Egyptians are the most capable of improvement. Their country might become one of the few bright spots of the Muhammadan world. But this prospect has been interrupted by a party who call themselves National, but who really dread improvement lest it should introduce European influence.

I have now touched on political Muhammadanism, first in regard to the Muhammadan world on the whole, and then in regard to each of the principal Muhammadan countries. I next propose to consider what sort of attitude Britain ought, as a Christian and a civilising Power, to maintain towards political Muhammadanism.

In the first place let us reflect for a moment upon the conduct of Britain as a Christian Power. We must, I fear, give up for the present the hope of converting any large number of Muhammadans to Christianity. The Muhammadan religion has not the many absurdities about it which Hinduism, the debased Buddhism, and several Pagan religions have. It is not likely to yield, as some of them are yielding, to the assaults of reason. Many parts of it are reasonable, and some parts are even noble.* It commands many of the feelings which lie deep in the heart of man at all times and under all climes. It has on the minds of its followers a grasp which will not be shaken. It is not utterly opposed to Christianity. It even regards Christianity as subsidiary to itself. A thoughtful Muhammadan considers a Christian to be much nearer to himself than the follower of any other religion. Of course there is really a vast difference, spiritual and other, between Christianity and Muhammadanism. But it is not easy to illustrate and explain that difference in a manner that shall at once strike the minds of ordinary Asiatics. The Christian advocate soon exposes the follies and saps the foundations of several among the heathen religions. But he cannot deal thus easlly with Muhammadanism. Having eternal truth on his side he must in the end prevail. Still, his victory may not be yet awhile.

* See 'Pearls of Faith,' or selection of Muhammadan Dicta, by Edwin Arnold.

Nevertheless, England may produce a great effect on Muhammadanism by showing the practical superiority of Christianity. We may hope, indeed, that she has already produced such an effect to some considerable extent. We must be prepared, however, to find that Muhammadans, like most other Orientals, are disposed to overrate our failings and underrate our merits. We may indeed desire that those with whom we have much intimate concern should—

> "Be to our faults a little blind,
> Be to our virtues very kind."

But, on the contrary, Muhammadans are apt to be very critical and suspicious regarding our faults, and to be unkind or disparaging regarding our virtues. Still, as claiming for ourselves superiority both in respect to our religion and our civilization, we are bound to display, above all things, charity. Many among us are but too ready to think ill of Muhammadans, as of all Asiatics. This vein of thought we must admit to be wrong. It is also impolitic; but when a thing is wrong, the argument is only weakened if impolicy is urged in addition. We stand in a peculiar position towards the Muhammadan world; and that position has its peculiar duties. While performing those duties we must be patient under misrepresentation. We must not be disappointed if, at first, we meet with ingratitude. Still, if we persist in well doing we shall win our way with the Muhammadans. They will evince gratitude if we succeed in giving them much to be grateful for. I could point to several instances of signal gratitude and loyalty on the part of Muhammadans who had received real benefits from the British Government. On the other hand, it would be difficult to produce equally signal cases of ingratitude.

Our primary care must be for those Muhammadans who are British subjects. It is not enough to preserve order among them, to protect their property, to secure to them the fruits of their industry, to give them just laws honestly administered, to render their taxation moderate, to develop the resources of their territory by public works, and so on. All this we do, not perfectly, indeed, but better than any native Power has ever done. The Muhammadans may be slow to admit this, and be too quick to carp and cavil. Still the plain fact does tell in our favour, and is raising our repute. But, as stated above, all this, though well in its way, is not enough for the Muhammadans who are British subjects. It is necessary to elevate them morally and intellectually. For this purpose the greatest agency is education. There is more difficulty in inducing Muhammadans to accept Western education than other Asiatic races. The Muhammadans prefer being taught even secular knowledge by teachers of their own faith. Though willing to learn English, they insist on learning those languages also in which the history of their faith and nationality is written. These predilections should be humoured as much as possible. While a part of their system is dying out amidst the progress of the age, some of their old institutions survive. It is important to preserve these, and to render them useful under the circumstances of the time. We should further give these Muhammadans, without grudge or stint, the benefit of all those sciences whereby we ourselves have risen to greatness. We should even train them gradually in the ways of self-government. In this the first step is to teach them how to manage their own municipal affairs. The sense of possessing rights which are really enjoyed under a settled Government, the hope of qualifying for the exercise of political privileges, the breadth of thought which is brought about by knowledge and science, must all tend to elevate the individual man. It is the aim of good government to raise every person among the millions. It is also essential to render them all the loyal citizens of a world-wide Empire, and the useful members of a vast society. We must do all this courageously, without fear of the consequences hereafter. Here, again, whatever be the mandate of Christian charity must be the dictate of true policy.

As previously stated, Muhammadanism has much that is irreconciIeable and implacable in its religion. Still even there, if we respect the endowments and grants made by our predecessors for religious uses, we produce a good effect. Some endowments, too, were made for the sake of Muhammadan education. If we take care that these are applied to uses which shall benefit the people under the conditions of the time, and shall also be such as the donors would have approved, our conduct will be appreciated.

After all, the Muhammadans have always a vague fear that a foreign Government may interfere with their religion. They know that this is just what they themselves used to do with their subjects of other religions. Thus it is their conscience which now makes them timid in this matter. Experience has probably convinced them that they have nothing to fear in this respect from force. But they imagine that education and other improvements will be turned into engines for moving the minds of youth away from the faith of the Prophet. Now, we must at all hazards communicate knowledge to them. Nevertheless, we must let them see that no unfair advantage whatever is taken in respect to religion. Their faith will have every reasonable chance of holding its own or winning its way if it can. Despite all their fanaticism, the argument that their religion has never been interfered with, that every opportunity has been allowed to them for maintaining their doctrines, will always carry weight with their minds in our favour.

This generous policy on the part of England in Asia is doing much to reconcile Muhammadan nations generally to the growth of European influence. It may, indeed, be said that nevertheless this influence is dreaded by them. Yes; but how much more would it have been dreaded if our enemies had been able to say that we interfered with religion! How easily might political movements have then been stirred up! As it is, the fanatics rather fear that the masses are becoming fond of the easy life they are having under their foreign rulers.

It is but just to say that, according to the best information, Russia is pursuing the same wise course in the several Muhammadan countries which have come under her sway. If she perseveres in this, her name will become in this respect as good as that of England.

So much for the Muhammadans who are the subjects of the British Queen, and who, as already seen, constitute half the Muhammadan world. Let us for a moment consider our attitude towards the other half—that is, towards those who are not British subjects.

In the first place, we must try to make them feel that, as a Christian power, we are not ambitious of grasping at dominion belonging to others. We are not consumed by "earth-hunger." We have enough to do in guarding from many possible dangers the dominion which has fallen to the lot of our Sovereign and nation. In several Muhammadan nations, not belonging to the British Empire, British interests have sprung up. These interests must be protected. We can never allow them to be injured with impunity. Even then, however, our first care should be to make the native State do its duty towards the British interests existing within its limits. This is preferable to our undertaking to execute the duty for ourselves. We should strive to convince the Muhammadans that we do not look on with secret satisfaction while they go the road to ruin, in order that we may step into their places. Rather do we desire to see them properly sustaining all the independence that still remains to them. We may pursue our own national advantage within our proper sphere, which is indeed large enough. We hope that they will have the sense to promote their own true advantage within their several spheres also. In doing this they should have the moral support of our sympathy, and occasionally even the material assistance of a friendly hand. But there again, such assistance should be tendered in such a way as not to destroy their self-reliance and their spirit of self-help. In short, let them feel that, whether they dislike us or not, we have no unfriendly sentiment towards them, and that we cherish for them that brotherly kindness which is an essential part of our Christianity.

Having considered the attitude of Britain towards the Muhammadans as a Christian Power, I have now to discuss her attitude as a civilising Power.

It has been already explained that Muhammadanism as a religious system, over-ruling the State, has still a warm and strong life. But it is stagnant or retrogressive respecting material improvement. In former centuries it did much for science. Its scientific services in the past are often remembered gratefully by its admirers. But nowadays it is nowhere in the race of invention, of investigation, of discovery. In effect it is as a dead weight of lead pressing down any attempt that may be made for material improvement.

Now in modern times experience shows that in some countries the white races gradually drive out the savages. How, exactly, the savages become extinguished none can say. But somehow they languish and dwindle until they die out. In the same way a superior civilization, if brought into contact with an inferior one, will kill it outright. If the inferior civilization is to preserve its life, it must improve itself. It must work in the lines of its superiors respecting material improvement and education. This rule will sternly apply to the Muhammadans. Their faith may survive, but their political system, if unreformed, cannot live alongside the European system. Its only chance for life is to reform itself. This truth is unpleasant to Muhammadans, and therefore they shut their eyes to it. Thence it becomes the duty of England, as a friendly Power, to make this point quite clear to them. Let them, at all events, be warned, in a conciliatory yet in a positive manner. If they will not hearken they will bring about their own destruction. The end may be long delayed, perhaps, but come it must at last.

Turkey in Europe supplies the strongest instance. After the Crimean war Turkey enjoyed the fairest chance of self-improvement which she ever had. That chance she has flung away, and perhaps it may never return. She possessed many provinces in Europe. These provinces, being in the valley or basin of the

Danube, were the finest in her whole Empire. But they required the same sort of improvement as that which was going on throughout most parts of Europe. As a basis of such improvement there were needed an honest administration and a certain degree of constitutional liberty. Such improvement and such liberty might have been allowed, and yet the Muhammadan authority might have been kept up. But the Turks could not, or would not, see this. They thought that if these boons were once granted the Muhammadan authority would be gone. They believed that their system could not live if the people began to have a voice in the management of the national affairs. The truth was that their system had some chance for life, if popular concessions were wisely made. But if these were not made, then it had no chance at all. The Turks, however, would not yield. Doubtless there were many excuses to be made for their conduct. Many things combined to turn them into a wrong course. The behaviour of this neighbour and of that neighbour was such as to rouse their suspicions and to set them against reform. Still, to reform, or not to reform, that was the real question which Turkey had to consider. She decided it in the negative. Then what was the consequence? After a series of events, now historical, she has been crippled by a ruinous war, and has lost most of her European provinces. She has been obliged, indeed, to part with full half of her whole Empire. Even the half that yet remains to her is grievously enfeebled by all that has happened. Nevertheless, all these misfortunes might have been staved off—perhaps might have been prevented altogether—by timely reform. No doubt, after such reform, the Turks would have had a more troublesome time of it in the Danubian provinces than they had ever known before. Still, they would have continued to exist politically. But they would not face the trouble, and consequently they have ceased to exist in that quarter. Thus a severe lesson has been read to them. Are they profiting by it? No; hardly at all as yet. Therefore dangers will gradually arise of the same sort as those which have already burst over Turkey with such a disastrous effect. It would be, perhaps, unfriendly to indicate in public the nature of such dangers. But they are arising just like clouds gathering in the sky. The true friends of Turkey—and there are many such friends among Englishmen—ought to warn her of this. Perhaps they are warning her, though she does not hearken. It is natural that she should be jealous or suspicious in respect to foreign advice. Still, there is the truth, to which she must bend —or else be broken.

The same remarks may apply in some degree to Persia. She has not, like Turkey, large classes of subjects claiming a reform of the national institutions. But her administration is feeble in the extreme, and is becoming gradually weaker. Of late there has been much comment on the encroachments of Russia upon the north-eastern frontier of Persia. What is the circumstance that has most favoured those encroachments? Why, the manner in which Persia herself has for many years past mismanaged her own frontier. The neighbouring Turkoman tribes, that were finally beaten by Skobeleff at the battle of Geok Tepe two years ago, ought properly to have been Persian subjects. But Persia found that they were hard to govern, and that their country was unprofitable. So she left them to their own devices. These devices of theirs did indeed prove horrid. For a regular system was established of plundering property and of enslaving human beings. The Turkoman horsemen used to cross over into Persian territory and ravage whole villages, carring off plunder on their pack-saddles, while the men and women were fastened by the hands to the horses' tails, and so dragged into slavery. The Persian Government did little or nothing to save its subjects from this maltreatment. The border line offered great facilities for defence and protection. Had a military police been organised the mischief might have been put down. But, being unopposed, the Turkomans grew bolder, and began to give trouble to the neighbouring Russian authorities. Then Russia was only too glad of a pretext for interfering. Accordingly she has interfered with marked effect, as all the world knows. She had, as her own officers acknowledged, ambitious motives in doing this. That is, she desired politically to open up a possible highway in the direction of British India. She also meant to obtain complete control over the north-eastern frontier of Persia. That has rendered the position of Persia lower even than it was before, and will make her obedient to the very nod or beckon of Russia. This fresh degradation of the Persian Government is owing mainly to its own fault in not restraining the Turkomans.

The Asiatic neighbours of Persia are as backward and uncivilized as herself, so they are not likely to embarrass her by showing any superiority. But then she has two other very progressive neighbours, namely, England and Russia. She also feels French influence in several respects. Europeans enter Persian territory for trade or industry and lay out capital there. The same thing is done by the Asiatics who are subjects of European Powers. This gives some little impulse to a sluggish country. It also adds to the responsibilities of the Persian administration. If oppression is permitted or extortion practised, an outcry arises. If the dissatisfaction is not removed, the quarrel ends in blows. This is exactly the sort of case which becomes the origin of war.

Recently, as we all remember, France has by force established her authority in Tunis. The Muhammadan Prince has been thereby reduced to a condition of dependence. If his conduct in these affairs be examined, it will be found that he brought the trouble upon himself by his own misgovernment. French interests had grown up in his territory, and French capital had been invested therein. Had he duly protected these interests, and preserved order throughout his dominions, he might have saved himself for a time at least.

There is not space to examine the origin of the recent trouble internally in Egypt. But similar causes will be found to govern that case also.

The fact is that nearly all the Muhammadan countries are unable to avoid contact with the progressive nations of Europe.

Arabia alone, being girdled by deserts, can keep herself free from such contact, for the present at least. She may preserve her originality and follow her own rude way for sometime to come. The Bedouin Arabs may continue to be the free lances of south-western Asia. Other Arabs are fond of migrating temporarily to civilized regions for trade and for service. They keep up their connection with their wild home in the Arabian uplands. If they live to return to it, they doubtless rejoice to find it unimproved, and unaffected by the civilization that is going on in the world around.

But the other Muhammadan nations cannot follow this course with any success at all. They often try to do so, but the attempt generally ends in disaster to themselves. Their geographical situation is such as to render their isolation impossible. Their people will be passing over in numbers to the neighbouring nations of Europe. Similarly the Europeans will be passing over to them. It is obvious that in these days men will be running to and fro on the earth. This constant migration backwards and forwards must involve certain consequences. Muhammadans who have resided abroad will often return to their own country, bringing with them new ideas. These ideas will relate to education, to good government, even to freedom. Europeans residing in Muhammadan countries will introduce ideas of the same character. There will further be more solid changes. Industrial enterprise will push its way to the inviting regions of Muhammadanism, and sometimes even to the uninviting ones. Capital, accumulated in European countries, will be seeking investment in Muhammadan quarters as in other foreign quarters. This will occur as surely as water rises to its proper level. Indeed, this must happen according to the laws of modern society. Whether the Muhammadans like it or not, they are powerless to prevent it. The Europeans could not prevent it if they would, but in fact there is no reason why they should wish to do so.

This inevitable process produces certain consequences which

the Muhammadans must face. If they fail herein, they must fall sooner or later. These consequences are that there must be a respectable administration for their own people, and an ordinary degree of protection for the foreigners who are carrying on trade or managing industrial concerns. But Muhammadan administration, instead of improving with the times, has become weaker than it used to be in former ages, and is often unequal to the task of dealing with the new interests which are springing up within its borders.

If, on the other hand, a Muhammadan Government succeeds in governing well, according to the requirements of the nineteenth century, it will certainly receive the sympathy of England, and probably of other European nations also.

Muhammadans are apt to deceive themselves by reason of the facility with which money in vast sums has been borrowed by them in the European money markets. They may fail to pay the interest of the debt; they may even repudiate a part of the principal. Yet there may be no political consequences to follow. The foreign Governments may not feel justified in interfering by force on behalf of those who have chosen to lend their money.

But the case is practically different with those who have established interests and laid out capital in Muhammadan countries. If these concerns are injured, either from violence of misrule, the case then becomes one of police management. Every Government in all parts of the world is expected to answer for order. If the subjects of any nation are specially maltreated abroad, if, as it were, a set is violently made against them, a remonstrance from their own Government is sure to follow. If, for instance, the British residents in any part of southern Europe, say at Odessa, or at Athens, or at Brindisi, or at Barcelona, had been suddenly maltreated or outraged, as the British were at Alexandria in the summer of 1882, serious political consequences would have ensued. This should be remembered as one of the many reasons which exist to justify the vigorous action which the British Government took in Egypt.

It is the part of true kindness, then, for Britain to do her best in bringing these truths home to the Muhammadan mind. She may do this in a conciliatory manner, so as not to wound the pride of Muhammadans. Let them feel that she has no selfish ambition; that she does not wish to annex them; that, on the contrary, she desires to see them independent and prosperous. She will in every sense wish them well; but her good wishes will be of little avail to them unless they, of their own accord, improve themselves.*

* The observations in this chapter regarding the Turks have recently been verified by me during a visit to Turkey.—R. T.

# CHAPTER XV.

## THE MAHRATTA NATIONALITY.

[*Reprinted from the 'Encyclopædia Britannica,' New Edition*, 1883.]

Native region of the Mahrattas — Originally mountaineers of the hill ranges along the western coast of India — Their physical characteristics — Their sturdy and patriotic temper — Their agricultural industry — Their landed tenures — Their condition under British rule — Greatness of their past history — Predatory foundation of their power — Unimproving character of their rule — Establishment of the Mahratta confederation — The Peshwas, or Brahman princes — Leading Mahratta States — Their military contests with the British power — Their incorporation into the British empire.

THE Mahrattas inhabit that portion of India which is known by the ancient name of Mahârâshtra (Sanskrit for the great kingdom or region). This large tract, extending from the Arabian Sea on the west to the Sâtpura mountains in the north, comprises a good part of western and central India, including the modern provinces of the Konkan, Khandesh, Berar, the British Deccan, part of Nagpur, and about half the Nizam's Deccan. Its area amounts to about 120,000 square miles, and its population to about twelve millions of souls, or 100 to the square mile. The population has increased greatly in the nineteenth century under British rule; but there had been much decrease during the seventeenth and eighteenth centuries owing to war and devastation. Frightful depopulation occurred from the famine which was at its height in 1400 A.D., and was called the Dùrga Dévi or the goddess of destruction. Much mortality was also caused by famine between 1801 and 1803. There was probably a period of high prosperity during the first centuries of the Christian era, under a number of petty indigenous sovereigns, among whom these wide territories had become parcelled out before the first invasion of the Deccan by the Moslems about 1100.

The etymology of the word Mahratta (or Marhatta, as it is written in the vernacular) is uncertain. The name does not indicate a social caste, or a religious sect; it is not even tribal. It embraces the people of all races who dwell in the region of Mahàràshtra, both high-caste and low-caste Hindus; it is applied, of course, to Hindus only. Thus there are Mahratta Brahmans, next Mahratta Kumbis or cultivators, and Mahratta Rajputs or warriors, though the latter have but a small infusion of real Rajput blood. The Mahrattas, then, are essentially Hindus in religion and in caste ordinances, not differing in these respects from the Hindus in other parts of India. They have a language of their own, called the Mahratti, a dialect of the Sanskrit, and this Mahratti is a copious, flexible, and sonorous tongue.

But the Mahrattas have always formed a separate nation or people, and still regard themselves as such, though nowadays they are almost all under British or Muhammadan jurisdiction; that is, they belong either to British India or to the Nizam's Dominions. A few states or principalities purely Mahratta,—such as Kolhapur and some lesser states clustering round it in the southern Deccan,—still survive, but they are under close supervision on the part of the British Government. There are indeed still three large native states nominally Mahratta, namely, that of Sindhia near the borders of Hindustan in the north, that of Holkar in Malwa in the heart of the Indian continent, and that of the Gaekwar in Gujerat on the western coast. But in these states the prince, his relatives, and some of his ministers or employés only are Mahrattas; the nobility and the mass of the people are not Mahrattas at all, but belong to other sections of the Hindu race. These states then are not to be included in the Mahratta nation, though they have a share in the Mahratta history, and are concerned in the extraneous achievements of that people.

In general terms the Mahrattas, as above defined, may be described under two main heads, first the Brahmans, and secondly the humble or low-caste men. The Mahratta Brahmans possess, in an intense degree, the qualities of the famous Brahman caste, physical, intellectual, and moral. They have generally the lofty brow, the regular features, the spare upright figure, the calm aspect, the commanding gait, which might be expected in a race maintained in great purity yet upon a broad basis. In modern times they have proved themselves the most able and ambitious of all the Brahmans in the Indian empire. They are notably divided into two sections—the Konkanast, coming from the Konkan or littoral tract of the west coast below the West Ghát mountains, and the Dèshast, coming from the upland or Deccan, on the east of the mountains. Though there have been many distinguished Dèshasts, yet the most remarkable of all have been Konkanasts. For instance, the pèshwas, or heads of the Mahratta confederation which at one time dominated nearly all India, were Konkanast Brahmans. The birthplaces of these persons are still known, and to this day there are sequestered villages, nestling near the western base of the Gháts, which are pointed to as being the ancestral homes of men who two centuries ago had political control over the Indian empire.

Apart from the Brahmans, the Mahrattas may be generally designated as Sùdras, or men of the humblest of the four great castes into which the Hindu race is divided. But, as indicated above, the upper classes among the Mahrattas claim to be Kshatriyas or Rajputs. They probably are aborigines fundamentally, with a mixture of what are now called the Scythian tribes, which at a very early time overran India. They have but a slight admixture of the Aryans, who victoriously immigrated from Central Asia and established the Hindu system.

These ordinary Mahrattas, who form the backbone of the nation, have plain features, an uncouth manner, a clownish aspect, short stature, a small but wiry frame. Their eyes, however, are bright and piercing, and under excitement will gleam with passion. Though not powerful physically as compared with the northern races of the Panjab and Oudh, they have much activity and an unsurpassed endurance. Born and bred in or near the Western Ghát mountains and the numerous tributary ranges, they have all the qualities of mountaineers. Among their native hills they have at all times evinced desperate courage. Away from the hills they do not display remarkable valour, except under the discipline which may be supplied by other races. For such organisation they have never, of themselves, shown any aptitude. Under civilized authority, however, they are to be reckoned among the good soldiers of the empire. In recent times they enter military service less and less, betaking themselves mainly to cultivation and to the carrying business connected with agriculture. As husbandmen they are not remarkable; but as graziers, as cartmen, as labourers, they are excellent. As artisans they have seldom signalised themselves, save as armourers and clothweavers.

Those Mahrattas who dwell in the extreme west of Mahàrâshtra, within the main range of the Western Ghắts, and in the extreme north of Mahàrâshtra near the Sâtpura mountains, are blessed with unfailing rainfall and regular seasons. But those who dwell at a distance from these main ranges, or among the lower or subsidiary ranges, are troubled with variable moisture and uncertain seasons, frequently, too, with alternations of drought and of flood. Periodically they are afflicted by scarcity, and sometimes by severe famine. They have within the last half century largely extended their area of cultivation. Their industry, which is chiefly agricultural, has grown apace. Their tendency is undoubtedly to increase in numbers; and, despite occasional depopulation from disasters of season, they have increased considerably on the whole. But in some districts, owing to the recent famine in 1877, and the sickness which ensued when excessive rainfall followed the drought, the population is at present stationary, while in others it has actually retrograded because epidemics and plagues of vermin were added to the misfortunes of season.

Among all the Mahrattas the land is usually held on the tenure technically known as "ryotwari." This tenure is now established under the British Government by surveying and assessing operations comprehended under the official term "settlement." It practically means peasant proprietorship. The proprietor, or ryot, is a cultivator also. His holding may be on the average twenty or thirty acres, divided into small fields. Of these fields he cultivates some, himself working at the plough, and his family weeding and cleaning the soil. He will also hire labour, and thus the farm-labourers become a considerable class. He pays to the Government direct the land tax, which is assessed on his holding for the long term of thirty years, so that he may have the benefit of his improvements. His property in the land is absolute; it descends according to the Hindu law of inheritance; it can be sold or otherwise transferred by private arrangement; it is pledged or mortgaged for debt, and money is largely borrowed on its security. It is liable to sale for default in regard to land revenue; and the Government as a creditor has the first claim. Thus, as a peasant proprietary, the Mahrattas are in the best possible position, and have been so for many years since the completion of the British settlement. Their only fault is a disposition to live beyond their humble means. They have thus been of late years led into debt, which has produced disputes between them and the money-lenders, ending sometimes in agrarian disturbance.

In the Konkan there are some superior proprietors termed Khotes. With this and perhaps some other exceptions, notably that of Nagpur, there are not in the Mahratta country many large landlords, nor many of the superior tenure-holders whose position relatively to that of the peasantry has caused much discussion in other parts of India. There are indeed many Mahratta chiefs still resident in the country, members of the aristocracy, which formerly enjoyed much more wealth and power than at present. They are sometimes in the position of landlords, but often they are the assignees of the land revenue, which they are entitled under special grants to collect for themselves instead of for Government, paying merely a small sum to Government by way of quit-rent. Under them the cultivators are by British arrangements placed in the position of peasant proprietors. The village community has always existed as the social unit in the Mahratta territories, though with less cohesion among its members than in the village communities of Hindustan and the Panjab. The ancient offices pertaining to the village, as those of the headman (*patèl*), and of the village accountant, are in working order throughout the Mahratta country.

The Mahratta peasantry possess manly fortitude under suffering and misfortune. Though patient and good-tempered in the main, they have a latent warmth of temper, and if oppressed beyond a certain endurable limit they would fiercely turn and rend their tormentors. Cruelty also is an element in their character. As a rule they are orderly and law-abiding, but traditions of plunder have been handed down to them from early times, and many of them retain the predatory instincts of their forefathers. The neighbourhood of dense forests, steep hill-sides, and fastnesses hard of access, offers extraordinary facilities to plunderers for screening themselves and their booty Thus gang-robbery is apt to break out, gains head with rapidity, and is suppressed with difficulty. In time of peace it is kept under, but during war, or whenever the bands of civil order are loosened, it becomes a cause of anxiety and a source of danger. The women have frankness and strength of character; they work hard in the fields, and as a rule evince domestic virtue. Conjugal infidelity, however, is not unknown among them, and here, as elsewhere in India, leads to bloodshed.

The peasantry preserve a grave and quiet demeanour, but they have their humble ideas of gaiety, and hold their gatherings on occasions of births or marriages. They frequently beguile their toil with carols. They like the gossiping and bartering at the rural markets and in the larger fairs, which are sometimes held in strikingly picturesque localities. They are utterly superstitious, and will worship with hearty veneration any being or thing whose destructive agency they fear. They will even speak of the tiger with honorific titles. They are Hindus, but their Hinduism is held to be of a non-Aryan type. They are sincerely devout in religion, and feel an awe regarding "the holy Brahmans," holding the life and the person of a Brahman sacred, even though he be a criminal of the deepest dye. They of course regard the cow as equally sacred. There are two principal sects among the modern Hindus—those who follow Vishnu and those who follow Siva. The Mahrattas generally follow Siva and his wife, a dread goddess known under many names. The Mahratta war-cry, "*Har Har Mahadeo*," which used to be heard above the din of battle urging the soldiers to onset with victorious *élan*, referred to Siva. All classes, high and low, are fond of the religious festivals, the principal of which, the "*Dasserah*," occurs in October, when the first harvest of the year has been secured and the second crop sown. This has always been held with the utmost pomp and magnificence at every centre of Mahratta wealth and power. The people frequently assemble in bowers and harbours constructed of leafy boughs to hear "*kathas*" recited. These recitations are partly religious, partly also romantic and quasi-historical. After the hearing of them, national resolves of just resistance or of aggressive ambition have often been formed.

Apart from the Mahratta Brahmans, as already mentioned, the Mahratta nobles and princes are not generally fine-looking men. Their appearance, notwithstanding jewellery and rich apparel, is still that of peasants. There certainly are some exceptions, but there is general truth in what was once said by a high authority to the effect that, while there will be something dignified in the humblest Râjpût, there will be something mean in the highest Mahratta. Bluff good-nature a certain jocoseness, a humour pungent and ready, though somewhat coarse, a hot or even violent disposition, are characteristics of Mahratta chieftains. They usually show little aptitude for business or for sedentary pursuits; but, on the other hand, they are born equestrians and sportsmen. As a rule they are not moderate in living, and are not unfrequently addicted to intemperance. Instances of licentiousness and debauchery have always been found among them. They have generally sprung from a lowly origin, and they have been proud of this fact even after attaining greatness. For instance, three Mahratta chiefs, each of whom established a large kingdom—Sindhia, Holkar, and the Gaekwar—declared the lowliness of their birth. Holkar was the descendant of a shepherd; Sindhia boasted of having begun life by keeping his master's slippers; and by his very title, the Gaekwar perpetuates the memory of his progenitor having tended the cow (*gàe*). Mahratta ladies and princesses have often taken a prominent part in public affairs and in dynastic intrigues; in some instances their conduct has been of the highest type, in others their influence has been exerted for evil.

Though they have produced some poetry, the Mahrattas have never done much for Oriental literature. Nor have they been distinguished in industrial art. Their architecture in wood, however, was excellent; and the teak-forests of their country afforded the finest timber for building and for carving. They had also much skill in the construction of works for the supply of drinking-water on a large scale, and for irrigation.

On the whole, the Mahrattas will hardly be regarded by Europeans as being among the most interesting of the Indian races. The admirable 'History of the Mahrattas,' by Captain Grant Duff (1826), may possibly awaken enthusiasm, as written under personal advantages and with a living knowledge which will never again be possessed by a historian of the later Mahratta times. At all events, a strange interest gathers itself around the Mahratta history.

In the first place the Mahratta country is for the most part strategically important as well as highly picturesque. Some parts of the Deccan are indeed almost irretrievably ugly. The stretches of low hill have long been disforested, and even laid bare of lesser vegetation, and the champaign tracts are treeless as far as the eye can reach. Still much of the Mahratta country lies in the bosom or near the skirts of the Ghát mountains. The geological formations may be popularly described as consisting of trap, basalt, and indurated lava in magnificent layers. The black precipices, scarped for thousands of feet, and striped with marks of the layers, are superb. The summits, though generally flat with horizontal outlines, are often broken into towers and cones. The vapours from the Arabian Sea are propelled by the south-west monsoon against these mountain-tops, and produce an excessive rainfall. Hence arise a luxuriant vegetation, and the spectacle (at certain seasons) of numerous cascades tumbling down the perpendicular flanks of the mountains. The forests have suffered during ages from wasteful cutting; but of late years a system of conservancy has been established, and many great forests remain.

The mountains stand in the midst of a fertile and populous country; on both sides of them are rich valleys, cultivated plains, numerous villages, and large towns. Thus insurgents or warriors had here a complete military base, with sources whence supplies could be drawn, and strongholds for organizing power or for securing refuge. This hill country has been regarded by strategists as one of the strongest, in a military sense, to be found in India. It extends over nearly 500 miles from north to south, and has at least 20 fortresses, which in uncivilized warfare were virtually impregnable if resolutely defended, and which, though of course unable to resist a scientific attack in these times, would yet prove difficult of approach. Several of these are surrounded with historic traditions. In former times there was no road worthy of the name across these mountains. No means of passage existed save steep rugged pathways for footmen and pack animals. Within the last generation the

British Government has, in Oriental phrase, lifted up the veil of these mountains, piercing them with well-made roads and with railways. There are now seven of such roads, and two lines of railway open, a third being projected. Guns and troops as well as goods and produce can now be moved up and down these once impassable mountains.

It is the range of the Western Gháts which enabled the Mahrattas to rise against their Muhammadan conquerors, to reassert their Hindu nationality against the whole power of the Mogul empire, and to establish in its place an empire of their own. It is often held that in India British conquest or annnexation succeeded Muhammadan rule; and to a considerable extent this was the case. But, on the other hand, the principal power, the widest sovereignty, which the British overthrew in India, was that of the Mahrattas.

During the earlier Moslem invasions in A.D. 1100 and in subsequent years, the Mahrattas do not seem to have made much resistance. They submitted to several Muhammadan kings under the changing circumstances of those times. They were despised by their conquerors, and were called "mountain rats" in derision. It was against the Muhammadan king of Bijapur in the Deccan that Sivaji, the hero of Mahratta history, first rebelled in 1657. Sivaji and his fighting officers were Mahrattas of humble caste, but his ministers were Mahratta Brahmans. When the Mogul empire absorbed that kingdom he defied the emperor. He imparted a self-reliant enthusiasm to his countrymen, formed them into an army, and organized them as a political community. His mountaineer infantry, though limited in numbers, proved desperately courageous; his cavalry was daring and ubiquitous. Having once overcome the Hindus in almost all parts of India, often after heroic resistance, the Moslems had not for centuries met with any noteworthy uprising. Sivaji, however, planned their expulsion, and before the end of his restless life made much progress in the execution of that design. The new Mahratta state which he founded was maintained under various vicissitudes after his death. Still Mahratta resistance, once aroused by him, was never extinguished, and the imperial resources were worn out by ceaseless though vain efforts to quell it. The great Mogul emperor's impoverished and enfeebled successor was fain to recognise the Mahratta state by a formal instrument. The Mahratta king, a descendant of Sivaji, was a *roi fainéant*, and the arrangement was negotiated by his Brahman minister, whose official designation was the pèshwa. The office of pèshwa then became hereditary in the minister's family, and grew in importance as the Mahratta kingdom rose, while the king sunk into the condition of a puppet. Thus the Mahratta power was consolidated throughout nearly the whole of Mahàrâshtra under the Brahman pèshwa as virtual sovereign, with his capital at Poona, while the titular Mahratta raja or king had his court at the neighbouring city of Sattara. Despite his political insignificance, however, the raja was still venerated as the descendant of Sivaji.

Then several chiefs carved out principalities of their own from among the ruins of the Mogul empire. Thus Raghuji Bhônsla established himself in the tracts lying underneath the southern base of the Satpura range (namely Nagpur and Berar), overran Orissa, and entered Bengal. Dammaji Gaekwar descended from the Western Ghâts upon the alluvial plains of Gujerat around Baroda. Takaji Holkar subdued the uplands of Malwa beyond the Vindhya range on the north bank of the Nerbadda. Madhaji Sindhia obtained possession of large tracts immediately south of Agra and Delhi, marched into Hindustan, and became virtually the master of the Mogul emperor himself. Princes of Sivaji's own family founded a dominion at Tanjore, in the rich delta of the Kaveri, south of Madras.

But these principalities, though really independent respecting internal administration, and making war or peace with their neighbours according to opportunity, yet owned allegiance to the pèshwa at Poona as head of the Mahratta body. On state occasions, heads of principalities would visit Poona by way of acknowledging the superior position of the pèshwa. On the other hand, the pèshwa was careful to obtain the sanction of his nominal sovereign at Sattara to every important act of state. Thus a confederation was formed, of which the Brahmin pèshwa, or head, was at Poona, governing the adjacent territories, while the members belonging to the lower castes of Mahrattas were scattered throughout the continent of India. Such was the Mahratta empire which supplanted the Mogul empire. The Mahratta power grew and prospered till it embraced all India, with certain exceptions. Its culminating point was reached about 1750, or about a century after Sivaji first rebelled against his Muhammadan sovereign.

Its armies drew soldiers from all parts of India. The infantry was not of good quality; but its cavalry was really an enormous force, numbering fully a hundred thousand in all. The horsemen were splendidly audacious in riding for long distances into the heart of a hostile country without support, striking some terrific blows, and then returning rapidly beyond reach of pursuit. They could truly boast of having watered their horses in every Indian river from the Kaveri to the Indus. If attacked, however, in a competent manner, they would not stand; and afterwards, in conflict with the British, whole masses of them behaved in a dastardly manner. As their ambition grew, the chiefs began to organize their troops after the system learnt from the English and French. In this way several Frenchmen—De Boigne, Perron, and others—rose in the Mahratta service to a position dangerous to the British. But the new system was unsuited to the Mahratta genius; it hampered the meteoric movements of the cavalry, which was obliged to manœuvre in combination with the new artillery and the disciplined battalions. Mahratta elders hence uttered predictions of military disaster which were in the end more than fulfilled.

While the Mahrattas collected vast quantities of treasure and valuables, the ordinary revenue of the confederation hardly exceeded ten millions sterling annually. Large amounts, however, were drawn by feudal tenure-holders, which never appeared in the public accounts. The area and population under the dominion or the contiol of the confederation could hardly have been less than 700,000 square miles and 90,000,000 of souls.

The rapid and amazing success of the Mahratta confederation rendered it the largest Hindu sovereignty that ever existed in India. But it lacked the elements of true greatness. It was founded by plundering expeditions, and its subsequent existence was tainted by the baseness of this predatory origin. With the exception of the pèshwas, its chiefs were little more than freebooting warriors, for the most part rude, violent, and unlettered. Their custom was to offer their neighbours or victims the alternative of paying "chouth"—that is, one-fourth of the ordinary revenue, or being plundered and ravaged. Thus the Mahratta chouth came to have an ominous significance in Indian history. Desultory efforts were made to establish a civil government, but in the main there was no administration formed on statesmanlike principles. The pèshwas, on the other hand, as Brahmans, were men of the highest education then possible in India. But they were absorbed by the direction of military and political combinations, and by intrigues for the preservation of their own power; and, even allowing for all this, they failed for the most part to evince the civil capacity which might have been anticipated. While several displayed commanding abilities, and some possessed many virtues, one only attempted to conduct an administration in an enlightened manner, and he died prematurely.

There were at the same time powers existing in India to keep the Mahrattas in check, and it has just been mentioned that some parts of India were excepted from their depredations. The British power was rising at Calcutta, Madras, and Bombay. The nascent Sikh power prevented Mahratta incursions from being permanently successful in the Panjab. As the Mogul empire broke up, some separate Muhammadan powers rose upon its ruins. The Nizam of the Deccan established himself at Hyderabad, comparatively near the headquarters of the pèshwa. Hyder Ali was proclaimed Sultan of Mysore in the south. Ahmed Shah Abdali burst upon India from Afghanistan. The Mahrattas bravely encountered him at Panipat, near Delhi, in 1761, and were decisively defeated. The defeat, however, did not essentially shake the Mahratta empire. It was collision with the English that broke that wonderful fabric to pieces.

The first collision with the English occurred in 1780; it arose from a disputed succession to the pèshwaship. The English Government at Bombay supported one of the claimants, and the affair became critical for the English as well as for the Mahrattas. It was at this conjuncture that Warren Hastings displayed his political genius and rendered signal service to his country.

The next collision happened in 1803. The pèshwa had fallen into grave difficulties with some of the principal members of the Mahratta confederation, namely, Sindhia, Holkar, and the Bhonsla raja of Nagpur. He therefore placed himself under British protection, and this led to the great Mahratta war, in which the Marquis Wellesley displayed those talents for military and political combination which have rendered him illustrious. It was during the campaigns which ensued that General Arthur Wellesley defeated Holkar and the Bhonsla raja at Assaye, and General Lake won the victories of Farôkhabad, Dîg, and Laswari over Sindhia and Holkar. The three confederates, Sindhia, Holkar, and the Bhonsla, concluded peace with the British Government, after making large sacrifices of territory in favour of the victor, and submitting to British control politically. Thus the Mahratta empire was broken up. It was during these events that the British won the province of Orissa, the old Hindustan now known as the North-Western Provinces, and a part of the western coast, comprising Gujerat.

The third collision came to pass between 1816 and 1818, through the conduct, not only of the confederates, but also of the pèshwa himself. During the previous war the pèshwa had been the *protégée* and ally of the British; and since the war he had fallen more completely than before under British protection and guidance, British political officers and British troops being stationed at his capital. He apparently felt encouraged by circumstances to rebel. Holkar and the Bhonslas committed hostile acts. The predatory Pindaris offered a formidable resistance to the British troops. So the pèshwa ventured to take part in the combination against the British power, which even yet the Mahrattas did not despair of overthrowing. After long-protracted menaces, he attacked the British at Kirki, but failed utterly, and fled a ruined man. Ultimately he surrendered to Sir John Malcolm, and was sent as a state pensioner to Bithûr, near Cawnpur. Thus the last vestige of the Mahratta empire disappeared. The British, however, released the raja of Sattara from the captivity in which he had been kept during the pèshwa's time, and reinstated him on the throne. Owing to these events, the British Government became possessed of the Konkan and of the greater part of the Deccan.

It remains to mention briefly the fortunes of each remaining member of the once imperial confederation. The principality of Sattara was held to have lapsed in 1849 by the death of the raja without lineal heirs, and was annexed by the British Government. The Bhonsla raja of Nagpur and Berar was obliged to surrender Berar to the Nizam, as the ally of the British, in 1803. Berar then remained under the Nizam till 1854, when it came under British administration, though it is still included in the Nizam's dominions. The raja of Nagpur died without lineal heirs in 1853, and his territory, being held to have lapsed, was annexed to the British territories. The house of Holkar has, during the last sixty years, remained faithful to its engagements with the British Government, and its position as a feudatory of the empire is well maintained. In Sindhia's territory, by reason of internal feuds, the British had to undertake measures which were successfully terminated after the battles of Maharajpur and Panniar in 1843. But, on the whole, the house of Sindhia has remained faithful. Sindhia himself was actively loyal during the war of the mutinies. The Gaekwar gradually fell under British control toward the close of last century, and his house has never engaged in hostilities with the British Government. The Gaekwar Khande Rao signalized himself by loyalty during the troubles consequent on the mutinies of 1857. His successor, Malhàr Rao, was deposed by the British Government on account of gross mal-administration. An adopted son has ascended the throne recently. The expèshwa lived to old age at Bithûr, and died in 1851. His adopted son grew up to be the Nana Sahib, of infamous memory, who took a leading part in the war of the mutinies.

# CHAPTER XVI.

## BIRTHPLACE AND CRADLE OF MAHRATTA POWER.

[*Speech delivered before the Royal Geographical Society, in London, February* 1882.]

Imperial achievements of the Mahratta nation — Sivaji the founder of their power — His birth, education, and early habits — Amasses plunder in mountain fastnesses — Openly defies the Muhammadan Power after assassinating its Envoy — Revenges his father's wrongs — Performs exploit against Muhammadan Viceroy — His escape from Delhi — Retakes the Lion's Den fortress — His reign and death — Situation of his tomb — National spirit aroused by him — Political control subsequently established and maintained by the British.

THE subject of my speech this evening is the geography of the birthplace and cradle of Mahratta power. This geography is in the first place illustrated by a map, which has been prepared by the Society's draughtsman, Mr. Sharbau; it is further illustrated by a series of pictorial illustrations, prepared by my brother, Lieutenant George Temple, R.N., and enlarged from sketches made by me upon the spot.* Though the subject of my speech will be partly political, still it will not infringe upon the rules of this Society, and it will after all be in a great degree geographical, because its object will be to show you how, owing to the peculiar geographical features of the country, a despised and abject race rose to dominion over what has subsequently become the British Empire in the East.

At the time of which I speak, just over two hundred years

* These have been engraved, much reduced, for this report of the speech, by Mr. Whymper.

ago, about the year 1650—that is, a hundred years before the battle of Plassy, and two hundred years before the war of the Indian Mutiny—the Mahrattas had been subjected for full five hundred years to the Muhammadans. They were an aboriginal race, of very humble, I may say unprepossessing, aspect; rather short, clumsy, mean-looking little men: they were thoroughly despised by their Muhammadan conquerors, who called them the mountain rats. But the hour came for them to rise, and with the hour came the man, and the leader. Owing to the extraordinary advantages offered them by the country in which they dwelt, they, in a short time, rose victoriously against their foreign rulers the Muhammadans. They first dethroned the Great Mogul in his imperial palace at Delhi; they fought the Afgan and Persian invaders of India; they worried the Portuguese at Goa; they threatened even the early British Governors of Bombay: they were visited by European embassies in some of the hill forts depicted in our illustrations; they obtained a dominion from Cape Comorin, near Ceylon, right up to the Himalayas. They truly boasted that their cavalry watered their horses in the river Kaveri, not far from Ceylon, and as far as the Indus opposite Peshawur. They fought the English in many stand-up fights. They even threatened us to such a degree that we had to build a ditch round Calcutta to defend ourselves from them. You have often heard Calcutta called the City of the Ditch: against whom was that ditch constructed? It was against the Mahrattas. Such, then, was the splendid imperial position obtained in the course of one century by this abject, despised race. And what was the cause of this astonishing success? It was, first, the martial quality fostered by the mountains, and in the second place the immense military and political advantages offered by the mountain fastnesses and strongholds. Such is the main topic upon which I shall offer you historical, pictorial, and topographical details.

I must first ask you carefully to consider the map prefixed to this address. You will observe the western coast with the great city of Bombay. That coast district is called the Konkan. Then you will perceive a long line of dark mountains running from north to south: those are the Western Ghats. To the east of these Western Ghats you will see the country called the Deccan, the capital of which is the city of Poona. Now I must remind you of the contour and configuration of this remarkable country. Taking it from west to east, you will first observe the coast-line, then there is a great wall of mountain, 2000 feet high on the average, rising in its peaks up to 5000 feet. From this average altitude of 2000 feet there gradually slopes eastwards the plateau of the Deccan, so that the Konkan being on the level of the sea, there is a wall of mountains, and above that there is the great table-land of the Deccan, 2000 feet above the sea, gradually becoming lower as you proceed eastwards. Then notice exactly the line of the Western Ghats. I have explained to you their altitude, 2000 feet on the average, rising up to peaks of 5000 feet.

I must ask you to remember these details, because upon such remembrance will depend the interest with which I hope you will follow the stirring scenes I am about to describe. Then the geology is very remarkable. Time does not permit me to explain the various processes of geological denudation which have caused these hills to present the form of a great wall—literally a wall. The wall may be broken; it may be in sections; but, after all, a wall it is, and a wall it will remain, I suppose, to the end of the world. The geological formation is of the plutonic kind, commonly called trap: in many parts it consists of layers of indurated lava. The importance, politically, of these mountains is in this wise: first, they nourish a resolute, enduring, daring, I may say audacious spirit among their inhabitants; secondly, they offer strongholds and fastnesses to which these inhabitants can resort whenever they are pressed by an enemy; and thirdly, and perhaps most important, they lie between fertile countries. The country to the west, the Konkan, is one of the most fertile parts of India and one of the most densely inhabited. The country to the east, the Deccan, is also fertile and populous. Consequently, the men of the hills can make rapid raids for marauding or plundering purposes, just as the eagle swoops from its eyry upon the quarry. After these sudden descents they can rapidly carry off plunder, treasure, and the like, to the hills, and once they are there it is very difficult to approach them. They are, therefore, able readily to establish a predatory power which cannot be extirpated or exterminated. You will perceive what immense political advantages these mountains offer, and how it is that they become truly the cradle of greatness, power, and empire.

This being the physical, topographical and political character of the hills, I have to remind you that the leader of the Mahrattas and the founder of their empire was Sivaji. I particularly beg you to remember the name in order that you may follow the stories I have to tell. Recollect that Sivaji flourished a little over two hundred years ago, one hundred years before Clive won the battle of Plassy, two hundred years before the Indian Mutiny. I am anxious to impress these facts well upon your minds, in order that you may follow my narrative.

After this preface, I will ask you to go straight to the pictorial diagrams. The first illustration to which I shall invite your attention (No. 22) is the hill fort of Junnar, where Sivaji was born. I should explain that the hill itself is called Sewnar, but nowadays takes the name of Junnar, from the town which lies at its base. You will see the town in the illustration, on a plain, and you will note rising above it precipitous mountains. You will also see Junnar clearly marked upon the map just behind the main crest of the range. It is the first instance which I have to mention of those peaks of 4000 or 5000 feet which I have already alluded to. You will see what a rugged precipitous place this is, and what a fitting spot it was for a hero to be born in. I must ask you to remember Sivaji's father, Shahji, because I shall have to mention that person hereafter. I must ask you also to remember that Sivaji's mother was a Mahratta lady of remarkable spirit and energy. Presently I shall have to say more about her.

Sivaji's education was, in the modern sense of the term, rather neglected by these parents, that is to say, he was never taught to read and write. Though in after years he became the sovereign of a great kingdom, he never could put the sign manual to his decrees. But he had an education of a different kind, in those days a much more practical education, for he was

FIG. 22.—JUNNAR; THE BIRTHPLACE OF SIVAJI.

taught to be a splendid shot with the gun and with the bow; he was a wonderful rider; and he learnt from poetical recitations all about the ancient history and the religion of his country. He used to hear of these things from the recitals of bards and people of that kind who sang before him regarding all the heroes of the Hindu race. Thus his mind became imbued with lofty notions of Hindu nationality, and with that spirit of patriotism which urged him to resist the foreign rulers, the Muhammadans.

Among his equipments and accoutrements there were three things which I must select for mention. The first was what is called the tiger's claw. This was an iron instrument as near as possible like the claw of a tiger, with very sharp points, which could be fastened inside the palm, so that a man might have the claw inside his hand, and yet show the outside, and nobody would suppose there was anything in it. Another thing was his sword, which was called Bhawani, after the name of a Hindu goddess; it really was a fine Genoa blade. The third article was a coat of mail which he would wear generally under a cotton dress, and in hot weather under a muslin dress; so that he would appear to be a very mild character indeed, though in reality underneath the cotton folds there was this famous sword, which was to the Mahrattas what the sword of King Arthur, "Excalibur," is in Tennyson's poetry, and inside his hand there was the tiger's claw. I beg you particularly to remember these three articles of equipment.

There were two persons among his attendants whom I must mention. One was the tutor named Dadaji, an old Brahman, with whom Sivaji was left, when Shahji, the father, went to the wars, and the mother was carried off into captivity by the Muhammadans. Then Sivaji and his tutor took a certain house in the city of Poona. I must ask you to remember that house particularly, because you will hear more of it presently. Next, among his henchmen and attendants was a man named Tannaji Malusra. I will only ask you to remember Tannaji, because Malusra is merely the name of the village which gave birth to Tannaji, as brave a man as ever adorned the annals of the Mahratta race. Malusra is just the sort of village to give birth to a hero. Its frowning rocks, its lofty trees, its flowing brooks, in fact everything about it, conspired to fill the imagination with heroic ideas.

Such being Sivaji's education and early surroundings, I must ask you to bear in mind that in those days this part of the Mahratta country was in the Muhammadan kingdom of Bijapur.

Now Bijapur was a magnificent city; its ruins are among the finest in the country. It still has a dome which is the marvel of architects, admitted to be the finest dome or cupola ever yet constructed by any nation. Thus Bijapur was then the Muhammadan capital. Well, Sivaji's father had a large grant of land from the Bijapur sovereign. The father having gone to the wars, Sivaji, who was then a young man, and his tutor were left in charge of this property. Then Sivaji began to plunder.

FIG. 23.—TORNA; WHERE SIVAJI STORED HIS PLUNDER.

He would rob neighbouring villages, and thus get a little money and valuables together, which he would store in the fort of Torna, depicted in our illustration (23). Torna is a highly picturesque place, built just upon the crest of the range; in the distant background of the sketch you will see another hill, to which I shall have to ask your attention immediately; that is the hill of Rajgarh. Sivaji first stored his plunder at Torna; and this really formed the original accumulation of money with which he began his political and military operations. But Torna was a large open hill on the top, steep at the sides no doubt, but it had a very large and flat summit, and therefore was not perfectly defensible against regular troops. So, after a time, when Sivaji became more ambitious, he abandoned Torna and went to the neighbouring hill of Rajgarh, the

FIG. 24.—RAJGARH; THE HILL OF THE KINGDOM.

top of which he thoroughly fortified. Rajgarh forms the subject of our illustration (24). The summit of the hill seen in the distance in the preceding illustration (23) is this same Rajgarh; you see the strongly fortified site represented in the illustration (24). Now, Rajgarh means the Hill of the Kingdom. Torna is a common local name; Sivaji gave no royal name to that, because it was only a place for storing plunder. But as he grew a little bolder and richer, he fortified Rajgarh, and gave it the ominous name of the Hill of the Kingdom. It was then that he conceived the idea of establishing a dominion. It was about the time when he was occupying Rajgarh that Dadaji, the tutor, became rather old and timid, and he said to Savaji, "You are only knocking your head against a rock by attempting to resist the Muhammadan power; you are putting your neck into a noose. For God's sake give these things up and live quietly on your estate. Obey your father, who is a worthy servant of the Muhammadans in the wars, and do not think of these ambitious things." Sivaji merely smiled and said, "I know my own business." Dadaji afterwards became sick, and drew near to his end; and when the shades of death began to gather about him, and his brow became cold and clammy with the sweat of approaching dissolution, he sent for his young master and said, "I now see it is no good offering you advice to keep quiet. After all, take the advice of an old man on the brink of the grave, and fulfil your destiny! Go in at the Muhammadans; I hate them more than you do; go in and win. Only remember, if you win, to think of your own religion; remember your ancestral gods; consider the Brahmans and the priests, and cherish the Hindu religion. Drive these Muhammadans back into Central Asia, and once more let it be India for the Hindus."

I am not exaggerating; some such speech, as I have described to you, was uttered by Dadaji on his death-bed to Sivaji; and I can hardly imagine a more fit subject for an historical picture than this Dadaji on his death-bed giving advice to the future hero and the coming king to fight the battles of his country. The breath was hardly out of the body of Dadaji when Sivaji began to fulfil that behest, and the first thing he did was to take the fort of Sing-garh. When I say he took it, I believe that he really won it by bribery, and that he gave some of his hoarded plunder to the Muhammadan commander, and so obtained the surrender of the hill. In those days it was called by another local name, with which I shall not trouble you; but Sivaji, having obtained possession of the hill, gave it the name of Sing-garh, which means the Lion's Fort. However, he did not mean that: he meant the Lion's Den. I shall have a good deal more to say about Sing-garh presently.

Now I must ask you to turn to illustration 25. Sivaji, having made up his mind to rebel against the Muhammadan power, which was then represented by the kings of Bijapur, the then king of Bijapur called him to account for his conduct. Sivaji, of course, gave evasive answers. A council of war was thereupon held at Bijapur as to what should be done. A Muhammadan commander, named Afzal Khan, stood up before the king of Bijapur and said, "O King, if you will give me 2000 horse and 5000 foot, with some artillery, I will go against this mountain rat" (as Sivaji was called), "and within two months I will bring him before your Majesty in an iron cage." Well, the order went forth, and Afzal Khan marched leisurely from Bijapur towards Partabgarh, which at that time was one of Sivaji's forts. Sivaji had moved to Partabgarh from Sing-garh, and was there when this Bijapur expedition was launched against him. When Afzal Khan approached the place (Partabgarh), Sivaji sent some ambassadors in unpretending guise, and said, "I hope you are not thinking of making war against me: I am a very humble person: if you will only come to visit me in my fort any morning, you will see what a quiet creature I am, and I shall be able to give satisfactory explanations, and show that I am, as I ever have been, a loyal subject of the king of Bijapur." Afzal Khan thought that, after all his warlike preparations, he was going to have a walk over; so he said to Sivaji, "Well, the only objection I have to coming to your fort is the character of the hills, which are very steep, and the forest, mark you, is uncommonly thick and impervious; I do not see how I am to get through it." Sivaji said, "Do not trouble yourself about that; I, your slave, will cut a road through it to the foot of Partabgarh, my humble abode." The Muhammadans agreed to this apparently amicable proposal. The rough places over the mountains were made smooth for them, and a very convenient path was cut for them. When they got to the foot of Partabgarh, a fine broad place was cleared by the Mahratta woodsmen for the encampment of the Muhammadan army. They were made as comfortable as possible; but remember that they were surrounded by rocky hills and thick forests, and inside the thickets Sivaji's marksmen lay hid in ambush. Having got them there, Sivaji formed a plan for murdering the Muhammadan commander and surprising his army. The project was to induce Afzal Khan to come with a single attendant to meet Sivaji just outside the gates of Partabgarh, and then Sivaji would gladly hand over the keys. Sivaji said, "I will come with just one single attendant, and I hope your Highness will honour me by doing the same: you can easily kill me if you like." The Khan said he would be very happy to do as he was requested.

I must ask you to observe the configuration of Partabgarh, as represented in our illustration (25). You see that, on the crest of a lofty eminence, there stands a towering fortress. Partabgarh is in the dip of the Western Ghât range. There is a dip, then the great fort, a dip, and then the range goes on again. The fort stands up boldly against the horizon. In the background on the left is a distant view of the Arabian Sea. I ought to mention that from all these high points on the Western Ghats you have a splendid view over the sea. In the morning, the time which our illustration represents, the sea is like a pale sea-green lake; in the afternoon it glitters radiantly towards the declining and setting sun.

I am afraid that the drawing cannot possibly represent fully the beauty of the scene, but you will readily see that it is a place of consummate beauty. There it was, on this autumn morning, in this fair scene of nature, that the desperate and bloody deeds meditated by Sivaji were carried out. Now, in the evening before the meeting, Sivaji's nerve failed him. I do not quite know why, but all men of this kind are a little superstitious, and suffer qualms of conscience, and he felt rather uneasy about the crime he was to commit in the morning. So he went to the little temple at the top of the hill, and asked his mother to meet him there. He laid his misgivings, his

FIG. 25.—PARTABGARH.

forebodings, before her, and asked her in a filial way for her maternal advice. He said, "Shall I really kill this man in the way I have planned; and when I have killed him, shall I really order all my men in the thickets to fire upon the Muhammadan encampment?" And she said, "Yes; I have in this very temple consulted the goddess Siva, the goddess of destruction, remember, after whom you are named." She said she had seen a vision, and the goddess had commanded her to see that not one Muhammadan, if possible, should escape alive. Then she said to him, "Now, my son, you act worthily according to your mother's advice, and take my maternal blessing." Then she solemnly gave him her benediction. Of course, after that he felt a little more comfortable in his mind, and gave the orders to his men.*

I have explained to you that the Muhammadans had been enticed to go through the thicket. They had had an encamping ground prepared for them in the middle of the forest. In that forest lay concealed all Sivaji's mountaineers, several thousand of these Mahrattas. Their orders were that as soon as a signal gun should be fired from a bastion of the fort—the forest all around being alive with men—the Mahratta troops were to fire upon the Muhammadan army. These orders were delivered with coolness and precision by Sivaji after he had received the maternal blessing, that is, early in the night. In the morning the Muhammadan commander, Afzal Khan, came forth from his encampment, and marched up to the rendezvous, the place marked by a greystone tomb in the foreground of our illustration, where he was murdered, as I shall explain to you. Sivaji also advanced from the fort. The gateway from which he issued is marked on the illustration as a little dark spot in the wall. As he came, the Muhammadan commander and his followers said, "What a mild, humble-looking person he appears." He advanced with a sort of hesitating step, as if he were a timid man. With him there was only one man, but that one man was the redoubtable Tannaji whom I have already mentioned. As he came on, the Muhammadan commander advanced to meet him with a single attendant as agreed; and in that sort of patronising way which Muhammadans of rank have, held out his arms to embrace him, with, "Hot morning, Sivaji," &c. Then Sivaji bowed his head humbly beneath the Muhammadan's arms, and drawing close up to his body, with the tiger's claw already described, he dug into his victim's bowels: then out came the dagger, followed by one desperate stab: then out

* See the graphic work by Meadows Taylor, entitled 'Tara.'

flashed the sword, that Excalibur I have previously described. I need not say that the Muhammadan and his single follower were very soon despatched by Sivaji and Tannaji, especially as Sivaji had underneath his muslin garment the coat of mail already mentioned. Thus was the deed done. That very tiger's claw, that very sword, that very coat of mail, that very muslin dress, are to this day religiously preserved from generation to generation by the Mahrattas, and it is unpleasant to see the veneration with which they are regarded. I assure you, never were the sword, or the hat, or any of the relics of Napoleon or Frederick the Great of Prussia venerated so much by the French or Germans, as these relics of Sivaji are to this day by the Mahrattas. Thus fell the Muhammadan commander. He was buried where he fell, and the Mahrattas had the grace afterwards to build a tomb over his remains—the tomb which you see sketched in the foreground of the illustration. As the Khan fell, the signal gun was fired from the bastion; then of course the Muhammadan army, who were at breakfast in the encampment, were fired upon from all sides by the Mahrattas concealed in the forest; and you can imagine the destruction, the struggle, the misery, the flight, which ensued. From that moment I need not say that Sivaji became an open rebel against the Muhammadans; and this event has always since been remembered in Indian history as the first blow struck by the Hindu nationality against the Muhammadan conquerors.

The next point in Sivaji's history to which I have to ask your attention is connected with the illustration (26), which is that of the fortress of Vishalgarh. The sketch which served as the original to the illustration, was taken in the height of the rains, just after one of the violent showers that caused the brilliant cascades to go tumbling over the precipices. Now, bear in mind that Sivaji had become, by the event I have just described, an open rebel against the Muhammadan power. Well, the first vengeance of the Muhammadans fell upon Sivaji's father, Shaji, already mentioned, who was quite

Fig. 26.—Vishalgarh

guiltless of the crimes which his son had committed. He greatly regretted all that had happened, and made every possible apology, but the Muhammadans would not listen to such excuses, and ordered him to be seized. It was rather difficult to seize a man of that kind; however, the seizure was arranged through the agency of another Mahratta named Baji, who had an estate at a place called Madhol. Baji showed a friendly demeanour towards Shahji, and asked him to an entertainment at Madhol. Shahji came, suspecting nothing, and was seized, and sent to the Muhammadans at Bijapur. He was confined in a dungeon, and threatened with all manner of dreadful things—that his eyes should be put out, that his tongue should be cut to pieces, and similar inflictions, after the fashion of those days. However, the dutiful son, Sivaji, gave up some of his hoarded plunder, and bribed the Muhammadan gaolers. So Shahji got out of gaol, and fled, but in flying he sent a message to Sivaji, and said, "Sivaji, if you love me, pay that fellow (Baji) out." Sivaji replied, "Never fear, sir; you will visit me some day, and then you shall hear all that I have done to him."

Soon after this the Bijapur king determined to send another expedition, this time against Vishalgarh, where Sivaji then was, hoping that it would be more successful than the last against Partabgarh. The command of this expedition was given to this very Baji. The troops were to move out towards Vishalgarh, and Baji, naturally enough, went on ahead of his army, and thought he would spend two or three pleasant days at home at Madhol. Intimation of this came to Sivaji at Vishalgarh, and he then determined upon one of his daring marches.

Madhol is just 100 miles from Vishalgarh, and although a very uninteresting town, is strongly fortified, with a high wall of black stone all round it, I should say about 60 feet high. You will observe, marked with a dotted line on the map, the road to it from Vishalgarh, which indicates the straight manner in which Sivaji marched to it. For really in these rushes and dashes Sivaji flew very like an arrow from a bow, or a shot from a cannon.

One fine morning Sivaji and a picked body of horse and foot appeared before Madhol, quite surprising the Madhol people. How Sivaji got over the 100 miles in so few hours it is difficult to say; but certainly he appeared early in the morning, as I well ascertained on the spot from the Madhol people, for the tradition of course still survives. He himself started not later than the previous afternoon from Vishalgarh. I suppose the only way in which he could have got there was this, that he ordered men to assemble in the wild country at different points beforehand (on a certain night in the dark half of the moon, as their expression was). They would go unobserved and concentrate at different places on the line of march, Sivaji remaining at Vishalgarh, and all the world supposing that he was up in his mountain fastness. He would then start in the afternoon, ride rapidly say for 50 miles, get to the rendezvous at 8 o'clock, and would accomplish the rest of the march during the night; and so he appeared before Madhol in the grey of the morning. His men were excellently good hands at escalading; they thoroughly understood rope ladders and grappling irons, and so they climbed the wall in no time; and the Muhammadans in Madhol were completely surprised. In a few moments Baji's palace was surrounded; he himself was dragged out, and brought before Sivaji. Out flashed the Excalibur, and down dropped Baji's head upon the ground. There was no more bloodshed, but then began one of the most relentless and ruthless plunderings of which the Mahrattas were ever guilty, and which is remembered vividly by the Madhol people to this very day, as I can personally attest. In about two hours the whole of Madhol was cleaned out absolutely, nothing remained. Sivaji went off with the jewels, the coins, and the fine articles, all fastened on to the saddle-bows of his cavalry; and he returned straight to Vishalgarh.

This was a very unpropitious beginning for the Muhammadan expedition against him, and I need not trouble you with the military particulars of all that followed. However, Vishalgarh was not taken, and Sivaji remained entirely master of the situation.

I have mentioned that Shahji, the father, obtained his liberty, and somehow in a short time managed to make peace with the Bijapur king, and to visit his son at Vishalgarh. He had not seen this redoubtable, this tremendous son of his, since he left him almost an infant in his mother's arms at Junnar, so of course the meeting between the son and the father was rather touching. Sivaji, this truculent fellow, came forward to meet his father. The father was riding upon a fine horse; the son would not ride; far from it. He went forth on foot several miles from the fort to meet his parent. He would not sit down in the paternal presence, and he humbly related to his father how he had fulfilled his behest, and had with his own hand cut off that treacherous Baji's head, and scrupulously plundered Madhol to the last farthing. He hoped, as he had received his mother's blessing last time, to receive his father's blessing this time, which I need not say was abundantly given him. But the father being of a practical turn of mind, criticised Vishalgarh, and said it was not a very advantageous position; he thought that it might be commanded and taken by the Muhammadans, and suggested to Sivaji that he should establish his fortress in a better situation, indicating Raigarh, which you will see on the map. So Raigarh afterwards became the seat of the Mahratta kingdom. From that place went forth decrees which had validity right over the continent, and the establishment of Raigarh was due to the sagacious father who visited his son at Vishalgarh after this Madhol affair.

I must now call your attention to illustration No. 27, which represents Sing-garh, already mentioned. You will see the city of Poona in the middle distance, with the river in the foreground. From this river are drawn many fine canals for irrigation, involving geographical problems with which I have not time to trouble you. In the distance stands up like a rigid square, Sing-garh, or the Lion's Den.

At the time which the narrative has now reached, the Bijapur kingdom had been subdued by another Muhammadan power, which was no other than the Mogul Empire. Therefore to the king of Bijapur had succeeded the Great Mogul, and the Great Mogul had a viceroy at Poona. The city of Poona was then regarded like Peshawur in our days, as an important frontier position. The Western Ghats were to the Moguls what the North-Western frontier is now to the British, and Poona was to them just what Peshawur is to us; so they had a Muhammadan viceroy at Poona supported by a force. Sivaji, on

FIG. 27.—DISTANT VIEW OF SING-GARH.

the other hand, was at Sing-garh. The viceroy considered that Sivaji was a very dangerous neighbour, dreaded that something awkward would happen, and took particular precautions that no armed men should be admitted into Poona, which happened to be at that time an open city. Sivaji nevertheless determined to do a daring deed which should flagrantly insult the Muhammadan viceroy. His idea always was to do an audacious thing which should have a great moral effect on the whole of the country round, and in that way to flout the Muhammadan authority. He acted as follows. As he could not get into the city armed, he managed to go apparently unarmed, with some thirty followers. He, and they of course, had arms concealed under their cotton dresses. He joined a marriage procession which was entering the city, and thus contrived in disguise to enter unobserved with the crowd. The bold project was facilitated by the fact that the Muhammadan viceroy had taken up his viceregal quarters in the very house in which Sivaji had been brought up, under his tutor Dadaji. I have already spoken to you about that house; and I told you that a tale would hang on it. In consequence of this, Sivaji thoroughly understood the ins and outs of the dwelling. Mixing with the crowd he and his thirty followers entered the city and remained quiet till the dead of the night. He knew a particular way through the kitchen window, whereby an entrance for armed men could be found; and thus got within the dwelling. The viceroy, of course, according to the Muhammadan fashion, was sleeping with his staff on one side of the house, and the ladies of the family were sleeping on the other side; so, after Sivaji and his men had entered by the window, they had to pass not far from the ladies' apartments, and one of the ladies heard the sound of men moving. She instantly shrieked. The shriek reached the viceroy and his staff; but before they could do much, Sivaji and his men made a rush and were on them. The viceroy was in such a hurry that he was jumping out of the window; and as he had got his right hand on the window-sill letting himself down, Sivaji came up with the Excalibur and just cut off his fore and middle fingers. The viceroy naturally let himself down extremely quick after that; and immediately afterwards there was a row all over the city. Sivaji and his men had decamped in the darkness and confusion; and, arrived at the outside of the town, gave notice to others of their party, who had planted beacons from point to point on the way to Sing-garh, to pass on the signals for illuminating the peak of that hill-fort. Sing-garh is a very conspicuous object from Poona, and thus the inhabitants learnt at midnight that the redoubtable

Sivaji had found his way into the viceregal palace, had cut off the viceroy's fingers, and was illuminating Singgarh in honour of the event. This was a thoroughly insulting mode of procedure, recounted in after times with glee by the Mahrattas. The next morning the viceroy sent his Afghan cavalry against Sing-garh. You may imagine the sort of swaggering way, the proud, bombastic manner, in which the Muhammadan cavalry would behave, stroking their beards, twirling their moustachios, and saying they would soon bring Sivaji back in chains, and so forth. The cavalry went, and approached Sing-garh. Of course there was a puff of smoke from the top; then a cannon-ball in the middle of a squadron of horse. Presently from behind a rock, or tree, a little spit from a Mahratta musket, and a Muhammadan saddle was emptied. In a very short time the cavalry came back utterly crestfallen, with half their number killed or wounded, and the Muhammadan viceroy the next day sent in his resignation to the Emperor. He could not possibly have signed it, because he had lost two fingers of his right hand. This was an insolent exploit, which is to this day freshly remembered by the Mahrattas.

I shall have to revert to Sing-garh directly; meanwhile I ask your attention to Bowragarh, depicted in illustration 28.

Bowragarh is one of the grand situations on the crest of the Western Ghats, from which you have a distant view of the setting sun over the sea. It was in that neighbourhood that some of Sivaji's piratical exploits by sea were performed. He was great not only on land but at sea. He used to plunder all the rich flourishing seaports on the coast, and carry the plunder, as usual, to the hills. On one of these occasions, while he was sailing with all his plunder from one part of the coast to the other, he was overtaken first by contrary winds, and then by a severe storm, and he became extremely indisposed. It is an extraordinary thing, but after this, for a time, he quite lost his nerve.

The Muhammadan Emperor having heard of the manner in which his viceroy had been insulted, sent a large force of Rajpût soldiers against Sivaji. There again Sivaji was a little superstitious. He had a kind of fear of these Rajpûts as being high-born warriors. The Mahrattas are low-caste men themselves, and they have a veneration for upper-caste Hindus. He was rather afraid of the redoubtable Rajpût soldiery, and was very much indisposed by the storm at sea. So he lost his resolution and determined to surrender a number of his forts. Among

FIG. 28.—BOWRAGARH.

others he surrendered this very fort of Sing-garh, after which he went up to pay his respects to the Muhammadan Emperor at Delhi. The Emperor detained him on various excuses, and then subjected him to confinement. However, he soon escaped. He used to have capacious baskets of fruit and flowers sent to and from his place every day, and one fine morning he put himself into a basket and was carried out under the belief that the basket contained nothing but fruit and flowers. Outside the city he met the redoubtable Tannaji. Thence he and Tannaji escaped in disguise, and actually walked all the way, hundreds of miles, from Delhi to Poona. After that they declared that they would rebel openly and for ever against the Great Mogul.

Recollect that Sivaji had just before given up Sing-garh, but he was still at Raigarh, already mentioned. His aim now was to retake Sing-garh, and the retaking of that place was entrusted to Tannaji. It was planned that Tannaji should escalade Sing-garh with a thousand men. If he succeeded in taking the place, he was to light the thatch of a storehouse which was on the top of the fort. This burning thatch making a flame would be seen from Raigarh, and Sivaji would know that Sing-garh was taken.

Tannaji, with his thousand picked men, advanced against Sing-garh. When I say "advanced," I mean that what they really did was this: the men in the different villages got orders to rendezvous at the foot of the Sing-garh precipice. I know that precipice well, and so do many other Englishmen, and it truly is an awful place. For hundreds of feet this black trap rock forms an absolute wall as straight as possible. Well, Tannaji had the ladders of rope and the grappling irons with him, and with those rope ladders up they went. There are many military men present, and I put it to them whether that is not a very daring, dashing thing to do, and whether it could be surpassed by any troops in the world. Alexander and his Macedonians used to do something of the same kind.

In this way Tannaji and 300 out of the thousand ascended the rock. Why he took only 300 men with him I never was able to ascertain; but it was a somewhat unfortunate arrangement. At any rate, he left 700 men under the command of his brother as a reserve, with instructions to move up if they should have an impression that anything was going wrong. So Tannaji and his 300 men reached the top in the dead of the night to surprise the Rajpût garrison. When they had climbed to the top they were quite unobserved, but somehow one of the soldiers of the garrison suspected he heard something, so he peered about, and came quite close to them. A deadly arrow answered his inquiry, but as he fell dying he uttered a cry. This cry alarmed the sentinels, and in an instant a blue light was lighted, which displayed Tannaji and his 300 men. Of course there was nothing for it but to go in at the fast-mustering garrison. Tannaji charged them, and was immediately killed. Seeing him killed, the men lost heart, and tried to get back to the ladder and down the precipice again; but the sound of firing had alarmed the reserve, and every one of them had come up also. They met the 300 retreating. Then Tannaji's brother showed himself a worthy brother. He made a speech to the men, which is not a bad specimen of Mahratta military eloquence, and I will endeavour to repeat it to you. He said to them: "Come, men, you must go on, for I tell you I have cut the ladders; there is a precipice behind you, and there is the enemy in front; moreover, there is among the enemy the dead body of your common father." I should mention that it is usual for Mahratta troops to style their commander their father. He added: "If you do not rescue the body it will be buried by low-caste men."

This was an argument which was irresistible to Mahrattas; they rushed on with their war-cry and overcame the Rajpûts. Some of the Rajpûts were killed, but the greater part of them jumped over the precipice, and there they lay, mangled bodies, at the bottom. The signal fire was then lighted with the thatch of the store-house, and Sivaji at Raigarh knew that Sing-garh was retaken.

The authentic tradition is that when, next day, Sivaji heard that this fort had been recaptured at the price of the life of Tannaji, he burst into passionate wailing and lamentation. I cannot possibly attempt to reproduce it, but you can imagine the sort of language which a man of that fiery passion and energy would use. He said something of this kind: "The lion's den is taken, but the lion is killed; what have I gained by winning a fort and losing such a man as Tannaji?" Such was the end of the life of the bravest and most faithful of Sivaji's dependants.

This completes the story of the adventures of Sivaji and his followers. I hope I have made it clear how the rugged nature of the country fostered this daring, this gallant spirit both in master and in men.

The next illustration (29) represents Raigarh. By the map you will perceive that this place is situated on the western or

FIG. 29.—RAIGARH.

Konkan side of the mountain range. The enemy of the Mahrattas was on the east; therefore, for a Mahratta fastness it was a great thing to be on the west of the range, for this military reason, that this arrangement placed the crest of the range, the high peaks, and the rugged mountain roads, between the Mahrattas and the enemy. Therefore Raigarh, according to the sagacious suggestion of Sivaji's father, was occupied as the last and the greatest of the Mahratta strongholds. There it was that

Sivaji established himself finally as sovereign of Western India. You will observe the way in which the place is arranged. In the foreground there is a little lake or tank on the summit of the mountain. This sort of lake is constructed in this wise. You first try to hit upon some point where there is likely to be a spring, some point on the top of the mountain, but which has some higher peaks near it; consequently the water collecting from the higher ground will form a spring. Then over this spring you make a quarry, whereby you obtain the stone for your palace or your fort, and with the same operation you excavate an artificial tank to secure your water supply. The ascent of Raigarh is exceedingly steep. Of all the ascents I have ever made in India, the Himalaya included, that of Raigarh is the worst. It is not only that the side is very steep, but the heat is most trying. If you ascend any other peak on the crest of the range, you do so from a tolerably good climate, but in ascending Raigarh you have to start in the heat from the level of the sea.

It was here that Sivaji established his dominion and reigned. Here, too, he died at the early age of fifty-three, after having rebelled, plundered, fought, and ruled for about thirty years. In this fort he collected the wealth and riches of half India; treasures in Spanish dollars, sequins, and the coins from all southern Europe and all Asia. Here, after his early death, he was succeeded by a son, who committed horrible crimes, and who died an equally horrible death.

On the top of Raigarh is the tomb of Sivaji. You may be aware that the Mahrattas do not bury their dead; no Hindus do; they practise cremation, and the ashes are buried in the tomb. I myself on one November day carefully examined the tomb of Sivaji. You may think I am romancing, but those who know that part of the Deccan will bear me out when I say that, at that season of the year, there is a particular blue flower —I have forgotten its name—of the most tender and delicate beauty; it grows on all parts of those hills where the soil is rich. I suppose they put rich soil over the tomb of Sivaji, for when I was there it was one mass of these tender blue flowers. A more poetic contrast you can hardly imagine, than that a bloom of such exquisite delicacy should be covering the grave of a man so desperate and violent, yet so great and statesmanlike, as Sivaji. Thus the hero was buried on the summit of his hill, commanding a view of the scenery fraught with associations of his deeds, and within sight of the Torna and Rajgarh, where his dominion was founded, and which he loved so well.

Sivaji was not only a bold man, such as I have described him, but he had peculiarly the power of arousing enthusiasm in others, and he was the man who raised an abject, subject race from nothingness up to empire. If it had not been for him there might have been no Mahratta uprising; but that uprising, on the other hand, would never have been possible if it had not been for the rugged and mountainous country which forms the subject of our geographical lesson this evening. But, besides that, Sivaji was a great administrator: he founded many institutions which survived for more than one century, during which his successors enjoyed imperial power; and the official titles of all his state departments and departmental officers are preserved among the Mahrattas to this day. So much for Sivaji and his biography.

I will ask your attention now, in conclusion, to the two pictorial illustrations numbered 30 and 31. The first of these (30) represents the scenery of Mahabaleshwar (Arthur's Seat), the summer residence of the Bombay Government and its principal officers, and of the ladies and gentlemen who form the society of Western India. It is close to Partabgarh, which I have already described, in the midst of the Mahratta country; and now, where all these desperate deeds were committed of old, there are picnics, while Badminton, lawn tennis, and the like are being played. You will see that along the rocks there are traces of the indurated lava lying layer upon layer, one over the other. The whole is, as it were, a series of regular horizontal stripes from end to end. In the middle distance there stands up the very Partabgarh which I have been describing to you this evening, and in the distance, as usual, there is the Arabian Sea.

FIG. 30.—ARTHUR'S SEAT AT MAHABALESHWAR.

The last illustration (31) represents the Bhore Ghat incline, the view being taken at the height of the rainy season. The Western Ghats, rising straight up from the sea-coast, catch all the clouds and vapour as they rise; which clouds are condensed into torrents, buckets, sheets of rain; and thus after one of these rain-storms the whole mountain-side is covered with waterfalls and cascades. It is through or along the mountain-side that the railway runs with magnificent engineering works; and this brings me, in conclusion, to the great difference there is now in the state of things in these Western Ghats as compared with Mahratta times.

I have shown you how difficult, in a military point of view, was the topography of these mountains. Now the British are

FIG. 31.—THE BHORE GHAT INCLINE.

penetrating them in every direction with roads and railways. First of all, consider the roads. Where before there was a rugged mountain pass which a mule or a pony or a single pack-bullock could just laboriously ascend or descend, there is now a regularly engineered road with complete gradients, levels, zigzags, and the like, up which wheeled carriages pass by hundreds and thousands during every traffic season, and by which also artillery can move. Thus you see what a great political engine one of these roads is. Consider for a moment the number of roads the British Government has made in these hills. I will enumerate them to you as they are marked on the map. First, there is the Thall Ghat Road; next the road opposite Junnar; the Bhore Ghat Road; the road opposite Rajgarh; the road opposite Partabgarh; those opposite Vishalgarh, Goa, and Karwar; so that you see we have pierced these mountain fastnesses by what may be called the resources of civilisation. Besides these, we have two lines of railway, one running from Bombay by the Thall Ghat towards northern India, the other from Bombay by the Bhore Ghat towards Poona and the Madras coast; besides which a third, under the auspices of a British Company, with the assistance of the Portuguese Government, is about to be made from the coast at Goa eastward. In this way the arrangements of the British Government are very different from, and I hope vastly superior to, those of its Mahratta or Muhammadan predecessors.

Lastly, the spirit which I have been describing to you, as prevailing among the Mahrattas in the Muhammadan times, survives to this very hour. These qualities depend upon the topography and the physical surroundings. To this day the Mahrattas are within sight of these everlasting hills, and they have the same spirit and courage as their forefathers. You say, "Have we had any recent proofs of this?" Well, we had some very unpleasant proofs so recently as 1879; for, would you believe it, owing possibly to the excitement caused by the war in Turkey, possibly also—one cannot tell exactly—in consequence of the occurrences in Africa, a certain amount of excitement arose among the Mahrattas: plundering began exactly in the same way; though we had an army and all our modern resources at Poona, nevertheless gang-robbery set in; men of rank were murdered, large quantities of property were carried off right up to these very hill fastnesses which I have been describing to you, and I assure you it took all we knew in the Bombay Government to put that affair down in the course of two or three months. Some leaders came forward; regular bandits were organised. One of these actually called himself Sivaji the Second.

On the other hand, these Mahrattas are good men in their way. You cannot altogether blame them for asserting their nationality now and then; but as long as you manage them well and assert your physical and moral superiority, they are thoroughly brave fellows, and will do your work for you. We must remember that the races who once furnished the soldiers of Sivaji, and who used to be called the Mawulis of the Deccan and the Hetkaris of the Konkan, are now wearing the British uniform, and that the descendants of Sivaji's soldiers have carried the British standard, not only in India and Afghanistan, but also in Persia, in Abyssinia, in China, and in the Mediterranean.

In conclusion, let me say that I want you to carry home not only a vivid idea of this beautiful scenery, but a geographical, a political, and an historical lesson. The lesson is that human character is greatly formed by physical surroundings; that so long as we choose to hold empire over such a country as that of Western India, we must be vigilant, and must figuratively, as well as actually, keep our powder dry; that if we are vigilant our empire is safe, and that if we are neglectful it is in danger. For depend upon it, if any serious blow were to be struck at our power by sea or land in any part of the world, excitement would once more arise among these very Mahrattas. Therefore, gentlemen, I hope, as members of the Royal Geographical Society, you will realise this lesson, that geography has its noblest function in describing the theatres of human action, and that he who would understand history aright must have a sound basis of geographical knowledge.

# CHAPTER XVII.

## PERSONAL TRAITS OF MAHRATTA BRAHMAN PRINCES.

[*Paper read before the Royal Historical Society, in London, June* 1883.]

Death of Sivaji, the founder of Mahratta power — His son Sambhaji comes to a tragic end — Adventures of the next king, Raja Ram — Degeneracy of his successor Shao — Origin of the Pêshwas as hereditary Prime Ministers — The Mahratta confederation — Character of the Pêshwas as Brahman sovereigns — Vishwanath the first Pêshwa — His successor Baji Rao I. the Brave — Third Pêshwa, Balaji the Great — Next Pêshwa, Madhu Rao the Good — Succeeded by Naraen Rao, who was murdered while young — Raghunath, the uncle, disputes the succession — British interference in Mahratta politics — Madhu Rao Naraen next Pêshwa — Baji Rao II. the Bad — Last of the Pêshwas — Greatness of the Pêshwa dynasty — Conduct of Brahman sovereigns in the diplomatic, the military, the civil, and the ceremonial branches of their administration.

THE essay which I am about to read should be taken as a continuation of a speech delivered by me before the Royal Geographical Society in February, 1882, regarding the "birthplace and cradle of Mahratta power." The subject of the speech was in a great degree geographical, and the intention was to show how history is affected by geography. The subject of this essay is an analysis of human character as exhibited in vast spheres of action. Nevertheless, for a due understanding of the men it is necessary to bear the geography in mind, for the significance of the events cannot be apprehended without a general idea of the physical surroundings.

The characters now to be summoned before you in historic

order were once the ruling spirits of the Mahratta dominion. The origin of that dominion was in all respects strange, and in some respects romantic. The organisation, thus established, ultimately spread all over India, which then probably comprised, as it certainly now comprises, one-seventh of the human race. The importance of the subject should induce us to observe the men who were the instruments of such national achievements as these.

The life of Sivaji, the founder of Mahratta dominion, has been set forth in the speech. This address refers to those who came after him, inheriting his idea, preserving its power, and extending its effect for weal or woe, but, alas, more for evil than for good.

Just two hundred years ago, that is in the spring of 1680, Sivaji died in his fortress-palace at Raigarh. As already described, he had run the most successful career ever displayed by a Hindu in war and politics within the time of authentic history. The ultimate inheritors of his power were equally successful; but they, though men of his nation, did not belong to his lineage, nor even to his caste. The successors of his line and race mounted his throne only to prove their degeneracy.

Of these lineal successors the first, Sambhaji, began and ended his reign under circumstances indeed awful. Immediately after being installed in royal authority at Raigarh, he called his widowed stepmother before him, loaded her with insults, and ordered her to death by starvation in a dark dungeon. He caused one of his father's trusty lieutenants to be flung from the precipices of Raigarh, and another to be tied to the feet of an elephant. These horrible executions were even exceeded in horror by the end which befell himself. After leading his troops in the wars then pending with the Moguls and the Portuguese, after wielding his father's famous sword in battle at one time, and at another time pursuing his foes with cavalry into an estuary till his horse swam in the rising tide—he succumbed to intemperance. One evening, while drunk with ardent liquor, he was surprised and seized by a party of Moguls in the garden of his summer-house at the foot of the Western Ghât Mountains. By the irony of fate he was dragged up the rugged roadways and along the undulating plains, which were the very scenes of his mighty father's exploits, till he reached the camp of the Mogul emperor, Aurangzêb. The enforced sobriety of this melancholy march settled his resolve to die with words on his lips of rage against his captors. When offered mercy by the emperor, he refused in terms of studied insult—as coming from a Hindu captive to a Muhammadan conqueror—and was straightway led forth to have his eyes seared with red-hot iron, and his tongue cut out.

The next or second successor was Raja Ram, also a son of Sivaji. His heritage in Western India was overrun by the Moguls, and he had to fly to Southern India in disguise, accompanied by a little party of followers, whose names are famed in Mahratta history, and who braved questioning by torture in order to screen him in a hair-breadth escape when suspicion of his rank had been aroused by the fact of his feet being washed by a servant. Arrived in Southern India, he set up a phantom court within a fortress there. Beleaguered by the Mogul troops, he again escaped, passing through their very lines at night, and took the field at the head of a Mahratta army. But he died at an early age from the rupture of a bloodvessel, caused by over-exertion on horseback during a protracted march—leaving a memory stained by one crime only. For he procured, on the lonely bank of a hill-stream, the assassination of Santoji, one of his staunchest followers, who was the most dashing officer that ever commanded that Mahratta cavalry which next, after the Mongol cavalry, was the most wonderful known in the annals of war.

Thus the immediate successors of Sivaji led lives both rough and short. The third, Shao or Sahû, passed through a long life of pampered idiotcy, having failed to inherit either the genius of his grandfather or the brute courage of his father. As the infant son of Sambhaji, he was after his father's fall, carried off to the Mogul camp. Having tragically executed the father, the Mogul emperor was kind to the child in a peculiar manner, causing him to be nurtured in the companionship of slaves, and under the enervating influences of the seraglio. During the changeful politics of that day Shao was released, and ascended the Mahratta throne as a feudatory of the Moguls, whom his grandfather had spent a lifetime in defying. He reigned a *fainéant*, as a puppet of those about him, and was afflicted by an hallucination respecting a faithful dog that had saved his life in a tiger-hunt. He would seat the animal on the throne beside him, place his own turban on its head, sit bare-headed in its presence, and have it carried with pomp in a sedan-chair. During his lucid intervals, however, he emitted sparks of a strange wit. Among his witticisms there was one which became historic, and bore a marvellous significance. He once said that the Mahrattas had reconquered India from the Muhammadans, and handed it over to the Brahmans. This saying of his is the key to the main portion of the address which I am now delivering.

During Shao's reign, the ministry led the armies, conducted the diplomacy, administered the provinces, distributed the rewards. The head of the ministry was the Pêshwa, one of the several functionaries instituted by Sivaji himself. The word pêshwa is of Persian origin, and signifies "the foremost": in Mahratta politics it is equivalent to prime minister or premier. The Pêshwaship, or premiership, became hereditary, and lasted for five eventful generations. The Mahratta kingdom founded by Sivaji in Western India was not the only one. Several other kingdoms were subsequently founded by Mahratta chiefs. These chiefs combined in one confederation under the Pêshwa as hereditary minister of Sivaji's kingdom. Thus the Pêshwa administered directly that particular kingdom, and directed the federal affairs of the confederated Mahratta kingdoms, which in their totality bore the general name of the Mahratta Empire. During the wars which led to the establishment of the British Empire, the negotiations were conducted with the Pêshwa. Thus it was the Pêshwa, as the representative Mahratta, with whom

Warren Hastings or the Marquis Wellesley contended in the Cabinet, and Lake or Arthur Wellesley in the field, while the Mahratta sovereigns of Sivaji's line were guarded in a palace-fortress as the shadows of a great name. But such was the respect paid to hereditary status, even in an age of violence, that each Pêshwa on his accession had to receive investiture from the titular king descended from Sivaji.

Now, while the Mahratta chiefs were men of a humble and unlettered caste, the Pêshwas were Brahmans of the highest and most cultured caste. The Pêshwa family sprang from a little village, which may still be seen nestling near the base of the Ghât mountains in the littoral tract known as the Konkan. This family founded and preserved for more than one hundred years a dynasty, which presided over the fitful fortunes of India, and of one among the most populous empires in the globe. This then was a Brahman dynasty, and as such was perhaps unique in the diversified history of India, almost all, if not absolutely all, other dynasties having belonged to lesser castes or races.

Consequently the individuality, the character, the idiosyncrasy of these persons—who were quite different from all other Indian sovereigns, and who also became bound up with the fortunes of British dominion—must have a peculiar interest for English students. I proceed then to sketch the characteristic traits of the several Pêshwas. As there were seven of them in succession, the portraiture of each one must be brief. In Indian history Brahmans appear as men of letters in the council-chamber, as financiers or administrators; but though potential factors, even arbiters, in politics, they are generally found to be wire-pullers exercising covert authority. In this crucial instance of the Mahratta Empire, they are seen to be the ostensible leaders everywhere, whether indoors or out of doors, and to be the possessors of overt responsibility. In this exalted capacity, then, what manner of men did they prove themselves to be? That is the question to be answered in the following review.

Irrespective of early Pêshwas, who were only ministers, the

founder of the hereditary Pêshwaship was Balaji Vishwanath, who was appointed Pêshwa in 1714, and whom, to prevent confusion of names, I shall call Vishwanath. He was more like a typical Brahman than any of his successors. He had a calm, comprehensive, and commanding intellect, an imaginative and aspiring disposition, an aptitude for ruling rude natures by moral force, a genius for diplomatic combinations, a mastery of finance. But having an over-refined physique and delicate health, he shrank from contact with the violence of those scenes in which his imperial ambition constrained him to mix. Among other defects, his horsemanship was timid and awkward, and that was a real misfortune in the Mahratta dominions. Nevertheless his political destiny propelled him into affairs wherein his misery must have been acute. He had a sharp brush with the pirates on the coast near Bombay. Once in the uplands of the Deccan he was captured, and subjected to the Mahratta discipline of a horse's nose-bag, full of glowing ashes or of hot pepper, being fastened over his nose and mouth. Once he eluded capture by hiding for several days in the wilderness. More than once he was threatened with death, for which he doubtless prepared himself with all the stoicism of his race, when a ransom opportunely arrived. At length, in 1720, he was deputed as plenipotentiary to Delhi, to wring by power of menace and argument from the Moguls a recognition of Mahratta sovereignty. During these complex and far-reaching negotiations his sensitive nerves were shaken by civil broils and street tumults. However, he carried victoriously all his diplomatic points, and brought back to Western India a political instrument which is one of the most noteworthy state documents in Indian history, and constituted the Magna Charta of Mahratta dominion. Regarding this as his political testament, he took leave of his countrymen, simply saying that his health was feeble. With not more dignity did Cardinal Wolsey lay his bones in the monastery, than did this Brahman Pêshwa proceed towards his country seat to sink into premature death, with the consciousness that a Hindu empire had been erected over the ruins of Muhammadan power, and that of this empire the hereditary headship had been secured for his family.

He was succeeded in the Pêshwaship by his eldest son, Baji Rao I., to whom he had given that manly training, the want of which he knew to have been a grave drawback in his own career.

Baji Rao I. then, as the second Pêshwa, entered on his imperial duties in 1721. His position was environed with difficulties; the new-born empire had to be consolidated and developed; the Mahratta confederation, full of discordant elements, had to be held together; the Muhammadans, still retaining many parts of India, had to be kept at arm's length; the Hindu spirit had to be sustained after the shock of a recent invasion from Persia. For such an hour Baji Rao was quite the man. In the first place he possessed all the special qualities of his caste; he had an imposing aspect, an engaging manner, a winning address, a scheming mind, and a fertility in resource. He frequently displayed a commanding eloquence that fired the patriotism of his countrymen during success, and raised their drooping spirits under reverse. In that age there was no such device as *verbatim* reporting, but some of his outbursts are known to have been fine and grand. His correspondence, too, was considerable, and fragments of it remain, enough to show that some of his despatches must have been almost as impressive as his speeches. Though inferior to his father in business and finance, yet he had been a confidant in the negotiations conducted by the first Pêshwa. He was thus able to gather up, unravel, and hold together the scattered or complicated threads. With these, which may be called indoor qualifications, he combined perfectly the outdoor qualifications essential to his position. As a rider he was hardly to be surpassed in a country where horsemanship was regarded as the first of accomplishments. His *métier* was perhaps that of a cavalry leader, but in battle he would be with the infantry also, and was ready to supervise siege operations as well. Though far from being foolhardy, he was ever forward in action and eager to expose himself under fire if the affair was arduous. He was inured to fatigue, and prided himself on enduring, while supreme chief in his political or military capacity, the same hardships as his soldiers and sharing their scanty fare. If they had to subsist on parched grain carried in their pouches, and munched as they rode along, he would insist on doing the same. He was moved by an ardour for success in national undertakings, by a patriotic confidence in the Hindu cause as against its old enemies, the Muhammadans, and its new rivals, the Europeans, then rising above the political horizon. He was distinguished by a toleration the reverse of Brahmanical. Besides his Brahman wife, he married a Muhammadan, whose son he brought up in the mother's religion. He lived to see his Mahrattas spread terror over the Indian continent from the Arabian Ocean to the Bay of Bengal. Entangled incessantly in military and political combinations, he heeded the civil administration but little. He strove in a general way to find administrators who would maintain the institutions of Sivaji, but that was all. If he possessed any constructive ability in these matters, he never allowed himself any opportunities of showing it. His state finances were left in a straitened condition. He died, as he had lived, in camp under canvas among his men; and he is remembered to this day among Mahrattas as the fighting Pêshwa, as the incarnation of Hindu energy. His death, like that of his father, was premature, no doubt owing to ceaseless exposure under the vicissitudes of a tropical climate.

His eldest son, Balaji Baji Rao, obtained the succession as third Pêshwa in 1740. To prevent confusion, I shall abbreviate his name to Balaji.

The accession of Balaji to power was signalized by financial worry. The disorder of the finances has just been mentioned, and it will be readily understood that the public creditors were legion. Some of them resolved to subject Balaji to the famous process of "Dharna," whereby they sat fasting at his gate, enforcing by rigid Hindu custom a similar abstinence on him. The scandal, as well as the inconvenience, of this procedure being immense, the treasury pledged its credit to raise a loan for liquidation.

Balaji's character was formed on the same lines as that of his father, and his disposition moved in the same direction. But, though a man of skilful address, of influence in council, and of ability in the field, he was inferior to his father both as a soldier and as a politician. He well knew how to utilize the talents of those about him, and some of his greatest successes were won for him by his lieutenants. Still, he was ever to the front, organizing or supervising, and he saw the Mahratta power attain its zenith. It was under him that the Mahratta cavalry, fully one hundred thousand strong, could truly boast that they had slaked their thirst in every stream that flowed between Cape Comorin and the Himalayas. But he did not take, perhaps he was not capable of taking, any steps for rendering this widely-extended dominion advantageous to the people. He allowed Mahratta rule to continue to be what it had been from the first, more an organization of plunder than a system of administration. It was indeed the most unimproving rule on a gigantic scale that has ever been seen in India—a country which at various epochs can afford many instances of misgovernment. Personally, he was unscrupulous, in this respect morally inferior to his father and grandfather. There is a strange instance of this in the manner whereby he worked with Brahmanical persuasiveness on the superstitious pride of a royal Hindu widow, inducing her to burn herself on her husband's pyre, in order that she might be removed out of his way for a political purpose. In his private life there was a coarse wildness specially unbecoming to a high-caste man. After a career in his estimation brilliant, the end came to him in sadness. When the Afghans advanced from Afghanistan upon Delhi, he sent the flower of the Mahratta army to oppose them. At the head of that army were his trusty cousin and his eldest son. His father, in like emergency, would himself have gone with the troops of the first line, but he remained with the second line encamped in Central India. While in camp in wait for tidings, he intercepted a banker's private messenger, who was the bearer of a letter which indicated, by metaphors relating to jewellery, that something serious had happened to the Mahratta host. Among other enigmatical expressions there were these words: "Two pearls dissolved." The Pêshwa must have asked his beating heart what this could mean. But the enigma was soon solved sadly for him. The dissolution of two pearls signified that his son and cousin had been slain in battle. In due course official details reached him, telling how the Mahrattas, having been cooped up in their entrenchment at Panipat, near Delhi, till they were nearly starved, had clamorously rushed forth to fight, and had been ridden down or crushed by the superior weight of the Afghan soldiers and the Turkoman horses. He retired to his tent literally with a broken heart. Unable to withstand his chagrin, he marched homewards to Poona and died in the temple he had previously built on the margin of a lake. The fact that such a man should thus be mortally affected by a not irretrievable disaster, may seem strange to us in hardier climes. It is to be accounted for by the nervous sensitiveness produced in him by tropical conditions, and other instances of the tendency are to be found in the Pêshwa dynasty.

He was succeeded in 1761 by his second son, Madhu Rao, as the fourth Pêshwa, then only seventeen years old.

Now, in some of the characters just depicted there has been found virtue of the secondary type, energy, courage, enthusiasm, patriotism, and the like; but in none of them is to be seen virtue of the purer, nobler, loftier quality. In the character now to be described there is virtue of the best stamp.

Mahdu Rao, then, the young Pêshwa, was, it will be remembered, brought up as a Brahman of the bluest blood. In his faith he was sincerely devout, so much so that, when engaged in state affairs, he sometimes caused embarrassment by retiring for the mystic meditation prescribed by his religious rules. While thoroughly realizing the responsibilities of his position, he was deferential in his manner towards older men; but still he never let them forget his sovereign rank. His temper, though hot, was generous; if treated with any disrespect, on account of his youth, by rough Mahratta councillors, he was prompt to resent; but when he felt himself to be wrong, he was anxious to make reparation. In such moments he would use the language of friend to friend rather than that of sovereign to subject. For a short time he was under the political tutelage of an uncle, Raghunath, whom he knew to be clever and unprincipled. From such leading-strings he soon emancipated himself, and, by the time he was twenty-one years of age, he had become the real controller of his imperial affairs, whether military, political, or civil. He had already distinguished himself in battle, personally rescuing his uncle from a critical situation. In trying moments he evinced not only presence of mind, but also a proud consciousness that by him an example should be set to all around. He chose ministers with discrimination, some of whom justified his choice by their subsequent achievements. He enforced strictness in the service of the state, and strove to procure honesty so far as that was procurable in a corrupt age. If an instance occurred of bad faith in high places, he would denounce it with a frankness surprising to those who lived in evil times. Though obliged to keep the uncle out of positions which afforded opportunities of doing harm, yet he showed the utmost consideration towards his relative. When two of his officers, during a siege, wanted to fight a duel over a quarrel, he told them instead to scale the deadly breach, promising to decree in favour of the disputant who should first plant the national flag upon the rampart.

He was the first Pêshwa who bestowed assiduous care on

the civil administration, not attempting innovations, but insisting on time-honoured institutions being made practically efficacious, instead of being treated as good in theory but defective in practice. His care extended to the fiscal, the judicial, and the general departments. All men in his day knew that the head of the State was personally master of the work, was the friend of the oppressed, and the foe of the oppressor, was anxious to extend a charitable equity to all alike, and was choosing agents who would carry out his beneficent orders. His thoughtfulness and considerateness were untiring, and were often shown in a signal or graceful manner. For instance, he conferred benefits upon the descendants of the cavalry leader Santoji, already mentioned as having been assassinated by Sivaji's successor, in order that such tardy justice as might be possible after the lapse of a generation should be done. All the while he was engaged in war and politics. He had to hold his own against the Nizam of the Deccan; to drive back Hyder Ali, of Mysore, afterwards famous in British annals; and to retrieve that disaster at Delhi which had grieved his father to death. While greatly superior to his predecessors as a civil ruler, he was not inferior to them as a warlike commander. While he was present in the field, the army of Hyder Ali, that had become the scourge of Southern India, was more than held in check. His lieutenants were just retrieving the Delhi disaster, when his own health, always delicate, gave way.

Soon the good officers throughout the empire, who had been appointed by him, were dismayed by the news that he was sinking under incurable consumption. Anticipating death, he adjured his uncle to protect the next Pêshwa, who would be a boy, to avert disunion from the reigning family, and save the empire from distraction. What reply he received we know not; at all events, he was allowed to die in hope; we shall soon see how cruelly that hope was belied. True to the habits of his race, he retired to a rural village near

Poona, and died quietly in the twenty-eighth year of his age, during the autumn of 1772; and that village is to this day regarded by the Mahrattas as one of the most classic spots in their historic land. His childless widow, to whom he was devotedly attached, burnt herself with his corpse, to satisfy her grief as well as to obey the behests of her religion. This is an instance of those who are virtuous in their joint life, and to whom death brings no separation.

That Madhu Rao, a Hindu prince, should have done so much in so brief a life as his, under such disadvantages and despite such temptations—that before being cut off in the heyday of his career, he should have evinced such capacity as this, not only in affairs susceptible of management by youthful genius, but also in matters ordinarily demanding the experience of riper years—is truly astonishing. Indeed he is for ever to be revered, as the model prince, the "flos regum," and as one of the finest characters that the Hindu nationality has ever produced.

Dying childless, he was succeeded by his brother, Narâen Rao, as the fifth Pêshwa, then only eighteen years old.

But Narâen Rao was, a few months after his investiture and installation, assassinated in broad daylight within his own palace at Poona, vainly clasping his arms round the neck of a faithful servant. The uncle, Raghunath, already mentioned, being present at the murder, might have saved the victim, but would not; and indeed his conduct was so dastardly as to cause suspicion of privity to the design. The murdered youth left a widow, who shortly afterwards gave birth to a son.

This son was, while yet an infant, proclaimed and invested as the sixth Pêshwa, under the name of Madhu Rao Narâen. He, like his father, scarcely reached the age of manhood. During his minority the affairs of the Pêshwaship were piloted through endless shoals and breakers by a helmsman of wondrous skill and resourcefulness, the famous minister, Nana Farnavîs. But the minister's mind was absorbed in a never-ceasing combat with political conjunctures. Though most competent to deal with emergencies and to baffle intrigues, though methodically industrious in business, he did little or nothing for the civil administration which had been so much improved during a recent reign, and which consequently relapsed into its pristine inefficiency.

Meanwhile the boy Pêshwa was growing up. During boyhood he showed signs of an ardent and generous disposition, and his fondness for wild sports gave promise of a military capacity like that of his ancestors. He was present at a battle between the Mahrattas and the Muhammadans, wherein both sides behaved feebly. The Mahrattas, however, gained the advantage, and began to boast of victory, but he reproached them for boasting, and lamented that the standard of merit should have fallen so low as to justify exultation over a paltry success. Having attained the age of twenty, he longed to act for himself in his sovereign capacity, and chafed under the strict though necessary control still maintained over him by his constitutional advisers. There is an oil-picture extant, representing him seated on his cushion of state, and gazing with expectant curiosity into the grave, careworn, and lofty countenance of the great minister. He had indeed attained his majority according to Hindu law. But at that moment the Mahratta Empire was menaced by perils from without and by factions from within. The minister and his colleagues justly decided that the handling of a complex mechanism could not be entrusted to a wayward and impetuous youth. But the young Pêshwa could see only with the eyes of unsatisfied ambition. He forgot that through weary years this sagacious minister had guarded the throne against foreign and domestic foes, had prevented the powerful members of the Mahratta confederation from reducing the Pêshwa to a condition as insignificant as that of Sivaji's descendants, had frustrated the diplomacy of the French, had resisted the rising power of the British. He thought merely of breaking loose from the political tutorship of his minister.

While in this mood he became affected by the super-sensitiveness characteristic of his race. Impatient of his powerless position, and aggrieved by a durance which was but imaginary, he refused to appear at the ceremonies and state functions at which his presence as Pêshwa was needed. In seclusion he brooded desperately over his fancied wrongs till he resolved on self-destruction. Yet he thought that before dying he would for once appear in all his glory. So during the autumnal festival at Poona, the greatest of the social and religious occasions of the Mahratta year, he rode in the morning along the line of his troops on parade. In the evening he held a state reception with the utmost splendour. Shortly afterwards he deliberately threw himself from the balcony of his palace. On being lifted up with fractured limbs from the marble floor, he bequeathed with dying breath the succession to his favourite cousin, Baji Rao II.

This event happening in 1795 was the second tragedy which had been enacted within the palace of the Pêshwas at Poona. This beautiful structure saw two of its masters, father and son in succession, die a violent death in the flower of their age. It was a noble edifice, built of teak-wood beautifully carved. It thus constituted one of the finest specimens of timbered architecture in India, and around it were gathered the threads of imperial affairs and the associations of history. It survived till the other day, when just four years ago the torch of an incendiary was treacherously applied to it, and the old woodwork burnt like tinder.

Among the troubles, which beset the minority of the late Pêshwa, was a disputed succession. The uncle, Raghunath, was actually proclaimed Pêshwa, but was never acknowledged as such by the Mahratta nation. He induced the British to interfere in support of his rival claims, and to justify that interference, obtained enough support from some of the members of the Mahratta confederation. It was this interference on his behalf that led to the extension of British power in Western India, and drove a wedge into the heart of the Mahratta Empire. He is the man who figures in those transactions during the time of Warren Hastings, which led to what is known as the first Mahratta war. He possessed military virtue, and the power of inspiring some of his immediate followers with a devotion of which extraordinary instances are recorded; but he was otherwise destitute of merit. Suffering many vicissitudes, he once took refuge with the British, and once was imprisoned by a Mahratta chief. At length forced to live in seclusion on the banks of the Nerbadda, he died from ennui and humiliation while yet in the vigour of his life. He was the instrument of various crimes in which his wife was the prime mover. This princess had remarkable abilities perverted to the pursuit of ambition by criminal means. She affords one of the numerous instances of Mahratta ladies acquiring wonderful influence in public life—of whom some worked eminently for good and others for evil. She was the mother of Baji Rao II., cousin of the late Pêshwa, and to this son were transmitted her own evil qualities. He, then, is the Baji Rao II. to whom the dying Pêshwa bequeathed the succession.

He was the seventh and was also, as will presently be seen, the last in the line of the Pêshwas. A brief description of him will conclude the portrait-gallery which I have been exhibiting in this address.

In most of the preceding characters there have been interesting traits; in some there have been elements of greatness; in one there has been absolute virtue. But in the picture now to be drawn of Baji Rao II., the shadows will prevail, scarcely relieved by a ray of brightness.

During the early years of his reign, that is, from 1795 to 1800, the reins remained in the able hands of his minister, the Nana Farnavîs already mentioned. But the administration was engrossed by war and politics, then urgently pressing, and extended to nothing beyond. In all that related to civil affairs or to the progress and contentment of the people, it was feeble when not actually harmful. It lost all vestige of honesty and efficiency after the death of the great minister in 1800.

The Pêshwa Baji Rao II., thus left to his own evil devices, took men of the vilest character into his counsels. He personally set the worst example. With some noteworthy exceptions, the private life of his predecessors had been respectable; but his conduct was scandalously vicious. Under a handsome aspect and a polished manner, he concealed a cruel and revengeful temper. He would sit in the balcony of his palace and watch barbarous sentences executed. It need hardly be added that he was a master hand in deceit, and betrayed his supporters all round. He was innately skilful in ingratiating himself with others before they discovered his real disposition. Manliness had generally been possessed by his race, but he was at heart a coward. He was miserably superstitious, and the neighbourhood of Poona is still shaded by groves which he planted in expiation of his crimes. He was tormented by the ghost of the murdered Pêshwa, whose murder he ascribed to his father and mother, the uncle and aunt of the victim. He possessed only one of the attributes of his ancestors, namely, eloquent persuasiveness. When, as a youth, he wished (for some selfish purpose) to stimulate into madness the morbid self-consciousness of his cousin, the late Pêshwa; when he essayed to make Mahratta chiefs believe in him, despite untoward appearances; when he tried to cajole Arthur Wellesley or to mislead the British envoy, the famous Mountstuart Elphinstone; when he strove to lull the British force at Poona into a sense of security that might precede swift and treacherous destruction; when he sought favourable terms from his captor, Sir John Malcolm;—his command of touching and impressive language never deserted him.

He was one of those men who, judged by their own conduct, seem to be devoid of conscience, and are found to distinguish between right and wrong only by the language they use regarding the conduct of others. His political position was always critical, and its successive crises could hardly have been surmounted even by virtue and genius. But he infinitely aggravated its inherent difficulties. He contrived to set the great feudatories of the Mahratta empire against himself and his favourites. He threw himself into the arms of the British, and entreated their support. When that support was rendered, he enjoyed its advantages for a time with much satisfaction; but soon he tired of it and intrigued against his allies. Finding that intrigues were unavailing, he compassed the secret destruction of his benefactors, including Mountstuart Elphinstone the envoy and the British force cantoned near Poona according to formal treaty. With this view, he strove to corrupt the native soldiers of the British force, and thought he had succeeded; but this project was frustrated by the fidelity of the men. Having laid his train, as he supposed, completely, he sent a private message to two European officers, for whom he had an old kindness, warning them to secure their own safety, as their countrymen were going to be destroyed to a man. This friendly intention on his part throws just one gleam of light over the blackness of his character. It was an anxious moment for Mountstuart Elphinstone. The terrace in his official residence near Poona may still be seen where he paced during the watches of the night, straining every sense in the direction of the city, and awaiting the attack which at daybreak would be delivered against his little force with what might prove to be overwhelming numbers. The attack, however, failed as utterly as it deserved to fail. This decisive action is known to history as the battle of Kirki, and was fought in October, 1818. Standing in the balcony of the temple set on a hill near Poona —the very place where his grandfather Balaji expired, as will be remembered—Baji Rao II., the last of the Pêshwas, saw the charges of his half-disciplined multitudes repulsed by a little force under the guidance of British skill and valour. From that moment nought but flight and ruin remained to him. His territory then passed under British rule, and became that

Deccan of the Bombay Presidency regarding which so much has been heard in British annals. Ultimately captured, after many arduous adventures, he was sent to reside as a state prisoner, under easy restraint and with a liberal pension, on the banks of the Ganges, in British territory, at Bithur near Cawnpore. He was devoid of the honourable sensitiveness that had characterized his ancestors, and lived to a childless and dishonoured old age, in an obscurity which made people forget the historic associations with which his life had been connected. He died in 1851, and left an adopted son, who became the Nana Sahib so infamously known during the Indian mutinies in 1857.

Thus seven Pêshwas have passed under review between 1714 and 1818, just a century. Of these sovereigns two died before really attaining manhood; three were great; one was both great and good, but he, too, died before his greatness was fully developed; and one was utterly bad. Hence we see that the line of the Pêshwas produced four great sovereigns in succession of the Brahman caste, namely, Vishwanath, reigning from 1714 to 1720; Baji Rao I., reigning from 1721 to 1739; Balaji, reigning from 1740 to 1760; and Madhu Rao, reigning from 1761 to 1772. Inasmuch as the Brahmans have preserved purity of descent more than any race on earth except the Jews, as they established several thousand years ago an intellectual superiority over their countrymen which has been transmitted through many generations, it might be expected that Brahmans attaining to sovereignty would evince a marked capacity in their imperial position. Accordingly these four Pêshwas fully realized this expectation. None of the many lines of Hindu sovereigns in India has ever shown a series of sovereigns equal to the Pêshwas. The historical student will immediately inquire whether four sovereigns equal to them can be found in any of the Muhammadan dynasties of India. It may be answered that in one only can a parallel be seen, namely the dynasty of the Great Mogul. The four Mogul emperors,

Akber, Jehangir, Shah Jehan, and Aurangzêb were as great as the four Pêshwas; and of these Akber was both great and good.

In India the capacity of a sovereign is to be observed in the four main departments of state, the political or diplomatic, the military, the civil, and the ceremonial. Now, Brahman sovereigns would be sure to be adepts in political combinations and in diplomatic management. The Pêshwas were such adepts to a degree hardly to be surpassed in any age or country. The effect of their whole bringing up was to endue them with an ability to contrive or design, and with an insight into the thoughts, sentiments, passions, or foibles of others. Regarding war, whether in military administration, or in strategy, or in the command of troops in the field, it might have been anticipated that they, as Brahmans, would prove deficient. On the contrary, however, in each and all of these respects they proved themselves to possess the brain to control, the courage to execute, the fortitude to endure. In the civil administration it might have been supposed that they would evince a decided superiority to all other princes. Being essentially educated and lettered men, raised mentally much above the level of their countrymen, and endowed with all the culture known to their age, they ought to have consolidated the institutions of their country, imparted an impulse to administrative business, and promoted the education of the people. On the contrary, however, three out of the four great Pêshwas failed to do any of these things with efficiency, partly because they were preoccupied by war and politics, but partly because they wanted the philanthropic and enlightened disposition for the doing. The fourth began to do all these things nobly well, and would have done much more had his pricelessly valuable life been spared. He, too, was immersed in war and politics; and the fact that he nevertheless attended to the civil administration shows that, where the will exists, there is a way for a ruler to attend to all branches of his work alike. In the ceremonial department, which is peculiarly important in an eastern country, it might have been foreseen that Brahmans, being gifted with beauty of appearance, dignity of mien, excellence of manner, and power of elocution, would hold their courts with becoming grandeur. This the Pêshwas certainly did with consummate effect.

On the whole, while unsparingly indicating the misdeeds or shortcomings of these several characters, I have striven to do justice to their merits. It is essential that Englishmen, when judging the native Indian character, should be alive to its virtues as well as to its faults. If we are to improve upon the rule of preceding dynasties, whether Hindu or Muhammadan, if we are to govern the natives successfully, we must, while striving to correct their faulty side, learn to appreciate that virtuous and most interesting side of theirs which a civilized administration will develop.

# CHAPTER XVIII.

## THE TEMPERANCE MOVEMENT AMONG THE BRITISH IN INDIA.

[*Speech delivered before the Temperance Association at Liverpool, February,* 1881.]

The liquor laws of India — Question of temperance among Europeans generally in the East — Among sailors in Indian ports — Among European soldiers in India — Sailors' homes and soldiers' recreations — Temperance movement in the capital cities of India — Order of Good Templars in the East — Statistics of temperance in India — Temperance essential for sportsmen and travellers — Special danger of intemperance in the tropics — Experience derivable from military history and scientific exploration.

I HAVE been asked to speak before you on the subject of Temperance, and I will take up that portion of the subject which relates to the welfare of your countrymen in the East. Happily the matter—however important it may be in some parts of Asia, for instance, China—has not greatly affected the natives of India. The excise laws in India are framed to repress the consumption of drugs and spirits, while raising the revenue. Faults sometimes occur in this, as in all other human arrangements; but wherever the excise has been found incidentally to encourage intemperance, a remedy has been applied. With the Europeans in India, however, the case is somewhat different. You can but too readily imagine that with them the same tendency to indulge in alcoholic drinks is developed there as here in Britain. A century ago this tendency was excessive; the authentic accounts of the harm and the scandal, which used thence to arise, afford encouragement in that they show how great an improvement has been effected in recent times. We must be thankful for the change which, in this respect, has come over the manners of Europeans in the East, both in the upper and in the humbler classes. Still the memory of past intemperance clings to the European name in the East, tarnishing the brightness of an otherwise brilliant escutcheon, and lowering the grandeur of a mighty prestige. Moreover, despite all the improvement which may be justly claimed, there is unhappily enough of intemperance still perceptible to sustain the evil memory I have alluded to. Thus, intemperance is still regarded, though in a mitigated form, as the national vice of the British in the East. It is still one of the things which has to be inquired about in the character of an applicant for employment; it is still one of the points towards which the apprehensive glance of the employer is turned. After all the abatement and diminution that can be fairly estimated, there is yet very much to be lamented, and there is but too large a scope for the work of temperance advocates in the East.

Here, at Liverpool, your thoughts will naturally turn in the first place towards the sailors of that mercantile marine, which, centred in this the largest port in the world, is the very life of the Eastern seaports. Well, as regards temperance or intemperance, you know that to our sailors the well-known line is peculiarly applicable—

> "Cœlum non animum mutant qui trans mare currunt."

In former days there were many allurements offered to thirsty sailors coming ashore under a hot sun, by the taverns of Calcutta or Bombay, punch-houses as they were called apparently from punch the drink, with tempting maritime names like "The White Cloud," and so on. In those days as nowadays it was necessary to let the men go ashore; but whenever they went, almost all of them (doubtless with some honourable exceptions) fell more or less into mischief from intemperance. This mischief was reckoned as among the inevitable contingencies, necessarily inherent in the nature of things. Indeed there was but too much reason for this view, inasmuch as when a man landed on a tropical strand he really needed something to drink, and he could not obtain beverage anywhere, save in places that lured him to intemperance. For this state of things the responsibility in part rested with the authorities and with the leaders of society in those days, inasmuch as no better places of resort were provided. But of late years institutions named "Sailors' Homes" have been provided at the principal Eastern seaports. The Sailors' Home at Bombay was inaugurated during the visit of His Royal Highness the Duke of Edinburgh, and that at Calcutta by the late Lord Lawrence. These homes are truly fine structures, architecturally attractive to the eye of the passer by—which externally is an important feature. Internally they are spacious, convenient, clean, and salubrious. Their scale of expenses is in all respects adapted to the humble means of the seaman. Their influences and surroundings are calculated to wean men from evil and lead them towards good. They answer nearly all, if not absolutely all, the objects which the advocates of temperance have at heart. They do not indeed fulfil all the requirements of the total abstainers, because they have "bars" where liquor is sold, under well-supervised regulations that guard against and effectually prevent intemperance. They are thus frequented by many men who buy liquor at the "bars" in strict moderation and remain in a well-arranged home, but who in the absence of such "bars" would go to taverns for liquor immoderately, and would remain there in disorderly surroundings. At all events public opinion is not yet ripe for prohibiting "bars" in Sailors' Homes, though it ensures the existing "bars" being maintained on temperance principles. Now these homes have proved quite successful. They do not as yet attract all the sailors, of whom some still resort to the taverns. But they secure very much of the seamen's custom and proportionately diminish the business of the old taverns. Every man who resorts to the "homes" is so far kept out of harm's way. Owing to this and to other causes there has been, and is still going on, a happy improvement in the habits and customs of seamen at the Eastern seaports.

Similarly with the European soldiery in the East, all the moral and material improvements of recent years tend to check the intemperance once so fearfully prevalent, and to promote temperance. With this view the old rules and practices regarding the canteens and the serving out of spirits to the men in quarters, on the march, or on service, have been revised. The access to the native liquor shops has been rendered more difficult than formerly. Endeavour has been made to prevent it altogether, but seldom with complete success. In former days one cause, among others, why the men resorted to places affording temptations to intemperance was the want of recreation grounds during the daylight and of reading rooms during the dark hours. Nowadays recreations of all sorts are provided out of doors, and indoors there are reading rooms, well-stocked and well-lighted. Both indoors and out of doors soldiers' industries are encouraged, and periodical exhibitions of their handiwork are held. The improved education of the men before they enlist, and the instruction compulsorily afforded to them after enlistment, have caused the British soldiery to be a body of men educated at least in an elementary degree. All this disposes them to follow those pursuits and to frequent those places, which instead of alluring people to mischief, offer inducements towards those things that are good, among which things temperance is in the foremost rank. Those who, seeing the European soldier in India as he now is, remember what he was, say, thirty years ago, are from the bottom of their hearts thankful.

Nevertheless, it must be sorrowfully admitted that intemperance still exists in the European army of India. Military crime, as it is technically termed, is not indeed prevalent, but there is much more of it than, all circumstances considered, we should expect to find. Now of that crime the greater part is directly or indirectly caused by drink. There is no statement more fully attested by the best military authorities than this, by such men as Lord Napier of Magdala, Lord Strathnairn, Lord Wolseley. If it were not for drink, the amount of military crime in the European army of India would be small and insignificant. Whatever be the merits or demerits of the native soldiery, it is allowed on all hands that their conduct is exemplary. One cause of that happy result is this that their national habits indispose them to intemperance and predispose them to temperance. Thus, when all allowance has been made for the effect of recent improvements, there remains the solemn and melancholy fact that, in the course of a year or two, thousands of European soldiers have been sent to prison, or otherwise punished, who never would have fallen into trouble but for drink. Hundreds of soldiers nurtured in the quiet happy homes of Britain and brought out to India at a heavy cost to the State—who in the ranks would be of value to the public service—are languishing in military prisons, because they had yielded to drink, and so drifted into the evil courses that flow therefrom. Irrespective of moral and political advantages, it would financially pay the Government to incur considerable expense in order to prevent the waste of public resources thus caused through intemperance.

But, besides efforts by the State, there is much of persuasion, of indoctrination, of exemplification, which can be effected only by private exertions and by benevolent agencies. In this respect the Temperance movement is by no means backward in its work among the soldiery. Indeed the abstainers are constantly preaching total abstinence among the men, and enrolling fresh members in their ranks. In the European forces of India there were, in 1875, 4350 men who had joined this movement, and of these the greater number had taken the pledge of total abstinence. By 1880 this number had risen to 10,880, an increase by more than double in five years. The last-named number is equal to one sixth of the total forces. Further, in each of the three Presidencies into which India is divided, the European section of the army has temperance associations allied with, though actually distinct from, the total abstinence societies. In the Presidency of Bengal there are fifty-seven of such associations, in that of Madras twenty, in that of Bombay twenty-three. Each of these associations may have from fifty to 100 members. This movement, in combination with all the improved surroundings which I have mentioned, is producing an excellent effect.

Thus, one way and another, the military service is becoming a far more desirable profession than it used to be, and much better calculated to attract young men of fair character and ability. Indeed, a youth born in humble circumstances at home, and by nurture or education inclined towards good, might enlist in the army and proceed to India. Arriving there, he would find abundant influences tending towards the good ways in which he had been brought up, and supporting him in his resistance against evil. He would have ample scope for his abilities, and he would fast rise in the service. He would have opportunities of laying by money in the soldiers' savings banks, which are established in every military station and cantonment.

The Temperance movement in India is happily not confined to the European army. It has extended to the Europeans who are there called civilians in contradistinction to the soldiery. Thus in Calcutta the Temperance societies have 560 members, in Bombay 600, in Madras 200. For the Europeans in India generally, there is a League having 500 members, and an Order of Good Templars having 1000 members. The figures are relatively more important than they might at first sight appear to be, because the civil population of Europeans is both scanty and scattered.

On the whole, taking the European soldiers and civilians together, it is probable that the members of Temperance associations, under one form or another, in India, are not less than 16,000. This result is fraught with blessings to our countrymen generally in the East, and will help in lessening (though hardly in removing) that which unhappily is a blot on our national character.

Influential meetings are often held, and are largely attended, not only by the friends of the movement, but by strangers who go to listen. Though I do not myself belong to any of the Temperance associations, yet I have sometimes attended on these occasions, and both at Calcutta and at Bombay I have addressed meetings—not so large indeed as the vast Liverpool meeting before which I am now speaking—but still very considerable both as regards numbers and earnestness.

On such occasions, indeed, I cannot undertake to present the higher considerations relating to this grave matter, which considerations can be better urged by reverend gentlemen who will speak with religious authority, or by those who devote themselves to the subject. I can only state, when specifically requested to do so, the arguments which occur to the mind of one who has seen service and gone through hard work.

Now, as a practical fact, there is no doubt that in the East those who are to endure the stress of hot weather, the rapid alternations of heat and chill, of drought and damp; who are to preserve freshness under long-sustained fatigue; who are to maintain a sturdy spirit, a steady nerve, a brightness of mind, despite bodily exertion and physical exhaustion; who are to stand severe intellectual strain with brain-force unimpaired by tropical conditions—must be, if not absolute abstainers, yet very temperate, must take very little wine, still less of ale (for what is called beer in India is really bottled ale), and of spirits the smallest modicum diluted in water. Such persons—who include nearly all, if not absolutely all, the men who in the East are successful in war, politics, administration, trade, industries, learning, literature—are actually examples of temperance "in excelsis," although they do not join temperance associations. Though they do not preach yet they practise, and their conduct perhaps has more effect on the community and gives more solid support to the Temperance movement than anything they could say or write. Doubtless there may be exceptions to the rule which I have indicated, though I doubt whether the exceptional cases to the contrary, which might be adduced, would stand close criticism. But the rule, as a general fact, stands as clear as noonday throughout the East.

Again in the East there are two pursuits so interesting as almost to constitute professions, namely, sport and travel. These are peculiarly attractive to the manhood of Britain, because they exercise body and mind together, and demand all sorts of capacity. They involve exposure generally, risk often, and danger sometimes. For these temperance is essential; indeed they can hardly be pursued without it. The fact of there being a spice of danger in most Eastern sports, renders them attractive. But if the danger is to be surmounted, there must be that absolute coolness which belongs only to the temperate. Wounds or other injuries are sure to be suffered; for rapid and complete recovery, in an eastern climate, that bodily condition is needed which, again, the temperate alone possess. The best books that are published regarding the wild sports of the East, usually contain specific warnings to young sportsmen on this head, and remind them that if they are to spear the boar as he rushes, or take sure aim at the tiger as he bursts forth, or come to close quarters with the bear, or bring down the chamois and the wild sheep on dizzy heights—they must be strictly temperate; and that unsteadiness in these critical moments may cause not only failure but even disaster and death. Again, whenever a small party of travellers undertake a really arduous march in the Himalayas or other mountainous regions, they form necessarily a little temperance league among themselves, for they will probably carry with them neither wine nor beer, but only some spirits to be diluted with the water of mountain springs; and for stimulants they will rely mainly on tea or coffee.

But besides the cases of everyday life in sport or travel, there are numerous instances to be found in contemporary history. Consult the journals of celebrated travellers in Asia, and you will find that after their dire fatigues, in great altitudes, in blinding storms, in ice and snow, in utter exposure all day, in the slenderest shelter at night, in acute distress from rarefied air—the stimulant they crave is not liquor but tea. Examine the reports made by surveyors who have for scientific explorations made the highest ascents ever attempted in mountain ranges, or the records left by those who are the martyrs of science, and after labours nobly borne have left their bones in places almost inaccessible—and you will read the same story.

Doubtless, in small quantities, beer may be wholesome enough in the East as elsewhere, wine in moderation may be a harmless luxury, or may have the dietetic advantages which Liebig ascribed to it, and spirits may at times be medicinally useful. Still there is the limit of moderation which is but too likely to be overstepped, and the line of safety which is but seldom observed. If the history of Indian pathology could be exactly written, many ailments attributed to climate would be found attributable to causes alcoholic rather than climatic. I wonder how many inflamed livers, ascribed to the tropics, how many so-called sunstrokes, are really due to alcohol, not perhaps taken in excess, but merely absorbed in minute quantities from day to day.

Lastly, if historic works on recent wars be consulted, it will be found that in Afghanistan, Europeans, frost-bitten, half-frozen, worn out with toil, hunger and anxiety, have been recruited, not with liquor, but with tea; and that in Abyssinia European troops, accidentally deprived of the commissariat rum ration, have marched and worked all the better without it, and have been improved in health for the want of it.

Though keenly alive to the evil produced by intemperance in the United Kingdom, greater probably than that produced by all other causes put together, and to the excellent effect produced in counteraction by the temperance movement in its various forms, I will leave these matters to be treated by other speakers who are more qualified than myself by experience and special knowledge. But as regards Oriental experience, I have thought it my duty to comply with the request that I should say what I know as a man of the world from a practical point of view, in the confidence that considerations relating to the welfare of our fellow-countrymen in the East, will be acceptable at the great port of Liverpool, where countless eastern interests are concentrated.

## CHAPTER XIX.

### PRINCIPLES OF BRITISH POLICY IN EGYPT.

[*Reprinted from the 'Contemporary Review' for October* 1882.]

Relations of England towards the Muhammadan world — Sovereignty of the Khedive and suzerainty of the Sultan in Egypt — Accord between England and the European Powers — Dismantling of Egyptian forts — Reduction of the Egyptian army — Reorganization of the Egyptian troops — Reformed police — The Bedouins to be kept in check — Retention of the British garrison — Civil government of Egypt — Maintenance of the British Control — Representative government among the Egyptians — Judicial administration — The Public Debt of Egypt — Suez Canal to be used by England in war and peace — Hydraulic works of improvement in the valley and delta of the Nile.

THE object of this article is not to discuss the causes which led to the British military operations in Egypt,* but to examine the principles which should guide British policy when these operations have been crowned with success. Having extinguished by force the rebellion of Arabi and his party, England has for the moment a commanding opportunity; then how ought she to make use of it? That is the question.

Now this question is doubtless engaging the anxious attention of nearly all the Muhammadan world, that is, the Muhammadans in Turkey, in Persia, in Arabia, in Afghanistan, in India, in Northern Africa. There are still two important bodies of Muhammadans, namely, those dwelling in Central Asia, who

* It will be seen that this article was written before the fall of Tel-el-Kebir, but its main purport is still applicable.

are under Russian domination, and those inhabiting certain parts of the Chinese Empire, whose political thoughts can hardly be gauged. It is probable, however, that the Chinese Muhammadans do not trouble their minds on the subject. After all abatements, the number of Muhammadans who are seriously exercising their minds in this matter, must be great, comprising as it does a total population of nearly one hundred millions. There is no need for pausing to show how England has under her direct administration or her political control about half of this large aggregate. Her interest, then, in the Muhammadan world, if judged by the numerical standard of a census, would appear to be much greater than that of any other Power. Thus she has every motive to conciliate the Muhammadans, inducing them to confide in her benevolent will and loyal intentions.

It is important to bear this in mind when considering the main questions as above set forth. In reference to that question the first point is the maintenance of Muhammadan sovereignty and rule in Egypt. From the outset, then, the British authorities have proclaimed the maintenance of Muhammadan rule as represented by the Khedive. On his part the Khedive has commanded his subjects to loyally co-operate with the British authorities, and has declared Arabi a rebel in arms against his lawful master. The Sultan of Turkey is prepared to issue a proclamation to the effect that Arabi is a rebel. Further, to the Sultan there is allowed the option of sending a body of Turkish troops to co-operate with the British in Egypt at the seat of war. These proceedings certainly set England right with the Muhammadan world at large, and place her in the position of one who is battling for her Muhammadan allies (the Sultan and the Khedive) against an insurrectionary party. It also establishes the contention that Arabi is a rebel, notwithstanding any sentiments of nationality or feelings of fanaticism which may temporarily have gathered round him. There has undoubtedly been much in his conduct to attract the admiration and sympathy of many classes among Muhammadans generally. It is therefore of much consequence to so arrange the language of proclamations or other authoritative proceedings that he may be made to stand in his true position, namely, that of an insurgent against his legitimate lord. This is apparently being done quite effectually, and will produce a favourable effect upon Muhammadan opinion everywhere.

Happily the Khedive stands well in British opinion, as having played an exceptionally difficult part with loyalty and fidelity. But this public opinion has been dubious respecting the Khedive's suzerain, the Sultan of Turkey. On the one hand, all Englishmen who are acquainted with Constantinople, will considerately make allowance for the Sultan on account of the cruel difficulties which environ his political position. On the other hand, there is no disguising the violent probability that the recent troubles in Egypt have been indirectly encouraged by some classes in Turkey, and even fomented by some parties there. It were superfluous to recapitulate the reasons why the conduct of the Turkish Government during some stages of the negotiations is held to have been unsatisfactory, and to have been guided by the idea of impeding or retarding the British operations. These circumstances have injuriously affected Turkey's position, though it may yet be retrieved by behaviour which shall be worthy of acceptance as clearly good. If, then, it shall be found possible, with political consistency, to overlook the Sultan's shortcomings in the past, with a view to his co-operation in the immediate future, and thus to maintain the recognition of his suzerainty over Egypt—this will have a good effect upon the Muhammadan world, or more particularly upon that part of it with which England is directly concerned. The Sultan indeed holds a very high position among Muhammadans, though it is well to avoid making too much even of that position. He being (as will be readily remembered) of the Sunni sect, Persia, being of the Shia sect, will not pay reverence to him. Afghanistan too, as was proved by the experience of the last Afghan war, regards him but little. Still his office and person are venerated by most among the influential Muhammadans of India, his prestige is still maintained in Turkey, and probably there is a religious party on his side in Arabia. If then England shall find herself able, with the approval of Europe, to set the Khedive on a throne of real power, and to preserve the suzerainty of the Sultan, she will be held by the Muhammadan world to have done well. It would be a mere truism to state how many contingencies may hinder the accomplishment of any such design, as of many other good and wise designs.

Next, in the future settlement of Egypt it will be most desirable to obtain, not only the formal acceptance but also the cordial approval of the European Powers, and to avoid anything which may even bear the semblance of lawlessness or violence. Besides the high considerations which are too manifest to need recapitulation, it may be remarked that any step which should deviate from the comity of nations or from the best principles of international law, would be likely to produce bitter consequences hereafter. Aggressive ambition, on the part of one great Power, arouses similar tendencies among other Powers. It is obvious that there are several, perhaps many, Oriental regions which offer temptations and enticing opportunities to one or other of the great Powers for that sort of interposition which ultimately leads to domination. Though England is far from claiming any exclusive interest in the East, where other Powers also have interests, still such movements may prove embarrassing more or less to her, and occasionally might even be dangerous to her legitimate interest. She should therefore eschew giving the least encouragement to them by any example in her own conduct. If after being compelled to draw the sword in a just quarrel, and having secured advantages in Egypt of which the equitableness is unquestionable, England shall abstain from undue self-aggrandizement, shall carry with her the sentiments of the European Powers, and shall show that her work is done, not only for her own interest but for the interest of others also,—for the sake of the native ruler of Egypt, of the Egyptian people, and of all Europeans, to whatever nation belonging, who may carry on trade or industry in the Nile valley,—then she will possess an additional vantage-ground in political controversies hereafter. Her objections will continue to carry the moral force which happily they have always commanded, if in the future aggression shall be attempted by any Power upon those Oriental regions which are exposed to interference or to attack. Justice in argument does not indeed prevail invariably when such conjunctures arise, and material as well as moral forces are called into play. Still, the Power which has moral force on its side possesses a fulcrum which it is advantageous to keep and disadvantageous to lose.

Then, if England, with the approval of Europe, shall maintain the Muhammadan sovereignty in Egypt, the point will arise as to how this rehabilitated sovereignty shall be rendered safe for the future.

The primary step will be to secure the persons of Arabi and of his principal supporters, civil or military. Judgment in the case of each individual will doubtless be meted out after quasi-judicial inquiry, and to some a punishment more severe than banishment or imprisonment may possibly have to be awarded. But, at the least, the leaders will have to be detained as State prisoners for such time as may seem proper. For such detention there are several British localities conveniently available. To leave these men at large, or in any place from which escape would be practicable, might jeopardize the success of military and political results that had been won by blood and treasure.

This done, the disbandment would follow of the Egyptian troops that had fought against us and also against their lawful sovereign. Such a measure would, however, by no means suffice. For there is needed a revision of the establishment to be allowed in future to the Egyptian army. One of the fundamental causes of the troubles in Egypt is the maintenance of an army which, on the one hand, can never be adequate for external defence against a European Power, but which is quite strong enough to overawe the native Government and to set up an internal disturbance. The Egyptian Government has for many years past been borrowing money in the European markets, and has been devoting a part of these funds to military armaments of various sorts, arms of precision, cannon of modern invention, forts with scientific engineering, and the like. These very things are now being used against England, and most of them were made in English factories. This, of course, is one among the many instances which occur of the eagle being hit by shafts winged with his own feathers. Again, though the Egyptian troops may fight with their own unassisted courage and endurance, still, much of their discipline, tactics, and manœuvres arise from European training. If, then, the continuance of this system shall be allowed after the new settlement of Egypt, the renewal of troubles in some form is, humanly speaking, quite probable. The occurrence will be only a question of time and opportunity. In vain will Arabi and his kindred spirits have been overcome. Other Arabis as bad, or worse, may arise, with other spirits more evil still. The Khedive, then, on being restored to real authority, should be required to reconsider existing forts, deciding which should be dismantled and which retained, and to revise the strength of his ordnance, so that it should not be excessive. British consideration should be specially given to those forts which were strongly constructed and placed in commanding positions, and which might therefore prove dangerous if they fell into evil hands. The peace establishment of the Khedive's forces, after the conclusion of military operations, should be so limited that practically it shall never become dangerous to order. If he be guaranteed, as he doubtless will be, against outer foes, then his military force for internal order should be comparatively small, and should be composed very differently from that Egyptian force which has evinced some prowess in contest even with British arms.

Moreover, financial necessity dictates that reform in Egypt

should begin with a permanent reduction of its army. In past years the military expenses, though not extraordinarily great, have yet been greater than the over-burdened treasury could afford. The naval and marine expenses, too, have been considerable. In future years these several expenses, if not curtailed, would prove intolerable to an impoverished finance, and would render both the Administration and the people incapable of recovering prosperity, of recouping some of the losses that have been sustained, and of bearing the additional burdens which in several ways will be brought about by the present troubles.

Further, the site of overgrown forces, maintained without a definite object, is of itself provocative of mischief, in that it fosters martial aspirations among the Egyptians, and induces some fanatical classes to vainly imagine that their country can withstand the demands of civilization, and resist the influences of a progressive age.

On every ground, then, political, administrative, financial, an excessive strength of the Egyptian army is to be deprecated. But if that army is thus strictly limited, a really effective police will have to be organized. Such organization should be sufficient to strengthen the constabulary in keeping the peace, but not sufficient to enable the men to combine for mutiny or other disorderly purpose. The limitation of the military forces will add much to the importance of the police.

Again the prominence of the Bedouin Arabs in the deserts which impinge on the east side of Egypt, is a noteworthy feature in the present troubles. Their predatory habit and instinct have long been well known; but they are playing a part greater even than that which would ordinarily have been expected of them. They assemble apparently from all parts of the desert, and hang upon the borders of the cultivated delta, even venturing sometimes inside the inhabited tracts. Being often well mounted and evincing the active endurance which usually pertains to the sons of the desert, they inflict damage, inspire dread, and elude pursuit. It remains to be ascertained how far Arabi relied on Bedoüin co-operation when he dared to brave constitutional authority. Probably this reliance was considerable, and is partly justified by the event, for the Bedouins have proved useful allies to the rebels. The desert tribes then, despite any chastisement which they may now receive, will probably become more enterprising and formidable than they were before. It may be possible to arrive at some understanding with the head men among their tribes or clans, and even to enlist some of them on the side of order. Under any circumstances, it will be essential to display before them a resolute front. At all points accessible to them, a good system of police patrolling will be needful, while at some points military detachments may have to be employed.

The Khedive may ask for the presence of some European force, naval and military, for a time, to enable him to set his house in order. England is primarily interested in providing that the Khedive's authority, having been re-established by her at great cost, shall not be pulled down again. In the decision of this question the other European Powers will probably claim a voice. As the phrase, *beati possidentes*, is nowadays publicly used in Europe, it will perhaps be admitted that, if a foreign garrison is with the consent of Europe to be temporarily maintained in Egypt, the troops composing it should, under the circumstances, be British. Such a temporary British garrison need not be large, indeed might be comparatively small, if the Egyptian forces shall be kept at a reduced strength. The stations for the garrison would be Alexandria and Cairo, at both which places healthy cantonments can be found. It may well be held that the stay of such a garrison should be as brief as possible, if a feeling of self-reliance is to be restored to the native government. However cautious and moderate the diplomatic management may be, the presence of foreign troops must inevitably detract somewhat from the nationality and autonomy which presumably England desires to preserve for

Egypt. Such nationality too, while productive of moral good to the people, is quite consistent with loyalty and fidelity towards the Powers that have befriended and protected the Egyptian Government. Nevertheless, for the present, the maintenance of a British garrison in Egypt is absolutely necessary for overawing the fierce and unruly spirits that still lurk in all the centres of the Egyptian population, for ensuring general obedience to that authority which is about to be restored, for securing the safety of the Europeans who have been wrongfully driven away by recent disturbances, and who will be invited to return to their occupations.

For the civil administration of the country the Egyptian Government will require instruction and guidance. The manner of affording such guidance will probably have to be decided by England, after consulting the other European Powers. Still, for conducting this administration, Egypt should be taught to rely on itself mainly; assistance it may have for a time, but it need not expect to be kept permanently in leading-strings.

The principal requirements of civil administration in Egypt, as in any other Oriental country, have sometimes been partly fulfilled, but doubtless more often have been left unfulfilled. They are so well known that it may suffice to recapitulate them in a few words. In them are comprised a comparatively honest collection of the revenues, whereby the State receives its own fully, and the people do not pay more than is due; in other words, the prevention of peculation, whereby the State is cheated, while the tax-payers are overcharged; the concession of adequate salaries and the assured prospect of promotion, whereby, in combination with other good influences, a body of trustworthy officials is raised up; the assessment of the taxes on land at moderate rates for long terms of years; the extension of the reforms which have been already begun in the judicial system; the better diffusion of the popular education which has existed during many generations; the maintenance of the public works for communication and for irrigation, wherein the Egyptian Government has of late made progressive strides; and the undertaking of new works, for which Egypt offers facilities not surpassed in any country of the world. It were easy to show how all these things could be devised for Egypt by the British Government, which has acquired a noble experience elsewhere. But that would really imply nothing less than British administration, which under existing political conditions is assumed to be out of the question. The British military operations were undertaken on the express basis of maintaining the Khedive's authority,—in other words, the Native Government; and that precludes the idea of British administration, which could hardly be contemplated except under an alteration of the surrounding conditions politically. Nevertheless, if progress towards these administrative results or something like them be not effected, Egypt will be in constant danger of falling into trouble. The propelling influences of the nineteenth century are so potent, the demands of an advancing civilization are so inexorable, that an Oriental country in a prominent position, as Egypt is, cannot practically stand still. It may march in company with the age and so hold its own. Or it may resist these complex agencies and try to stand still; but stagnation will soon turn to retrogression, and then the decline towards the final fall proceeds at an accelerated rate. There are some remote or isolated countries in the East where stagnation may endure for many generations without the national system being broken up. But the delta of the Nile is not one of these; and in consequence of her noble situation (irrespective of many other causes), a national Egypt, if unreformed, unenlightened, and unimproved, cannot last very long. If it be desirable, as it actually is desired, to maintain a Native Government in Egypt, then order, retrenchment, progress, and improvement are essential conditions. It should be the object of England, then, to teach the Egyptians how to acquire these things for themselves.

It would not be possible to instruct the Egyptians in the art of government by introducing British officers into most of the important offices in the interior of Egypt, as has been done in British India. Such officers would doubtless effect much good, but they would virtually do the work, and the Egyptians would be inapt at learning so long as a foreign agency was at hand to perform the business for them. It is the sense of responsibility which quickens the faculties of men, and necessity is the parent of self-help. Let the Egyptians be impressed with the consideration that there must be a decent administration, if they are to remain a nation, and that they must work out the problem for themselves, then they will soon begin to learn. The notion of a Ministry, in which each member is the responsible Minister for some Department of State, has taken some root in Egypt. Although some Khedives seem to have treated their Ministers as secretaries only, still the heads of State Departments will practically be the depositaries of much real power. Whatever may be the character of Egyptian statesmen generally, there have been honest and capable persons among them. Here then is a ready-made school for Egyptian statesmanship, and if the Khedive will really search for capable men, he will doubtless find them more and more among the rising generation of educated Egyptians.

Then there is the chamber of representatives, known as the Assembly of Notables or Delegates. The institution of this Assembly some years ago is one of the most noteworthy experiments yet made in any Oriental country. Whether the mode of election was rude and informal or not, the members were elected. When they first met they had only a vague notion of their future functions as virtually a controlling body in the State. They seem, however, by degrees to have warmed to their work, and to have passed some important votes on public questions, which votes were respected by the executive power. This chamber, like many other reformed bodies, must have been paralyzed by the recent events; still its resuscitation ought to be a primary object when a new settlement of Egypt comes to be made. There may be difficulty in arranging an efficient system for conducting the elections; but as the Egyptian Government had the courage to begin some years ago, it should persevere, when its general functions are restored after the conclusion of military operations. As all Englishmen know, institutions of this description do not attain any large growth in a generation, even in a century. Still, new constitutions have a great advantage in the dearly bought experience of the most advanced nations. There does not seem to be any clear evidence as to what the duties of the Egyptian Assembly have been. The following passage may be extracted from the work of a very competent observer (McCoan's 'Egypt as it is,' p. 117):—

"In 1866, the Khedive revived the defunct Assembly of Delegates, one of the inchoate reforms projected by Mehemet Ali, but which had not met since his death. This germ of an Egyptian Parliament consists of village sheikhs and other provincial notables, elected by the communes, and assembles once a year to receive from the Privy Council a report on the administration during the twelvemonth. Its function is also to consider and advise on all proposed fiscal changes, new public works, and other matters of national concern that may be laid before it. It has, of course, no legislative power; but in practice its recommendations are received not merely with respect, but are often acted on by the Government."

Now the political growth of this Assembly may be judiciously fostered; and there is a hopeful chance of its voice being raised on behalf of the improvements already enumerated, most of which tell in favour of the people. It will ventilate grievances, and will give expression to the griefs of millions who are practically inarticulate. It will operate to some extent as a check on the corruption and peculation which are the prevailing vices in the official circles of almost all Eastern countries, and from which Egypt is not as yet exempt according to impartial testimony. It will probably be jealously opposed to all expenditure, without much regard to the reasons which may justify or necessitate the outlay; as experience in other Eastern countries, under foreign rule, has shown that whenever the natives are able to make their voice heard, they object unsparingly to the public expenses incurred by their rulers. It will be likely to follow the same method with the indigenous ruler, in the belief that the disposition to incur expense on improvements is really inspired by European example. Thus its financial influence, though in many respects tending to wise economy, will in some respects be harmful as hampering beneficent expenditure on public improvement. But it is not likely in the immediate future to be allowed by the Government to exercise a Parliamentary power over the State purse. Without, however, possessing such a power as that, it may by criticism of annual budgets, and on other occasions, obtain considerable influence over the finances. In British India the ultimate power in effect rests with the Government; still, new taxation cannot be imposed without votes by the Legislative Councils, of which non-official persons, both European and Native are members, and of which the debates are free and public. Though in practice the Government can appoint official members enough to ensure a majority, still the feelings of the non-official sections of the Councils are much regarded. A similar result would doubtless ensue if some plan of this sort were to be tried in Egypt. Either, as in British India, the Government might be empowered to appoint official members; or if that were deemed unsuitable for Egypt, the Government might retain the power of overruling the decision of the Assembly. This might *primâ facie* appear to be an arbitrary procedure; but the tendency would be for the assembly to win its way more and more, and for the Khedive to become less and less disposed to override its decisions. Moreover, the freedom and publicity of its debates would soon stamp a mark on State affairs, even though its decisions were not final. The consciousness that men may say publicly what they think and feel (within reasonable and well understood limits) must produce among Egyptians the same effect as that which it has long produced among European nations, and which it is beginning to produce in British India.

Again, respecting ordinary legislation much more may be done by the Egyptian Assembly than seems to have been heretofore attempted by it. There appears to be a judicial machinery in Egypt which, if not good as yet, is surely improvable. Whether it has any reasonably framed laws to administer, or any comprehensive code to follow, except the Korân, may be doubted. In many departments of social life, the Korân commands the affectionate obedience of Muhammadans. But the advance of civilisation in Egypt will be creating a host of contingencies for which no system of Oriental law makes adequate provision. This civilisation too will virtually establish a reign of law, and participation in law-making is found in British India to have an excellent effect on the native mind. There, nothing is done in civil administration without law, and the legislation is conducted in the councils mentioned above, though a scientific shape is given to the laws by English jurists. Much legislative experience of a peculiarly suitable kind has thus been amassed, by which Egypt may profit, if she will.

But in a country like Egypt the enactment of laws will be only one step in good government. Another important step is to secure competent and honest administrators for giving effect to the laws. Now Egyptians, if properly educated, well paid, and placed in assured positions with favourable prospects, will surely evince honesty and ability. This has been found the case in British India, and a different consequence is not likely to arise in Egypt. It must indeed involve some expense, but the cost will be repaid a hundredfold by the results of honest administration.

Once more, British India affords an example applicable to Egypt, in respect to the working of the elective principle in municipal corporations on a large scale. Many of the great Indian cities have their municipal affairs managed through bodies elected by the ratepayers. Notably the two cities of Calcutta and Bombay, with a joint urban population of nearly one and a half million of souls, have municipal corporations consisting mainly of elected members, chiefly natives. These two corporations together administer revenues of more than half a million sterling annually, and levy the local taxes. At first the ratepayers were apathetic respecting election, but by degrees they learnt their power, and now the system is either becoming popular, or at least mitigates the unpopularity which at the outset attends municipal improvement among an Eastern population.

Some administrators, possessing much old experience in the East, may be sceptical as to the practicability of inducing a Native State like that of Egypt to govern really well. But, in British India, the practicability of this is nowadays satisfactorily demonstrated. In past days, even during the preceding generation, there was much misrule in the Native Indian States. But during the present generation, owing to British influence, many of these Native States are fairly governed, and some few are managed nearly as well as the British territories. The number of States thus ruled respectably is increasing from time to time. Individual talent and personal originality are perhaps better educed in the Native States than in the British territories. These States have produced and are producing many native administrators of an excellent type, among whom some may even be termed statesmen. All this augurs well for Egypt, as showing that, with some judicious guidance at first, she may ultimately become proficient in the art of self-government.

It were needless to make more than a brief allusion to the necessity of conciliating the priesthood and the fanatical classes in Egypt, who muster in especial strength at Cairo with its many mosques of historic interest or modern splendour. Much injury would be wrought to the cause of secular progress if the classes concerned in the religious ministrations of Islam were to imagine that the Khedive, under foreign influence, would gradually withdraw that countenance and support which they have long been accustomed to receive from their rulers. There ought, however, to be no reason for fearing any untoward conjuncture in this respect. The Native Government if left to itself will scrupulously regard the religious establishments and maintain their endowments. No British counsellor would ever advise it to do otherwise. The priesthood will probably claim a share also in the national education, and that need not at all interfere with the secular and scientific instruction. On this condition, then, such participation may fairly be conceded to them.

There seems to be no apprehension in Egypt as to any inequality between Egyptians and Christians before the tribunals, or as to any disabilities being inflicted upon Christians, such as those which have unhappily prevailed in Turkey. In Egypt the European community has already become an important member of the body politic. Whether Europeans be numerously employed in the public service for the future or not, there will probably be many Europeans engaged in trade and industrial enterprises. The outrages at Alexandria and Tanta will have given a shock to such undertakings, and it is hardly possible to say whether the distressed Government of Egypt will be able to fully pay the indemnity justly due to the sufferers, though doubtless each European Government will do its best on behalf of those sufferers who belong to it. Whether such compensatory efforts be successful or not, European energy will revive on the restoration of order. The closed factories will be re-opened, the suspended works will be resumed, and the external trade, already reckoned at fifteen million sterling annually, will increase. The presence of non-official Europeans in Egyptian jurisdiction will serve as a motive power in the country, and will operate in favour of reform and justice. They will form a class that must be treated fairly by the Native Government; and the Egyptians in general, observing this, will demand similar treatment, which sooner or later must be accorded.

In the future settlement of Egypt the question of the public debt will inevitably obtrude itself. At the present time the foreign holders of Egyptian securities do not seem to attract the sympathy of the British public. Indeed, the sentiments of many thoughtful Englishmen are apparently adverse to the claims of the bondholders. The terms on which the Egyptian loans were contracted are deemed by many to have been excessive, in favour of the European lenders, and against the Native Government. Such opinions have received some confirmation from official reports, and from other authentic or semi-official statements. Nevertheless the Egyptian Government contracted these obligations of its own free will and with its eyes open. Although many abatements had to be made from the claims of the creditors, still there was such a residuum of equity in the matter as to induce England and France some years ago to sanction a special arrangement being made by the Khedive. According to that arrangement, English and French officers were appointed by the Native Government to exercise a Financial Control for the fulfilment of the obligations concerning the Public Debt of Egypt. For this purpose the debt was reviewed, and presumably reduced to the amount which, under the circumstances, was deemed just and suitable. The Control thus exercised by foreigners, though technically limited to the management of the National Debt, did virtually improve the civil administration of the country. However diverse the opinions of well-informed persons may be as to the propriety of thus controlling the affairs of the Public Debt, there appears to be a consensus of opinion that the Control has produced immense and untold benefit to the Egyptian people.

It will be said, no doubt, that recent events have shown how adverse many Egyptians are to this Control. It is indeed very difficult in an Oriental country to gauge the opinion of the people. Two things may, however, according to Eastern experience, be surmised with some confidence—first, that the humbler classes, cultivators, artisans and traders, will be in favour of the

Control as a system which ensures to them a comparatively just Government and moderate taxation; second, that several classes, official or other, will be hostile to this system, because it impedes or prevents the illicit gains which, hydra-headed, are sure to be rife in Egypt as elsewhere in the East. These considerations may perhaps be found worthy of the attention of those who, in the first instance, are impressed with such high-sounding phrases as "Egypt for the Egyptians," and "the National Party." If the Egyptian classes, from whose mouths these cries proceed, could be exactly analysed, it might possibly be discovered that the agitation has but a limited significance. In this agitation there are doubtless several elements, among which national aspirations and religious sentiments must be reckoned; one element, however, consists of special interests which would be deemed objectionable, and will not be avowed. Among the enemies of the Control, and in the rebel camp itself, there may be individuals who, however misguided have patriotism in their hearts.

Be that as it may, there remains the fact that this Control was deliberately sanctioned by England and France, and has operated for several years with undoubted benefit to Egyptian credit and to the native population. Its abandonment, then, in the future settlement would at the least be difficult, unless something equivalent shall be substituted. Those who have heretofore been in favour of this Control will hardly be convinced that the recent disturbances afford a justification for its relinquishment. These events may, however, necessitate its reconsideration and modification. The conditions of the debt do indeed seem to have been reviewed carefully before the Control was established, and the Egyptian Government renewed its obligations. Still, if those whose views are entitled to respect shall think that there is anything immoderate or injurious in these conditions, they might be allowed an opportunity of vindicating that opinion. Or if the Control should be found to have in practice gone beyond its limited sphere, and to have interfered more than was absolutely necessary with the Egyptian autonomy and administration, then the rules of conduct might be modified. At all events if the existing control be abandoned the British Government must see that an adequate substitute is provided.

Lastly, as regards the Suez Canal, some eminent authorities connected with the Canal Company seem to object to this great work being made the base of military operations. Several interesting arguments have been adduced in favour of that view. But, whatever may be the value of that contention under certain circumstances and conditions, there is no doubt that the British Government, proceeding with the consent, indeed at the declared request, of the Khedive, is altogether entitled to use the Canal for suppressing by armed force a revolt in Egypt. The British commander is acting on behalf of the lawful ruler of the country, the Khedive, against proclaimed rebels. The Canal is unquestionably in Egyptian jurisdiction. Though constructed by French genius and enterprise, and in a large degree with French financial resources, still it belongs to Egypt, and is in part at least sustained by Egyptian resources. The British Government too has, as will be immediately recollected, acquired in it a not inconsiderable share. Its channel then is legitimately available to the Khedive and his British allies for the purpose of suppressing a rebellion against his authority. This limited proposition seems so clear that the bare statement of it may suffice.

But respecting this important water highway other international questions are understood to have been raised. The phrase, "neutralization of the Suez Canal," may sound strangely to British ears, and there may be doubt as to its exact import. If it mean that the Canal may be closed against British ships of war or military transport, then it surely will not be allowed by the British Government and nation. The reinforcements for the British troops serving in India and other parts of Asia, the munitions of war, the ships joining the British squadrons in

Indian and in Chinese waters, pass through the Canal. The British mail service for India, China, and Australia, and a large part of British commerce with those regions, use the Canal highway. Potent as these interests are in time of peace, their cogency and urgency would be enhanced in time of war. Manifestly England must command the freest passage during peace, and it appears impossible that her discretion or her action should be fettered during war. Whatever privileges she uses ordinarily would doubtless be claimed equally by other nations. In the event of war it were perhaps vain to anticipate the form or forms which questions might take. The only point that need be presumed is this, that England must be free as regards her own action in the Canal for her military safety.

In conclusion, if hereafter the finances and resources of Egypt shall enable the Native Government to undertake enterprises beyond the limits of Lower Egypt, then magnificent schemes for utilising the river-water only await the means of execution in what may be termed the middle valley of the Nile. Beyond that again, in the upper valley of the great river, in the basins of the White Nile, the Blue Nile, and their tributaries, there is a productive area abounding in natural resources capable of sustaining a great population, but as yet scantily inhabited by tribes who, though now fierce, are not untameable. In this wondrous region a beneficent work can be performed, if the Egyptian Government shall fortunately acquire the power of performance. In this work Samuel Baker and Gordon have been the pioneers. If it languish for a while, it may be resumed hereafter. Then, if it be pursued to its legitimate conclusion, the results will be the suppression of slavery and the production of endless benefit to the human race in Northern Africa.*

* Since writing the article I have visited Egypt; and my information, gathered on the spot, confirms all that is stated in this chapter.—R. T.

# CHAPTER XX.

## ASPECT OF PALESTINE IN 1883.

[*Reprinted from the 'Evening News,' London, July* 1883.]

Peculiar benefit from travelling in Palestine — Best season for journeying — Atmospheric effects in stormy weather — Character of the scenery — Scriptural associations of the Holy Land — Relating to the Old Testament — Relating to the New Testament — Number and variety of sacred places — Holy sentiments gathering round them — Historical associations — Cave-cells and rock-hewn tombs — Antiquarian remains beyond the Jordan — Phœnician remains — Greek and Roman ruins — Herodian buildings — Monuments of the Crusaders' æra — Divisions of the present population — The modern Canaanites — The Jews in the land of their race — Political considerations — The Turkish administration — The Christian missionary establishments — Influence of the great European Powers.

Having recently returned from a pilgrimage to Palestine, I proceed to describe briefly the aspect of the Holy Land during the early part of the present year (1883).

In the first place, intending travellers would do well to consider beforehand the object for which they undertake a journey that, for Christians, is quite unique in its character, being wholly unlike any other journey that can be undertaken by them. If, after having heard reports, or seen illustrated books regarding 'Picturesque Palestine,' they proceed to the Holy Land in the same frame of mind as that in which they would visit Italy or Greece, or even Egypt, they may be disappointed, and may find their glowing anticipations suddenly chilled. It is this sort of disappointment which has in Palestine been sometimes called "disillusion." A little forethought would soon convince a cultured man that brilliant expectations must not be formed respecting the aspect of Palestine, seeing that the Land has not any Alpine features, being in altitude of mountains about equal to Great Britain; had never any exuberant vegetation, and has been denuded of the forests it once possessed; had but few fine examples of ancient art, and has long ago lost most, though not all, of the architectural monuments which existed; in short, has all the external drawbacks which are to be expected in a country that for ages was subject to war, devastation, revolution, and misgovernment. If, then, a man's mind is bent upon the glories of nature and the beauties of art mainly, to the exclusion of other subjects, he should hardly resort to Palestine. If he does, he will probably return declaring that there is but little to be seen there.

But if his mind be imbued with biblical, scriptural, and historical associations, with the sentiments relating to the traditions of the early Christians and of the religious bodies into which Christendom has since been divided, then Palestine will more than repay even the utmost labour that he can devote to its study. To him a pilgrimage to Palestine is the most instructive and interesting task which can be undertaken upon this earth. However wide his experience may be of travel in various lands, it will all pale in significance as compared with the experience which he will gain in the Land of the Book. However bright his visions may be of sunny climes in other quarters of the globe, they will be like "ineffectual fires" after the memories which are left in his soul by the sacred scenery.

It is from this point of view, then, that I shall endeavour humbly to portray, with the imperfection which is inevitable, some of the lessons to be learnt from a tour in Palestine. The imperfection, too, is aggravated by the circumstance that, while the subject is ineffably great, the tour must, from the character of the climate and country, be short.

At the best the tourist can have only eight weeks at a time for his tour, namely, two months in the spring and two months in the autumn. The winter is too rainy, snowy, and tempestuous for travelling, while the summer is too arid, sultry, and feverish. Ardent travellers, braving the midsummer heat of this land, have sometimes left their bones there. It is difficult to choose between the two seasons of spring and autumn, each season having its special advantages. In spring the vegetation bursts into a brief awakening after a long slumber, the young crops are waving in the valleys, the fruit orchards are rich with blossom and foliage, the rugged hillsides are gay with wild flowers. But then there is the liability to showers or even rain-storms, that vex the traveller, who is necessarily a dweller in tents. In the autumn, on the other hand, the weather is much drier and more settled—a great comfort to the tourist as he marches. But then the vegetation has become parched, and the rich colouring of the landscape has been reduced or lost.

It is always to be remembered that, with the exception of some thirty miles of carriage road between Jaffa, on the Mediterranean coast, and Jerusalem, there are no roads. The only mode of transit is on horseback, even for ladies, though, under unusual circumstances, a sedan chair or a litter can be arranged for an invalid. But the whole country is threaded by bridle-paths, which, though rocky, muddy, or steep in parts, are quite practicable for an ordinarily good horseman or horsewoman. The horses, too, gallant and enduring little animals from the regions beyond the Jordan, are all that can reasonably be desired in respect of speed, steadiness, and surefootedness. Complete facilities also exist nowadays on the spot for hiring interpreters, muleteers, servants, tents, baggage animals, and for obtaining supplies of food.

I was obliged by circumstances to essay the journey somewhat before the advantageous time — that is, during the last days of winter and the first days of spring—and was, in consequence, exposed to some storminess of weather and some vicissitudes of climate. But for the consequent discomfort (such as it might be considered) there was ample compensation in the atmospheric phenomena which were witnessed, and in the cloud effects setting off the sacred landscape or stirring the imagination of the beholder. It is at such moments that grand things are beheld. The tempest gathers up in black masses behind Jerusalem, while gleams of heavenly light irradiate the city; the Mount of Olives is aglow in the effulgence of sunset; the Dead Sea in the morning is as dark as Erebus, and at eventide is an azure-emerald expanse contrasted with a rosy splendour upon Nebo and Pisgah; a deep gloom settles upon Carmel, while thunder rolls around the mountain; the great Hermon, the place of the Transfiguration, pierces the skies with a snow-clad pyramid; the Jordan rushes along in muddy whirlpools; the brook Kishon suddenly becomes an unfordable torrent; the lake of Gennesareth is lashed by furious gusts into waves like those of the sea; the hail rattles with impetuous descent on the uplands of Galilee. It may be truly said of those who are on the hill-tops of Palestine in bad weather during wintry months, that they see the wonders of the Lord.

At such times the tourist should be wary; the wet rocks may be slippery for the horses feet; the clayey soil of the Esdraelon plain may be turned into a quagmire; the brooks and the ravines may be surcharged with rushing water; the shore of the Mediterranean may be dotted here and there with treacherous quicksands. Even if the traveller passes through all this without harm, there is always some risk of the baggage being injured or lost. Nevertheless, English ladies year after year successfully encounter these hardships; though delicately nurtured at home, they march through Palestine despite the fatigue, being doubtless sustained by the mental stimulus which springs from surroundings of matchless interest.

It would be generally thought better to avoid journeying too early in the year before the spring, with its comparatively settled weather, shall have set in. For the tourist, April is, on the whole, the best month, and constitutes for him the very cream of the year. Then the sky, though finely diversified by clouds, is for the most part azure; the ground is carpeted by "the tender grass that springeth up with clear shining after rain"; the wild flowers are seen to exceed the array of Solomon in all his glory. Later on, the month of May is quite tolerable, though the temperature of course becomes hotter, and the lady traveller will become sunburnt. After that month the heats of summer gradually supervene, until the sky becomes like brass and the earth like iron.

Still, at the best, the tourist ought not to reckon on uninterrupted fine weather, and must be prepared for the discomforts of wind and wet in very small tents. For the tents obtainable in Palestine are not like those to which British people have been accustomed in India, and are unavoidably distressful during a rainfall. The question then arises whether the tourist, under stress of weather, can find some shelter better than that of tent canvas? Well, he usually can. The country being interspersed with villages, some cottage can almost always be turned into a lodging for a few hours of the night or the day, even for ladies. But such lodgment is undoubtedly fraught with discomfort. Far better than this, however, is the shelter afforded by the convents and monasteries (of the Greek and the Latin churches) which are to be found in most parts of the Holy Land. These institutions are very hospitable to European travellers of all races and of all religious communities. The reception given by the abbots and friars to the way-worn or storm-battered tourist is friendly and gracious, being manifestly inspired by the sentiments of Christian kindness. There is in their bearing that dignified simplicity which arises from the contemplation of things beyond this material sphere. The stone staircase, the long corridor, the vaulted bedchamber, are refreshing to the eye and invite repose. Such are the conventual buildings at Bethlehem, at Marsâba (near the Dead Sea), at

Jericho, at Nablûs (near Samaria), at Nazareth, at Tiberias (on the margin of the Sea of Galilee), at Acre, and at Sidon. Among these structures, the monastery of Marsâba, built on precipitous heights in the wilderness of Judæa, is one of the most weird and wildly picturesque features in the land.

Hospitable kindness is also dispensed in emergency by the establishments of the Anglican missions at Bethlehem, at Nablûs, and at Nazareth. Mention need not in this respect be made of Jerusalem, for there the European hotels afford ample accommodation.

It may further be satisfactory to travellers to know that British medical aid can be obtained at Jerusalem and at Nazareth. In event of sickness or of accident, the sufferer or the invalid, if on the Mediterranean side of the Jordan, can, without any serious delay or difficulty, be brought within reach of medical treatment locally, and then carried to one of the points on the coast, such as Jaffa, Haifa (near Carmel), or Beyrout, where the steamers touch from week to week. But if he have penetrated beyond the Jordan, then he can neither obtain aid locally, nor can he be transported easily to the coast.

Throughout the Holy Land there are places which not only invite, but constrain the student or pilgrim to pause and linger. But this is emphatically not the Land for him who is a lover only of the picturesque without reference to other considerations. Nevertheless the Land abounds with subjects in detail which accomplished artists have deemed worthy of their pencil and brush. There are also views which, though not at all to be placed in the first or even the second rank of picturesqueness, are yet absolutely fine; such as the prospect from the top of Olivet, overlooking Jerusalem; from the mountains overhanging the Jordan valley, near Jericho; from the heights surrounding the plain of Esdraelon; from the beetling crags of the promontories between Tyre and Sidon.

Opinions will differ as to the charm or otherwise of a sojourn at one or other of the principal places. To many, Jerusalem, though indescribably interesting for a visit, would seem depressing for a lengthened residence, as the memory of woes unnumbered is recalled at every turn. Wandering amidst the scenes of moral and material desolation, the pilgrim says inwardly, Lord, how long? and wonders when the Almighty voice, speaking comfort to the Holy City, will pronounce that her iniquity is pardoned, and her warfare accomplished. Bethlehem, however, standing on an eminence in the midst of a cultivated plateau, and facing towards the blue mountains of Moab that bound the horizon as with a wall, will be admitted by all to be cheerful. Nazareth, too, nestling beneath heights whence the eye can range from the violet-coloured Mediterranean to the snow-white Hermon, is truly a pleasant habitation.

The travelling arrangements of these days facilitate the journey from England to Palestine, in a degree which would have seemed incredible to the last generation. The easiest and the quickest way from England is by Brindisi and Alexandria. By this route, a traveller, leaving London with the weekly Indian mail, may start on Friday evening and arrive at Jerusalem on the evening of the Saturday week, which represents a journey of eight days merely. The only fatigue is the railway journey of two days and nights, but even then there is sleeping accommodation in the railway carriage. The rest of the journey is by sea from Brindisi to Alexandria, thence to Port Said (head of Suez Canal), and to Jaffa, the port for Jerusalem. From Jaffa there is a drive by carriage of eight hours to the Holy City.

Having thus mentioned some of the points which concern the tourist in Palestine, I proceed to treat briefly of the biblical and scriptural associations relating to the Holy Land.

A primary advantage of the journey is this, that thereby the reading of learned books, which at home may seem difficult, becomes vitalised and energised; indeed, endued with a new light and a fresh interest. The mind is at once receptive, and points, which were apprehended with dulness before, are now vividly impressed on the imagination. However well read a man may have previously been, he will find his knowledge systematised and his ideas perfected by a tour in Palestine.

The intending traveller ought to perform his preparatory reading, or at least refresh his memory, and verify the facts in his books, before he touches the shore of Palestine. Once arrived there, he will enjoy only the scantiest leisure for study. As explained already, climatic reasons will cause his tour to be rapid and urgent. He will probably be riding or standing about from morning till evening; and he will retire early to rest, as he must rise betimes. Apart from the many works to which learned persons refer, there are three books which a well-informed tourist should read, in part at least, before he starts—namely, Tristram's writings, Robinson's travels, and Thompson's 'The Land and the Book.' He would do well to carry with him Stanley's 'Sinai and Palestine,' and Farrar's 'Life of Christ,' as both these books are written in a manner which fixes the eye and assists the memory. If he fails to do this, he must at all events take the Palestine exploration survey map, and one or other of the recognised handbooks by Murray or Baedeker. The handbook of Baedeker contains accurate information in a compact form; but it is, from its nature and composition, somewhat too condensed to be attractively interesting. The handbook of Murray is more expansive, and is written in a literary style; the work is the fruit of study on the spot, and affords much delightful reading. It is therefore better suited than any other handbook for the cultured traveller. Above all things the pilgrim should always have in his pocket a Bible, which he can open on the instant as he rides along, and to which he can at need refer without dismounting from his horse. Of all possible guide-books for Palestine, the first and the last is the Bible itself.

At the outset the traveller will be disappointed, perhaps even shocked, by the superstitions which have sometimes gathered round the holiest things in Palestine. Occasionally he will be told silly tales which are quite unworthy of Christian intelligence. But he can shut his ears to that which his understanding plainly rejects, and can shake off the temporary disturbance which may have arisen in his thoughts.

Sometimes, too, he may deplore the unseemly and violent disputes which spring up between the members of the several religious Orders. For instance, it is melancholy for him to see Turkish sentries (who are necessarily Muhammadans) mounting guard at Bethlehem over the very spot where, according to Christian tradition, Jesus was born. On inquiry he will learn that this strange arrangement has been rendered necessary by the contests between some of the monks. But the unfavourable impression will soon wear off as he observes the religious discipline prevailing in the monasteries throughout the Land, and the quiet, saintly lives led by the monks at large.

Further, although some Holy Places are indicated by tradition only, which cannot be precisely verified, or which are even rendered doubtful by scientific inquiry, still an exceeding interest attaches to them as being the spots venerated by devout Christians during many centuries, and consecrated by pious memories of many generations. For instance, some of us may not feel assured that the place known to Christendom as the Holy Sepulchre is actually the spot where Our Lord was buried and rose again, still we revere the place, remembering how many historic persons and how many pilgrims, men and women, whose names, as we believe, are written in the Book of Life, have knelt and worshipped there during successive ages.

The list is very long indeed of places which are mentioned in the Bible, but which have not yet been identified by modern research.

But apart from all places regarding which any reasonable doubt may exist, there is quite a wealth of known sites which are indissolubly bound up with the record of both the Old and the New Testament. Respecting these sites there is historic certainty based on scientific inquiry. Imperfect, then, must be the knowledge that fails to appreciate such scenes; hard must be the heart, and dull the imagination that is not touched by them.

Respecting the Old Testament, the most antique site is Bethel, a short day's march, say about ten miles, north of Jerusalem. From the heights surrounding Bethel the spectator looks down into the valley of the Jordan on the one side, and can just descry the sea-line of the Mediterranean on the other. Here he sees the eminence whence Lot and Abraham, casting their eyes to the right and the left, decided on the division of the Land between them. Here he sojourns close to the fountain where the cattle of Abraham used to drink, and Sarah filled her water-pitcher, to the spot where the Patriarch encamped, where Jacob dreamt of the ladder ascending to heaven, and where Jeroboam set up his unhallowed altar. Around the Dead Sea may be seen traces of the sulphurous and bituminous elements which, ignited by volcanic agency, destroyed Sodom and Gomorrah with almost instantaneous conflagration, and turned the then smiling or fertile basin of the Dead Sea into a truly death-like wilderness. The mound may be distinctly observed, which is still called Dothan, and which bore that name in the days when the sons of Jacob sold their brother Joseph to the Ishmaelite caravan on its way to Egypt. On the site of Joshua's Jericho there is a pleasant resting-place to-day, amidst the irrigated gardens which are but the feeble successors of the famous gardens that once made Jericho one of the queens of the East, and the envy of surrounding tribes. Climbing the stony heights of Ai, we may discern the wooded hollow where the Israelite soldiers lay in ambush before delivering their assault. At Shiloh we have the very spot where the Tabernacle, with the Ark of the Covenant, was set up, and near which the twelve tribes were assembled yearly for their sacred festival. Here is a structure raised in subsequent ages, and now ruined; a tall and aged terebinth tree overhangs the ruins, stretching its withered arms and weeping, as it were, with its dependent branches over the desolation of what once was the holiest of holies. At moonlight in Ajalon, the moon seems to stand still over the valley once terraced with fruit gardens, but now covered with the *débris* of destruction. We may ascend the commanding hill of Mizpeh, where the assembled Israelites elected Saul to be king, swearing fealty to him, and the hillock of Gibeon, where Solomon received from God the promise of wisdom and understanding. There are yet the pools whence the greatest of Jewish monarchs brought water by aqueducts to the Holy City. The barley crops still grow on the very fields (near Bethlehem) where Ruth gleaned in the lands of Boaz. The torrent-bed in the vale of Elah still has smooth stones, of the same sort as those which David chose for his sling in the combat with Goliath. Gilboa may be identified, where the victorious Philistines charged uphill, crushed the Israelites, slaying both the king and the heir apparent, and where David uttered his poetic lamentation over Saul and Jonathan. The caves may be traced in one or other of which Elijah received sustenance from the birds, and the brook Cherith still runs pellucid. On the summit of Carmel is to be seen the place where Elijah bade his servant watch for the little cloud rising from the sea; and whence Elisha descried the Shunammite coming across the plain to him for succour on behalf of her lost son.

In and about Jerusalem itself, despite the superincumbent *débris*, together with the confusion caused by sieges, by spoliation, and by the Moslem conquest, we may perceive many points that have been consecrated by the record of the Old Testament. There are still to be observed the tomb of David on the top of Zion; the hollow dividing Zion from Moriah; the quarries whence the stones were taken for the sacred edifices; the subterranean structures beneath the Temple itself; the valley of Jehoshaphat and the ravine of Kidron between the temple site and Olivet; the rock-hewn village of Siloam; the gloomy Tophet, horrid with memories of Moloch sacrifice; the vale of Hinnom, walled in with rocks and adorned with olive-groves; the King's gardens, whereby the last of the Hebrew sovereigns escaped for the moment from the besieging Assyrians.

From one view on the road between Samaria and Galilee we behold a scene fraught with the memories of both the Old and the New Testament. At one comprehensive glance the eye takes in Carmel, Gilboa, Tabor, Little Hermon, Jezreel, and at the same moment Nazareth, Galilee, the hills of Tiberias, with the Great Hermon overlooking all. Perhaps there is no other view on earth which commands so many sacredly classical points as this.

In the Old Testament the sacred topography is set forth in but few words, and yet with such marvellous fidelity that identification after several thousand years is satisfactorily possible. The inspired writing, in this as in numberless other respects, commands our veneration and serves as a model for human thought. In the New Testament the notice of localities is not always specific in an equal degree.

Nevertheless, if we cannot identify for a certainty the eminence of Calvary, and cannot know exactly the site of the Crucifixion, yet we have a reasonable conviction regarding the sites of many among the events of Our Lord's life on earth. We note, with the confidence arising from scientific geography, the spot where He must in childhood have gone daily with His Mother to draw water from the fountain at Nazareth; where He received baptism from John on the bank of the Jordan; where He endured Temptation on the arid top of a scarped hill; where He propounded the practical doctrines of Christianity near the Lake of Gennesareth; where He chose His disciples from among the fishermen of the then thriving shore, whose fisheries are now extinct; where He ministered constantly at Capernaum, Chorazin, Bethsaida, and Magdala, whose sites are now overgrown with thistles; where, standing on Galilean uplands, He pointed to a city built on a hill; where He unfolded the spiritual character of Christianity to the woman at the old well (now dried up and ruined) near the base of

Gerizim; where He laboured for good among cities freshly embellished by Herod, Jericho (the new), Samaria, and Tiberias; where stood His favoured village of Bethany; where, to avoid the malice of the Jews, He rested awhile among the stony heights of Ephraim; where, looking at the rocky eminence near Cæsarea Phillippi (now Bânias), He declared that on Peter the Church should be built as on a rock; where, on His last and triumphant entry into Jerusalem, He paused at the angle of the road whence the Temple burst into full view, and then wept aloud over the fate of the City; where, after receiving the judgment of Pilate, He moved with the death procession towards the place of Crucifixion.

It is manifest from the configuration of the country that the so-called roads—they are really footpaths or bridlepaths—must be the self-same tracks as those by which Our Lord passed to and fro during His life on earth. Such are the lines or ways which now lead, as they must have then led, from Jericho by a sublime glen up to Bethany at the head of a long valley commanding a prospect of the trans-Jordan mountains, from Jerusalem past Bethel and Shiloh to Samaria, from Shechem by Engannin and Jezreel to Nazareth, from the heights over Nazareth by Cana of Galilee and Magdala to Capernaum. When the traveller, passing laboriously along such tracks from sunrise to sunset, considers Whose eyes gazed on this landscape, Whose feet climbed these rocks and trod this dust, Whose head bore this vertical sun or this pitiless storm, Whose wearied limbs rested in this shade, Whose lips drank of this rill or this fountain, Whose voice resounded amidst this scenery, Whose words caught up every image suggested by the habits of this people, the fruits of these fields, the flowers of these banks, the birds of this air—then he feels his mind lifted out of its poor self, and his "darkness lighted with the blaze of the bright ranks that guard the eternal throne."

Having touched on the sacred and scriptural associations of

Palestine, I propose next to touch upon the secular and historical, apart from the religious, associations of the Land, as they present themselves to the traveller of to-day.

Now, in respect to ancient history, though Palestine has often been the unhappy hunting-ground where imperial hunters have striven for the price of dominion, though it has been successively overrun by Assyrians, Persians, Egyptians, Greeks, Romans, it has fewer architectural remains than might perhaps be expected by the traveller. The tribes dwelling between the Jordan and the Mediterranean—whom the Jews dispossessed partially, but never entirely — left but few marks on the Land. The plain of Esdraelon, the scene of the future Armageddon, stretching from the base of Carmel, near Acre, on the Mediterranean, right across to the valley of the Jordan, near Ramoth Gilead, divides the Galilean uplands from the hilly plateau of Samaria and Jerusalem, and is, on the whole, the most sacredly classical plain on the earth. But it has no architectural remains to rivet the traveller's gaze, although in the vigorous words of Canon Farrar, "it had been for centuries the battle-field of nations—Pharaohs and Ptolemies, Emirs and Arsacids, Judges and Consuls, had all contended for the mastery of that smiling tract—it had glittered with the lances of the Amalekites, it had trembled under the chariot-wheels of Sesostris, it had echoed the twanging bowstrings of Sennacherib, it had been trodden by the phalanxes of Macedonia, it had clashed with the broadswords of Rome."

One class of objects is, however, to be found all over Palestine, and it consists of the caves, sometimes natural, but mostly artificial. These were occasionally excavated in order to serve as cells for hermits. But usually they were sepulchres, and from early ages the prevailing practice was to bury the distinguished dead in rock-hewn tombs. Here and there the hill-sides, or the rocky flanks of mountains, are honeycombed, as it were, with these cell-caves or tomb-caves. These excavations are not, indeed, at all to be compared with the rock-cut chambers of India, but are strangely interesting, and carry back the beholder's mind to the days of old.

But, if the antiquarian remains between the Mediterranean and the Jordan be scanty, still, beyond the Jordan, that is, on the eastern, or Arabian, side of that famous river, they are comparatively abundant. Here, amidst the tribes, whom the Israelites overcame before advancing into the Promised Land of Canaan, in the country of Nebo and Pisgah, of Gilead, Bashan, and Rabbath Ammon, are to be seen the remnants of hoar antiquity. Here, too, may be traced several cities evidently the seats of a lost civilization. We are often unable to conjecture by what race or what nationality they were founded. It is to this region that the operations of the Palestine Exploration, having proved very successful in the Holy Land on the Mediterranean side of the Jordan, were recently extended. They were at the outset resisted by the wild tribes of the neighbouring deserts, and then were for a time suspended by the order of Turkish authority. Such an interruption, ordered by the Turks, was naturally very unpopular with the scientific world in England, and occasioned some remark even in political circles. Allowance, indeed, ought to be made by us for the embarrassment of the Turks in such a case as this, for they dread the responsibility which would attach itself to their administration if the European explorers were murdered or outraged. Still it does seem monstrous that in the Trans-Jordan region—which is not wholly desolate, being partially cultivated and having even some towns —certain wild tribes should be able to stop explorations of high interest to the scientific public, and, what is more, to the Christian world.

Then, adjoining Canaan, and generally within the limits assigned by the Old Testament for the heritage of Israel, the Phœnicians have left on the face of the country countless marks of their mighty handiwork. These marks, if abandoned to the ordinary process of ruin and decay, would prove to be well-nigh indelible. But the ruthless hand of man himself has been directed, with inauspicious skill, to obliterate the traces of human art and industry during the "juventus mundi." The antique cities. with their abundant masses of masonry, have been used as stone quarries by the builders of modern cities. The deeply-laid foundations have been torn up, the massive bastions undermined, the rounded pillars overthrown, the wondrous monoliths broken up, in order to provide materials for the structures of to-day. Heathen temples have been rifled of their bevilled basements, and despoiled of their tapering columns, for the purpose of beautifying Christian churches. The spoliation is actually stimulated by the consideration that the ancient masonry is greatly superior to any work which is executed in modern times. It is not so much that equal work cannot be performed nowadays, for within certain limits, anything is possible to engineering science, but that the cost would be almost prohibitory.

Thus, the traveller, riding along the beautiful coast from Acre northwards, past Tyre and Sidon, to the Lebanon, finds the whole way strewn with monuments of ages prior to the time of authentic history. His eye will be caught by a fountain, or a reservoir, or a cistern, or a terrace, or a paved floor, or a pedestal. Here he perceives that the jutting headland of wave-washed rocks was once crowned with summer houses for the enjoyment of sea breezes. There he stumbles over the *débris* of cities with long frontages and palatial edifices, regarding all which there is nothing known. At every step a mysterious voice seems whispering in his ear, "siste viator:" "stop, for thy tread is on an empire's dust."

At Tyre he can trace the points of its strategic and commercial topography; the old city built on the main land of the coast; the tight little island which was the seat of maritime superiority and where an almost invincible citadel was fortified; the sheltered harbour lying between the island and the shore, where the finest fleets of ancient commerce used to anchor; the approaches whereby Alexander the Great with his Greeks beleaguered and subdued the Tyrian might; the causeway which the Macedonian besiegers piled up with earth right athwart the strait between the coast and the island, in order that they might pass on the final assault of the sea-girt fastness. The city site is quite uninhabited now. But on the ground which was once the island, and is now the little peninsula, there is a town which, by its insignificance, mocks the pristine grandeur of Tyre.

At Sidon, on the contrary, the traveller can find nothing to remind him of the mighty past. A pleasant Syrian town, overlooking a sunny strand, a modern and picturesque fortress on a rock in the sea, connected with the town by an arched causeway, environs of orange groves, bending with the weight of golden fruit, and backed by the spurs of the Lebanon range—represent that which has succeeded the Sidon which was the mother and the queen of ancient commerce.

North of Sidon and near Beyrout, after an ascent of several hundred feet up a hill known as that of Derah-al-Kalaat, the traveller reaches a wonderful situation. On the summit he finds the ruins of a Phœnician temple; its massive pediments form a bold foreground, and its columns of amazing girth stand up majestically against the azure sky. Whichever way he turns he perceives a background worthy of the architecture; looking westwards he sees at his feet, far beneath him, the promontory and city of Beyrout projecting into the blue Mediterranean; looking eastwards he sees the hills, darkling with pine forests, and surmounted by the dazzling snows of the Lebanon peaks. Rarely is such a foreground combined with a background so lovely and diversified as this.

At Baalbec again, at the period which intervenes between winter and spring, when the heaviest snow usually falls, a wondrous combination of foreground and background is to be seen by the traveller. The ruins—which are among the most famous of ancient times and represent structures originally raised by the Phœnicians, and subsequently built over by the Greeks and Romans—rise up magnificently in masses of reddish-grey. In ordinary seasons, their long shadows under an eastern sun are cast upon an arid drab-coloured ground, and their background consists of hills, bleak, sterile, with yellow ochre hues. But the aspect of these unattractive surroundings is changed at this particular season, when winter asserts itself strongly before yielding to spring. Then the low hills are temporarily snow-clad and the whole ground is whitened with snow. Consequently the shadows of the lofty pillars are flung in dark grey upon the snow-white ground, and the sombre mass of primeval architecture is contrasted with a background of snowy hills which at sunrise are lit up with a fire of golden splendour, and at sunset are glowing with roseate tints.

After the Phœnician remains, there are monuments, though of a lesser calibre, belonging to the Greeks and the Romans. Following up his victory over the Persians on the banks of the Issus, to the north of Syria, Alexander the Great marched down the Tyrian coast. Then, having reduced Tyre, after the stoutest resistance that he ever encountered during his world-wide conquests, he determined on making a military road-line along the mountainous sea-shore. So he began a road which his successors carried on, and which the Romans completed. This roadway still serves for the traveller; it passes over the brows of several precipices whose bases are lashed by the raging surf. But though it has been left quite untouched and unimproved by modern administration, yet so well was it engineered in classic times, and so securely was it then constructed, that the rider of to-day passes along it without a qualm of misgiving, despite its apparently dangerous situation.

Next, under Roman auspices, Herod the Great became a mighty architect. It is strange that he, a man of the vilest disposition and the basest habits, should in this respect have evinced taste and culture. In fact, however, his efforts in this direction are attested by the rows of pillars on the hill-top of

Samaria, the structures on the margin of the Galilean Sea, the buildings at Herodium near Hebron, and the remnants of the new Jericho, where he built for delectation those palatial summer-houses in which he closed a mis-spent life by an agonising death.

In Herod's time, just before and after the Christian era, Cæsarea, on the Mediterranean, just north of Jaffa (now called Kaisariyah), Cæsarea Philippi, near the foot of Great Hermon (now called Banias), Tiberias, on the Sea of Galilee (now called Tabariyah), Neapolis, near Samaria (now called Nablûs), were the rising towns and the fashionable watering-places, the resort of all who were wealthy, and the centre of all that was gay in a pleasure-seeking age. The classic lovers of fashion in that day little recked of the religious movement then beginning in the neighbouring villages, which was destined to shake the world. The architectural work, begun by Herod, was carried on by the Romans. Of this work the half-obliterated traces may be discerned by the traveller of to-day.

But beyond Canaan the Romans pushed their administration across the Jordan into the heart of Moab and its adjacent regions. There the traces are to be observed of Roman causeways, theatres, aqueducts, quadrangles, fanes, and fortifications.

When rapid inroads were made upon the Roman Empire by the followers of Muhammad, mosques were, of course, erected in Palestine. Of these mosques one only can be placed in the first rank, namely, the mosque of Omar at Jerusalem, built on the very site of the Jewish Temple. This mosque—though not equal to the fairest edifices erected in honour of Islam, such as those at Delhi, Agra, Constantinople, Broussa, Cairo, Isfahan, Samarcand—is yet grand in size and rich in ornament. Its noble dome is now the most conspicuous object in Jerusalem, just as the Duomo is in Florence. In many places there are subterranean grottos of amazing picturesqueness, tenanted by ascetics of Islam and visited by Muhammadan pilgrims. Some of the Muhammadan cemeteries, too, attract the travellers' attention, such as that under the walls of Jerusalem, just outside the old enclosure of the Temple; and that established among the ruins of Tyre, where funerals belonging to a modern civilization are held amidst the sepulchres of antique nationalities, and the associations of death in its various forms are perpetuated from age to age.

When the rule of the crescent in Palestine was for a time interrupted by the soldiers of the Cross, the Crusaders enriched the Land with churches, chapels, and hospices, all of which are now, with but few exceptions, in ruins. Nearly every site that has been consecrated by the record of the Old or the New Testament, is still marked by the remains of some edifice dating from the Crusades. If the traveller stands on the ridge of Bethel, or rests by the well of Jacob, or broods over the desolate Shiloh, or mounts the hill of Samaria, there, right under his eye, will be the fragments of hewn stones, once piled up by the pious and heroic hands of mediæval chivalry. In the neighbourhood of Nazareth he may study the rendezvous where the last Christian King of Jerusalem mustered his forces for the final struggle with the Saracens—the battle-field where the European knights in heavy armour and mounted on sluggish horses, under a fierce sun, were beaten by the light-armed horsemen of Islam on their swift-footed steeds—the memorable hillock where the defeated Christians rallied round the Cross, their standard, and were slain as they stood. He remembers, too, that this hillock is the very place which some of the best authorities believe to be the Mount of Beatitudes. How wonderful is the thought that this terrific scene, for a long time fatal to Christian rule in the Holy Land, should have been enacted on the spot where the Sermon on the Mount was preached.

To this period pertain the monuments left by the Templars and the Knights of St. John of Jerusalem, who were truly the magnates of Christian chivalry. The ruins of the religious buildings belonging to the Order of St. John attest the greatness of its organization. At Ascalon, however, dedicated to the memory of the English Richard, the lion-hearted king, and at Acre, the supreme scene of knightly heroism, there is little to remind the traveller of that glorious history.

The Turks, after a possession of several centuries, have not succeeded in setting up any noteworthy monuments of their rule in Palestine.

But within the last hundred years the disputes between rival sections of the Turkish nationality have invited the interference of European Powers. The traveller, midway in the Esdraelon plain, sees the place where Napoleon's troops, under Kleber, contending against fearful odds, were victorious over the Turks. At Acre he hears the well-remembered tale of the British bombardment under Napier. It is melancholy for him to reflect that amidst scenery consecrated by the Gospel of Peace, there should have been heard the thunder of French and British artillery.

Having thus sketched briefly the Holy Land, I shall next advert to the people who dwell in it.

The inhabitants of Palestine to-day bear the same name as that which is familiar to us in Egypt, that is, "fellahin," or plural of fellah. Now the fellah of Palestine, like the fellah of Egypt, is the peasant proprietor, the son of the soil. In Palestine he is the descendant of the aborigines, to whom the Old Testament has given a deathless celebrity.

Travelling in the region between the Mediterranean and the Jordan, we behold the peasants toiling in their fields, we reflect that they are the Canaanites of to-day, and we call to mind the chequered fortunes which their race has undergone. Their ancestors were the Philistines, the Amorites, and the Jebusites. Before the Jewish invasion, these tribes worshipped their gods with rites generally barbarous and often shocking. After that event they were not all converted to the Jewish faith; on the contrary, they but too often perverted the Jewish nation to their religious practices. When the Assyrian power and the Persian monarchy subdued their land, they were doubtless as apt to follow strange deities as they had proved unwilling to believe in the one true God. In some tracts they yielded sullenly to the Jewish invasion, in others they were forcibly dispossessed. But they often turned to rend their invaders, and the chief tribe among them, the Philistines, held their own all along the Mediterranean coast, and thus confined the Jews to the mountainous tracts inland. With almost ceaseless struggle they maintained their nationality until the Greek conquest under Alexander the Great, when they, doubtless, were obliged to add the Hellenic deities to their pantheon. Under Alexander's successors they must have passed through a dreadful time, dwelling on the battlefield between the Græco-Egyptian dynasty on the Nile and the Græco-Assyrian dynasty on the Euphrates. At length they came under the settled sway of Rome and admitted the Latin deities to the celestial categories. Under the Herodian dynasty they had religious peace, and did not suffer themselves to be disturbed by the Christian movement. When the Roman power was Christianised, they still failed to be turned towards the pure faith of their rulers, and remained quietly in their idolatry. Their rest was rudely disturbed by the Muhammadan irruption. Their former conquerors had either left them to the enjoyment of their religious observances, or had been satisfied by their allowing to the gods of the new ruler a share in their veneration in company with their original gods. The Muhammadan conqueror, however, would accept no compromise whatever. Under him the one god, absolutely indivisible, must alone be worshipped. At the point of the sword he compelled the Canaanites to acknowledge the unity of his god. Having accepted this faith compulsorily in the first instance, they afterwards adhered to it willingly and *ex animo*. There is something in the faith of Islam which has always induced nations to cling to it fanatically, although they have been brought into its fold, not by conviction, but by force. Thus the Canaanites remained Muhammadans till the time of the Crusades. Whether the Crusading

Power, having won the dominion, converted them largely to Christianity, there is no certain knowledge, but it probably did not. They must have suffered sadly during the final contest between the Christians and the Saracens, and, after the utter defeat of the King of Jerusalem and the chief of the Templars, between Nazareth and Tiberias in A.D. 1187, they, at all events, relapsed into Islam, in which persuasion they have remained devotedly to the present moment.

Owing to war and misrule, their numbers have been cruelly thinned, while the fiercer, sturdier and wilder portions of their character have been hardened. They have independent feelings, but are destitute of the aptitude for social organization whereby alone their independence could be secured. The circumstances of their country conduce to isolation; the hills hard to traverse, and the raviny valleys tend to divide tribe from tribe, and hinder anything like national federation. Thus they have always been the prey of more organized races. Habituated to resist oppression as best they might, they have had their disposition soured; and to an external observer they present a somewhat unamiable appearance. Charitable consideration ought, however, to be given to their past sufferings and to their present disadvantages, while their sturdy industry is always to be admired.

The traveller, to the south of Jerusalem especially, is struck by the countless signs of former agriculture and habitation, as compared with the waste lands and the scanty villages now to be seen. The truth is, that those tracts where agricultural capital is needed have become deserted or neglected; while those tracts which can be cultivated by labour only, and without expense, are still fertile and well tilled. In those palmy days, when the Land flowed with milk and honey, long lines of walls, one above the other, were constructed along the steep hillsides with the stones that lay about in abundance. Thus terraces were formed which gathered up and retained the productive soil, the real "humus." Thus, too, were arranged the olive groves, the fig orchards, the vineyards of Palestine, which made its agriculture and horticulture famous for all ages. Those who have seen the terraced culture in the Lebanon or in the Himalayas, can readily imagine how beautiful must have been the same culture in Judæa of old. But such culture as this essentially requires capital, both to maintain the long succession of terrace walls and to keep open the irrigation channels. With warring and plundering, however, capital makes wings for itself and disappears, the terrace walls become dilapidated, and the fertilising watercourses choked up. Down come the torrents of rain, and the water, instead of being husbanded for human use, proves actually destructive. For it tears up the fertile surface, and carries off the "humus," which is no longer retained by the terrace walls. This is the process by which the gardens of Judæa, immortalised by Scripture, have been almost irreparably swept away.

But in the flat vales or in the champaign, where the soil has been from the configuration of the country, permanently maintained by nature, the cultivation is still excellent, and is pushed on to its utmost limits, even to the very verge of the unculturable waste. Thus it is that the littoral tract of Sharon, the plain of Esdraelon, the valley at the foot of Gerizim, the plateau around Bethlehem, the level areas amidst the Galilean hills, still display waving harvests as of yore.

In the valley of the Jordan, and in the eastern region beyond it, the people are the Bedouins, or the Badawis, the descendants of the Moabites and the Amalekites, and of the tribes that mustered under the standard of Og, King of Bashan. They have the virtues which usually characterize the sons of the desert. Though capable of a certain sort of self-government locally, they are thievish in temper, and look upon their neighbours' property as a natural hunting-ground. In their own homes they are better cultivators than might at first thought be expected. Beyond the Jordan, indeed, there is much cultivation and habitation to astonish those who may have regarded that region as a part of the great wilderness.

Though the Muhammadan Canaanites are not likely to be fanatical from their own disposition, their priesthood consists largely of foreigners from Arabia or Turkey, and these priests communicate a tinge of fanaticism to the population in many places, as may be perceived by every traveller.

There is still a small colony of Samaritans, who are interesting ethnically, but are not of any national or tribal importance.

In the thoughts of those who are considering the people of Palestine, the Jews will be uppermost. That several among the Jewish tribes never succeeded in winning the heritage which was allotted to them in the Promised Land under the Theocracy, is to be understood from the language of the Old Testament. This fact is, perhaps, best realised by those who travel in the country. The Jews, indeed, occupied the central territories, and possessed the general dominion of the Land; but over many divisions of it they had only a partial hold. Their territorial tenure having been interrupted by the captivity, was to some extent restored under Ezra, but was again depressed under Alexander's successors, until it was rehabilitated under the glorious *régime* of the Maccabees. When they were exterminated or expatriated after the capture and destruction of Jerusalem by Titus, they never returned in force to their native Land, which must for ever be endeared to them by associations of divine significance, and by valorous records of which even the most permanently successful nations on earth might be proud. Indeed, all the influences, which affected the Jews, also cherished a patriotic valour and a poetic temperament.

They retained, indeed, a hold upon Tiberias for some centuries after the Christian era, and in mediæval times they occupied Safêd (between Nazareth and Capernaum), both which places they rendered illustrious by Rabbinical learning. Otherwise they have never colonised, or reoccupied as cultivators, their ancestral Land. There are, indeed, a few thousands of them (the number is said not to exceed 12,000) now in the Land, gathered in the four cities deemed holy, Jerusalem, Hebron,

Tiberias, and Safêd. These are really immigrants, in birth and language foreigners, coming from all parts of Europe and some parts of Asia. Many come to sojourn as pilgrims, and many to lay their bones in the sacred soil. Their demeanour in Palestine is instructive to the student of human nature as showing the intensity which affection can acquire and the depth to which sentiment can penetrate. They mourn over the ruins of their once beautiful Safêd, crowning the most conspicuous site in Palestine, but overthrown by an earthquake in 1837. They love the consecrated earth at Tiberias, where the great Rabbis of the mediæval school repose. They kiss the rocks at Hebron, near Macphelah's cave, in reverence to that tomb of their patriarch forefather, which they are precluded by the Muhammadans from entering. They silently approach the stones which remain of Solomon's Temple at Jerusalem, and read the penitential psalms of David with tears and sobs. Once a week, on Fridays, they meet at this venerated spot to wail with passionate lamentation, and to pray that the kingdom, of which the monument is before their eyes, may be restored. In the valley of Jehoshaphat the vast number of their graves compared with the paucity of the living inhabitants of their race, shows how for many generations they have come in the evening of life to Jerusalem as their final resting place—*vedere e poi morir*. Seeing all this, the traveller realises the fact that "to them the very dust is dear." Indeed, it has been said of them, with literal accuracy, that "they moisten the stones of Jerusalem with their tears, and whiten the sides of Olivet with their tombstones."

Visions still float before the mind of Christendom respecting beneficence to be displayed towards the Jews in their own land. Missions have been established for their conversion to Christianity. Projects have been formed for their colonisation. Public works have been designed with a view, among other things, for their immigration. Long rows of cottages have been charitably built to accommodate the poorest among them. But whether these well-meant efforts will produce any large result, no man can say. Recently, when the Jews suffered persecution in southern Russia, and were either expelled or fled from that land of their adoption, there was some hope that they might be settled in Palestine. But the Turkish Government of the land does not seem to have encouraged the plan, and failure has ensued, be the cause what it may. Nothing, then, is occurring as yet to lift even a corner of that veil of obscurity which hides the immediate future of the Jewish race.

In the appearance of the people who now dwell in Palestine, there is much to attract the poet's eye, and to employ the painter's brush. Hardihood and endurance are stamped on the aspect of all classes. At some places, too, there is much physical beauty to be seen among the peasantry, as at Nazareth and Hebron. The habits and ways of the people, assembled in groups, are picturesque in the extreme. A painter, having a poetic insight and a masterly hand, might be thankful to have an opportunity of depicting the Jews pressing their foreheads reverently against the massive remains of Solomon's Temple—the Christians crowding the sacred bathing-place of Jordan at Easter-tide—the Latin priests chanting mass in the dimly lighted chapel in the subterranean tomb of the Virgin—the worshippers of the Greek Church kissing the stone-cut grave, where with the eye of faith they see their Lord buried—the women drawing water at sunset from the ancient fountains of Nazareth and Cana of Galilee—the armed parties, decked with eastern paraphernalia, winding round the base of Gerizim—the Moslem pilgrim sinking exhausted before shrines in the cave beneath the very site of the Temple—the caravan trending slowly along the glorious glen that leads down from Bethany to Jericho—the black tents of the Bedouin encampment, dotting under the mid-day glare, the sterile heights of the Judean wilderness and facing towards the distant mountains of Moab.

Having thus briefly described the Holy Land, its sacred and historical associations, and the people who dwell in it, I shall, in conclusion, advert to its political conditions.

The Land, it will be remembered, is under Turkish rule. That *régime* has been confirmed since 1840, when England took an active part in aiding the Turkish Sultan against the Egyptian Khedive, and bombarded Acre with the fleet of Napier and Stopford. Morally, then, England has been, in part at least, responsible for the consequences resulting to Palestine from Turkish rule. If these have not been good, they are, perhaps, not worse than the consequences would have been had Egyptian administration been permanently established there.

Among the many Turkish Pashas who have appeared in Palestine, many have doubtless been fair examples of the Muhammadan gentleman. Some, however, have exemplified the evil effect which the uncontrolled exercise of despotic power may have upon human nature. An instance of this forces itself on the attention of the traveller at Acre. His eye is caught by a mosque of some interest and beauty which is called the mosque of Jezzâr Pasha—a strange title, for Jezzâr in Arabic means butcher. Why, he asks, is it called the mosque of the butcher prefect? It appears, on reference and inquiry, that this was a real title assumed by a barbarous Turk, who with hardihood and capacity rose to power, who gloried in deeds of cruelty and blood, who combined fanaticism with ferocity, performing a pilgrimage to Mecca, and finishing a mis-spent life by building a mosque in honour of the religion which by his conduct he had dishonoured.

During the first half of the nineteenth century much disorder existed in Palestine; highway robbery was rife, the roads were often unsafe even for British travellers, and instances occurred recalling the immortal memory of the Parable which told of the wayfarer left for dead by robbers who was tended by the good Samaritan. English ladies occasionally underwent trouble from thieves and danger from bandits. But within the last twenty years the police administration has been much improved; and travelling is now practically safe from the Mediterranean coast to the mountain ridges which overlook the Jordan valley. But descending thence towards the Jordan the traveller must take with him an escort consisting of one or two Bedouins on foot, civil, active fellows and capital guides among the mountain paths. If he crosses the Jordan and penetrates into the interesting regions beyond, the strength of his escort must be increased. But if he passes beyond a certain geographical line in those regions, then no escort that he can reasonably take will ensure safety. In general terms it may be said that Turkish rule answers for order with tolerable efficiency west of the Jordan, but not to the east of the river, and that the absence of social control in that trans-Jordan quarter is discreditable. Indeed the slight control, which has been of late years attempted by the Turks there, is understood to be productive of harm rather than of benefit to the people.

The gradual growth of Christian establishments in the Land, the rapid increase of British and American tourists, and the augmented vigilance of public opinion, have caused the Turkish authorities to set their administrative house in order according to their feeble lights. It is not likely that nowadays any flagrant instance of misrule will occur; on the contrary, there will be found to prevail a certain degree of external propriety. Upon a closer inspection, however, it will be seen that the Government fails to bring into operation those influences which cause the creation and the application of capital, or the organization of productive labour. The old industries of Palestine have perished or are languishing, and the elaborate agriculture, which once adorned the slopes of the classic mountains and the everlasting hills, has shrunk to a shadow of its original self. In the great days of old, the arid portions of the landscape were relieved by the abundant olive-groves which, unlike the sickly grey tinted groves of southern Europe, have a rich dark green. Of these innumerable olives, some were planted in the hill-side terraces needing outlay of capital. Others grew at the bottom of the valleys, and could there be maintained with but little expense. Now those olives, which can be maintained only at some expense, have passed, or are gradually passing, away; those which can be maintained without appreciable cost survive, and thus in many places there are still to be seen splendid olive-groves yielding profitable fruit in something like the wildness of nature. This example is typical of the condition of Palestine generally.

Nothing is done for the making of roads in a rugged, but naturally rich territory, peculiarly needing "communications" for its development; and wheeled conveyance is practically unknown. The forests once formed a rich heritage with which the Creator endowed Palestine; but in most parts the Land has been deforested, and in consequence has become almost denuded of vegetation. The oaks under which patriarchs rested must in the fulness of time have passed away, leaving no successors, for there is hardly a trace of them now. The woods of Carmel and Tabor have been grievously thinned. The terebinths that once clothed the low hills near the mouth of Kishon are fast disappearing. The local supplies of fuel are becoming dearer and scarcer, and the importation of wood from without is increasing. Those who know the wood-markets of Jerusalem will say that the people, having used up the trunks and branches, are now exhuming the roots! Nevertheless, there is an extraordinary supply of fuel available within fifteen or twenty miles from Jerusalem, if only the means of conveyance were available. For the Jordan every winter brings down large quantities of dead trees, great and small, which have fallen from the sides, flanks, and spurs of the Hermon group of mountains. The rushing water flings these trunks and branches on the shore of the Dead Sea, where they lie and waste away, adding an additional feature to the deathlike aspect of the scene. The descendants of the cedars of Solomon and Hiram still exist, but are restricted to a comparatively narrow area. The forests of Bashan and Moab have, it is understood, been much less destroyed, doubtless because, being east of the Jordan, they are more beyond the reach of destructive agencies.

Nor is there anything done by the Provincial Government for the moral improvement or for the education of the people. Educational agencies are, indeed, at work in several parts of Palestine, but these are under European direction and are supported by European funds. Whether the English mission for the conversion of the Jews does or does not effect much for that particular object, it is certainly effective and beneficent in educating many waifs and strays among the poorer Christian children, and also the children of Muhammadans. In short, to its special work it wisely adds the general work of a mission in foreign parts. Similarly, the Church Missionary Society has establishments at Zion, at Bethlehem, at Nablûs (near Samaria), and at Nazareth. The Society for Promoting Female Education in the East has an excellent institution built on the brow of the height overlooking Nazareth, where girls of various Oriental nationalities, both Christian and Muhammadan, are collected in spacious and salubrious buildings. The education given there, under the supervision of Miss Dickson, is excellent, and by means of it seeds of good are sown among long-neglected races. A branch institution of this society has been set up at Bethlehem, with a fair promise of usefulness. Equally excellent, and larger in scale, are the educational institutions at Beyrout, the Syrian Protestant College, the American Mission, the Bible Schools under Miss Mott,—all which institutions are producing an effect upon the rising generation of Syria. Numerous schools for religious instruction, under European and American supervision, have been established in the interior of the Lebanon district, in the heart of the mountains. The educational funds in this portion of Syria, come partly from Britain but mainly from America. The Turkish Government, while doing nothing itself for popular education, yet offers no opposition whatever to the operations of these foreign agencies, and may be said to afford them some encouragement indirectly, as it protects them from the fanaticism to which they would otherwise fall victims.

Besides these, there are other institutions for humane and charitable uses. An ophthalmic *hospice* has been established recently at Jerusalem, under English auspices, for the curing of the eye complaints from which the people of Palestine suffer. It promises to be of immense service, and to illustrate the practical virtue of Christianity.* The Edinburgh Medical Mission has an efficient establishment at Nazareth. At Beyrout is the Institution of Prussian Deaconesses, and there also the Prussian Hospital is supported by the Order of St. John.

The Turkish Government doubtless regards with mixed feelings the influx of foreigners, who come partly for touring, but chiefly for religious or educational purposes. It cannot but be glad of the constant flow of money from these sources into an impoverished country. So large are the religious establishments at Jerusalem (belonging to the several Christian communions) that the management and custody of their funds afford employment to banking firms established for their sake alone. There is neither trade nor industry at Jerusalem; who, then, asks the traveller, are the customers for the bankers? and he is told, the religious bodies. To the west of Jerusalem on the Jaffa road an European suburb of considerable importance is growing up; fortunately, it is on that side of the Holy City where no sacred or historical associations exist. Prominent in this quarter is the Russian cathedral and convent. Here, too, the several European Powers maintain their Consulates. The English Consul especially, Mr. Moore, is well known to all his countrymen who travel in Palestine, for the readiness and courtesy which he displays, and for the accurate acquaintance he possesses of the Land and the people. The growth of European influence must work much good for the indigenous inhabitants, and must serve as a check upon misrule, though it cannot energise a feeble administration. Despite its material advantages, it must in some respects be distasteful to the natural pride of

* One of the prime movers in this benevolent enterprise is Sir Edmund Lechmere, of Worcestershire.

the Turks and other Muhammadan races. Many writers, having travelled in the country, affirm that since the era of Islam a torpor and a decadence, unknown even in the most troubled ages previously, have settled down upon Palestine; they mention the cities and the towns which existed before that time, and ask, where are all these now? Others will say that Palestine, though she is the "widowed queen," bereft of all her best resources, still has her inherent capabilities, which can be developed by good government. Given, they will declare, fifty years, nay, even twenty years, of British administration, and the wilderness would begin to blossom like the rose. All this may be true enough, and it may be quite right to bring out the truth; but the inference cannot fail to be displeasing to Muhammadans, who regard Jerusalem as second only to Mecca itself in sanctity, and allow it to be called by no name save Al Kuds, or the Holy.

But if the Turks can succeed in governing, perhaps not in an enlightened manner, yet with some degree of respectability, and in holding their empire together, they need have little fear from British ambition in Palestine. For though the Land is intensely interesting, it has but little value politically in comparison with the two neighbouring countries, Egypt and Syria. The importance of Egypt to England has become too manifest to need explanation. The importance of Syria, though lesser in degree, is still considerable. A portion of Syria, adjoining Palestine and surrounding the Lebanon, comprises the high road from the Mediterranean at Beyrout to Damascus. This line of communication is very much under the influence of France, as a French company engineered the road and maintains an efficient wheeled traffic along it. Still, Damascus, though in itself valuable, is hardly a goal of national ambition, for the communication thence to the Euphrates valley is difficult. The adjoining part of Syria, and the northernmost, which comprises the line from Alexandretta (near the ancient Antioch) to Aleppo, leading towards Bagdad on the Tigris, is most important to England. If she secures this line—which includes the best approach from the Mediterranean to Mesopotamia and the Persian Gulf, thus commanding an alternative overland route to India, second only in importance to the Egyptian route—she would feel less concern in the Damascus line, and still less in the country of Palestine, for the present at least, that is while the Turkish dominion is preserved.

In respect to all these questions the Turkish Government may be sure that many Englishmen, from a reasonable regard for their own national interests as well as from loyalty towards an old friend and ally, hope for the maintenance of the Turkish Empire in such a tolerable condition as may ensure stability and permanence. In other words it is hoped that the Turks will learn to govern their widely extended territory well enough to admit of their continuance in power, under the conditions which the opinion of an enlightened age will demand. But, at the best, the hope, however earnest, is a hope only. There is in many minds much misgiving lest the Turkish Empire should fall to pieces from its own dead weight. We desire, indeed, that this contingency may be long delayed, and that the Eastern Question may sleep yet awhile. But if such a contingency were to happen, then the future of Palestine would become a matter of anxiety to England, in common with other Powers, on political grounds. England would feel much less interest than some other Powers in the ecclesiastical questions touching the Land and the Holy Places. In those questions France and Russia would be primarily concerned, on behalf of the Latin and the Greek Church respectively. The memory of the dispute between the Latin and Greek monks regarding the repairs of the Church of the Holy Sepulchre, which led to the Crimean war, suggests forebodings as to what might happen. It is thought by many that (under a contingency which we hope may not happen) France would desire for the sake of the Latin Church to hold Palestine, but Russia would intervene. Or Russia, for the sake of the Greek Church, would desire to hold Palestine, but France would intervene. In either of these events (both of which are much to be deprecated) it is probable that French intervention would be more potent than Russian, as Palestine is accessible by naval force chiefly. From any dispute of this nature between the two Powers there would arise much anxiety to England on account of her adjacent interest in the East. This is indeed an example of the complications which might spring out of the Eastern Question if that were unhappily to be opened again. That it may yet remain closed will be the prayer of those who desire the peace of the world.

The position of England respecting Palestine may indeed be affected by the inchoate project for a ship canal to run from the Mediterranean shore near Acre by the valley of the Jordan to the Dead Sea, and thence to the head of the Akaba Gulf, a branch of the Red Sea. This project would serve as an alternative route to India, and would answer much the same purposes as those to be answered by a second canal through the Isthmus of Suez. There is no space here for discussing the geographical and engineering topics connected with this scheme. To many earnest people the thought of Scriptural sites, Jericho, Capernaum, Magdala, being submerged, is melancholy indeed. Probably no insuperable difficulty will be encountered until the neighbourhood of the Gulf of Akaba is reached, although there is something unique in the conception of filling up the depression of the Jordan and the Dead Sea with 1200 feet of water, in order that the inland lake thus to be formed may be raised to the level of the Mediterranean. The real difficulty may possibly arise in that section of the line which lies between the Dead Sea basin and the Gulf of Akaba; and this section remains to be examined accurately by engineering surveys. The result of such surveys must be awaited, before a judgment can be formed regarding the practicability of the scheme.

# CHAPTER XXI.

## SOCIAL SCIENCE IN THE BRITISH EMPIRE ABROAD.

[*Presidential Address delivered before the National Association for the Promotion of Social Science, at Huddersfield, October*, 1883.]

Extent of the British Empire abroad — Social science, as pursued in the United Kingdom, is applicable to the Colonies and to the Eastern dominion — Standard of physical comfort — Improvement of dwellings — Quality of food supply — Purification of water — Sanitation, drainage and sewage — Vital statistics — Hospital management — Production and distribution of wealth — The tenure of land — Emigration from India to the Colonies — Forestry and forests — Mental and moral training — National and popular education — Art culture — Ethical instruction — Social organization — Law Reform — Prison discipline — Reformatories and industrial schools — Friendly societies and savings banks — Support of the destitute — The Temperance cause — The Agents General for the Colonies — Local self-government in the East — Conclusion.

THE subject of my address is the application of social science to the British Empire abroad. To help us in raising our thoughts towards the height of a great argument, let some leading facts be called to our recollection. The area of this empire, at home and abroad, more than 8 millions of square miles, may fail to convey a definite idea; but the total of the population is instantly suggestive, as it amounts to 315 millions of souls. This population, too, is increasing at the rate of 2½ millions annually; in other words, by 25 millions every decade, or 50 millions in every twenty years. The total revenue amounts to 170 millions sterling yearly, and the external commerce of the United Kingdom, with all its colonies or dependencies together, to nearly 1000 millions sterling in annual value. These facts shew the empire to be the greatest and richest that the world has ever seen. It may also prove to be nearly the most numerously peopled empire as well; at all events, the number of its people is enormous. Out of that population, about 33 millions, equal to one-tenth, are in the United Kingdom, and therefore fall directly under the influence of social science, as we, subject to correction, understand the term. The remainder are either colonies, who, though giant offspring, may yet look to the mother country for some guiding example; or else alien, though loyal races, whom the British Sovereign has taken under parental protection in three out of the four quarters of the globe. From our point of view, then, each one at home who succeeds in improving, or neglects to improve, himself, will influence, for progress or for stagnation, nine other persons his fellow-subjects abroad; every result which we realise in the United Kingdom may be ultimately multiplied nine times in the foreign empire; and if we were to be nationally listless or inefficient here, then a similar listlessness and inefficiency would settle there among vast nationalities in scattered regions. Surely this consideration will help us to gauge the weight of our responsibilities under Providence, the grandeur of our opportunities, on behalf of ourselves as forming a mighty nation, and for the sake of other nations that are politically connected with us. Besides those colonies that are of our own flesh and blood, and for whom we feel as for ourselves, there are the almost countless tribes among whom the poorest, the most abject, has a bodily frame to be sustained, a mind to be enlightened, and a spirit to be moved. Thus regarded, the sphere of our study is indefinitely widened, and the magnitude of its scope becomes enlarged to an extent almost indescribable.

In many parts of this foreign empire the British Government leads up by its good administration towards the very results at which our Association, in common with many other associations, is aiming. But the administrative successes of the Government alone will not suffice. It is not enough that the State should secure external peace and internal order, should guard property and ensure to every man the fruits of his labour, should develop trade and promote material improvement, should enact laws and provide a trustworthy judiciary, should diffuse a sound education and encourage physical science—all which things are done well on a vast scale. We all feel that something more is imperatively needed. That something, then, is to be supplied by those studies to which the Association gives the name of Social Science, and to which other names have been, or may yet be, given.

We shall immediately find that all the social questions which have been agitated at home are, with hardly any exception, pertinent or applicable to the foreign empire, and that some additional questions belonging to our subject have arisen abroad.

When recapitulating the subjects on which this Association has spoken or written within the last quarter of a century, I shall not presume to claim for it any undue share in the credit of the reforms and improvements to which it has contributed advocacy. We duly remember that the force of events and the growth of opinion have helped to confer these benefits on society; and that other associations besides ours have applied their shoulders to the wheel of progress. But we can never forget the great names that have belonged to our annals, and we are content humbly to follow where Brougham, Russell, and Shaftesbury have pointed the way.

The aim of our study (by whatsoever name it should be called) is to render mankind not only prosperous materially, but also happy and wise, as individuals and as members of an organized community. Though we may have faith that there is a Light that can irradiate even the darkest prison-house, still for the most part we know that happiness and wisdom cannot be attained without a reasonable degree of physical comfort. It is practically vain to inculcate morality upon those who are huddled together in squalid tenements. It is impossible to obtain proficiency from half-famished scholars whose brain-power is enfeebled by hunger. The standard of physical comfort, then, has always been kept before the student's mind, and may constitute the primary division of my address.

Herein the foremost topic has been the improvement of dwellings. For this object something is being attempted at home, though we are saddened by the thought of how much remains to be done. Now, in India or in Egypt the self-same need presents itself to philanthropists. Amidst the villages, the peasants pen up the cattle inside the dwelling-houses. Amidst the largest cities, the artizans are crowded together in the compartments of houses many stories high, wherein to all the miseries which exist in our cool latitudes there are added the heat and malaria of the tropics. The dwellings of the poorest classes, close to the centres of civilization in the East and the West, often exemplify terribly the eastern proverb that the darkness is deepest right underneath the candle! In the colonies, again, we hear that while the settler dwells in the comparative discomfort of draughty huts, with chinks that admit the outer air, he remains healthy. But when the squatter population begins to congregate into villages, and cottages of another sort are built, then typhus and zymotic disease appear.

Again, the quality of food supply is a matter with which our studies are rightly concerned at home, and this object is almost, though not quite, equally important abroad. Respecting adulteration of food, there is not the same temptation in the thinly peopled and abundantly productive colonies as in a densely peopled island like Great Britain. In the East the natives have not yet acquired much proficiency in that dark science, though they might prove but too teachable if once this black art were to gain ground at home. For instance, on one occasion when a malignant disease broke out in the port of Calcutta, the native contractor for the supply of water to the shipping was found to have adulterated the pure liquid from the waterworks with some impure fluid from the river! Still, irrespective of what may be termed artificial evil, imagine the natural evil to which articles of food or drink are liable in the tropics—such as the exposure of meat in the burning heat of an Oriental city, or the fish in coast districts where fish is extensively cured, and where the curing is but too often imperfect. If the pure and wholesome quality of food for the masses of humanity congregated in the British metropolis is a theme for study, equally must this be the case for a city like Bombay, where 700,000 people are compressed into a little island situated at some distance from the main sources of sustenance. Again, the subtle conveyance of poison through the medium of milk causes solicitude here. But the danger is even more active and urgent in the East, where, from the habits of the milkmen, the milk is but too frequently affected by poisonous ingredients. If time permitted I could give signal instances of valuable lives being lost from milk-poisoning, not by any evil design, but simply through reckless ignorance.

The purification of water for drinking and for bathing has always been among the objects of our studies, and some benefit has accrued from persistent advocacy. There is dread lest impurity in this element should produce untold evils in the United Kingdom; but we know that in India it has produced more physical mischief than any cause whatsoever, and perhaps as much mischief as all other causes put together could produce. In the capital cities, the Indian Government and people in combination have constructed waterworks very much after the scientific models established in the United Kingdom, in every instance with a marked benefit to the public health. In the lesser towns of the interior waterworks have been or are being built; in every case some local diseases, believed in ignorance to be unavoidably endemic to the locality, disappear as if by magic. Still, among the villages in a vast country, some have water from running streams and others have not. Those which are thus destitute add to the natural difficulty by recklessly defiling what little water they have. Time does not admit of my adducing instances of the epidemics traceable to the state of the water, when the scanty tanks and wells had been reduced to their dregs. We see at home illustrations of wells being poisoned from sewage. I remember a case in the East where a large garrison of European troops was decimated and disorganized by cholera, which, after inquiry, was attributed to percolation from cesspools through the solid ground into the drinking wells. In times of famine, mortality has occurred, not only from the withering of crops, but also from the drying up of the drinking water. The State might convey food for famishing multitudes, but could not bring water for thirsty millions. Much of this evil is preventable by water supply provided during years of plenty, and here is a field abroad for that engineering science which has wrought wonders at home.

It were almost superfluous to call to remembrance the successful efforts put forth at home respecting sanitation, drainage, and sewage. We have but lately beheld the terrible example afforded by the cholera in Egypt. If this fell foe be generated somewhere else than in the localities actually attacked, and be, as it were, floating in the air, still its attack is generally, though not invariably, attracted by insanitation or averted by sanitation. The angel of death is, so to speak, hovering over a doomed land, and he descends on those spots which are the foulest. We can imagine what the physical surroundings of the Egyptians in the cholera-stricken places must have been, from our knowledge of the like conditions in other countries of the East. In India the capital cities have drainage works constructed in the manner which has approved itself to engineers at home, whereon some millions sterling have from first to last been expended, to the marked diminution (among other things), indeed almost to the prevention, of epidemic cholera, though sporadic cholera still appears sometimes. Drainage works are also undertaken in all the lesser towns of the interior,

But the faults of sanitation, still remaining in the great cities and the lesser towns, are legion; while the conduct of the rural people in most of the villages, in the matter of sewage, is so culpably fatuous as to be incredible to any save those who have witnessed it. Some attempt is made to diffuse a smattering of sanitary science among the rustics, but it is uphill work to reclaim a population from the habits of centuries. If anything could aggravate the regret with which this disposition of the people must be regarded, it would be the thought that the utilisation of sewage even in the smallest quantities is peculiarly needed for Indian agriculture, which ordinarily is very deficient in manure. Though much is attempted in this matter at some central places, yet in the country generally, quantities of sewage, which might have fertilised the fields, are left to breed poison for man.

As the proportion of the urban population to the whole people increases, and as the congregation of inhabitants into dense masses proceeds apace, there is no profession more vitally important than that of sanitary engineering. This profession at home has attained a considerable growth, and will thus afford the means of forming similar professions abroad. But still the faults in domestic as well as in public sanitation here are sometimes appalling, and cause new evils even worse than that which the arrangement was intended to obviate. How much more must this be the case abroad, in the rising colonies, where towns spring up with startling rapidity before proper arrangements can be made; in the East, where the work has to be done through native agency under novel conditions that breed mischief with perplexing effect. Already in the East the fear that sanitation, while averting some familiar diseases, is actually producing typhoid sickness, gives rise to a prejudice among the natives against Western sanitation. Nothing but a more rigid attention to sanitary engineering can set this right. So frequent are the sanitary faults of new-built houses in urban localities at home, that some authorities recommend the professional inspection of every new house before it is occupied, and private companies are formed for this purpose. This must be equally wanted in the colonies, and assuredly it is needed in the capital cities of the East.

The preparation of those vital statistics, which are essential to good administration, is doubtless accomplished well in the United Kingdom, perhaps in the colonies also; and the difference in the death-rate between town and country tells a terrible tale of the physical ills which humanity brings on itself by the conditions of social existence. In the East, however, this work has hardly advanced beyond its infancy. It is, indeed, hard to ascertain the facts of births, of disease and death, for so vast a population; and as yet they are but partially ascertained, though progress towards ascertainment is being gradually made. For the principal centres, and for some selected districts in the interior, the facts have become known, and they reveal death-rates that are always higher than those of Europe, and are sometimes miserably high.

Hospital management at home is a subject to which the attention of this Association has been constantly directed, and at its instance a conference of hospital authorities has recently assembled, whose deliberations will doubtless prove fruitful in results. This subject is of at least equal importance in the East, where the founding of hospitals, and the opening of provident and charitable dispensaries, are regarded by Asiatics as among the fairest features of British rule. If at home errors in management arise, and peculiar diseases are generated within the very walls of these institutions, how much more must this be the case in the East, where to inherent difficulties are superadded the tropical conditions and the habits of an Oriental people! I remember a case where an Eastern hospital, superbly constructed with a generous outlay, was plagued with gangrene and erysipelas manifestly produced within its precincts. At length inquiry revealed the proximity of certain underground drains. On the drainage being rectified the hospital recovered, and we all realised the scientific dictum, "*Cessante causâ, cessat et effectus.*"

In all matters relating to the public health, the Eastern nationalities must be brought under sanitary education. Unless they learn how to save themselves, and become imbued with a desire to practise what they learn, the utmost effort of the State for saving them will fail. Therefore sanitation must form a prominent branch in the national instruction, sanitary primers must be used in the schools, sanitary regulations elaborated by the native municipalities, and sanitary treatises circulated, so practical that he who runs may understand them.

Next after physical health and comfort, social science concerns itself with the production and distribution of wealth. In the general question relating to wealth, Free Trade and that which is termed Fair Trade are comprised. These matters are of peculiar interest and importance to the colonies, and have been frequently discussed by our Association, though they are fully dealt with by other associations whose work is more specialised than ours. We know that as regards the question of protection there is but one answer that can be given by economic science.

But in reference to material well-being there is the subject of the land. The study of that has always been regarded by this Association as specially within its province. Important as landed affairs are everywhere, to no part of the world are they more important than to the British Empire abroad.

We see the new doctrine propounded in some, though perhaps a very few quarters, in hostility to the existing property in land on both sides of the Atlantic. In that view the natural origin of landed property seems to be overlooked. In an Oriental nation the land belongs to him who first reclaimed it, and to his heirs or assigns. The right thus originating in labour, industry and enterprise, descends by inheritance throughout the East. A man then has power to sell or mortgage that which he or his forefather has rendered valuable, and in regard to mortage such power is commonly exercised. In the course of time small properties will be thus transferred by needy owners to others, and so large properties arise. Here, then, are an origination and a devolution, both most legitimate, and wholly opposed to the revolutionary ideas respecting property which are sometimes put forth. They are by themselves adequate to account for landed property as it exists in civilized countries, irrespective of the political means by which such property has at various times and places been created. In the East, the people, regarding this property as the most precious of their material possessions, have often seen it threatened and overrun by armed violence, but have clung to it with unsurpassable pertinacity. It has been recognised and confirmed finally in all the regions that have come under British sway. The legal recognition has been supported, too, with a registration of titles officially and judicially framed, and amended from year to year. This registration, in reference to its vast extent and its accuracy up to date, is the finest that has ever been framed anywhere; the Chinese registration may be as extensive, but is not so accurate. The matter is now being considered in the colonies, and much valuable information hereon has been presented to this Association by colonial authorities. Eminent among these is Sir Robert Torrens, a member of this Association, who has devised and has been instrumental in establishing for Australia a registration which may serve as a model for other communities.

In some Western countries we hear of anxiety respecting the landless classes, the millions who do not own even the smallest area of land; in others we learn that very small proprietors, who have nothing but land to live on, find their livelihood beset more and more with distress. In the East this anxiety has not heretofore been felt; the most important classes are landed, and not landless, and men can live on petty properties. The transfer and conveyance of the property have been greatly facilitated by British rule, and that which, despite the efforts of social science, is found difficult at home has been rendered easy abroad. Thus in many Eastern places land is gradually passing from the feeble and inefficient to those who possess capital and intelligence.

But even here a danger lurks, for in the East the complete recognition of landed property under British rule has afforded a title, on the security of which money can be easily raised. This facility has encouraged the peasant proprietors to borrow much too largely. Thus serious trouble has occasionally arisen and may yet arise. The danger has been aggravated by the British law of debtor and creditor, and may in future be mitigated by an improvement of that law. This particular law, however just in intention, works very badly, although in theory the fault may be hard to define. I regret that time does not allow me to do more than to mention this as a subject wherein the Association may exert its influence for the good of our fellow-subjects in India. The selfsame difficulty, too, is found to exist in Egypt.

It is to be regretted that all the troubles which have arisen in parts of the United Kingdom regarding encumbered estates are well known in parts of India, and the Indian statute-book has but too many instances of legislation in this direction.

The principle obtaining in the United Kingdom, whereby landowners can be lawfully compelled to combine for executing improvements affecting their neighbourhoods, has been applied to the East. Indian landlords have in some remarkable instances been thus induced to coalesce for banking off inundations or reclaiming swamps, to the benefit of their own estates and of the community.

Besides the proprietary, almost every conceivable form of tenancy and occupation is to be found in the East, and here is a field of study for this Association. For large classes of tenants occupancy rights have been legally secured, the power of transferring the tenancy has been acknowledged, the claim to compensation for improvement has been affirmed. But the claim can hardly arise, because practically the man cannot be evicted, and in event of dispute his rent will be judicially determined. There is, however, a still larger class of tenants-at-will, whose position, though much better now than formerly, is still far from satisfactory, and whose lot evokes the sympathy of philanthropists in England.

Emigration from India to the West Indies and other tropical colonies is needed not only for the colonial labour market, but also for relieving the density of population in overcrowded Indian districts. This gives birth to urgent questions affecting the welfare of the emigrants as settlers, and the interest of the colonists as employers. Regarding the comfort of the emigrants on their long sea voyages, every arrangement is made through a protector appointed by the Government. Similarly, encouragement is given to emigration from one part of India to another, especially those parts where new industries, such as the culture of tea and coffee, are being developed through European enterprise.

Time does not admit of our adverting to the landed questions which arise in the colonies, and of which many demand a consideration guided by economic science. The importance of such matters may be imagined from a single class of cases, where railway companies obtain large territorial concessions of lands adjacent to the line, or lines, which lands are sold to great land companies who are ultimately to settle colonists thereon. Other examples might be adduced, such as the difference between the systems of leasing and of free-ranging in the cattle ranches of North-west America, and the project for storing the water of rivers in the interior of Australia.

Before quitting this part of my address, I would say a passing word on forestry and the preservation of forests, a matter which deserves the study of this Association as vitally concerning the material welfare of India and of the colonies. The destruction of forests has caused anxiety in India, in Cyprus, in South Africa, in Canada, in the West Indies. I have no space here for describing the great department of forest conservancy in India—established too late for those fine forests which are gone irreparably, but still in time to save those which remain—or the preservative measures which are being adopted in the colonies. But the point which I would press upon you is this, that the destructive effects from which we have narrowly escaped—if, indeed, we have altogether escaped—are due to the fact that formerly educated people did not sufficiently think upon the importance of forests, not only for the national wealth, but also for the tempering of the climate and the retention of moisture in hot countries. Consequently there used to be much ignorance respecting the forests, an indifference to their injuries, and a too facile yielding to the obstacles which retarded their preservation. Even now it is only by rousing public attention at home, by discussions in our Association and other associations, that persevering energy in preservation can be secured abroad.

Having thus considered the primary subject of physical comfort and material well-being, we pass on to the central subject of this address, namely, mental and moral training.

Now, this Association has repeatedly discussed all that relates to national and popular education. It has treated of the questions whether education should be afforded to the poor gratuitously by the State, as is done in America, or whether some payment should be exacted from the parents, as in the United Kingdom—whether the schools under voluntary organization are preferable to schools under public management, as the Board Schools—whether the system of grants-in-aid by the State to private schools, according to the method known as payment by result, is to be encouraged. All these questions are, of course, equally applicable to the colonies. It is noteworthy, too, that they have all arisen in the East. In the two most populous countries of Asia, namely, China and India, we must remember that while the Chinese Government from ancient times has attended to education in a degree never surpassed in any age or country, the various native Indian Governments, with few exceptions, neglected this subject utterly. Even the British Government hesitated for more than half a century to essay the task. But within the present generation the Government has grasped this matter with its wonted vigour. Consequently all the questions above mentioned, and other kindred questions, have arisen and are still being agitated in the East. It is there held that while the State may properly defray educational charges for direction and organization, and contribute at the outset something towards the education itself, still the parents must pay all they possibly can, the principle of gratuitous education being rejected, and that the State contribution should take the form of grants-in-aid to private institutions. The policy is to render education self-sustaining, and to teach the parents to draw upon their own resources rather than upon the public taxes.

To this important principle there is a special exception, which has been advocated by this Association, and has been fully admitted in the East, namely, the system of free scholarships. The generous idea, in the United Kingdom, is that the boy of genius, springing from the humblest origin, should win, by competition in a primary school, a free scholarship that shall maintain him in a school of the next grade above, where he may win another scholarship to maintain him in a superior school, and so on till he reaches one of the universities, where, again, he may win the highest academic honours, which finally may prove the passport to success in any of the great professions. This idea has also found the strongest possible expression in the United States. It is equally current in the East; and every Asiatic subject of the British Crown has the selfsame chance proffered to him—a beneficent chance of which the very humblest are availing themselves to the happiest extent.

We all know the good effect at home of the compulsion, gently and indirectly applied to parents who neglect to send their children to school, so that most children of a school-going age are under instruction more or less. The gradual and cautious application of this principle is wanted in the East, where only a portion of the children are at school, and where the majority, despite the efforts of the authorities, stay away.

Among our Asiatic fellow-subjects it is peculiarly necessary to add physical science to the instruction already given in literature and philosophy, and to diffuse generally a scientific spirit. In this respect the State education has heretofore been defective, but, despite obstacles, there is a resolute attempt being made to remedy this defect.

The extension of technical instruction at home has long been advocated by this Association. In common with others, we thankfully note the progress which is beginning in the United Kingdom, of which the institution founded by the Livery Companies of London, the Engineering College at Cooper's Hill, and the technical school of which the new building is about to be inaugurated at Huddersfield under royal auspices, are recent examples. Notwithstanding the apparent backwardness of Great Britain in this respect as compared with the continent of Europe, it is probable that a vast amount of instruction is given in private establishments which never appears in returns or reports, while on the continent the technical teaching always pertains to a State or to a public corporation, and is consequently reported. If any one were to prepare from private information an account of all the technical instruction arranged by masters and by firms in our manufacturing districts, he would render a public service. Be this as it may, there is no doubt that in the East technical education is a crying want, which is as yet but partly satisfied; except in medical instruction, where the success has been signal, and in civil engineering, where success is beginning.

Art-culture has always been advocated by this Association as a fitting crown to the educational system. It is naturally much needed in the colonies, young, bustling, pre-occupied communities, where no classes have leisure. It has in the East presented problems as yet unsolved. The Asiatics have an indigenous art, which, though not scientifically directed, is yet, in genius, in perception, and in sentiment, peculiarly their own. This exceeding merit arises from the hereditary character of Eastern art, and the transmission of qualities from father to son, through many generations of artists. If we were to teach our art to the natives exclusively, they might be in danger of losing their own, which, so far as it goes, is better than anything that we can teach them, and which is indeed to be reckoned among the beautiful possessions of the human race. Still we can teach them one thing, which through all the preceding ages they have never learnt, namely, drawing objects correctly, whether figures, landscape, or architecture. Such drawing tends to rectify some of their mental faults, to intensify their powers of observation, and to make them understand analytically those glories of nature which they love so well.

From mental exercise we pass on to the still more important branch of moral training. This is a matter which during recent years even up to the present moment has engaged, and is engaging, the anxious attention of thoughtful and earnest people in the United Kingdom. There is no apprehension, on this head, respecting schools under private or voluntary organization, and we may trust that there will be no real ground for such apprehension in the schools under local public management, as the Board schools. But it is remarkable that this very apprehension has arisen in the East. Although indigenous education used certainly to be defective in this respect, yet the natives nowadays, if they cared to speak their mind, would say that in the schools under British rule sufficient care has not been directly paid to this matter. They would admit that indirectly, by instruction in the literature, the history, the civilization of the

West, much moral teaching is conveyed. They would, indeed, be not unwillingly compelled to such admission by the example of good conduct and improved disposition among those of their countrymen who had received this instruction. They would, however, wish that to this were superadded more of direct and formal instruction in ethics. Nothing would more tend to popularise Western education in the East than a conviction in the Asiatic mind that such education necessarily comprises a regular course of moral culture.

But moral culture extends in the East, as elsewhere, far beyond the schoolroom. There especially is it conveyed by the entire work of that Western civilization which permeates the action of the State in legislation, in the administration of the law, in the organization of the public service, in the adjudication of landed tenures. Above all is it communicated by the example of those Europeans who are truly representative men, and illustrate by their life and conversation the blessing offered by that civilization of which they are the harbingers.

We are not wanting in reverence to religion when we refrain from adverting to religious considerations respecting the East or other regions of the world, inasmuch as social science has always regarded these considerations to be above and beyond its sphere. Happily in the East, as even in the remotest parts of the earth, the Christian missions have done and are doing, with entire devotion, that which could not properly be undertaken by the State or by any secular organization.

Before quitting this division of my address it may be appropriate for me to say a word on female education. Although no question regarding what at home are termed "women's rights" is likely to arise in the East, yet the position of Hindu widows claims the sympathy of the lady members of this Association. The legal difficulty is indeed removed respecting the re-marriage of widows, yet social prejudice is stronger than law, and their condition is generally miserable, as child-wives are often widowed in childhood. Still, if they remain unmarried they may be employed as mistresses in the girls' schools which are being established in such numbers as to portend in the next generation a revolution which, though gentle, will affect Oriental society to its foundations. An impetus and a fitting direction can be imparted to this gracious movement of female education by British ladies at home, who may be stirred by the discussions on this subject to proceed themselves—as Mary Carpenter proceeded—or induce other ladies to proceed, to the East, where their presence may diffuse light amidst the secluded apartments of their Asiatic sisters.

I have now completed the primary and the central divisions of this address, namely, physical comfort and material well-being, then mental and moral training. I proceed thence to the concluding division, namely, social organization as applicable to the empire abroad.

This concluding division manifestly comprises law reform, the advocacy of which has always been a peculiar province of this Association. Most of the legal matters in the United Kingdom to which attention has thus been turned, such as commercial regulations, bankruptcy, partnership, juries, transfer of land and registration of titles, charitable trusts, law reporting, are all applicable to the empire abroad. The European jurists and legislators in the East have laboured in these very matters, which are seldom or never provided for by Asiatic codes, and their labours have been essentially lightened by the work of reformers at home. The projects of digests and of codification, which have been strenuously advocated at home with but an imperfect success, have, partly through this very advocacy, been perfectly carried into effect in the East. Indeed, enlightened, comprehensive, and searching legislation, well digested, consolidated, and codified, with the co-operation of eminent jurists in the United Kingdom and practical law-makers abroad, has become a leading characteristic of British rule in the East, until to every section of that vast administration both stability and continuity have been legally secured.

In the colonies the law reforms projected in the mother country are more easily carried into effect, because in those regions the social ground is less cumbered by the fragments of legal structures that have become dilapidated or have crumbled into ruins from disuse. Thus the hearts of reformers are more often cheered by progress in these new countries than in the old country. Moreover, those young communities have at their disposal experience dearly bought elsewhere with untold trouble, as a free gift to them from the past, and have no antecedent obstacles to hinder them in profiting thereby. From them, therefore, reformers at home have welcomed, and expect yet to welcome, novel suggestions in many branches of legislation.

Respecting the execution of the law, this Association has humanely advocated improvements in prison discipline in the United Kingdom, and has fearlessly grappled with the moral questions comprised therein. Now, every one of these multifarious matters concerns the colonies, and the remarkable reports transmitted from Victoria, regarding the prisons there, attest the colonial ability in this department. But more especially does this subject affect the East. The difficulties connected with prison management in our northern latitudes are but too well known. Infinitely are they aggravated in the East by the conditions of a tropical climate. The prison reformers in the East are almost disheartened when they see that, despite augmented ventilation, enlarged space, carefully adjusted tasks, a generously calculated diet, and surroundings superior to anything that the prisoners could ever have had in their domiciles —the prisons are often unhealthy, the normal death-rate is high, and epidemics baffle preventive skill, mainly owing to the depressing effect of incarceration upon the spirits of Asiatics, and the mischief generated in a tropical atmosphere by any congregation of human beings. The same question which arises at home regarding the classification of prisoners, the solitary confinement, the cellular plan, the good behaviour system, the educational instruction, the treatment devised for inspiring the wretched with remorse for the past and with hope for the future, is agitated in the East also. An additional difficulty has existed there, in that prisoners used to work on the roads by what was known as outdoor labour. The reformers caused indoor labour to be substituted. But the principle of indoor labour, though accepted at home long ago, was tardily accepted abroad, and is still regarded jealously by opponents. Again, the discussion at home regarding the rules under which tickets-of-leave should be allowed to prisoners under penal servitude, was followed by a similar discussion regarding the convict settlements on the islands in Eastern seas.

Reformatories and industrial schools have long engaged the attention of this Association. After these institutions had been established abroad, the authorities in the East lost but little time in adding reformatories to the category of pending improvements. There was, however, among the Indian authorities unnecessary hesitation in adopting the principle that reformatory discipline should be applied not only to those children who have been convicted of crime, but also to those who are ignorantly moving in vicious grooves that can have but one ending, namely, a criminal course.

Looking back to the eloquent addresses that have been delivered before this Association regarding the past state of crime and the criminal law even in Western countries, we may feel thankful in considering the humane wisdom of the penal code which has been given to the East, and the suppression of organized crimes which has been effected there by British jurists and administrators. But despite recent efforts, a good police, such as we happily have in the United Kingdom, is still one of the unaccomplished reforms of India.

The discussion regarding the public prosecutor in the United Kingdom is equally relevant to the East, not so much perhaps regarding the capital cities as the interior of the country, where unwillingness to prosecute is a peculiarity of the natives, and where consequently a special burden is thrown upon the authorities.

The recent growth of manufactures in the East has caused questions to arise regarding factory legislation. Although the factories are managed, on the whole, considerately in respect to the native workpeople, yet the risk of over-exertion in the close air of crowded buildings, in a heated and humid atmosphere, makes it necessary to protect young people of both sexes, and may render it desirable to extend the protection to adults also.

The organization of thrift has been advocated by members of this Association in common with other philanthropists in the United Kingdom. The result of our friendly societies—if only, through the action of the Legislature and the force of public opinion, they shall be well managed—will be one of the monuments of our national greatness. So also our savings banks are progressing apace, both those which exist under the auspices of the State, and those which are organized through private agency, of which the Penny Bank in this county of York—with its million and a half sterling, deposited in small sums by a million of depositors—is a signal instance. Still the average saving per head is less among us than among some Continental nations. Now in the East, although the form is different, the principle is the same. The natives are in several respects unthrifty and extravagant. Their expenditure on marriages, on festivals, and other social occasions, is commonly more than they can afford, and among the poor leads to embarrassment. Native reformers have urged, with but a modicum of success, a relaxation of the old customs which impose this burden. Savings banks have been established in all parts of the country by the Government, with a beginning of success auguring well for the future. The establishing of life insurance for the natives with the assistance of the State has been recommended (though in vain), as calculated not only to encourage thrift, but to bind the people with fresh ties to British rule.

The discussion regarding charitable endowments in the United Kingdom has extended, though in a much smaller shape, to the East. There was a signal instance in Bengal of an endowment, which had become practically ineffective, being applied to educational purposes in a manner consonant with the general intention of the founder, and approved by the community concerned.

The question regarding the property of married women, which was recently determined at home, and in which this Association took a most active part, has during ages past been settled in the East. Ancient Hindu lawgivers, in Sanscrit terminology, enacted effective safeguards for this object in favour of the wife. The Muhammadan law of dowry is celebrated as being particularly severe upon the husband.

It is a happy circumstance that the discussions so rife at home regarding the Poor Law have no bearing on the East, because there the poor do not require any public organization for their relief in ordinary times. During scarcity or famine, the infirm and destitute must indeed be sustained by the State, but on the cessation of the extraordinary distress they revert to their normal sustenance, which is afforded by private charity in their villages or parishes. The people of India have indeed their poor always with them, but the fact that ordinarily they do by voluntary and private action sustain the miserable without any State intervention or legal compulsion. redounds to their national honour.

As a consequence, the nurture of orphans by parish authorities, which causes grief to philanthropists at home, never occurs in the East. The orphans find foster parents, or else are received into the orphanages under private management, which have been organized there like the orphanages in the United Kingdom, of which there is a remarkable instance at Halifax, near the place of our present meeting.

The laws relating to the sale of intoxicating drinks, to which this Association, in conjunction with other bodies, has consistently attended, affect the colonies in common with the United Kingdom. Happily they are less important in the East, as Indian people are seldom intemperate; although, while I write, in one part of India at least, a question is arising which resembles the question of local option at home. But among our European soldiers and sailors in the East, the very bulwarks of our power, the question of Temperance assumes the highest importance. In no part of the British army are Temperance associations more efficient than in the European forces of India, to the marked diminution of military crime. In no ports of the British Empire are Sailor's Homes more conducive to the seaman's welfare than in Calcutta and Bombay.

The idea prevalent in the United Kingdom of forming associations for the promotion of the public weal, has been extensively imitated or adopted in the East. There also associations exist, not indeed so well-informed and influential as the Association which I am addressing, or as other societies which might readily be named, but still full of interest, as conducing to the moral culture, and above all to the self-education, of the Eastern people. In almost every district the educated natives organize societies for the advancement of objects bearing on social science. I myself have had to deliver an inaugural address to a Social Science Association formed by the natives of Bengal for their own improvement.

The presence in London of an Agent General, for each colony in the empire, may be utilised by this Association, as by all other associations that take a brotherly interest in colonial progress and happiness, for the acquisition of knowledge bearing upon the interest of the colonists—so far as that can be furthered by public opinion at home—and upon the good relations which we are all anxious to preserve between the mother country and the offspring of whom she is justly proud.

The example largely set in the United Kingdom of voluntary service, in civil affairs, rendered to the country by classes and by individuals, has been urged with some effect on our fellow-subjects in the East. The natives, becoming members of legislative councils, municipal commissioners, electors in municipal elections, school committee-men, jurors in criminal trials, assessors in civil causes, and honorary magistrates, are learning to take some interest and pride in the administration of their own country. This tendency will be further strengthened by the recent scheme for extending self-government under an elective system for the administration of the local funds in the Indian districts resembling the English counties. This scheme, though in some respects constituting a new departure, is in most respects an expansion of that which had previously existed.

Thus glancing at the principle of local self-government in the East, subject always to British control, I must conclude this, the last division of my address.

I have now touched upon the application of social science to the British Empire abroad in the three main divisions, namely, physical comfort and material well-being, mental and moral training, social organization.

I trust that the extension of our horizon, and the indication of many matters needing reform abroad, may not have bewildered you. For while unreservedly noting the evils which demand your attention, I have also adduced, for your encouragement, examples of blessings already produced.

My general summary will be followed by able addresses in each of the five departments into which this Association is divided. Papers will be read to you throwing light on some of the subjects mentioned in my address, and on many others besides, such as public prosecutions; the law of marriage and divorce; reformatory and industrial schools; the sale of poisons; the preparation for technical instruction; the higher education of those who have left school; the physical health of scholars; the spread of zymotic disease from infected food; the opening of museums and art galleries on Sundays; the application of art to textile manufactures. The names of those who will address you during this meeting constitute a guarantee that the time-honoured traditions of the Association will be thoroughly maintained.

But we must to-day lament that these traditions will no

more be actively sustained by two members of the Association who were among its ornaments, namely, William Farr, and Alexander Patrick Stewart. By the students of statistical science throughout Europe, William Farr was reckoned as among its foremost pioneers and its greatest expounders. By the medical profession Alexander Stewart was regarded as an accomplished worker, and by all men as a devoted advocate of hygiene.

Now let me finish, as I began, by reminding you that divers races in far off countries look to public opinion in the United Kingdom for direction in the higher paths of their social existence. It is for you to help in the formation of that opinion, which will be to them a beacon light for encouragement and a pole-star for guidance. Your countrymen abroad, indeed, possess originality of mind and energy of disposition, but amidst the distractions of a stirring life, the exhausting effects of torrid heat, and the obstacles to constant intercourse of thinker with thinker, they cannot elaborate schemes of progress with the efficacy which you, with your countless advantages, can command at home. But if you work out beneficent thoughts to sound and practical conclusions, you may be sure that the sentiment, which gathers strength here in Britain, will rapidly spread to the East and to the West. Thus the good seed sown at home may, by the Divine blessing, grow into a tree of wisdom overshadowing that Empire upon which the sun—the sun of benevolence and of charity—never sets.

FINIS.

# INDEX.